INRO and
other miniature forms of
Japanese Lacquer Art

1 *(Frontispiece)*. INRO. Emma, king of hell. Signed: Yamada Joka. Red takamakie decorated with aogai on a black
ground with mura nashiji. $3\frac{7}{8}''\times2\frac{3}{16}''\times1\frac{1}{4}''$. 4 cases and lid.

INRO and
other miniature forms of
JAPANESE LACQUER ART

❖

by Melvin and Betty Jahss

CHARLES E. TUTTLE COMPANY
Rutland, Vermont & Tokyo, Japan

REPRESENTATIVES

For Continental Europe:
BOXERBOOKS, INC., Zurich

For the British Isles:
PRENTICE-HALL INTERNATIONAL, INC., London

For Australasia:
PAUL FLESCH & CO., PTY. LTD., Melbourne

For Canada:
M. G. HURTIG, LTD., Edmonton

Published by the Charles E. Tuttle Company, Inc.
of Rutland, Vermont & Tokyo, Japan
with editorial offices at
Suido 1-chome, 2-6, Bunkyo-ku, Tokyo 112

Copyright in Japan, 1971
by Charles E. Tuttle Co., Inc.

Library of Congress Catalog Card No. 76-109406
International Standard Book No. 0-8048-0263-7

First printing, 1971

Book design & typography by Florence Sakade
Layout of plates by Shigeo Katakura

PRINTED IN JAPAN

❖ Table of Contents

❖ List of Illustrations

❖ Introduction

      WHEN JAPAN FINALLY OPENED HER DOORS TO THE OUTSIDE world in the mid-19th century, there emerged one of the most skillful, exquisite, and remarkable art forms ever developed by any country: that of Japanese lacquer. Today, it is startling to discover that what we now consider as avant-garde in modern art—such as abstraction, impressionism, and collage—had already been perfected by Japanese lacquer artists over 300 years ago.

Japanese art is best known for its superb craftsmanship as expressed through its three forms of miniature art, each created in a different medium. The first form and by far the most popular in the Western world is the netsuke. This is essentially a tiny sculptured wood or ivory figure. These exquisite carvings were made by a specialized class of artisans, a handful of whom are still carving to this very day. The second medium is that of miniature metal art, best expressed in sword ornamentation, such as the sword guard *(tsuba)* or knife handle *(kozuka)*. This art form was also done by very specialized artists who unfortunately no longer exist because of the ban on wearing swords since 1877. The third medium equally prized by the Japanese is that of miniature lacquer art, also created by specialized artists. It should be noted that Oriental lacquer is not in the Western sense a chemically prepared varnish but is a natural product which comes from the sap of a tree. The lacquer is applied in numerous layers, and its beautiful gloss is only obtained through endless polishings. Furthermore, the magnificent designs are accomplished through painstaking applications of layers of repeated dustings of fine metallic and colored powders onto the tacky lacquered surfaces. The art of lacquering has also fallen into disuse because of the decreased demand, as well as the expense and extreme length of time necessary for its production.

Japanese lacquer work represents the acme of artistry as well as of technical craftsmanship. Such artistry embodies the Japanese sense of aesthetic and decorative design in a colorful graphic form, while the craftsmanship is expressed through the use of an extremely difficult medium in which to work. Thus while lacquer art was originally adopted from China, even the adept Chinese craftsmen were unable to copy the high Japanese development of this medium.

Among the lacquered objects, the miniature pieces provided the greatest technical challenge, both in the difficulty of artistically presenting subject matter and design on relatively small irregularly shaped surface areas and in the miniature, almost microscopic, work entailed in such small objects. Of all the miniature lacquered objects the widely used inro is a perfect example of Japanese miniature lacquer art. This small bibelot, approximately $3\frac{1}{2}'' \times 2'' \times 1''$ deep, was essentially a multicompartment case worn suspended from the sash and served to carry seals, portable shrines, or powdered medicines. Inro were developed during the late 17th and 18th centuries, paralleling the height of development of Japanese lacquer art. The Japanese people did not wear or use any nonutilitarian objects such as jewelry. Therefore the artisan only worked on utilitarian objects. The inro, besides the sword, was the one exposed object worn mainly by the noblemen, samurai (warrior class), and merchants. It thus became the one "jewel" and expressed artistically in miniature lacquer form the aesthetic tastes of its patrons as revealed through the creative talents of the great Japanese lacquer artists.

Since Japanese lacquer is an extremely difficult medium in which to work, it often took months or even years to complete a single object. However, under the old Japanese feudal system time and money were of no significance to the lacquerer as each daimyo, or lord, subsidized his own artists. Only under such circumstances was it possible to have so time-consuming and costly an art flourish and prosper. However by the mid-19th century there was an overthrow of the feudal system and the loss of the patrons of lacquer art. These factors, combined with the commercialization of Japanese art forms in general, virtually brought an end to this magnificent form of art.

It is the purpose of this book to elucidate the history, technique, and development of this unique art form, about which so little has been written and for which Japan has become world-renowned.

We are indebted to many people for their cooperation in the preparation of this book. We would particularly like to thank Mr. Joseph U. Seo for his invaluable assistance and guidance not only in the translating of original Japanese sources and for clarifying previously uncertain data relating to lacquer artists but also for his expert judgment in obtaining and assessing the major portion of the objects which are illustrated.

INRO and
other miniature forms of
Japanese Lacquer Art

1 ❖ Characteristics of Japanese Lacquer Art

THERE ARE CERTAIN SIMILARITIES BETWEEN MINIATURE metal and lacquer art. Both were held in the highest esteem by the Japanese and were fostered by the imperial court and local wealthy feudal lords. Great metal and lacquer artists received honorary titles in spite of the relatively low social strata that these artisans held in Japan's feudal society. Both metal and lacquer arts were essentially graphic rather than sculptural, and yet they possessed subtle sculptural elements. Both of these arts utilized similar artistic techniques even though in entirely different media. They both made full use of color for decorative values: different-colored lacquers and different-colored metals. Yet in both forms at times color was minimized, as seen in plain iron sword ornamentation with just a touch of sculptural effects in the iron. The same applied to lacquer, where we might see a subtle simple black design superimposed upon a plain black lacquered background. Both metal and lacquer arts used combinations of flat, medium, and raised reliefs as well as encrustations. Art motifs and background effects were also often comparable. Finally all three of these art media slowly evolved over the centuries and reached the zenith of their artistic and technical development in the 18th century. Separate and famous schools of netsuke, metal, and lacquer artists evolved during the 17th, 18th, and 19th centuries. Each of these highly specialized art forms required years of assiduous training, and each developed numerous schools of different and overlapping artistic styles. Figures 17, 18, and 19 represent the simple subject of a pair of playful puppies as portrayed in each of the three miniature art forms by a master craftsman in each medium.

To the Western eye it is somewhat difficult to appreciate Oriental artistic presentation of subject matter and design in graphic form. This can only be realized by obtaining a thorough understanding of the tastes and the aesthetic development of the Oriental artist over centuries of maturation. The uninitiated, upon viewing an expert specimen of Japanese lacquer, may see what appears to be somewhat grotesque, exaggerated, and conventionalized figures and designs eccentrically placed over the surface area of the lacquered object. The design, more often than not, will flow over and envelop all sides of the object in question. Such artistic treatment of subject matter and surface area, unique in Japanese lacquer art, may at first appear disturbingly strange until we gain a better knowledge of Oriental and Japanese artistic concepts. Figure 2 represents a masked Noh dancer. What at first may appear to be a grotesque face on second glance becomes a powerfully expressive mask. The figure abounds with motion and energy. The clothes, upon closer scrutiny, are typically Japanese in treatment. It is not enough to represent an exquisite, colorful, detailed, designed robe, but also each part of the garment has a different motif in different colors. There are even slight ornamental variations within each motif itself. The motifs themselves have symbolic meaning, including the "seven precious things." The dancing figure is eccentrically placed on the surface area and is counterbalanced by the peonies. The flowers are done in encrusted raised mother-of-pearl similar to the face of the Noh dancer for heightened effect. Thus we see how the Japanese artist deliberately and thoughtfully presents his subject matter. Strength and motion are counterbalanced by delicate intricate ornamental design. The asymmetry of the overall design and of the details within the design artistically prevents boredom. The technical use of materials such as the mother-of-pearl and the red lacquer of the dancer's hair completes the artistic effect. One final effect should be noted: that of the subtle use of perspective completely different from Western techniques. The dancer appears to be leaping into the air. This effect is heightened by the peonies, which are on a lower level and appear to be rising above the ground although the ground itself is not portrayed. This is perspective in a vertical sense rather than one of depth. Yet the sense of depth is also present through the proportionately large size of the peonies, which appear as if in the foreground. Depth and perspective are also gained within the design itself by use of the flat and raised lacquer and the inlaid mother-of-pearl.

The development of such artistic concepts and aestheticism as related to Japanese lacquer was dependent upon five major influences, which through the centuries formulated these concepts. These influences are: 1) geographical, 2) Chinese, 3) religious, 4) feudal (political and economic), and 5) cultural. Together, these five factors formed and molded the customs, mores, and aesthetic values of Japan, which, combined with endless Oriental patience and supreme technical craftsmanship, produced the finest lacquer ware the world has ever known. All of the arts were influenced historically by the customs, aesthetics, and technical knowledge of the day along with Chinese and Buddhist influences. Similarly there was a certain degree of influence of the arts upon one another. Thus lacquer artists often adopted designs of famous paintings and prints. Similarly, metal artists often did encrusted work on inro, and netsuke artists occasionally made inro. On the other hand, lacquer became a uniquely independent and highly developed art form because of two major factors. The first was that lacquer art was practiced throughout the ages by a highly specialized class of artisans and their families. The second was that since this media involved so much time, effort, and expense, it could only be patronized by wealthy persons, such as the imperial household, the nobility, and the local feudal lords. Lacquer art was not only highly esteemed but naturally reflected the more subtle conservative aesthetic tastes of these patrons, being altered only by the 18th-century school of lacquer impressionists and in the 19th century by the more ornate, lavish, less artistic tastes of the rising merchant class. Finally it should be noted that, at the height of lacquer-art development in the 18th century, the influence of the traditional, conventional, and rigid dogma of Chinese art had already been completely modified, softened, and liberalized in relation to Japanese lacquer. Pictorially, decoratively, and in regard to technique, Japan now emerged unsurpassed and unrivaled in her lacquer art.

Geographical Influences

In most countries ancient art, because of limited communication and transportation, was physically and aesthetically dependent upon natural resources along with the inevitable influences of neighboring civilizations. This applied particularly to Japan, whose close proximity to the older Chinese and Korean civilizations resulted in adoption of their art forms and techniques along with assimilation of their culture, religions, mythology, and symbolism. Thus early Japanese lacquer was strongly influenced by Chinese art and lacquer through intercourse with China. However, when Japan closed her doors to the world from the mid-17th to the mid-19th century, entering virtually complete cultural and physical isolation, her lacquer art rapidly developed into a true Japanese art form both in technique and in artistic concept.

The physical restrictions, natural resources, and climate of Japan played a great part in the development of her arts. In regard to physical restrictions, for example, the absence of stone ranges, such as found in China, was responsible for the absence of large stone sculpture and stone architecture, with the exception of occasional small stone images and stone lanterns. The same reasoning may be applied to jade carvings, as jade is not indigenous to Japan, nor did Japan have any marble quarries. Similarly, ivory was not in common use until it became popular in the 18th century, after which it was imported in relatively large quantities. On the other hand, the field of metal art was stimulated by the discovery of gold, silver, and copper in the early 8th century. The local daimyo readily developed their own industries including that of mining metals. However, the amount of available gold was limited, so that pure good-quality gold was used only by the best lacquer and metal artists. The fine gold used by Korin, for example, was of a rich dark orange-yellow appearance in contrast to the diluted lighter yellow color of the inferior products of the late 19th century. Originally, up to the Nara period, woods were often imported from China for sculptural art. However, Japan soon turned to her own abundant native woods. The rainfall and humidity are responsible for the well-wooded, thick forests of Japan with their abundance of many varieties of woods. Light, well-seasoned, nonwarping woods provided the basis of lacquer work, while tougher, finer-grained woods offered themselves to the sculptural arts, such as that of the netsuke. The Japanese love of natural woods, including their shapes, forms, color, grain, bark, and even defects, is reflected and imitated in Japan's lacquer art. At other times the wood or bark itself was used for the lacquer ground.

The lacquer tree was not indigenous to Japan and was undoubtedly originally brought to Japan from China. The best lacquer is obtained north of the 36th parallel between latitudes 37° and 39°. In general, lacquer coming from the temperate zones, as in Japan and China, is superior to that of the tropics.

The subject matter of early Japanese lacquer was at first influenced by the neighboring Chinese art. These subjects were at first mostly religious or mythological, and the designs were of rigid, conventionalized patterns and arabesques with an overall symmetrical pattern. However, the innate love of the Japanese for their own landscapes, flowers and natural vegetation, plants, insects, and animal life, stimulated by Zen Buddhism, created an entirely new world of subject matter. This became most apparent by the 18th century. The beauty and softness of the Japanese countryside, in contrast to the more rugged Chinese terrain, also became apparent in their art. Flowers and trees indigenous to Japan, such as the iris, cherry blossom, chrysanthemum, plum blossom, and wisteria, were frequently depicted in pictorial form and often as ornamental or conventionalized powderings, such as the sixteen-petaled chrysanthemum used as the crest *(kiku-mon)* of the imperial house. Similarly, every detailed aspect of Japanese nature, both animate and inanimate, was carefully observed by the artist and portrayed either realistically or in accord with his aesthetic and religious concepts. On the other hand, an animal such as the tiger, not indigenous to Japan, was often represented quite inaccurately, being copied from prior inaccurate models or from Chinese portrayals.

The Japanese climate not only influenced the architecture of the Japanese but their art as well. In Japan the four seasons are sharply divided, each being about the same length of time. The lacquer artist, as well as the painter, was keenly aware not only of the distinct four seasons but also of the influences of the seasons on every aspect of nature. The lacquer artist, however, had a distinct advantage over the painter. He had at his disposal many more ways of portraying nature. Thus while the Japanese painter basically painted in black and white, using only washes and stroke pressure to obtain effects, the lacquer artist freely used all tonalities of color, such as when depicting autumn leaves, or expressed visual and tactile aspects of nature by using smooth or rough lacquer and enhanced the sense of depth by using raised lacquer or encrustations. Each one of dozens of lacquer techniques was at the disposal of the master lacquer artist in order to bring out his aesthetic concepts.

Chinese Influences

China both directly and indirectly exerted great influence on Japanese lacquer. The close proximity of Japan to China and Korea, with their intermittent political and commercial ties as far back as the 5th century A.D., brought the two countries into close cultural contact. This consisted of emigration of Chinese artisans (as well as Buddhist priests who were familiar with the fine arts) into Japan as well as emigration of Japanese priests, students, and artisans into China. Thus not only were various techniques of Chinese lacquer adopted in Japan, but of equal significance was the adoption of diverse Chinese Buddhist sects, philosophy, and aesthetics. Early Japanese lacquer—that is, from the 6th century to the 15th century—was patronized essentially by the Buddhist temples in addition to the nobility in Kyoto, and this art reflected both pictorially, symbolically, and ornamentally Chinese and Buddhist art. Similarly, in regard to subject matter, the Japanese artisans adopted Chinese mythology and folklore but gradually added to their ornamentation their own folklore and finally, by the 18th century, their own local realistic genre topics. Along with these changes in pictorial design and subject matter were major Japanese alterations in ornamental design. Japanese ornamentation, including background effects, added a tremendous deliberately pleasing and decorative effect to the more conservative, formal, and stiff Chinese art concepts.

While the use of Chinese subject matter was gradually altered to suit the more flexible and decorative Japanese taste, the Japanese maintained to a greater extent certain important basic Chinese aesthetic principles. These principles form the core of Oriental art in general. These aesthetic canons involved in artistic portrayal consist of 1) living movement *(sei-do)*, 2) spiritual elevation *(ki-in)*, 3) strength, 4) accuracy, 5) invention *(esoragoto)*, 6) foreshortening, and 7) contrast *(in-yo)*. While these canons applied to Oriental painting, they were also applicable, sometimes uniquely, to Japanese miniature lacquer.

Living movement is the transmission, through the strength of the brush stroke into the art object, of the painter's feeling of the true nature of the object portrayed. Such is the artistic personal pictorial representation of the infinite beauty and power of nature or the saintly expression of a Buddhist priest. These expressions are often exaggerated, especially by the Japanese artisan.

Spiritual elevation expresses elevation of sentiment and nobility imparted by a work of art, without which, no matter how technically perfect, it can never become a divine masterpiece.

It can be seen that if these artistic canons are accepted with a little excessive freedom, imagination, and individual leeway it is possible to obtain the more extreme effects seen in Japanese art. Thus living movement and invention, when carried to their extremes, might well result in extreme personal variation such as seen in impressionistic Japanese lacquer works as exemplified, for example, by Korin and Koetsu, but never seen in Chinese art.

Strength refers to the power of the brush stroke as imparted into the art object by the inspired artist. Such a nebulous effect may be obtained by various other means in lacquer art. Thus the use of "strength" in impressionistic lacquer was often obtained through contrasting large and yet simple encrustations of mother-of-pearl and pewter.

Accuracy consists of correctness of subject matter. A historical picture must be accurate concerning the dress, customs, and manners of the periods represented in the art object in question. Similarly, the various subjects themselves must be in keeping with each other—both in regard to the season, symbolically, and in regard to the other canons of art such as contrast.

Contrast *(in-yo)* is used in the broadest sense whether it refers to color, active and passive, or upper and lower. Thus it may be generally expressed, for example, by two birds, one with its beak closed and one with its beak open (symbolically representing the male and the female) or simply by two brush strokes in a leaf, one up and one down (Fig. 20).

Invention is simply artistic liberty used to heighten the effect, such as decreasing the number of branches of a tree or drawing the leaves relatively larger than the stems. Occasionally such relative disproportions have symbolic meanings as well, such as the relatively large head of a child indicating naïveté.

Foreshortening is rendering a picture more effective by means of a minimum of design and strokes to achieve the desired effect. Thus a simple bent twig of a tree against a moonlight background may prove far more effective than a detailed realistic landscape topography. Simplicity and foreshortening were especially evident in Japanese art under the influence of Zen Buddhism. Such influence is best exemplified by the lacquer, metal, and pottery objects of the Zen tea ceremony and even permeated the associated simple aesthetic Zen-influenced flower arrangements, gardens, and architectural format. To the Japanese connoisseur this abbreviated and yet powerful form of art is considered the epitome of art whether it be graphic or sculptural such as in the netsuke. Specifically, in regard to the small surface areas provided in miniature lacquer, great artistic ingenuity is necessary in order to portray subject matter in relation to this principle of foreshortening. The small irregular area provided by an inro or a *kobako* necessitates abbreviation of complete scenes and landscapes which would appear too crowded and cumbersome if shown in their entirety. A part of a tree, a few sprays of flowers with a distant glimpse of a mountain are more appropriate (Fig. 21). Such suggestibility of the whole by portraying the part forms the core of the aesthetic subtlety of the Japanese artist's mind. Foreshortening goes even beyond this point. It is the ability to select and portray part of a subject both effectively and artistically, with a minimal amount of detail, stripped of minute photographic realism, from which arise strength, simplicity, delicacy, and subtlety. This concept of art prevalent in 18th-century lacquer works gave way by the mid-19th century to elaborate, gaudy, overornate, naturalistic, commonplace subject matter portrayed with an excess of minute decorative detail. This trend was due to the popularization of the arts under the more ostentatious taste of the merchants and the banal demands of the masses. These radical changes in aesthetic ideals were reflected in all forms of Japanese art. Thus simple black-and-white ink painting gave way to the naturalistic Okyo school and realistic woodblock prints. Concomitantly, in sculptural art, the simply carved, strongly expressive early netsuke gave way to detail and technical perfection. Similar changes occurred in lacquer art as seen in the 19th-century Somada and Shibayama schools as well as in *makie* work.

In general, when the canons of Japanese art are properly used and applied not just to stereotyped religious and military subjects, but artistically modified and softened, using nature and other less stereotyped subject matter and combined with typical Japanese decorative effects, we reach the height of Japanese aestheticism.

So far the aesthetic principles of Far Eastern art do not differ essentially from those of Western art. However, definite differences exist concerning perspective and handling of subject matter, both pictorial and ornamental. Chinese and Japanese perspective is basically two-dimensional. Shading is considered inartistic. There are no graphic sculptural effects. Features of people are in two dimensions. Pictorially, Oriental artists used many subtle means of obtaining perspective which accomplished their purpose and at the same time aesthetically avoided the distortion of Western perspective. Depth is expressed by aerial perspective rather than linear. A landscape scene is depicted with all of the parts, both near and far, with the eye parallel to all parts of the scene rather than fixed at one angle. This contrasts with Western art, where distant lines tend to converge, giving an accurate linear scientific aspect to perspective, which, however, is not always too aesthetically pleasing. Perspective in Oriental art is, however, still artistically suggested by various other means. Thus distant objects are often partially overlapped by nearer objects or are drawn smaller or partially obscured by haze or clouds. A mountain at a distance has no ledge marks and a man no eyes. Objects in the foreground are accentuated by having darker tones, or by using raised encrustations or raised lacquer *(takamakie)* techniques. More distant objects are often depicted at higher levels in the design and in softer tones and occasionally using a flat lacquer technique, such as *togidashi*. Occasionally perspective is interestingly shown where the observer appears to be peering down at a landscape, and at other times the eye follows the landscape upward, each successive "level," however, being parallel with the eye at its own level (Fig. 22). Occasionally the eye is at one level, halfway up a mountain or where only the middle of a tree can be seen (Fig. 23). In regard to lacquer art, perspective is stressed in many ways. Shading is delicately seen in *sumie* lacquer imitations of brush-stroke painting, as often done on inro made by Toyo (Figs. 22, 209). Here the shading of various black and gray tones is obtained by the density of black dustings used, as well as by the depth of the black within the translucent lacquer plus the exact amount of polishing used. However, much more often perspective and depth are obtained by the three principal lacquer techniques of flat lacquer, slightly raised lacquer, and highly raised lacquer, the last almost approaching sculptural qualities. Furthermore, raised metallic, ivory, and stone inlays were often used both for decorative pictorial effect and for obtaining a sense of depth. Finally perspective was realized (as in *sumie* lacquer) in a much more subtle way, within the depths of flat lacquer itself, by means of soft shadings of slightly different-colored metallic dusts. By dusting these powders within different layers of the built-up lacquer, the effects of distance, clouds, mists, rain, etc., could all be obtained with perfect blending, softness, and beautiful delicacy unobtainable in any other Japanese art form (Figs. 149, 151). The same metallic dust has softly modulated different tones at different depths of the layers of lacquer (Fig. 24). The different sparkling brown, orange, and gold tones of *nashiji* lacquer are an example of such a technique, where the flecks of gold dust vary in color depending upon their depth within the semi-transparent lacquer.

The last major Chinese influence on Japanese art relates to subject matter. There are strict specific laws adopted from the Chinese painters for portraying various subjects down to the minutest details, including the actual sequence of each stroke. These techniques were adopted by the Japanese painters along with some secondary influences upon the lacquer artists. For example, there are 18 different ways (laws) of depicting the lines and folds of a garment. Thus the robes of "elevated personages" are portrayed by the fine "floating silk thread line" *(ko-ko yu-shi byo)*, the stiffly starched garments of the court nobles, samurai, and Noh dancers by the stiff "stretched iron wire line" *(tetsu-sen byo)*, and beggars' clothes by the coarse irregular "rusty nail and old post line" *(ketsu-to-tei byo)*. Similarly, specific techniques are adhered to in portraying landscapes, water, clouds, trees, birds, and flowers. Besides the adherence to these details and laws, specific overall aesthetic and spiritual effects (such as spiritual elevation and living movement) are of paramount importance. Thus pure copying of nature or of human subjects stripped of these aesthetic principles is considered unworthy. Besides, even from a practical point of view, scenic portrayals could not be directly copied from nature because of the media of the Oriental artist. In painting, corrections of ink strokes were virtually impossible, and the rapidity of working with such ink necessitated a mental image of the entire final product before the painting could even be started. Similarly, this applied to netsuke and lacquer art. While the netsuke artist might spend hours studying his subject, such as a wild animal, the final product was his personal artistic conception, using his own unique style, of the wild animal after months of inspired carving. Similarly, with the lacquer artist, who even though he might work from sketches, or from a famous painting, the final product would be his own personal conception evolving out of months of slow, tedious, technical work necessitated by his difficult medium. True imitation is not to be seen in any great Japanese artist's work.

Landscapes should reveal the powers and influences of nature, warriors should look bold, religious personages divine, women delicate and graceful, etc. Thus the body and anatomy are not of prime importance but rather the feeling and spirit of the individual depicted. In Chinese art individual facial expression and bodily movement was not stressed as in Japanese portrayals. These differences will be noted subsequently in describing what might be considered the purely Japanese pictorial and ornamental art form following its emergence from Chinese influence. Chinese ornamental design and techniques, along with the pictorial element, also strongly influenced early Japanese art. Chinese ornamentation, especially in lacquer ware, tended to be overcrowded and symmetrically arranged. These designs consisted essentially of fine networks of scrolls, tendrils, and arabesques along with conventionalized animals and birds, the latter often incorporated into medallions. However, the Japanese artist soon broke away from such stereotyped ornamental tradition. It was this particular field of decoration and ornamentation that the Japanese uniquely developed to the highest degree, revealing the full force of their ingenuity, aesthetic ideals, and supreme technical craftsmanship. The Japanese also adapted the Chinese use of calligraphy both as an art form by itself and as a supplement to other art forms. Thus a treasured scroll may consist entirely of finely executed characters, or a picture might inspire a poem to be appropriately written alongside of it. On the other hand, a poem might inspire a picture. Similarly, calligraphy was used to enhance a pictorial design by interspersing a few letters within the tendrils and leaves of the design itself. In the Japanese handicrafts, including lacquer ware, the entire design might consist of two or three Chinese ideograms or of a few characters alluding to a *waka* poem. Calligraphy itself, as with all Japanese arts and culture, depicts specific symbolism and aesthetic ideals. The interplay between poetry, calligraphy, the fine arts, symbolism, the drama, and literature again represents the close inter-relationship between Japanese culture and way of life.

Japanese lacquer techniques initially were copies of those found in the Chinese and Korean art products which were highly esteemed by their patrons. Gradually the Chinese techniques were incorporated into native taste and were modified and further developed in typical Japanese fashion. New techniques originated and were used alongside the older ones. Thus the relatively crude Chinese method of dusting of lacquer with metallic filings formed the basis of the highly developed Japanese *makie* techniques which the Chinese artisans themselves tried to copy in vain. Similarly, the technique of the heavily carved, busy, Chinese *choshitsu* lacquer never gained popularity in Japan as an exclusive technique for an object but was used more often as a supplementary technique for enhancing *makie* ware or, for example, on a netsuke or an inro to render the red hair of a witch or a *shojo* Kabuki dancer. The Chinese technique of mother-of-pearl inlay work was similarly adopted by the Japanese by selectively using this method in *makie* work for supplementary artistic and decorative effect. Thus a fish, done purely in *makie,* would have realistic glistening iridescent mother-of-pearl eyes (Fig. 3). Many of the older pieces of blue-green iridescent mother-of-pearl inlay work were subtly combined with *togidashi* lacquer technique. It is only with the relatively late Somada school that we begin to see mother-of-pearl used only by itself, reminiscent of the original Chinese technique. These late specimens, not typically Japanese in taste, permitted aesthetic beauty of design to give way to overornate, ostentatious, gaudy, overdecorated technical details. It might be mentioned that while the Chinese used encrustations of mother-of-pearl, jade, and soapstone, the Japanese expanded this technique to include various metallic encrustations which were done by metal (sword furniture) artists.

Initially Japanese art, including lacquer ware, was strongly influenced by the Chinese both in specific techniques and in subject matter, along with the aesthetic canons of presenting this subject matter. With the isolation of Japan during the Edo period, combined with the natural decorative instinct of her artists, a purely Japanese form of art and art values arose. Thus the harsh Chinese landscape gave way to the softer, more delicate, and loving Japanese portrayal of nature which was combined and balanced with the strong Japanese sense of ornamental design. Similarly, the Japanese artist, especially the miniature handicraft artist, depicted more of the finer details of nature in preference to overpowering landscape scenes. This stress placed on the realistic portrayal of the minutiae of nature became characteristically Japanese in feeling and flavor. The scope of subject matter also became much wider and more plebeian in taste by the 18th century, portraying every detail of Japanese living and customs. The Japanese placed more and more stress on the decorative element. Formalized early Chinese lacquer designs and arabesques of relative symmetry, or of crowded figures and landscapes, gave way to typical Japanese lacquer styles. The pictorial element became less crowded and more and more pleasingly asymmetrical. Human and animal figures were shown with less and less stylization and more naturalism. Humor and impressionism were introduced. The decorative element became more Japanese in style, being more varied, softer in feeling, and used not just as a background but as a counterbalance enhancing the pictorial element. The love of the Japanese artist for various textures, natural materials, and "defects" was displayed in Japanese handicrafts. In the miniature metal arts this appeared as the development of various *ishime* grounds. In lacquer art it appeared as the simulation of various textures in both the ground and the pictorial element. Thus lacquer was purposely made in appearance and texture to imitate the knots of wood, the rough bark of a tree, or even pottery or leather. By the late 17th century Japanese lacquer, in technique, ornamental design, and subject matter, had completely divorced itself from its original Chinese influences and had reached its zenith as a unique, purely Japanese art form.

By the late Edo period there was a sudden increased demand for art objects by the *nouveau riche*. The ultimate result was the degeneration of artistic values for the sake of technique itself. Art objects became more and more gaudy and ornate, entailing extremely detailed, elaborate techniques. Such mechanically perfect specimens were often done by special classes of technicians, such as mother-of-pearl inlayers, and were rarely signed.

Thus we see that it would be entirely false to state that the Japanese craftsmen were merely excellent imitators of Chinese art rather than truly inventive artisans themselves. This false impression was gained by naïve and uninitiated Western critics, mainly through poor commercial late examples of Japanese art exported specifically for "Western taste."

Religious Influences

The influence of religion, especially Buddhism, on early Japanese lacquer was considerable. All forms of Japanese art were in their infancy until the advent of relations with China and the introduction of Chinese art and techniques along with the introduction of Buddhism and Buddhist art.

In the 7th century Korean and Chinese artists had emigrated to Japan, and many Buddhist priests were quite conversant with the fine arts. Buddhism had rapidly spread from India, through Central Asia to China, and then to Korea. Thus early Japanese Buddhist ecclesiastical art was tinged with Indian sculptural influences as well as decorative designs. Japanese style and influence in lacquer art had not as yet developed. In the early Heian period (794–889) new Buddhist sects were introduced into Japan. These various sects opened their own workshops, utilizing lacquer artists for the temples and their hierarchies of gods. By the late Heian period, with temporary loss of contact with China, ecclesiastical art saw the true beginnings of its own national art forms and characteristics. In general, designs of the arts changed from the stiff, symmetrical, conventionalized arabesque and religious type of Chinese motifs to the lighter, more asymmetrical, more artistically ornamental Japanese style expressing rhythm, movement, and more typical Japanese subject matter. This change was not only reflected in ecclesiastical art but also in secular art, which had begun to emerge—as, for example, in the beginnings of the Yamato-e school of painting. Similarly, *makie* and *raden* techniques developed and were used not only for Buddhist art but also on household articles and furnishings. It should be noted, however, that many of the early Chinese diaper designs, conventionalized bird and animal forms, and arabesque patterns are used to this very day in Japanese lacquer art, but usually as a means of background or fringe decorative element supplementing the main pictorial motif. This contrasts with early Chinese carved lacquer, which used such designs usually as the central motif itself in an elegant but more formal symmetrical manner. The significance of Buddhist art was not simply the fact that Buddhism patronized the arts and that early Japanese subject matter was mainly Buddhist, but rather that the aesthetic concepts formulated by these newly adopted sects, ingrained in the Oriental mind, were naturally projected into the art forms. For example, the principle that all living things are endowed with spirit (and are therefore fit subjects for artistic portrayal) is part of the Buddhist philosophy of the transmigration of souls. The insignificance and transience of man along with the grandeur and infiniteness of nature similarly reflects Buddhist thought. The religious aspects toward nature are commonly depicted, represented often by a tiny insignificant human figure portrayed against awe-inspiring large rocky landscapes or a small hut tucked away in large rising mountain ranges.

The Japanese absorbed not only Buddhist philosophy but also the associated iconography, mythology, and symbolism. All of these factors became transformed into Japanese thinking and customs and of course secondarily into art expression. A considerable part of the subject matter of Oriental art centers about religion. This includes portrayal of the various gods themselves as well as portrayal of the various legendary (mythological) stories about them. Similarly represented, especially to the delight of the imaginative and expressive Japanese artisan, are Buddhist concepts of hell with its fierce demonology. This subject matter represented direct portrayal of Buddhist religion, but of greater significance are the offshoots of Buddhist art and subject matter representing aesthetic and philosophical concepts engendered by Buddhism. An example already noted is the Buddhist concept of nature and its subjects. Zen Buddhism stressed the importance of meditation in the presence of nature, out of which evolved the typical Japanese garden. Similarly the art of the tea ceremony, the *tokonoma,* and the symbolic art of flower arrangement were offshoots of Zen Buddhism. The tea ceremony in turn led to the development of tea utensils, including lacquer ware, metal ware, and pottery. The basic simplicity of Zen philosophy was reflected in the concepts of Zen art, and complicated iconography and religious sculpture was rejected by Zen Buddhism, which had become the official religion of the court. Chinese monochrome brush-stroke painting, applying to Zen philosophy, resulted in simple artistic paintings, expressing the painter's meditative enlightenment concerning the inner essence of various aspects of nature. This simple economy and strength of stroke and the elimination of ornamental detail to express the "inner truth" of the subject rather than photographic accuracy are still considered by the Oriental connoisseur as the quintessence of art in its purest form. This principle applied as well to the pottery and lacquer ware of the Zen tea ceremony. The pottery, such as Raku ware, was purposely simple, crude, and muted. Similarly, lacquer trays and tea jars were of the simplest effective designs done in subtle, soft, muted tones. This spirit was reflected in other lacquer articles made during these times, such as incense boxes.

With the complete popularization of the arts by the Edo period, portrayal of religious subjects was replaced to a great degree by portrayal of secular subjects; yet the aesthetic artistic principles based on Buddhist philosophy remained in these purely Japanese artistic creations. It is only with a basic knowledge of these concepts, along with an understanding of the previously mentioned principles of Oriental art, that true appreciation and critical evaluation of Japanese art can be achieved.

Influences of the Feudal System

The Japanese feudal system provided an almost ideal means for a development of the fine arts in which commercialism played absolutely no part. Briefly, the feudal system in Japan consisted of a balance of power, both economic and military, between groups of clans. The stress upon hereditary rights and ancestor worship not only perpetuated powerful families or clans in an economic and political sense but also was responsible for the development of the artisan class and long family lines of lacquer artists. Japan was ruled basically by four powerful factions:

1) the imperial household, including the emperor and the court nobility: descendants of the founders of the Yamato Province of the 7th century B.C.

2) the military government (*bakufu* or shogunate) headed by the shogun, or generalissimo, first established in Kamakura in A.D. 1192.

3) the local *shugo* (high constables), who ruled through the shogunate the local provinces or fiefs *(kuni)*. (The local military leaders, or daimyo, were descendants of the *shugo* and developed independent power by the 15th century A.D.)

4) the various economically and militarily powerful Buddhist sects, which hired their own mercenaries.

Historically, the Japanese feudal system evolved as follows: Japan was initially inhabited by numerous clans which ultimately came under the military control of one clan whose authority was centered in Yamato in the 7th century B.C., thus instituting the first emperor and the beginnings of the imperial household. By 71 B.C. the ruling emperor had allocated fiefs or provinces *(kuni)* to 77 of his children, marking the beginning of feudal land distribution in Japan. Shintoism, the religion of Japan at this time, basically professed that everything in nature was equally divine *(kami)* and that the imperial family was an intermediary between the spirits and the people. By the 7th century A.D. Japan was divided into provinces which were owned by different clans. During this period Buddhism was introduced. The imperial capital was moved to Nara in 710 and to Heian-kyo in 794. The local militarily powerful clans, such as the Soga and subsequently the Fujiwara family, often directly or indirectly controlled the imperial family. Meanwhile, newly introduced Buddhist sects also gained economic, political, and military power by hiring mercenaries. Much of the land was owned through a system of absentee landlords who were descendants of the court nobility. In order to protect their property, mercenaries were hired, so that by the 11th century there arose the military class *(bushi)*. War between the powerful clans broke out, the final conflict occurring between the Taira or Heike and the Minamoto or Genji. The latter ultimately gained ascendancy in 1185 and initiated the Kamakura period (1185–1392), the military government being set up in Kamakura. The head of this military government was the shogun, or generalissimo, and thus was established the *bakufu,* or shogunate government. The shogun appointed members of his own clan to rule the local provinces. These were known as *shugo* (high constables), although the right of administration was theoretically still in the hands of the court-appointed governors.

The Muromachi or Ashikaga period (1392–1573) was marked by continued strife between the emperor and such powerful clans as the Ashikaga. Meanwhile the *shugo* increased their local military power and became autonomous beyond the control of the shogunate or the imperial house.

They became known as daimyo (*dai,* great; *myo,* name). Art now continued to flourish under the patronage of the church, the court, the shogunate, and the local daimyo along with the stimulus of the newly introduced Zen culture.

It would seem almost paradoxical that a warlike feudal system dominated by the military class should be conducive to the fostering of art. This was true, however, for three basic reasons: military, economic, and love of art. The Japanese admiration of art and their keen aesthetic sense, associated with their love of nature, has already been seen to arise out of their religion and their adoption of the already highly developed art forms of their neighbors, China and Korea.

The initial patrons of the fine arts, including music, poetry, and calligraphy, were the nobility and the imperial court. As early as the Heian period the wealthy Kyoto nobility contented themselves with the refinements of all forms of art and aestheticism as aptly described in the *Genji Monogatari* and the *Makura no Soshi.* The highly artistic, delicate, almost effeminate tastes of the nobility were naturally reflected in the art commissioned by them. The wealth of the nobility was made possible by the feudal system, under which members of imperial lineage (nobility) were given hereditary land grants as far back as the 4th century A.D. and taxes were collected from the farming class who inhabited these fiefs. The power of the nobility was sustained throughout the centuries through the religious concept (Shintoism) of the divine origin of the imperial family. Even when stripped of political and military power, the nobility contented themselves with the pleasures of artistic enjoyment and endeavors.

The Buddhist church was also a great patron of the arts, mainly for the embellishment of its temples. Many of the priests were learned men who were fully conversant with the arts and often were artists themselves. Some of the priests brought into Japan the arts of China and Korea. The feudal system also permitted the military, political, and economic expansion of the Buddhist sects in many ways. The impoverished peasants preferred to give their land to the church and act as tenants for smaller rent, rather than pay the enormous taxes levied on them. The power of the church was further increased by the shogunate's acceptance of its tenets. Shintoism allowed its clergy to marry, so that the abbots became hereditary. Again, emperors who were in conflict with the ruling shogunate became nominal monks and called powerful clans to help them. The church as well hired mercenaries. From an aesthetic point of view Buddhist art was represented mainly by adornment of temples with lacquer, large sculptures in wood, bronze and lacquered images of deities, and religious paintings. The early religious art forms reflected Buddhist-Chinese-Indian artistry but later reflected Japanese overtones with more lifelike individual faces combined with motion as expressed in muscle and bone configuration, position of the extremities, and more naturally flowing draperies. Even political expediency played a part in the development of the arts. During the time of their political dominance in the 10th and 11th centuries, the Fujiwara family had been inculcated with art appreciation to the neglect of rule by military power. Minamoto Yoritomo, emerging as shogun in 1192, realized this and maintained the center of power in Kamakura in order to isolate the military class from the weakening influence of art in Kyoto. On the other hand, the shogunate often encouraged the arts to distract the warlike clans and also for economic reasons in establishing trade relations with China, Korea, and Southeast Asia. However, the economic advantages of such trade were readily capitalized on by the local daimyo, who rapidly developed their own industries and patronized their own artists. Thus during the Kamakura (1185–1392) and Muromachi (1392–1573) periods the arts were also patronized to a great extent by the shogunate and the local daimyo. The taste of these new art patrons was reflected in the changing art motifs of these years. There was a predominance of Zen Buddhist art, since Zen was adopted mainly by the samurai class. Along with this religious art there developed, as previously mentioned, the tea ceremony, the art of flower arrangement, and the art of the Japanese garden. The daimyo, in spite of their militaristic spirit, were quick to emulate the nobility and the shogunate in their art appreciation. They competed in lavishing every possible artistic luxury on their castles, their taste often being somewhat gaudy and colorful and certainly less delicate than that of the Heian nobility. The metal arts, including the making of swords and sword furnishings, flourished under the military rule. The firm establishment of the Tokugawa regime early in the 17th century was responsible for radical changes in art forms. The political expediency of reducing the power of all but the shogunate resulted in the suppression of the Buddhist church and in the isolation of Japan from trade and political relations with the rest of the world. The result was the decline of religious art in deference to secular art, the rapid development of Japanese art techniques divorced from foreign influence, and the development of art in the local provinces.

The feudal system was also responsible for the propagation of art families. Thus as early as A.D. 905 Emperor Daigo ordered that official lacquer artists should not be permitted to change their occupation and that they were to train students to succeed them. The subsequent class distinctions (including prohibition of intermarriage) following the introduction of Confucian philosophy resulted in further isolation of the artisan class. These artists lived in homes set aside on the grounds and under the patronage of their local daimyo. Furthermore, the importance, according to the Shinto religion, of perpetuating the family name resulted in artists' adopting adept students and giving them the right to use part or all of their family name. Incidentally, this in turn, is in part responsible for the confusion of signatures in identifying Japanese works of art. Well-known artistic families were appreciated, often given honorary titles, and patronized, so that quality of work took complete precedence over quantity and commercialism. It was also the custom for the daimyo and the shogun to commission specific articles to be made for them by the lacquer artists. These commissioned articles, even when made by a very great artist, out of deference to the lord were never signed.

The cycle became complete with the rise of the merchant class during the Edo period (1615–1868) and the almost total popularization and secularization of the arts among the common classes. Money, rather than produce, became the basis of exchange, and with the development of commerce and industry wholesale and retail dealers and moneychangers gained economic ascendancy. This *nouveau riche* merchant class began to patronize the arts. More schools were established, spreading education and culture among the common people. Poetry, the drama, and woodblock printing gained popularity among the masses. Art began to be mass-produced according to the tastes of its new patrons. Subject matter was expanded to appeal to the masses and to the wealthy merchants. Every aspect of everyday Japanese life became fit subject matter for Japanese art. Art objects became more photographically realistic and technically increasingly more detailed, ornate, and colorful, quite often at the expense of prior effective artistic strength and simplicity. By the end of the Edo period, along with commercialization of art, the military class was disbanded and the wearing of arms was forbidden, which ended the fine miniature metal art of sword furnishings. The modernization of Japan, including the wearing of Western dress, ended the need for inro. The daimyo were forced to return their fiefs in 1869. The decreased demand for and the loss of the feudal patronage of lacquer art, combined with the rising cost of living and labor, made it virtually economically impossible for an artist to devote the necessary time needed to create a superior piece of lacquer art.

Cultural Influences

Along with the political and economic reasons for art development under the Japanese feudal system was the basic love of art, "art for art's sake." Without this the natural outlets of artistic development under the nobility, imperial household, church, daimyo, shogunate, and merchant classes could not have been realized.

Art forms existed to a minor degree in the pre-Buddhist era. As soon as Japan became organized into provinces by settled tribes, governmental fostering of the fine arts was eagerly promulgated. As early as A.D. 701 the legal code provided for bureaus of lacquer artists and textile workers. The cultivation of lacquer trees was encouraged, and raw lac was accepted in lieu of taxes. Lacquer ware was even accepted instead of land grants.

Meritorious deeds were often rewarded by the shogunate with gifts of lacquer ware. Artists were held in high esteem and were widely patronized by the wealthy and ruling classes and were given honorary titles, such as *hogen* and *hokkyo*. Even civil wars and campaigns against neighboring countries did not adversely affect the development of the arts. In fact the art-conscious Hideyoshi brought back potters during his war with Korea between 1592 and 1598. Similarly, local strife, such as the conflict between the Taira and Minamoto clans at the beginning of the 12th century, resulted in the rebuilding of temples which had been destroyed. The war of Onin (1467–78) resulted in the destruction of Kyoto, but the city was soon zealously and artistically rebuilt. What, then, formed the basis of this aestheticism of the Japanese people? We have seen that there were numerous factors responsible for the molding of the Japanese love of art. The intermittent close ties with China caused ready absorption of the already long-standing and well-established art forms of China. The simultaneous rise of Buddhist art and Buddhist philosophy also played a large part. The natural emulation of the shogunate, daimyo, and finally merchant class of the culture of the nobility also played a significant role. Finally there was the establishment of various artistic Japanese customs and modes of living thoroughly subconsciously indoctrinated into the Japanese mind, both young and old. The Japanese custom of applying art practically solely to utilitarian objects, no matter how insignificant, brought art within the reach of all social levels. Finally, the natural craftsmanship and technical ability of the Japanese artisan helped foster the handicrafts.

Appreciation of art and nature and antiquity is instilled into Japanese children at home and in school. Special excursions are taken into the countryside, to beauty spots, to famous temples, and to adjacent historical sites. Appreciation and observation of landscapes and of animal and insect life is inculcated into the students. The art of miniature landscape garden arrangement traces back as far as the reign of Empress Suiko (A.D. 593–628), when stones of rare shape were presented to the court from China. Various forms of arrangement thus developed including *bonseki* (tray stone), *bonkei* (tray landscapes), *bonsai* (potted dwarf trees), *bonga* (tray pictures), etc. In some of these art forms dwarf trees are used; in others sand is used to symbolically represent water and earth; and even feathers are used to represent different types of waves (according to the season). The custom of employing "rare" stones *(kiseki)* of unusual shapes to represent mountains or other natural phenomena is also followed in these miniature landscapes, or they are used by themselves for the *tokonoma*. Beautiful natural and often grotesque stones are similarly seen in Japanese gardens and are often depicted on Japanese lacquer ware. Thus appreciation of the natural materials of nature and texture are enjoyed by all classes of society. This important feature is represented in the various handicrafts where lacquer or metal backgrounds were often made to imitate both the appearance of and the texture of earth, wood, stone, or the bark of a tree. Lacquer was even devised to imitate antique bronze or rough pottery (Fig. 4). The appreciation of texture itself was not just visual but tactile as well, as exemplified by the purposefully rough texture of pottery or the stress placed upon the soft rounded feel of an old netsuke. This idea went even further into love of "defects" and "crudeness," including those of nature. Pottery was purposely made with defects in an artistic sense and made to appear artistically "crude." The aesthetically crude appearance of an unadorned old iron *tsuba* (sword guard) is highly appreciated by the Japanese connoisseur. Defects in the grain of ivory were incorporated into the design of the lid of the tea caddy, and metals were purposely divorced from their regular artificial sheen by use of various patinas and ground techniques, such as *ishime*. Nature is similarly represented with natural defects and erosions. In painting, specific brush strokes depict special erosions of rocks and landscapes; woods are represented with cracks, worm holes, and decay; and leaves similarly reflect the blights of nature. All these facts combine symbolism and keen observation of nature with consummate artistic mastery and technical perfection.

The Japanese garden and art of flower arrangement, outgrowths of Zen Buddhism, combine the simplicity of Zen philosophy with artistic and symbolic treatment of nature. Every Japanese town has its gardens of chrysanthemums, plum blossoms, cherry blossoms, etc. Similarly, Japanese homes are constructed with landscaped gardens. The reception room always overlooks these gardens, and when the outer doors are removed, the garden becomes essentially part of the house. The garden also forms part of the architecture of the adjacent teahouse, permitting meditation in nature as an integral essential of the tea ceremony (another artistic outgrowth of Zen Buddhism). These gardens are carefully planned works of art and contain natural stones, including irregular, artistically placed steppingstones of different size, shape, and color. Evergreen trees and nonflowering shrubs and moss-covered ground complete the simple, quiet-toned monochrome picture. In the larger gardens, water in the form of ponds, streams, and even waterfalls is employed, but in smaller gardens these are symbolically represented by sand.

The art of flower arrangement similarly represents the Japanese aesthetic method of displaying flowers. This may vary from a single bud in a simple bamboo vase for the *tokonoma* to a more complicated specific symbolic type of flower arrangement depending upon the season or festival but at the same time remaining complementary to the *kakemono*. In general, the flowers and branches are asymmetrically arranged and placed basically at three different levels, the tallest representing heaven, the lowest earth, and the middle the "reconciling principle," man. This art, known as *ikebana,* is taught in nearly all the girls' schools as well as privately by flower masters.

The Japanese home itself also typifies the aesthetic principles of its inhabitants. The typical home is the epitome of simplicity, representing the transience of man's life on earth. Basically it consists of rooms which are separated by movable partitions of folding screens *(byobu),* single screens *(tsuitate),* and sliding and removable doors *(fusuma).* There are also, in lieu of windows, sliding doors called *shoji.* These are covered with translucent paper, permitting soft diffused light to enter the room. Incidentally, paintings look better in this soft light and lose their subtle shadings (washes) in stronger light. The partitions are removable so that the rooms may readily be changed at will, or a portion removed so as to allow a view of the veranda *(engawa),* which may be either open or closed, and the garden. No furniture is used except for such items as the mats on the floor, a low table, and built-in wall shelves *(chigaidana).* An integral part of the house is the tearoom *(chashitsu)* as well as the *tokonoma,* or picture recess. The main room or reception room faces the garden and contains the *tokonoma* and the *chigaidana.* The *tokonoma* is basically a recessed frame containing a platform, all of which is constructed of beautiful natural woods. On the wall of the *tokonoma* is hung a scroll *(kakemono),* and on the platform sits a floral decoration *(ikebana)* or some work of art, each chosen, as mentioned, according to the season or holiday festival. In general, the house is built to permit maximum ventilation in the humid summer weather. Also to be noted is the typical asymmetry not only in the house but even in the eccentric placement of the *tokonoma* and the *chigaidana* as well as the shelves of the *chigaidana* itself. The entire house stands in the middle of the garden, which in turn is surrounded by a wooden fence.

The home is uncluttered by furniture, and the woods used for decoration of the interior of the house are unpainted but carefully chosen for their beauty of grain, texture, and color.

The widely practiced tea ceremony *(cha-no-yu)* involves details of etiquette approaching those of an aesthetic art form. Prior to the actual drinking of the tea, the guests sit in an arbor of the garden adjacent to the small tearoom or teahouse. It is here that one meditates in the presence of nature and divorces oneself from worldly things. The tearoom is also arranged simply according to Zen philosophy. It contains quite unobtrusively woodwork of the finest grains of various natural woods. It also contains a *tokonoma* from which hangs a *kakemono* of simple brush-stroke painting, or just calligraphy, and an appropriate flower arrangement. Part of the ceremony consists of studying, examining, appreciating, and asking questions about the history of the scroll, the displayed art objects, and the utensils used in the ceremony itself. These include the teakettle, the tea caddy, and other objects used in the preparation and drinking of the specially prepared tea. Such objects are in simple taste and are often valuable art treasures. Even the approved manner of handling these objects of art in the palm of the hand (guarded with the opposite hand and held low) speaks for the loving care with which the Japanese regard fine art objects. The stimulus given to the metal, lacquer, and ceramic handicrafts for use with the tea ceremony has already been noted.

Poetry, calligraphy, brush-stroke painting, and musical dramas are all interrelated with one another and to the handicrafts as well. They all form part of the cultural and aesthetic background of the Japanese people. The children are taught the Japanese *katakana* and *hiragana* syllabaries and then the Chinese ideographs. This trains them in the use of the brush as well as in the art of calligraphy itself. Furthermore, it visually and artistically fuses written language with ideographs. It is also training for the accuracy and keen observation so necessary for the Japanese artist. A much-valued scroll may contain just calligraphy, or a picture may inspire a poem which is appropriately written on the scroll. The use of written characters intertwined in a lacquer picture alluding to a poem *(waka)* was common to both Chinese and Japanese art. Poetic or literary allusions are found in Japanese plays. Poetry reading and composition was popular among all classes of society. In the spring, people would stroll in gardens and arbors and improvise poetry on paper in honor of the wisteria or of springtime and attach them to the branches of the tree so that they would be read by other passersby. Similarly, an old custom consists of parties held for the purpose of viewing the moon, at which time poetry was written.

The various forms of drama revolve about mythology and folklore and are expressed by subtle symbolic mimicry and movement abetted by music, make-up, or masks, and magnificent costumes. The development of mask carving (14th–17th centuries) and stimulation of textile manufacturing can be attributed to these dramas. The popularity of the Kabuki drama was reflected in the *ukiyo-e* woodblock prints, which commonly depicted the actors and their costumes and headdresses. The costumes and headdresses of a popular actor often became the "rage" of the day. In the Gagaku, or oldest form of court music, grotesque and exaggerated facial expressions contrasted with the esoteric Buddhist sculpture of the corresponding era. The Noh drama, which developed during the latter half of the Kamakura period (1185–1392), was derived from the Sarugaku. The Noh became quite popular among the nobles and upper classes while the later Kabuki drama was more popular among the masses. In the Noh play the principal actor *(shite)* and the adjunct to the *shite (shite-zure)* wear masks. The most famous mask carvers stem from this time (14th–17th centuries). The essence of the Noh play is to bring out a sense of elegance, beauty, and simplicity as specifically expressed rhythmically and musically in the dances. This is effected through a minimum of stylized movement and lack of facial expression. The plots are simple and concern themselves with mythology, folk tales, and war tales. In general the Japanese drama expresses life and emotion artistically through symbolism and suggestion in a simple lofty aesthetic manner so characteristic of Japanese art in general, whether it be painting, the tea ceremony, or flower arrangement. The allusions in the drama to poetry, literature, mythology, and Shinto and Buddhist ideas again typify the close relationship of the various art forms among themselves and also to folklore, symbolism, and native religion in regard to subject matter.

Japanese music, like the other art forms, is not isolated but is also related to religious, dramatic, or festival occasions. Japanese festivals again reflect a mixture of folklore, symbolism, religion, and love of nature and various art forms. All of the festivals purposely fall on an odd day of an odd month, since odd numbers are "positive," lucky, and reflect the male principle. Along with each festival there are associated symbolic flowers. Similarly, the *tokonoma* is decorated not only according to the season but also according to the festivals. The Girls' Festival, for example, is celebrated on the third day of the third month and is associated with the peach blossom (a symbol of longevity). An appropriate painting for the *tokonoma* is one of *kamibina,* or paper dolls. The women wear festive clothing, and the girls take out their dolls for display. Appropriate gifts to the girls are dolls which are essentially works of art rather than mere playthings and are often family heirlooms. Similarly, the New Year is celebrated with an appropriate picture, such as that of Fukurokuju, a god of good luck. The houses are adorned with evergreens. To the right and left of the entrance to the house are placed red- and black-stemmed pines representing the female and male principles, together indicating happy marriage. Near the entrance is also placed a straw rope which is divided into specific odd numbers of strands dividing the pure from the impure. From the rope are suspended other symbolic objects. A painting of the *takarabune,* or treasure ship (Fig. 25), is placed under the pillow to bring happiness for the coming year. At New Year's actors perform religious dances and pantomimes, strolling artists draw, and wandering ballad singers appear.

We have seen to a certain extent how the various art forms pervade every aspect of Japanese life and customs. We have seen this in the Japanese love of nature, their early school training, their flower and garden arrangements, their architecture and *tokonoma,* their tea ceremony, their poetry, music and drama, and their festivals. Japanese art objects and art forms are basically utilitarian or related to other aspects of their culture, rather than an isolated art in themselves. This applies to the handicrafts that specifically combine utility and art. Even paintings are done to reflect religious and spiritual qualities rather than to be appreciated mainly for their face value. Conversely, utilitarian objects are usually in themselves works of art. Thus even so minor an object as a penny fan or inexpensive writing paper is made tastefully and artistically. Each Japanese home has its *tokonoma* with its art objects commensurate with the economic status of its members. This also applies to the tea-ceremony objects. Such art objects are highly treasured and tastefully displayed a few at a time, the remainder being carefully stored away in fine silk bags and in turn in a storage box. This box is often carefully made and signed by the artist, thus providing as well a document of authenticity. Art objects are displayed also to the taste of invited guests, the best objects being brought out for the most honored guests. This is not a sign of ostentation but of true appreciation by the household and by the guests as well. This close observation of works of art is in part responsible for the extreme detail found in most Japanese art objects. The objects are decorated and carved equally carefully from all sides, including the bottom surfaces, since their quality depends on their being beautiful from no matter what aspect they are studied. This applies even to the drama, where the pose of the actors must look equally artistic from all directions. The feel of the art object is of equal importance, such as the rough texture of Raku ware, the smooth glossy texture of lacquer ware, and the rounded soft oval feel of a good old netsuke. In general, Japanese art objects are pleasing from a distance as well as upon minute scrutiny. The minuteness of many works, whether it be painting, metal work, lacquer, or sculpture, is often undiscernible until a strong hand lens is used. It is only at this time that the technical finesse of the artist can be fully appreciated. The details of brush stroke, the minuteness of chisel marks and metallic inlays, the hairline quality of *chinkin-bori* can only then be truly appreciated. Yet a good artist does not satisfy himself with pure technical detail at the expense of artistic values, as was commonly done in the late Edo period. The simplicity of design, the minimal strokes used to achieve the desired effect are of primary importance. The canons of art should be adhered to with the utmost simplicity and yet effective aesthetic taste.

The Japanese custom of exchange of gifts was already established under the first Tokugawa shogun, Ieyasu. Japanese gifts are usually works of art and must be appropriate to the occasion. Thus, when a male child is born, the proper present to the family is a carp *kakemono,* the carp representing the epitome of perseverance and military spirit. Similarly when a female child is born a *kamibina* (paper doll) painting is presented. As a wedding gift, a painting of male and female mandarin ducks, symbolic of conjugal fidelity, is appropriate. As previously mentioned, gifts of lacquer ware were happily accepted in lieu of land grants as rewards for meritorious deeds for the government.

Japanese clothing also reflects Japan's decorative textile art. Such clothing varies according to the season. Valuable works of art are stored in precious brocades. Even the Japanese meal is aesthetically presented. Food is served in artistic lacquered and pottery cups and dishes placed on fine lacquered trays. The food is artistically arranged so as to be pleasing to the eye as well as to satisfy the appetite.

In summary, then, the Japanese culture is pervaded with aestheticism and the home with artistic utilitarian objects. To this very day a high percentage of luxury money is spent on items of art. A specific example of the close interrelationship between Japanese culture, mythology, symbolism, and art in everyday living is reflected in the carp. This fresh-water fish *(koi),* according to Chinese mythology, in the third month of each year (note the odd-numbered month) ascends the Yellow River. It fights its way up the cataracts (five gates) and finally leaps the Dragon Gate, which, if it can pass it, will transform the carp into a dragon. The symbolic association of the carp is therefore that of perseverance, the conquering of obstacles, and military spirit. This symbolic representation is introduced into Japanese life in many ways: to pass the state examinations is known as "leaping the Dragon Gate." At the Boys' Festival, celebrated on the fifth day of the fifth month (note positive, odd, or male numbers), it is customary to hang carp flags or carp-shaped balloons attached to bamboo rods and lines over every housetop to encourage its boys to rise to fame and fortune. When a male child is born a proper present to the family is a carp *kakemono.* The carp is also used at ceremonial banquets and cut up alive for *sashimi.* The fish is placed alive in a vessel during the meal, and then the carver passes the flat side of the knife blade over the body of the fish, which becomes motionless and submits to being sliced to the backbone. The carp in Japanese mythology is associated with such Japanese deities as the *sennin* Kinko, the household god Ebisu, and the priest Kensu. Kinko was a Chinese recluse who spent his life (twelve centuries) painting fish. He was led by a fish through the river world, and he returned riding on the back of a carp in view of his disciples. The smiling old bearded priest Kinko riding on the back of a carp is a favorite Japanese art motif. Another favorite subject of Japanese art depicts the carp struggling upstream (Figs. 26, 27). We see here that the Japanese gods themselves represented basically the idealistic and aesthetic principles of the life of the Japanese people. Thus the close association of the gods with nature, their love of artistic and meditative pursuits, their adherence to religious and Confucian philosophy, their gentleness and individual personalities, and even gentle humor, reflect the basic Japanese mind, which in turn created its own mythology and folklore, in its own "mind's eye."

With a comprehensive knowledge of all of the factors influencing Japanese art we can now outline what may be considered as the final evolution of its art motifs, both pictorial and ornamental. We have already noted the strong Chinese and Buddhist influences which gradually gave way to typical Japanese modifications in response to indigenous Japanese culture and aestheticism. We have also noted the various factors responsible for the ultimate development of this culture and aestheticism. Of what, then, when broken down, does this typical Japanese art consist? Japanese art may be broken down into three main categories: 1) general aesthetic concepts of art and art motifs, 2) treatment of subject matter or pictorial design, and 3) treatment of decoration, surface area and backgrounds.

The way in which Japanese artisans portray these three factors comprises the inner core of their unique art. We have already discussed the evolution of and influences upon Japanese aesthetic principles of art. We can now analyze the basic Japanese treatment of specific subject matter.

Subject Matter: General Principles

Generally speaking, subject matter in lacquer art is treated in an overall Chinese or Oriental fashion. This includes the traditional method of handling perspective in the two-dimensional form and the use of typical Oriental subjects, such as landscapes, details of nature, birds, animals, and gods. Yet there evolved tremendous changes throughout the centuries, ultimately creating a distinctly unique Japanese flavor which reached its sublime quintessence by the 18th century, with which period we are primarily concerned. We have already seen how the Japanese lacquerer handled perspective, both subtly with the use of simple flat lacquer and more sculpturally with the use of raised lacquer and encrustations. The second general distinction of lacquer art which deviated from traditional ink-stroke painting was the use of color. Color, as practiced in typical *sumie* painting according to the subdued aesthetic principles of Zen art, is of secondary importance, if to be used at all. Color in black-and-white, as in Chinese painting, is obtained by the amount of pressure of the brush stroke and by the "wash"—the more diluted the ink, the lighter the tone. Thus an endless variety of tones (washes) could be obtained, from a deep powerful black to a faint, delicate, hazy gray-white. In such a way both strength and subtlety could be achieved, including beautiful portrayals of mist, haze, and other vagaries of nature so dear to the heart of the Japanese.

Such washes were also, as previously noted, used to depict perspective. This black-and-white painting was only occasionally imitated by the lacquer artist or even the metal artist. In lacquer the design consisted of shadings of black lacquer against a gold or silver background. Toyo was famous for this style of decoration (Figs. 22, 209). The metal artist also occasionally imitated this technique, using the black alloy *shakudo* against a gray background of the alloy known as *shibuichi*. With the popularization of the arts in the Edo period, the more striking use of color became a predominating motif in the arts as exemplified by the detailed naturalistic *ukiyo-e* school. In general, lacquer art always stressed color effects to varying degrees. While it has been stated that pure lacquer colors could not be obtained because of the inherent amber tone of clear lacquer, the real reason is that the Japanese lacquer artist preferred soft, muted colors and tones to sharp "pure" colors, as much as the metal artist preferred various subdued alloys and "picklings" to sharp, shiny pure copper and silver. Thus in lacquer art greens are muted, revealing an olive tint; blues are light and soft, often a muted grayish color; and reds also are toned down or brick-colored. Many gradations of tones were used, so that a subtle green would readily blend with a delicate blue tone. In later lacquer works, such as those of the Somada school, special iridescent blue-green mother-of-pearl was used. Occasionally gold leaf was put under the mother-of-pearl to give a golden hue, a similar color effect being used for inlaid tortoise shell. In general, it is in more modern works that colors have become more pure, sharp, and harsh. The one exception to the use of pure color is *roiro* or the highly prized, highly polished, rich gleaming black lacquer used as a ground. Figure 6 shows an inro revealing very unusual colors rarely seen in Japanese lacquer, including a rich dark olive-green ground and rarely used yellow lacquer along with shades of fairly pure reds.

Contrasting with the more decorative colorful aspects of Japanese lacquer are a group of subtle lacquer techniques which appeal to the Japanese taste and ultimately to the Western connoisseur. Such simple subdued taste was in keeping with the Zen tea ceremony. This consists of the use of fine simple black designs very slightly raised on a rich black background, such as may be seen by the nature lover at night. Occasionally the design is done in a dull black finish on the black glossy ground. Rarely the black design itself is etched or slightly below the ground surface. At times the design imitates an old Chinese inkstick with "cracks" in the background surface. Variations of this technique use dark tones of brown or combinations of dark brown and black. It is almost impossible to photograph such specimens of art, for the design can often only be visualized by tilting the lacquered object so that the light strikes it indirectly (Figs. 28, 147).

Irregularity and asymmetry of subject matter presentation is much more distinctly Japanese. While the Chinese may present the natural irregularity of nature by a tree with asymmetrical branches, the Japanese will go much further and present an aesthetically pleasing asymmetrical picture in regard to grouping all of the subject matter involved. The hardest part of the Japanese artisan's pictorial effect is often considered to be the "blank space." At times the Japanese artist definitely exaggerated the asymmetry so that almost an entire scene may be depicted in a corner of a lacquer painting (Figs. 25, 29). Japanese artistic effects of foreshortening and suggestion have already been noted.

Pictorial Subject Matter : Nature

Nature itself is handled with less awesome and more affectionate care than in comparable Chinese representations. Landscapes are less intense and foreboding, softer and more gentle, an effect due not only to the sympathetic daily existence of the Japanese in the midst of nature but also to their gentler natural landscapes. Japanese landscapes are not only less foreboding, but the Japanese handling of every facet of nature is keener, for it is portrayed in a more tender, realistic, often humorous, and yet artistic fashion. The Japanese artist is particularly fond of depicting not only the effect of the different seasons on natural vegetation—such as leaves gently bending in the wind and the nuances of autumnal tints—but also the subtle modifications and effects of such ethereal aspects of nature as wind, rain, mist, haze, and moonlight. A favorite picture is that of a tiny leaf or two wafting downward in the moonlight. As mentioned, a night effect is quite imaginatively obtained on lacquer ware by using "black on black." The Japanese artisan goes so far as to observe and depict the different types of rain. Thus spring rain is depicted by thin slightly opaque lines and winter rain by heavy, closely placed, very opaque lines falling at different angles. Waves are similarly represented differently according to the different seasons. Thus there are peacefully long spring waves, rippling summer waves, rougher autumn waves, and choppy winter waves. Even the directions of the wind peculiar to each season were considered. In general, however, the Japanese artist inherited and retained many of the Chinese conventionalized methods of portraying waves and clouds. An exception is the artistic semiconventionalized cloudlike appearance of *nashiji* used for background effect (see *mura nashiji*, page 113). Wind is revealed by bending of blades of grass or of a bird helplessly drifting with sideward motion against a strong breeze. Even the direction of the wind may be ingeniously represented. The Chinese had already carefully noted the natural erosion of their massive rocks and landscapes. They were accurately portrayed by numerous specific brush strokes, such as "axe marks," which were quite effective and powerful. Such landscapes are now existent in Japan through the Chinese Yüan teaching of painting, which had some effect on the Japanese artisan, including the lacquerers of the Muromachi period (1392–1573).

Astute observation is noted in the Japanese portrayal of every aspect of nature: its minerals, vegetables, insects, and animals. As we have previously noted, the appearance and physical texture, and grain of natural objects are keenly observed and artistically copied in the various handicrafts, being portrayed either as part of the ornamental design or as the background. Figure 30 shows a delicate sprig of plum blossoms contrasted against a background of rough-textured lacquer imitating in a semirealistic way the bark of a tree. The deleterious effects of time and the seasons on nature are also a favorite Japanese theme. A rotting plant or vegetable being eaten by parasitic insects and the natural decay and color changes of a leaf are popular subjects. In general the Japanese artist would as readily depict a simple worm or bug as an imposing landscape. Occasionally, plant and animal life was portrayed in a very impressionistic manner. Impressionism is best seen in the Korin school of lacquer ware. This is strictly a Japanese innovation, since Chinese impressionistic lacquer ware did not exist. Finally we should note that, in representing nature, the various elements of subject matter are often symbolic and may refer to folklore and mythology as in Chinese art. The symbolic elements, of course, must be in keeping with each other, such as the representing of a fir tree with bamboo, cranes, or tortoises, all of which are symbols of longevity.

Pictorial Subject Matter: Human Figures

Human figures are also handled much differently by the Japanese artisans. True, there are the set Chinese laws for drawing robes, faces, and figures, but all this is modified by the Japanese taste for individualism, expression, motion, realism, and ornamentation. In the early art periods, facial expression, as exemplified by the scroll paintings of the Heian period in Japanese art, was disregarded, being secondary to colorful robes. Similarly the faces in early Japanese Buddhist art reveal lack of individuality. Subsequently a certain amount of stereotyped portrayal developed, warriors collectively being depicted as bold, or ladies as equally beautiful. Ultimately there developed individuality of sentiment and expression. Even gods were softened and humanized in distinction to the placid, esoteric Chinese faces. In fact there is a decided tendency for the Japanese to exaggerate facial expression. This found fruition in depicting the more fierce Buddhist gods and in the concepts of hell. The love of grotesqueness and exaggeration is best seen in the portrayal of various ghosts and hobgoblins so popular in Japanese mythology and folklore. Free vent of the imagination can also be seen in the innumerable types of carved masks as well as in strong facial expressions seen in netsuke. The full range of human emotion and expression is forcefully depicted: from fear, horror, ferocity, humor, and caricature to subtle nobility of spirit. Artistic portrayal of symbolic positioning is also typically seen in the theater. In either case the accepted pattern is for exaggeration of body expressions. Similarly, the masks used in the drama overplay facial expression. While exaggeration of expression was considered poor taste in painting, it ran rampant in the handicrafts, although to a lesser degree in lacquer ware. Along with strong facial expression the Japanese portrayed corresponding power and motion in the muscles, bones, and sinews and in the flowing robes of their subjects (Fig. 32). The stiff Chinese portrayal of robes, especially in ecclesiastical subjects, gave way to softer, more natural flowing lines or to more vigorous swirling, waving, flying ends of draperies and garments in depicting motion and vigor. Such powerful delineation was seen as far back in Japanese sculpture as in portrayals of the guardian gods of the Nara period, in which even the veins of the arms were made to stand out. The muscles of the face, neck, exposed shoulders, forearms, hands, legs, and feet are similarly well anatomically presented with strength and motion. At the other extreme the Japanese artisan would just as carefully paint or carve a serene Buddhist deity or lovely, dainty female with a quiet restraint in which motion and grace might be subtly suggested by a slightly upturned wrist or finger and gently flowing draperies (Fig. 7). Copying the nude figure, on the other hand, played absolutely no part in Japanese art, either in sculpture, painting, or the handicrafts. Human figures were often portrayed in Chinese lacquer art, not as individual entities but as expressionless, motionless, stereotyped, similarly dressed people standing in great numbers in crowded court scenes or amidst scenes of numerous rigid pagodas, houses, trees, bridges, etc. Such works typified the minutely but nonaesthetically carved Chinese *tsuishu* lacquer ware, which never became very popular in Japan.

Japanese humor and caricature played a considerable role in art as far back as the animal scrolls of the Heian period (794–1185). Not only are animals portrayed in a humorous vein; they are often whimsically shown imitating human characteristics and foibles. Typical examples range from the almost slapstick Japanese humor of a monkey seriously studying an inro with a hand lens or a woman intently picking fleas out of her kimono to that of the subtle, penetrating caricatures of Sharaku's woodblock prints of actors. However, humor played a more predominant role in the plebeian arts like that of the netsuke rather than in lacquer art (Figs. 186, 196). Humor in Chinese art is less common.

Subject Matter: Decorative

Of utmost importance in Japanese art, especially the handicrafts, are the specific Japanese principles and techniques of ornamentation. Early Japanese art consisted essentially of Chinese art motifs and designs dispersed in the Chinese manner and with backgrounds reflecting Chinese methods. The designs, especially in the handicrafts, were of scrolls and arabesques of Buddhist Chinese-Indian-Persian flavor. The same applies to designs associated with Buddhist iconography, such as the flame pattern seen in halos. Other motifs adopted from the Chinese included conventionalized ocean waves, clouds, and mythological birds and animals like the phoenix *(ho-o)* and the dragon *(ryu)*. However, such designs were gradually modified to Japanese taste. The birds were made more graceful, and in the case of the mythological Buddhist birds called *karyobinga* the human face evolved into that of a Japanese woman. These mythological animals and birds were transposed by Chinese art into stiff formal medallions and arabesques as part of the overall scrollwork of conventionalized patterns of tendrils and leaves. These ornamental patterns were quite densely and evenly dispersed over the entire surface area. Backgrounds in paintings were of dark, somber washes. But this formal, heavy method of ornamentation did not for long appeal to the Japanese artisan. By the Heian period, even though the designs were still essentially Chinese in origin, they became less profuse, more curving and delicate in conforming to the somewhat effeminate aesthetic taste of the nobility. In later eras the Japanese continued to adopt Chinese techniques of painting as well as techniques involving the handicrafts, but such methods were used mainly as a means of further enhancing their own decorative patterns. Subject matter became typically Japanese, portraying Japan's own folklore or incidents in the everyday life of its people. This subject matter was tastefully balanced by ornamental decorative patterns. Background effects, especially in the handicrafts, became more and more important in order to enhance the pictorial element. By the early Edo period (17th century) ornamentation had become more and more predominant. Finally, by the late Edo period (19th century), the accent on superfluous and detailed decoration completely overwhelmed many attempts at artistic pictorial effects.

What, then, were the Japanese ornamental techniques? There were both general and also more specific techniques. The general techniques were: 1) subject matter, 2) color, 3) shape, 4) disproportion and impressionism, 5) symmetry, and 6) surface area. The specific techniques were: 1) fretwork, 2) diaper patterns, 3) powderings, 4) medallion work, 5) designs, 6) materials and multiple techniques, and 7) background effects.

Subject matter was often chosen specifically for its decorative effect rather than for artistic accomplishment. This was particularly true in genre painting and in the handicrafts of the late Edo period. Instead of religious subjects and the spiritual, aesthetic portrayal of nature, subjects were chosen such as seen in *ukiyo-e* prints of beautiful women in colorful flowing robes. Similarly, flowers and scenes on gold backgrounds were depicted on the screens of the daimyo in the Momoyama period (1573–1615) for purely decorative effect.

Color, at one time considered of secondary importance, now became predominant in Japanese art. Black-and-white paintings gave way to colorful paintings or were combined with color effects. The technique of combining artistry and decorative effect reached its zenith in the Korin school (early 18th century). In metalwork simple artistic monotone ironwork gave way to the lavish use of color obtained by encrustations with gold, silver, copper, and various alloys, such as *shakudo, shibuichi,* and *sentoku.* Similarly, in lacquer ware *makie* techniques became more detailed, colorful, and decorative. Ultimately the *makie* was combined with blue-green iridescent mother-of-pearl and various colorful encrustations using tinted ivory, metals, coral, malachite, etc.

The shape of decorated objects became more varied, more ornamental, and more daring. Simplicity gave way to irregular forms, often to shapes simulating their pictorial element. Thus an inro depicting sea shells might be made in the form of a sea shell, or a Daruma in the shape of a Daruma

(Figs. 31, 103, 104, 212, 229). The use of disproportion for artistic decorative effect was seen especially in the Korin school. Here effects actually became impressionistic both in painting and in lacquer ware. Detail was minimal, and bold strokes were used to obtain the decorative effect. In lacquer ware large, strong, almost crude-appearing pieces of tin, pewter, lead, and mother-of-pearl would be encrusted in an impressionistic manner offsetting a few finely decorative touches (Fig. 8). To achieve such effects a flower may be proportionately greatly enlarged in eye-catching fashion and perspective purposely distorted. Such artistic liberties were taught to a lesser degree in Chinese art, where flowers and leaves were made relatively larger than the remainder of the branches or the tree trunk. Such disregard for proportion is often seen in netsuke—for example, a frog squatting on a relatively large leaf or, conversely, a large frog climbing out of a relatively small water bucket. Occasionally such disproportion was used for symbolic reasons rather than purely artistic ones.

Asymmetry has always been a keynote in Japanese artistic taste, evinced in architecture, gardens, flower arrangement, and all of the arts. The basically symmetrical arrangement of Chinese lacquer art was soon replaced in Japanese lacquer ware by greater and greater asymmetry both in pictorial effect and in ornamentation (Figs. 25, 29). Subject matter was displaced to one side or low down in a picture, often leaving a large completely blank area which was occasionally enhanced with a few ornamental leaves or blades of grass. Similarly, the details within the subject matter itself would be asymmetrically arranged to avoid visual boredom. Flowers and branches would show a variety of shape and form, the stems and leaves being carefully eccentrically placed. The designs on a robe may vary in pattern, shape, design, and color and yet form a decorative cohesive whole. The same applies to ornamental patterns. Here various geometric and scroll-like patterns may be scattered throughout or border the pictorial element. Such patterns similarly vary in design and shape and are eccentrically dispersed, often twisting at various angles and even overlapping one another. The perfect balance between such ornamental design and the pictorial element is typical of Japanese artistry.

The Japanese handling or ornamentation of an object of art is unique. To the Japanese artist the entire surface area must be a part of the design. The sides, bottom, insides, and edges of the object all enter into both the pictorial and the ornamental effects. Specifically by the Momoyama period (1573–1615) both the picture and the supplemental ornamentation began to flow over the rims, edges, and sides of the objects. The entire object, no matter what its shape, was part of the design. While the insides of boxes and their bottom surfaces did not usually contain the pictorial design, they were enhanced with fine lacquer, frequently of *nashiji*. The inside of the covers, however, usually revealed designs often finer than those of the outside (Figs. 9, 130, 131). Even the natural openings of an object, such as a *tsuba,* were often employed for decorative purposes or as part of the picture. The holes in the *tsuba* were artistically made use of by including them as part of the design or permitting the design to sweep through them as if they never existed. Similarly, in the kimono, the design incorporated the entire surface area, including the neck and the sleeves.

We now come to more specific Japanese methods of ornamentation, the simplest being variations of fretwork. Japanese fretwork, like the comparable ancient Greek fretwork, consists of repeated angular geometric designs such as the well-known key pattern, which is usually used as an ornamentation about the edges of the lacquered object. The Japanese frets, however, are usually intermittent rather than continuous. They are extended or reduced to suit the size and shape of the objects to which they are applied. Japanese fretwork is extremely diversified and is further developed in Japanese diaperwork.

Japanese diaperwork again illustrates the love of variety. Diaperwork is essentially a more complicated, diversified, and extended form of fretwork. The designs are again geometric in nature or combined with geometriclike conventionalized forms. The diaper is often used as a supplementary ornamental design to the main pictorial element or, most or all, the design itself may consist of pure diaperwork (Fig. 35). The diaperwork on Japanese art objects is usually of several designs. The surface of the object is divided up into asymmetrical spaces constructed by the intersection of straight or curved lines, by combinations of the triangle, square, circle, or multisided forms. Thus there may be displayed intersecting circles, hexagons, lozenge forms, fish-scale diapers, etc. Quite often varying irregular spaces are left between the diaper forms, or the diapers are effectively contrasted and broken up with delicate scroll or floral patterns. Diapers may be of pure geometric designs or of conventionalized patterns of flowers and foliage. Attempts are purposely made to disguise any repeated symmetrical pattern or diaper so that the varied diaper designs may be irregular or geometric divisions which often intersect each other at varying angles. Finally the diaperwork may be dispersed in the form of medallions, which is a unique Japanese method developed as an offshoot of powderings.

Powdering consists of a decorative effect obtained by distributing small conventional geometrical (often floral) or pictorial designs through a field (Fig. 37). Quite often the powderings consist of various Japanese heraldic crests. The Japanese technique, in contrast to Western methods, employs powderings which are irregularly distributed, while the powderings themselves are usually varied. These powderings may be irregularly scattered, combined in varying-sized groups, or made to overlap one another. This seemingly haphazard distribution of powderings, as well as medallion decoration, is in reality very carefully planned so as to render a flexible, pleasing, nonboring appearance. In general powderings are most commonly seen as small circles within which appear conventionalized designs of flowers, animals, and heraldic crests.

A higher form of development of powdering technique, unique to Japanese art, is the medallion system. The medallion is a geometrically outlined form filled in with more ornate decoration, such as landscapes, flower, animal, or figure subjects. These medallions are of various sizes and shapes, most commonly circles or segments of the circumference of a circle. Circular medallions are often formed by conventionalized birds and foliage which coil on themselves. The medallions are kept distinct from the background by having different material, color, or groundwork and usually have well-defined borders of geometric shapes. When the circular medallions are used alone they are usually of different sizes. Commonly medallions of different shapes and sizes, as well as different designs, are used. The medallions, like powderings, are asymmetrically distributed (Fig. 36). In typical Japanese fashion the irregular dispersal of powderings and medallion work against varied backgrounds and pictorial effects makes the entire surface area quite pleasing to the eye and does not induce boredom. Similarly, their dispersal on all sides of the object makes it pleasing from all directions. Upon closer scrutiny this effect is still maintained by the detailed and variegated designs within the powderings, medallions, background, and picture. In small objects, such as inro, however, the use of medallions and powderings is limited by the small surface area. These techniques nevertheless were used on inro. More commonly, such ornamentation was absent or was achieved by means of diapers, powderings, or medallions along the edges of the inro outlining the subject matter or decoratively placed on the risers, on the external cord channels, or on the top and bottom surfaces. This ornamentation was done in *makie,* mother-of-pearl, *chinkin-bori,* and other techniques (Fig. 10).

Special geometric designs were used by the Japanese artisan—for example, the oblique or zigzag line which divided the surface roughly into corresponding asymmetrical halves. These contrasting halves were usually decorated differently. This technique became popular in the Momoyama period (1573–1615) and was applied to textile and lacquer-ware decoration (Figs. 158, 229). There are specific names for some of these geometric patterns *(saya-gata),* such as *rinzu* and *asa-no-ha.* The *rinzu* pattern is essentially a series of straight lines resembling the well-known "key pattern." *Asa-no-ha,* which is commonly found on Chinese and Japanese *tsuishu* lacquer ware, consists of a series of circles whose points of intersection are connected by lines forming a star (Figs. 40, 74). This pattern was called the hemp-leaf pattern and was used for babies' clothing, indicating the desire for the baby to "grow with a strength like that of the hemp plant." In other cases the geometric pattern represents decorative effects by conventionalizing the pictorial elements. The popular Zeshin "wave design" is such an example and consists of a repetitive series of concentrically smaller arcs fitting within one another (*seigai-ha;* Figs. 11, 25).

In a broader sense special designs of the pictorial element itself were done in order to obtain a decorative effect. These consisted of arabesques and scroll designs of flowers, plant life, birds, and even animals. In their simplest form these designs were done as circular powderings. Heraldic crests of infinite variety were commonly used as decorative powderings and often represented the crest of the noble family for whom the lacquered object was made. In a still broader sense even an entire tree—for example, a pine sapling—was represented in a decorative, slightly conventionalized manner. In general, however, the Japanese lacquer artist preferred to limit conventionalized patterns purely as a decorative adjunct to the more individual aesthetic pictorial element, in contrast to the Chinese lacquer artisan, in whose work the entire surface area was more often than not composed of stylized conventionalized and geometric patterns.

In general the varied decorative effects that the Japanese artisan obtained were achieved through the numerous materials and multiple techniques that had been developed within each field of art. The final effect was a combination of the aesthetic decorative ingenuity of the artist using the numerous techniques at hand. Specifically in lacquer ware the artist had at his disposal all gradations of colored lacquer, various sizes of metallic powders and cut foil, from a fine powder to large heavy sheets, ivory, coral, mother-of-pearl and various metals and alloys for encrustation. These and many more techniques from completely flat to highly raised lacquer work could be used in an infinite number of combinations to achieve the ultimate desired pictorial and decorative effect. Under such circumstances it is no small wonder that the artisan by the late Edo period tended to overdo the ornamentation producing ostentatious, gaudy, detailed decoration at the expense of simple, strong, aesthetic pictorial effects.

Of considerable importance in the development of Japanese decorative effects was the stress placed on background. This does not involve the various powderings and designs which were often used as decorations on the backgrounds. More specifically it consists of the groundwork upon which the decorative and pictorial elements were applied. Such backgrounds, known technically as the "ground," received as much attention as the pictorial element itself. These grounds often involved special techniques including the artistic portrayal of special "textures." Many times the backgrounds were prepared by special artists, both in lacquer and in the metal arts. There were even special artists who devoted themselves to preparing even so specific a metal background as *nanako* (tiny circular pebbles). Similarly in lacquer ware, the background may be of a natural wood grain, seen especially in the works of Ritsuo, or it may consist of a rich velvety black lacquer, occasionally prepared by a special group of artisans. This black lacquer may be enhanced by artistic dusting of metallic powders *(nashiji)*. Quite often the lacquer ground may be made to simulate the bark of a tree, a rough stone surface, or the grain of natural wood or leather. "Rough" iron and "crude" pottery were so perfectly imitated in lacquer as to defy identification of the material unless inspected by handling (Fig. 5). Objects such as Japanese dolls were similarly so cleverly made of porcelain, wood, or papier-mâché as to defy visual identification of their actual material. Even wood was carved to simulate a more "woody" appearance by purposely accentuating the grain and carving out defects and knotholes. *Mokume* was a technique used by both lacquer and metal artists in which the grain of wood was artistically simulated. Such background techniques imitating texture and natural simple crude products of nature were highly esteemed by all the handicraft artists. In a similar fashion the metal artist attained background effects by carefully engraving, hammering, and chiseling as seen in the various types of *nanako* and *ishime* (see metal techniques). By such methods highly artistic background effects simulating stone surfaces, the skin of a toad, falling drops of rain, etc., were carried out. Furthermore, the use of copper, gold, and silver in metalwork (and as encrustation for lacquer ware) was further developed technically into the use of various alloys, and the patina of the alloys themselves was altered for artistic effects by boiling them in chemical baths. The result of these innovations was the magnificent black and gray patinas of such alloys as *shakudo* and *shibuichi*, which were used primarily for background color effect as well as for adding variety to the pictorial element. As noted before, the use of pure shiny silver, gold, or copper for either the background or pictorial design was considered as vulgar taste. This was another reason for altering the appearance of the metals.

In summary, all forms of Japanese art, and in fact everyday Japanese living and culture itself, consist of a complicated web of reciprocating influences. Nature, art, religion, mythology, culture, symbolism, aesthetics, and home life are not isolated, independently working factors but are completely interrelated. A masterpiece of painting or handicraft is not simply a work of art to be placed in a museum but the symbolic representation of the artist's inner religious and aesthetic feelings toward his subject matter. In turn, we have seen how the artist's concepts were basically formulated by the above-mentioned interrelationships forming the background of Japanese aestheticism. Thus to the untrained eye, a simple picture of a stalk of bamboo merely represents an artist's sketch of one small aspect of nature. This is furthest from the truth, and such lack of understanding almost totally destroys the aesthetic value of the picture beyond its decorative effect. The bamboo, typifying constancy and upright conduct, is to the Japanese a paragon. Because the bamboo stalk grows close to the parent stem it is considered an emblem of family loyalty. The bamboo permeates every aspect of Japanese life. It is used in housing, for various utensils, as a food, and even as a medicine. To the Oriental eye, the bamboo is represented in spring with its leaves spread out joyously, or in rainy weather hanging down despondently, or wildly crossing its stems in windy weather. Symbolically the bamboo also represents longevity, constancy, and upright virtue. This symbolism is expressed in the upright conventional way of drawing bamboo and bamboo leaves. Symbolism is further reflected as far as minute specific rules for drawing every detail of the bamboo. Such details not only represent what is considered most appropriate artistically but also include symbolic strokes of calligraphy and references to nature. Thus the various horizontal lines on the bamboo stalk are similar in appearance to such Chinese characters as those for "positively," "heart," "second," and "eight." This close correlation between calligraphy and art has already been noted. The stem of the bamboo is similar in appearance to rats' tails, and the seven-leaf arrangements (odd numbers are favored) appear as "fishtails," "goldfish triple tails," and the "swallowtail." These cross references to nature reveal the harmony between art and nature and between all created things.

The bamboo is also associated with various mythological and folklore stories, such as the "Seven Sages in the Bamboo Grove" (Fig. 119). As in all Japanese art the bamboo is represented in keeping with the season and in symbolic accordance with the rest of the pictorial element. Thus it is often depicted giving refuge to the tiger during a storm and is symbolically associated with the crane representing long life, fidelity, and constancy. Finally the bamboo is presented in accordance with the previously mentioned canons of Japanese art along with whatever decorative elements and acceptable artistic license the artist may choose.

Thus we have seen that constant intercourse between nature and daily life was an integral part of Japanese cultural expression, and it was this combination that produced the various pictorial and decorative elements of Japanese lacquer ware, which evolved into a unique national art form.

2 ❖ History of Japanese Lacquer

THE HISTORY OF JAPANESE LACQUER CONSISTS OF THE VARIous political, religious, and economic stimuli throughout the centuries which founded and fostered this branch of Japanese art. This chapter concerns itself basically with the historical influences on three major phases of lacquer art: 1) the overall development of lacquering and lacquer schools, 2) the origin and development of the major lacquer techniques, and 3) the development of lacquer design and subject matter.

Ancient Period (to A.D. 552)

The basic art of lacquering originated in China. It was subsequently introduced into Japan, where it flourished and gradually developed its own characteristics. Unfortunately we have only scant knowledge concerning the details of lacquer techniques during the Ancient period. Relics of lacquered bowls, combs, and amulets dating from the Jomon period and the Ancient Burial Mound period have been recovered. Red and black lacquer was already in use, although lacquer was probably used mainly at this time as a preservative for wood and leather articles rather than for ornamental purposes. Mention is made in the old records of a clan of lacquer workers called *nuribe* or *urushibe* as well as the establishment of an Imperial Lacquer Department in the period of Emperor Koan (392–291 B.C.). Decorative figures and ornamentation were already being done at this time. A book written in A.D. 380 mentions red and gold lacquer and a work appearing eight years later mentions gold lacquer as well as powdered gold lacquer, or *nashiji*.

Asuka (Suiko) Period (552–645)

With the introduction of Buddhism into Japan about 552, lacquer art received a substantial impetus. Black, red, yellow, and green lacquers were used, and the ornamental designs revealed the influence of the Chinese Six Dynasties and Han dynasty periods. Lacquer art was employed mainly for the decoration of important buildings, Buddhist images, and temples and was used on priests' robes. Also Japanese envoys to China wore lacquered leather armor. In 607 Prince Shotoku sent a mission to China to import Chinese culture, including all of the handicrafts. Knowledge of these handicrafts was to be developed in the following Nara period as applied to Buddhist art.

Nara Period (645–794)

Emperor Kotoku, whose reign began in 645, took an interest in lacquer art and established a special department employing the best artisans. Inferior lacquer was officially banned. There is a record of an order from Emperor Temmu (673–86) for red lacquer cabinets. Mention is made of the appointment of twenty government lacquerers under the reign of Emperor Mommu (697–707) who were ordered to study lacquer works and to sign their names to their articles. In 701 a legal code was set forth which included the establishment of an office of the Guild of Lacquer Workers (Nuribe no Tsukasa), which became part of the Ministry of the Imperial Household. It also ordered every landowner to plant lacquer trees in accordance with the area of his land and accepted lacquer in lieu of taxes. At this time princes and chief government officials were given crests to be painted in lacquer on a wooden tablet indicating their rank and office.

With the free exchange between Chinese and Japanese artisans in this period, many new lacquer techniques were adopted, showing the influence of the T'ang dynasty. Among these techniques were mother-of-pearl (raden), oil color (yushoku), sheet design (hyomon), gold-and-silver picture (kingin-e), powdered gold (makkinru), and the beginnings of makie techniques, including chiri-makie. These methods were used separately or in combination and were applied to wood imported from China. During the Nara period dry lacquer (kanshitsu) and lacquered-hide techniques were copied from the Chinese. In the former the wooden base was covered with layers of lacquered hemp cloth and, when dried, the wooden frame was removed. These methods were used not only for small objects, such as boxes, but also for large Buddhist figures. While these techniques were subsequently abandoned, the use of cloth and hide as a basis for lacquer is seen in early inro. Here the bodies were made of ox leather or even of thin dog or cat skin further stiffened with paper or cloth. Occasionally the rims alone were made of leather, the bodies being of thin wood.

The greatest demand for lacquer was for use in the temples, on the images and even on the beams and walls. However, lacquer was also beginning to be used on furniture, boxes (including sutra boxes), musical instruments, and sword scabbards. The motifs were influenced by the Chinese and were essentially of symmetrical formal scroll and arabesque designs interspersed with conventionalized flowers, leaves, and birds. The objects were heavily decorated, with minimal free background space. By the time of Emperor Shomu (724–48) lacquer had reached a high level of perfection. In 756 among the presents given to the Todai-ji temple by the empress Koken were some musical instruments, a *go* board, and mirrors, all gold-lacquered and encrusted with mother-of-pearl.

Heian Period (794–1185)

Very little is known about early Heian lacquer ware since few specimens remain from this period. In general, the later Heian period is noted for the patronage of the arts by the new Buddhist sects and by the emperor and the nobility. With the temporary loss of contact with China in 894, Japanese artists started to develop their own techniques and designs and to decorate utilitarian articles in addition to religious ones. In the early 9th century the Lacquer Department was incorporated into the future Public Works Department. In the 10th century lacquer ware was apparently no longer restricted to the official governmental lacquerers, since lacquer articles and lacquer juices from some of the provinces (Mino, Kozuke, and Echizen) were received by the government in lieu of taxes. In the late Heian period (Fujiwara, 898–1185) the nobility indulged in luxurious living, causing an increased demand for such lacquered articles as screens, folding screens, and other furniture to adorn their homes. Temples continued to be lavishly decorated and even had their beams and ceilings decorated with *makie* lacquer. In 905 Emperor Daigo issued strict regulations for the official supervision of the methods of making lacquer. It was also ordered that official lacquer artists would not be permitted to change their profession and were to train students to succeed them. In 947 a law was passed requiring all chief court officers to carry a sword with the sheath encrusted with mother-of-pearl, and in 987 all court ladies decorated the margins of their robes with mother-of-pearl, marking the beginning of such decorations on costumes. The emperor Kazan (reigned 984–86) was an amateur lacquerer and encouraged the fine arts. The priest-artist Chonen sent his disciple Ka-in to the emperor of China in 988 to present gifts of his lacquer work. Similarly in 1073 lacquered objects were sent to the royal house in Korea.

In 1087 the temple Chuson-ji was built in Mutsu Province and was decorated with *nashiji* and encrustations of mother-of-pearl. During the civil strife between the Taira and the Minamoto in the 11th century the art of lacquering fell into complete decadence, the priests remaining as the chief lacquer artists working around Kyoto. They introduced the technique of *ashide-e,* or calligraphy, dispersed within the pictorial design (Fig. 41). In 1129, on the 50th birthday of the emperor Horikawa, two famous lacquer artists Norisue and Kiyohara no Sadayasu were honored by being invited to the imperial banquet. In 1142 the entire furniture of the palace of the emperor Konoe was done in *nashiji* with rich encrustations of gold, mother-of-pearl, and stones of five colors. In 1169 the *kuruma,* or carriages of nobles, were decorated with *hyomon* lacquer. In general, lacquer was now used for many types of smaller and larger utilitarian objects, such as ink-stone boxes, fan boxes, cosmetic kits, comb boxes, desks, sword sheaths, clothes boxes, musical instruments, saddles, lanterns, food and drinking vessels, religious scroll boxes, etc. Many of these objects were exported to China and Korea, but in general the exportation of lacquer ware was prohibited up until the Meiji Restoration (1868), when Japan emerged from isolation to enter the modern world.

Technically *makie* was becoming increasingly finer as was sheet design and mother-of-pearl, while the older Chinese method of oil color was discarded. Other techniques now used were *togidashi makie, makkinru, hiramakie,* and *heijin makie* ("even dust"). The introduction of *aokin-fun* (gold-silver powder) and *maki-bokashi* (graduated sprinkling) improved the shading techniques. The *ikakeji* method (heavier dusting than *heijin*) developed, and the Somada style was mentioned during this time in the *Genji Monogatari.* Colored glass inlay was even done, although rarely. Boxes were edged *(okiguchi)* with lead, pewter, and silver, as ordered by Emperor Kazan in 986. *Nashiji* was used as early as A.D. 905.

Artistically lacquer design followed the general art trends of the time. They expressed the delicate, simple, graceful artistic taste of the nobility along with the beginnings of a more Japanese type of design copied from the newly established Yamato-e school of painting. Nature was beginning to be portrayed more realistically and pictorially, and the overall design was balanced simply and more artistically over the surface of the object. This contrasted with the previously portrayed highly conventionalized patterns of scrollwork and vegetation, densely and evenly distributed over the surface purely in the form of decorative patterns and arabesques. Nature, however, was still represented symbolically—a characteristic that permeates Far Eastern art through tradition, mythology, folklore, religion, and teachings of the laws of Oriental painting. Similarly, the portrayal of human and animal figures became Japanized and changed from that which produced the stylized, calm, expressionless, stoic Chinese faces and figures to that which depicted softer figures expressing rhythm and movement and displaying more individual facial expressions. Such trends were foretold especially in the early Japanese Buddhist sculpture, which was often lacquered to give the figure an added softness and a quiet grace.

Kamakura Period (1185–1392)

Japanese art, which had formerly been patronized only by Buddhist sects and the nobility at Kyoto, now found new patrons in the shogunate established at Kamakura and in the rising warrior class. Lacquer products of the era of Emperor Gotoba, who reigned from 1183 to 1198, were preserved in the temple of Hachiman in Kamakura. Such articles are decorated with birds or chrysanthemums encrusted with mother-of-pearl. It is noted in old records that Minamoto Yoritomo's (1147–99) wife Masako had great admiration for lacquered objects. The Kamakura school of lacquer came into existence during this time. The re-establishment of relations with Sung China presaged the influence of Zen Buddhism on Japanese art, which was felt mainly in the following Muromachi period. In 1315 the temple known as the Hideyoshi-ji was decorated with lacquer by famous lacquerers, including such artists as Kiyomitsu, Morichika, Moriuji, Yoshinaga, Tomoshige, Tomonage, Kunitomo, and Morihiro. During the 14th and 15th centuries, besides the Kamakura lacquerers, Kyoto again started to produce lacquer work. Technically, silver powder was not used as in the Heian period, giving works more strength at the expense of finesse. *Hiramakie* (flat design) and *takamakie* (raised design) developed along with new powders: *hirame-fun* (flake gold), *nashiji-fun* (fine aventurine gold), and *kirigane* (cut gold). *Makie* powders showed a greater range from coarse to very fine, and mother-of-pearl was often used alone and more intricately, especially as seen on saddles. Two special types of lacquer techniques developed during this era. The first was Kamakura-bori originated by the sculptor Koben, and was copied from Chinese carved lacquer. The second was the Negoro-nuri technique (Sho-o era, 1288–92) developed by the priests in the monastery of Negoro in Kii to produce red-and-black-lacquered eating and drinking vessels. In 1585 their temple was destroyed by Hideyoshi, and the few survivors fled to Kuroe in the province of Kii, continuing their production of lacquer ware for a short time.

The various lacquer techniques were often used to illustrate popular poems *(waka)* by incorporating into the design various Chinese characters of the poem. This poem (or song) picture technique was called *utae* and was probably Japanese in origin, although it was also practiced by the Chinese artisans.

Japanese art, including that of lacquer ware, continuing under the influence of the Yamato-e school, tended to veer more toward secular subjects, and nature was portrayed more realistically. Through the influence of the military spirit, works were stronger in appearance, sharper, more detailed, and form and lines were stronger and more angular. The omission of shadings of silver powder during this period and the use of various gold powderings and flakes in both subject matter and background, along with a profuseness of subject matter, resulted in less delicate and more gaudy pictorial designs.

Muromachi (Ashikaga) Period (1392–1573)

Japanese art during the Muromachi period was influenced essentially by Zen Buddhism, the renewal of trade with China, and the continued patronage of the arts under the shoguns Yoshimitsu and Yoshimasa. The overthrow of the Kamakura *bakufu* involved the destruction of the town of Kamakura, the shogunate being returned to Kyoto. In the 14th century two retainers of the Ashikaga family built castles at Sakai in the province of Izumi, thereby attracting lacquer artists to this area and inspiring new developments in the lacquer art. Yoshimitsu re-established trade with China through the Chinese port of Nimpo, and the local provinces also traded with China. Japanese Zen priests went to China to study, bringing back Chinese Zen culture. Many Chinese art objects were thus imported to Japan, including Sung and Yüan paintings and the new techniques of Ming lacquer ware, all of which were highly prized by the Japanese. Yoshimitsu (1358–1408) built the famous Kinkaku (Gold Pavilion) in Kyoto and retired there to indulge in Zen art and Chinese painting. Similarly Yoshimasa (1435–90) retired after two years as shogun to devote himself to religion (Zen) and art. He built the Ginkaku (Silver Pavilion) at Higashiyama in Kyoto. He took an interest in painting, music, calligraphy, drama, and the tea and incense ceremonies as well as the lacquer and metal arts. He employed Shuko and Jo-o to design new lacquered tea utensils, such as the *natsume* (tea jar). These were used in the summer in contrast to the pottery jars employed during the winter. He also employed the lacquerer Koami Docho (Michinaga), who often used for his designs the works of famous painters, such as Noami, Soami, and Tosa Mitsunobu. Also serving Yoshimasa was the lacquerer Igarashi Shinsai, whose style was later adopted by the Kajikawa family. The descendants of Shinsai and Michinaga were the outstanding lacquerers of the late Muromachi period. In general Japanese artists, including lacquer artists, began to be known by name during the Ashikaga period along with the beginning of the development of lacquer art schools and families. The lacquer works of this period were appropriately called Higashiyama pieces after the location of the Silver Pavilion. Japanese lacquer was being exported to China, where it was so highly appreciated that between 1426 and 1457 Chinese workmen came to Japan specifically to learn the art of *makie*, but they were never able to master the Japanese techniques or artistry in this particular medium.

Meanwhile the importation of Chinese lacquer ware resulted in the adoption and development of new techniques which the Japanese lacquer artists characteristically perfected and incorporated into their armamentarium. An example is the Chinese carved lacquer *(choshitsu)*, also known as Pekin or cinnabar lacquer, which was adopted by the Japanese (see *tsuishu, tsuio, tsuikoku,* and *hashika-bori*) by a lacquerer called Monnyu who lived in Kyoto during the reign of Emperor Gotsuchimikado (1464–1500). He also introduced the *guri* lacquer technique of carving into layers of different colors. During the Muromachi period relief *makie* further developed and was combined with burnished *makie*, such as *shishiai togidashi*. Silver and vermilion lacquer were also used. The old mother-of-pearl technique tended to give way to the new Ming-style thin shell. During this period, however, mother-of-pearl technique was replaced mainly by gold and silver sheet-design lacquer including *kana-gai* technique. Kamakura-bori, which was employed in Kamakura, was popular as well as *chinkin-bori*, both of which were of Chinese influence. The Chinese *chinkin-bori* is known as lance-gold *(tsang-chin)* and had been popular since the Sung period (960–1279). In general the gold grounds were still rough, being polished by stone, and the grains of gold still projected beyond the lacquered surfaces. This point is important in determining the age of the lacquer. The technique of Shunkei-nuri, or transparent lacquer, was invented by the lacquerer Shunkei of Sakai in the province of Izumi at the end of the 14th century. Part of the stimulus to lacquer-ware production came from the tea-ceremony lacquered articles as well as those for the incense ceremony (Fig. 42). Lacquered cosmetic kits and especially inkstone (writing) boxes were popular during this period.

Pictorially the designs of this period were not only affected by freer shapes and the beginnings of Japanese lacquer asymmetry and new techniques but also by the influence of the strong brush strokes of the Chinese Sung and Yüan paintings in the portrayal of rocks, tree trunks, and flowing water. This Chinese influence was incorporated into the Yamato-e style, which continued to develop. Furthermore, the simplicity of Zen art also affected lacquer designs, which became simpler and more artistic than in the preceding period. The designs of the lacquer ware of this period were also adopted from the Kano school as well as from the graceful Tosa school of painting. Previous to the Muromachi period, designs were principally either of birds or flowers, but now landscape designs, temples, and human figures were introduced.

Momoyama Period (1573–1615)

The Momoyama art period was so named because during this period Hideyoshi built Fushimi Castle in Momoyama in the southern part of Kyoto. The culture of the Momoyama period was influenced essentially by the spirited patronization of the arts by the military rulers (Nobunaga, Hideyoshi, and Ieyasu) and the local daimyo, along with cultural contacts with China, Korea, the South Seas, and the West. The civil wars between 1570 and 1592 temporarily dispersed the lacquer artists and burned down their workshops, and once again lacquer art fell into temporary decadence. With the reunification of the country through subjugation of the powerful daimyo and Buddhist sects, art and culture continued to prosper. Trade with Portugal, Spain, Holland, and such Southeast Asian areas as the Philippines and Java flourished and to a certain degree furnished new art motifs and lacquer techniques. Relations with China were maintained, and, as a result of Hideyoshi's invasion of Korea in the last decade of the 16th century, new techniques of pottery and mother-of-pearl work were imported from that country.

Hideyoshi himself was a great patron of the arts and the tea and incense ceremonies. He introduced the custom of rewarding patriotic deeds with gifts of lacquer which were highly valued. This custom continued with several other shoguns. With the suppression of Buddhism, art became more and more secular. The end of feudal warfare brought about increased prosperity through foreign trade as well as increased trade and communication among the provinces. The local daimyo lived in luxury and patronized the fine arts, including the tea and incense ceremonies. They surrounded themselves with fine artists and maintained large castles which were resplendent with fine paintings, screens, lacquer, and metalwork. The castle towns subsequently became thriving commercial areas with the beginning of the new merchant class, which similarly began to patronize the arts, especially in the following Edo period. Lacquer ware, however, was still done mainly in Kyoto, rather than in the provinces, as would happen in the following Edo period.

Lacquer art and artists were patronized by the shogunate, especially Hideyoshi. There developed a gradually increased range of utilitarian articles, including personal articles along with household furniture and utensils, which were appropriate for lacquer decoration. Among such articles were meal trays with legs, eating and drinking bowls, cups and jars, tables, chairs, lanterns, cabinets, chests, shelves, etc. Hideyoshi employed the lacquerers Seiami and Hidetsugu II for making lacquered tea boxes. He also awarded a diploma of merit to the lacquerer Nagakiyo and commissioned his son Choan to supply lacquer articles for the enthronement ceremony of the emperor. Both of these men were members of the famous Koami lacquer family. Examples of fine lacquer work of this era include that done for the Tsukubusuma Shrine, the Sambo-in temple and the Kodai-ji temple in Kyoto, which was the mausoleum built by Hideyoshi's widow. The *makie* work of this period is also known as Kodai-ji *makie*. This period saw the beginnings and development of the *inro,* the *zushi* (miniature portable shrine), and the *natsume* tea jar, all of which added great stimulus to miniature lacquer art.

Technically flat *makie* was mainly employed. *Nashiji* was used not only for background but also in the pictorial design, known as picture aventurine *(e-nashiji)*. Untouched sprinkle *(maki-hanashi)* was also in favor giving a more sparkling effect, as well as relief *makie* sprinkled with gold dust on the raised design *(maki-abise)*. *Kana-gai* and *hari-bori* (needle carving) continued to be used, and the older Chinese lead-oxide-oil technique *(mitsuda-e)* was repopularized from the influence of Chinese lacquer and oil paintings. New methods were also being employed. These included *kimetsuke makie,* or relief *makie,* the design being ornamented with flakes of gold or silver, a development of the older *hyomon* technique. *Gyobu nashiji* (named after Gyobu Taro) became popular. Lacquer wares from Siam *(kimma-de)* and the South Sea Islands *(koma-de)* were imported and adopted by the Japanese artisans. In the former the designs were carved out and filled with colored lacquer, and in the latter the lacquer designs consisted of circles of different colors. *Chinkin-bori* (sunken gold carving) technique became popular, especially in Nagasaki, during the Kyoho era (1716–35) and Wakasa-nuri (marbled color effect) began to be used in imitation of the Chinese Zonsei lacquer. Artistically, Japanese lacquer ware by the end of this era and in the early part of the Edo period reached its zenith. Lacquer during this period was often called *jokei-in* after an appellation of the shogun Tokugawa Tsunayoshi. Designs, techniques, backgrounds, ornamentation, and subject matter became typically Japanese. Technique, especially in *makie,* had become more varied, detailed, and perfected. The various methods were combined to obtain optimum artistic effect. Pictorial designs were relatively purposely simple and proportionately combined with artistic ornamentation. Pictorially the designs of the Momoyama period consisted mainly of autumnal plants, chrysanthemums, and paulownia designs in the Yamato-e style. By the end of this period and the beginning of the Edo period, there was a tendency for stronger more abstract impressionistic effects under the Koetsu and Korin schools. Artistically entire surfaces, large or small, were treated as a whole. Designs were gracefully and asymmetrically dispersed, flowing over the edges and rims of the lacquered surfaces. The designs were varied, each surface having different but blending patterns and ornamentation. Varied diapers and ornamental powderings including family crests *(mon)* were used to enhance the entire pictorial effect. Occasionally, as previously noted, contrasting pictorial halves using a diagonal or zigzag line were designed as in the kimono of the day. Relatively uncommon was export lacquer ware produced under European guidance of designs appealing to the Western taste and including such articles as backgammon boards and Catholic religious boxes.

Edo Period (1615–1868)

The Edo period was marked by over 250 years of peace resulting from the firm control of the Tokugawa shogunate over the local daimyo, the imperial house, and the Buddhist sects, combined with the virtual isolation of Japan from the rest of the world, with the exception of China. The arts in the first half of this period continued to flourish under the patronage of the local daimyo and the shogunate in Edo. However, toward the end of the Edo period, because of the increase in commerce and industry, all types of art became popularized and secularized under the patronage of the newly rising wealthy merchant class *(chonin)* as well as the common folk.

With the transfer of the shogunate to Edo, lacquer artists were attracted to Edo from Kyoto. Many lacquer artists were summoned by the shogunate, including Koami Naganori of Kyoto. The shogunate even established a lacquer workshop, calling it *okoyaba,* or small workshop. Edo lacquer ware ultimately surpassed that of Kyoto, both of which stressed elaborate *makie* techniques. The lavish use of gold and *makie* with technical perfection continued. Concurrently there developed the Koetsu, Korin, and Ritsuo schools, which stressed stronger, simpler, impressionistic, and more artistic lacquer ware. Here the artistic effect was obtained by the use of relatively large encrustations of lead, pewter, shell, or porcelain. Excessive ornamentation and minute, photographic, crowded, pictorial detail gave way to simple effective suggestibility. During the early 19th century court lacquer was stimulated by Tokugawa Ienari (1773–1841), who stressed lacquer work associated with popular holidays, such as the miniature furniture used during the Boys' and Girls' Festival days. During this period also, lacquer design was influenced by the realistic nature-loving aspect of the Maruyama (Okyo) school of painting. By the mid-19th century, designs adapted from the colorful *ukiyo-e* school of painting and woodblock prints were used on lacquer work, including scenes of Hiroshige's *Fifty-three Stations on the Tokaido* (Fig. 151) along with pictures of typical *ukiyo-e* women and Kabuki actors with their resplendent colorful robes (Fig. 43). Many of the later generations of famous lacquer families—for example, the Shunsho—copied these designs, but these works can hardly be compared with the subtle, toned-down *togidashi* lacquer work of the earlier artists of the Shunsho family. However, along with these trends many lacquer artists still preferred and copied the more quiet, subtle designs of famous artists of their times, such as Hoitsu (Figs. 21, 223, 233).

Ultimately technical detail and perfection became paramount for the ornate, luxurious taste of the newly established merchant class. Encrustation became minute and of innumerable types of materials heavily spread over the entire ornamental surface. Tinted ivory, mother-of-pearl, malachite, coral, soapstone, gold, silver, metallic alloys, all minutely carved, were inlaid in the lacquer base. This technique of heavily encrusted work of minute detail, originated in the early 19th century, was known collectively as Shibayama work. The works were usually in poor artistic taste done for commercial purposes by special workers rather than by true lacquer artists and were usually unsigned. By the late 19th century such articles were commonly made specifically for export porposes. It is through such export items, including commercially exported netsuke, *okimono,* porcelains, and late woodblock prints that Japanese art has been often unfairly and falsely judged. It should be noted, however, that some excellent examples of Shibayama work exist (Figs. 49, 65, 129).

With the patronization of the arts in the provinces through the local daimyo, and their increasing popularity among the plebeian class, the handicrafts, including lacquer ware, rapidly developed in the local provinces. Specific metal and lacquer techniques were developed and became known by their provincial origins. New methods were also developed from older similar Chinese techniques. All of these new techniques placed very little stress on *makie,* which had already reached its maximum development and perfection.

A new type of greenish-blue iridescent thin shell work in imitation of Ming and Korean shell work became popular. It was introduced by the lacquerer Chobei about 1620, using *awabi,* or sea-ear shell *(aogai).* This method was now extensively used by the Somada school in the early 19th century, the entire design being made up of tiny iridescent pieces of shell imbedded in a rich black lacquer background (Figs. 44, 78, 80, 160). This style, too, ultimately degenerated into overdetailed ornateness. Different techniques of carved lacquer in the Chinese manner were introduced. These included *guri,* Zonsei-nuri, and Zokoku-nuri. Zonsei-nuri was originated by the lacquerer Zonsci of the 17th century, and Zokoku-nuri by Tamakaji Zokoku of Takamatsu, in Shikoku, in the mid-19th century. Other new methods included multicolored lacquer techniques, such as Tsugaru-nuri, made for the daimyo of Tsugaru in Hirosaki, and Wakasa-nuri, made in the province of Wakasa. The carved *tsuishu* lacquer was made in Edo under the shogunate's patronage by the descendants of the Tsuishu family. Various types of transparent lacquer techniques also developed in other provinces—for example, Hida Shunkei in Hida, Noshiro Shunkei in Noshiro in Akita Prefecture (both in the mid-17th century), and Ukitsu-nuri, made by Ukitsu in Nagoya in the mid-19th century. Other provincial techniques were Aizu-nuri in Aizu-Wakamatsu, Kuroe-nuri in Kii, and Awano Shunkei in Ibaraki. *Chinkin,* known as Wajima ware, was made in Noto Province in the mid-Edo period. An oil-painting technique was practiced in Etchu Province under the local name of Jogahana, which was originated by Hata Jigoemon Yoshinaga in the Momoyama period. The special lacquer-painting technique called Johoji lacquer was done in the village of that name in the province of Mutsu.

Various schools of lacquerers and outstanding lacquer families arose during the Edo period. The Koami, Koma, Kajikawa, and Tsuishu (Yosei) families were just a few, all of whom worked for the court and the shogunate (Figs. 45, 46). Various schools using encrustations, such as Somada and Shibayama and the impressionistic school of Koetsu, Soetsu, and Korin, have already been mentioned. Famous individual artists who flourished throughout the Edo period included Shiomi Masanari, Iizuka Toyo, and Igarashi Doho, the originator of Kaga *makie*.

The variety of lacquer techniques during the Edo period was applied to a similar expanding variety of forms and subject matter. Besides inro, innumerable types of articles were lacquered, including eating utensils, such as bowls and cups; personal utensils like hair combs, powder brushes, pipes and pipe cases; and various boxes, such as tobacco boxes, tobacco cabinets, pipe sheaths, jewel boxes, cosmetic boxes, needle boxes, string boxes, tea boxes, shell boxes, perfume boxes, incense boxes, lunch and food (picnic) boxes, etc. Similarly, the designs and subject matter of the lacquered articles revealed more variety. Subject matter was greatly expanded and included now every aspect of nature from complete landscape scenes to a single flower or insect (Figs. 47, 48). Animals, fish, fowl, fruit, or a single leaf was fit subject matter. Similarly, along with the conventional portrayal of gods, heroes, warriors, famous poets, mythological creatures, and other legendary characters, more commonplace subjects and scenes from everyday Japanese life were depicted (Fig. 49). However, extremes of banality did not exist in lacquer ware as in the more popular, less expensive art forms, such as woodblock prints and netsuke. Many of the painters of the popular schools made books of sketches *(shita-e)* which were used as designs for small lacquered articles, such as inro. Lacquer techniques also expanded to include clever imitations of natural wood, such as *mokume* and *shitan-nuri*. Clever artists would also have lacquer simulate various metals, such as iron or old bronze, or various types of pottery. Metal (sword furniture) artists would combine their talents with those of the lacquer artist by adding various types of beautiful carved encrustations (Figs. 66, 93, 94). *Takamakie* was commonly used to copy works of great masters of painting. Ultimately, by the end of the Edo period, lacquer ware lost its simple artistic effect and degenerated into detailed overornate pictorial designs as a result of the lavish demands of the rich merchant class and the increased volume of production using less expensive techniques. Finally, with the fall of the Tokugawa shogunate in 1867, the loss of patronage of the arts through the breakup of the feudal system, the disbanding of the samurai class, and the rise in commodity prices resulting from increased trade with the Western world, the costly art of lacquering completely degenerated. The last outstanding lacquer art school in Japan was headed by the famous artist Shibata Zeshin (1807–91), who followed the fine traditions of this great art of the famous lacquer artists of the past (Figs. 12, 50). After the 19th century the great schools of lacquerers ceased to exist, there remaining in the interim but a handful of good individual lacquer artists.

Modern Period (1868 to present)

During the Meiji era (1868–1912) the emperor Meiji, aware of the decline of lacquer, ordered the establishment of a *makie* factory in the Imperial Household Department and used Kawanobe Itcho and other lacquer artists to work for him. Inferior lacquer, made basically on a small factory scale, was exported on a commercial basis to the West. Many well-known Occidental art lovers at the end of the 19th and the beginning of the 20th century became interested in the Japanese handicrafts, including lacquer, and famous collections were thereby formed. Subsequently many were broken up at auction or dispersed to Western museums. Special exhibitions were held by the Japanese to reveal to the rest of the world the wonders of their lacquer art. Unfortunately, however, economic and cultural circumstances prevented the regrowth of Japanese lacquer art. The Tokyo Fine Arts School, established in 1887, includes a Lacquer Art Department whose first chief was Ogawa Shomin. Subsequently this position was held by Kawanobe Itcho and Shirayama Shosai (1853–1923), the last, and perhaps the greatest of Japan's modern lacquer artists (Figs. 143, 219). Shosai, Zeshin, and Taishin were also appointed as court artists.

During the early part of the 20th century the working lacquer artists were divided into two groups. The first group were those whose pictorial designs were strongly influenced by Western modernistic art and the other group consisted of those who followed the traditional Japanese style of lacquer art. Among the modern school were Yamazaki Kakutaro, Tsuji Koten, and Matsuoka Taiwa. Among the classical school were Yoshida Jun'ichiro, Takano Shozan and the well-known lacquerer Matsuda Gonroku, who is still alive at the present time.

2. INRO. Noh dancer portraying a shojo. Signed: Kanshosai. Noh dancer in takamakie with encrustation of mother-of-pearl on a roiro ground. $3\frac{1}{16}'' \times 3\frac{1}{4}'' \times \frac{7}{8}''$. 3 cases and lid.

3. INRO. Dried fish and foliage. Signed: Toyo. The fish is done in silver takamakie, with the eye inlaid in mother-of-pearl on a roiro ground. $3\frac{1}{4}'' \times 2'' \times \frac{7}{8}''$. 4 cases and lid.

4. INRO. Tea bowl and kobako. Unsigned. The tea bowl is in orange and brown takamakie simulating the coarse texture of Raku ware. The kobako is in dark-red lacquer in imitation of guri lacquer on a gold ground. $3\frac{1}{2}'' \times 1\frac{7}{8}'' \times 1''$. 5 cases and lid.

5. OPPOSITE SIDE of inro in Fig. 4. Colored takamakie in medium relief, simulating a tea caddy partially enclosed within its brocade bag. Note the clever portrayal of the drip glaze, ivory lid, and silken cord of the bag—all realistically executed in appropriately textured lacquer.

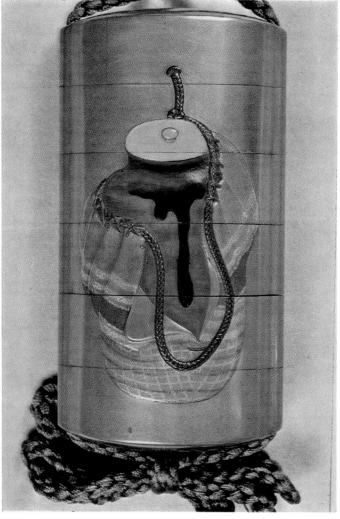

6. INRO. Pheasant. Signed: Kajikawa Bunryusai. The bird is executed in red, orange, and yellow togidashi on a dark-green ground. The rocks, tree, and stream are done in silver and gold togidashi highlighted with tiny pieces of aogai. $3\frac{3}{8}'' \times 1\frac{7}{8}'' \times 1''$. 4 cases and lid.

7. SAYA INRO. Court lady. Signed: Shunsui. Design in iroe togidashi on roiro ground; sheath in gold hiramakie. $3\frac{3}{8}'' \times 2\frac{1}{4}'' \times \frac{7}{8}''$. 4 cases and lid.

8. INRO. Goose on a veranda (illustrating the story of Ogishi). Style of Tsuchida Soetsu. The goose is executed in slightly raised vertical strips of inlaid mother-of-pearl. The veranda is in low gold taka-makie, mother-of-pearl, and pewter on a reddish-brown ground. $3'' \times 2\frac{5}{8}'' \times 1''$. 2 cases and lid.

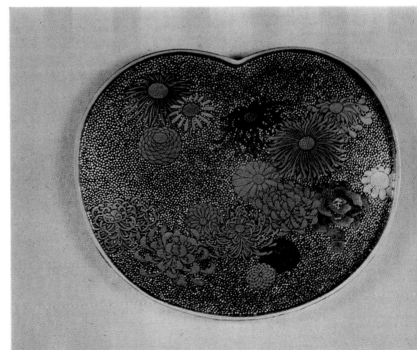

9. KOGO (inside cover of kogo in Fig. 29). Design of various types of chrysanthemums in shades of gold and silver togidashi on an oki-hirame ground.

10. INRO (bottom surface). Close-up of geometric designs in minute Somada-style iridescent aogai shell, silver, and gold.

11. INRO. Sea shells. Signed: Shibata Zeshin. Note the typical Zeshin wave design done in brown lacquer against a dull tea-green ground, with foliage and shells in gold lacquer and flat aogai shell. 3″ × 2⅛″ × 1″. 4 cases and lid.

12. INRO. Dragon and clouds. Signed: Zeshin. The design is in the style of the Myochin armorers, imitating to perfection a rust-iron ground. It is executed in low relief. $3\frac{5}{16}'' \times 2\frac{13}{16}'' \times \frac{3}{4}''$. 3 cases and lid.

13. INRO. Musical instruments. Signed: Kajikawa. The instruments depicted are the biwa (center), the koto (top), and a drum (right). Note the beautiful brown mokume imitating wood grain on the biwa. The ground is in cloudlike mura nashiji. $3\frac{1}{4}'' \times 2\frac{3}{8}'' \times 1''$. 4 cases and lid.

14. INRO. Samurai on a horse. Signed: Kajikawa. The design is in gold, silver, red, and black low takamakie on a lustrous red-gold gyobu nashiji ground. The technique used inside the lid and the lips is also gyobu nashiji. $3\frac{5}{8}'' \times 1\frac{7}{8}'' \times 1''$. 5 cases and lid.

15. INRO. Praying mantis and autumn plants. Signed: Hasegawa Shigeyoshi. The large leaves and gourds are done in tiny gold mosaics of oki-hirame. The praying mantis is in gold and green takamakie. The ground is a magnificent red-blue-green iridescent mosaic of flatly encrusted aogai shell, further illustrating the oki-hirame technique. $4\frac{3}{16}'' \times 2\frac{1}{8}'' \times 1\frac{1}{4}''$. 4 cases and lid.

16. INRO. Phoenix. Signed: Kajikawa. The phoenix is seen flying over the branches of a paulownia tree and a rivulet. Some of the leaves and parts of the bird are done in gold hyomon technique, the remainder being in gold takamakie. The rivulet is done in togidashi and the adjacent shore in kirigane. The ground is in gold fundame. $3\frac{3}{4}'' \times 1\frac{7}{8}'' \times \frac{15}{16}''$. 5 cases and lid.

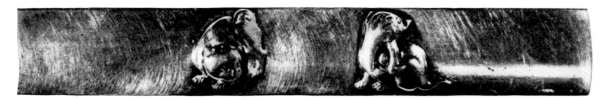

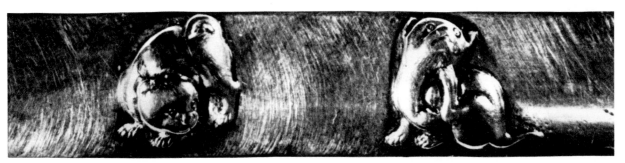

17. Kozuka and enlargement. Two puppies. Signed: Goto Shunjo. Silver ground with high repoussé in silver and tiny inlaid gold eyes. $3\frac{3}{4}'' \times \frac{5}{8}''$.

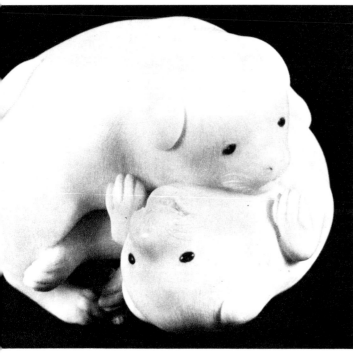

18. Netsuke. Two puppies. Signed: Kaigyokusai. Finely carved ivory showing two playful puppies in rounded form with encrusted red eyes of hornbill. $1\frac{1}{4}''$ high.

19. Inro. Two puppies. Signed: Koma Kansai. Two puppies in low takamakie, one in silver, the other in gold, on a gold gyobu ground. $3\frac{5}{8}'' \times 2\frac{3}{8}'' \times 1''$. 4 cases and lid. Matching lacquer manju netsuke: $1\frac{3}{8}'' \times \frac{3}{4}''$.

20. INRO. Crows and tree branches. Signed: Umehara Koryusai. Gold fundame ground with design in sumie lacquer technique. $3\frac{3}{8}'' \times 3'' \times 1''$. 4 cases and lid.

21. INRO. Cherry blossoms. Signed: Yoyusai (after a design of Hoitsu). Flowers in low gold takamakie on a gold fundame ground. $2\frac{3}{4}'' \times 2\frac{1}{4}'' \times \frac{7}{8}''$. 3 cases and lid.

22. INRO. Landscape. Signed: Kanshosai (Toyo). Design in sumie lacquer technique on a gold fundame ground, imitating the Sesshu style of painting. The picture is framed in aogai against a red-and-gold background simulating a brocade mounting. $3\frac{5}{8}'' \times 2\frac{1}{16}'' \times 1\frac{1}{4}''$. 4 cases and lid.

23. INRO. Pine tree. Signed: Kanshosai. Design in gold togidashi on a black ground. $3\frac{1}{8}'' \times 2\frac{1}{8}'' \times \frac{7}{8}''$. 4 cases and lid.

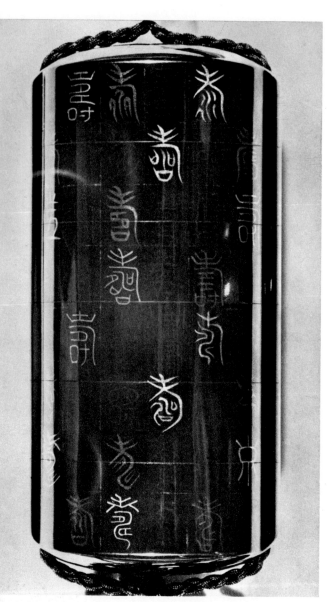

24. INRO. One hundred ju characters (antique versions of character for longevity). Unsigned. The characters are in gold or silver togidashi on a roiro ground and are applied at various levels in the layers of lacquer so as to produce varying tonalities of color and depth. $3\frac{3}{4}'' \times 1\frac{7}{8}'' \times 1\frac{1}{16}''$. 5 cases and lid.

25. INRO (tobacco-box shape). Takarabune. Signed: Zeshin. On a tea-green ground the various articles carried by the treasure ship are executed in low gold takamakie with inlaid mother-of-pearl and gold kirigane. The waves are done in the typical style of Zeshin. Note also the overall asymmetry of design. $2\frac{3}{8}'' \times 2\frac{3}{4}'' \times \frac{5}{8}''$. 1 case and lid.

26. INRO. Carp leaping up a waterfall. Signed: Yoshi Kane-tomo. The carp is in encrusted mother-of-pearl in high relief. The waterfall is done in silver makie on a gold yasuriko ground. $3\frac{1}{2}'' \times 2\frac{3}{8}'' \times \frac{5}{8}''$. 4 cases and lid.

27. DETAIL of inro in Fig. 26, showing encrusted carp and intricate carving of the mother-of-pearl. Note the impression of motion created by having part of the tail of the fish submerged beneath the falling water.

28. INRO. Chrysanthemums. Signed: Koma Kansai. The chrysanthemums are in low black takamakie on a roiro ground. $2\frac{5}{8}'' \times 2\frac{3}{8}'' \times \frac{7}{8}''$. 3 cases and lid.

29. KOGO. Tea-ceremony house. Signed: Morikazu. A heart-shaped kogo with an extremely asymmetrical design created by alternating rectangles of silver and black. The remainder of the design is in gold takamakie on a roiro ground. $3'' \times 3\frac{7}{8}'' \times \frac{3}{4}''$. (See Fig. 9 for inside cover.)

30. Inro. Plum blossoms. Signed: Tatsuke Takamitsu. The branches are executed in light-brown takamakie, with the buds in high relief of encrusted mother-of-pearl. The ground is in dark-brown coarse-textured lacquer (sabiji) simulating the bark of a tree. $2\frac{1}{8}'' \times 2\frac{1}{8}'' \times 1\frac{5}{16}''$. 2 cases and lid.

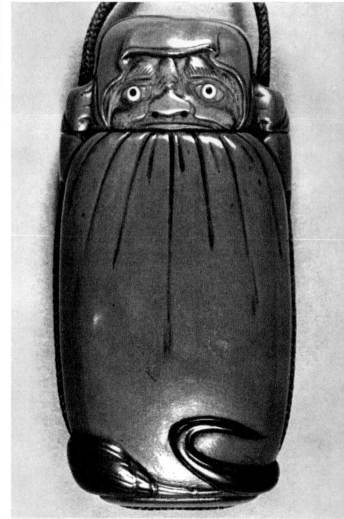

31. Inro. Daruma with fly whisk. Signed: Eisen. The Daruma is in red lacquer with a carved wooden face and inlaid ivory eyes. $3\frac{5}{16}''$ $\times 1\frac{11}{16}'' \times 1\frac{1}{16}''$. 1 case and lid.

32. INRO. Nio temple guardian. Unsigned. The design is executed in gold togidashi on a roiro ground. $3\frac{3}{8}'' \times 2'' \times 1\frac{1}{4}''$. 1 case and lid.

33. DETAIL of inro in Fig. 32, showing e-nashiji on robe of Nio temple guardian.

34. INRO of Fig. 32 opened to show accompanying zushi. Typical two-section inro used to carry a portable shrine.

35. NETSUKE. Unsigned. Lacquer manju with ground of diaper-work in geometric patterns created by inlaid iridescent mother-of-pearl and gold kirigane, which sets off a fan-shaped medallion design of an egret perched on a boat under a crescent moon. $1\frac{13}{16}''$ $\times \frac{15}{16}''$.

36. INRO. Floral and religious symbols. Unsigned. The design is created by the use of overlapping asymmetrically placed medallions in shades of gold hiramakie and low takamakie on a gold fundame ground. $3\frac{1}{2}''\times 2\frac{1}{4}''\times 1\frac{3}{16}''$. 4 cases and lid.

37. INRO. Two men neck-wrestling. Signed: Nakayama. Design in typical Shibayama style of colorful high encrustations of mother-of-pearl, soapstone, and ivory on a gold lacquer ground. This is encircled by powderings of crests on an oki-hirame ground. $3\frac{5}{8}'' \times 2\frac{11}{16}'' \times 1\frac{1}{4}''$. 2 cases and lid.

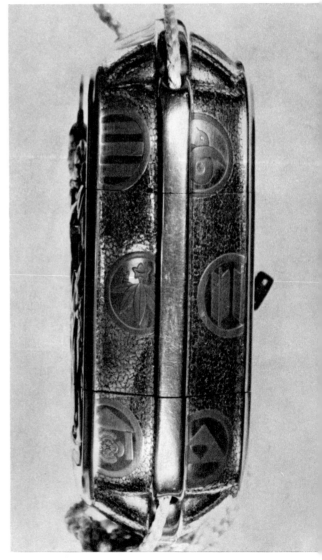

38. SIDE VIEW of inro in Fig. 37, showing various circular crests in silver and gold hiramakie against a gold gyobu ground.

39. INRO. Chinese scepter and leaves. Signed: Keigai. The design is encrusted on natural sugi wood. The scepter is executed in carved tsui-shu, and the leaves are in mother-of-pearl and gold takamakie. $3\frac{1}{4}'' \times 2\frac{3}{8}'' \times \frac{7}{8}''$. 3 cases and lid.

40. DETAIL of inro in Fig. 39, showing enlargement of encrustation in carved tsuishu lacquer in asa-no-ha pattern.

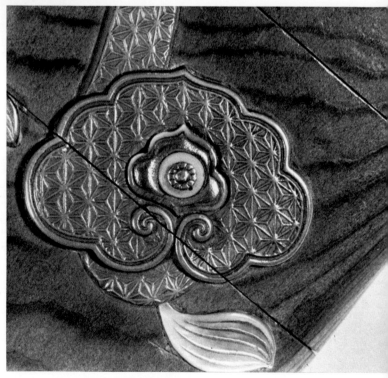

41. SUZURI-BAKO (inside cover). Unsigned. Middle Edo period. This detail
reveals the ashide-e technique within a
design of flying sparrows and cranes executed in gold lacquer. The ideograms signify longevity.

42. KOBAKO. Chrysanthemum design.
Unsigned. Muromachi period. The stylized design of the chrysanthemums is
done in gold lacquer with fine black outlines on a gold ground. The rims are in
pewter. $2\frac{1}{8}'' \times 2\frac{1}{8}'' \times 1\frac{1}{2}''$.

43. INRO. Ukiyo-e figure. Signed: Shunsho. The design, executed in green, red, and gold togidashi, depicts a graceful lady on a roiro ground. $3\frac{1}{2}'' \times 2\frac{1}{8}'' \times 1''$. 4 cases and lid.

44. INRO. Boy beating a drum. Unsigned. Somada school. Design executed in typical colorful iridescent aogai shell along with silver and gold inlays on a black ground. External cord channels and top and bottom surfaces are also decorated in geometric patterns of aogai shell. $3\frac{1}{2}'' \times 1\frac{7}{8}'' \times 1\frac{1}{4}''$. 3 cases and lid.

45. INRO. Mount Fuji. Signed: Koma Kansai. Design in medallion form showing Mount Fuji surrounded by clouds and waves. The summit of the mountain and the clouds are done in silver lacquer, the ground of the medallion in gold, and the ground encircling the medallion in gold oki-hirame. $2\frac{15}{16}'' \times 3\frac{1}{16}'' \times \frac{7}{8}''$. 3 cases and lid.

46. INRO. Praying mantis and fan. Signed: Kajikawa. The design is executed in gold in low takamakie on a gold ground. $3\frac{1}{16}'' \times \frac{3}{4}'' \times 1\frac{1}{16}''$. 4 cases and lid.

47. INRO. Stag beetle. Signed: Jitokusai (Gyokuzan). The design is in a highly polished tortoise-shell-colored lacquer in low taka-makie on a gray-black coarse bark ground. $3\frac{1}{8}'' \times 2\frac{3}{16}'' \times \frac{3}{4}''$. 4 cases and lid.

48. INRO. Peony. Signed: Toshi. The single flower is executed in moderate relief in black takamakie on a gold oki-hirame ground. $2\frac{1}{8}'' \times 1\frac{3}{4}'' \times \frac{5}{8}''$. 3 cases and lid.

49. INRO. Rooster and chicks. Signed: Shibayama Yasumasa. The design is done in colorful raised mother-of-pearl, coral, and gold inlays on a natural ground of sugi (cryptomeria) wood. $3\frac{7}{8}'' \times 2\frac{3}{8}'' \times 1''$. 3 cases and lid.

50. INRO. Daruma. Signed: Zeshin. The design represents a sumie painting and is executed in red and black togidashi against a gold background. The overall ground is a reddish brown. This unusually constructed inro has a long lid completely enclosing 3 cases. $2\frac{5}{8}'' \times 1\frac{13}{16}'' \times 1''$.

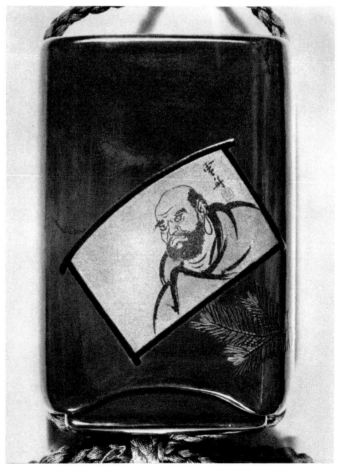

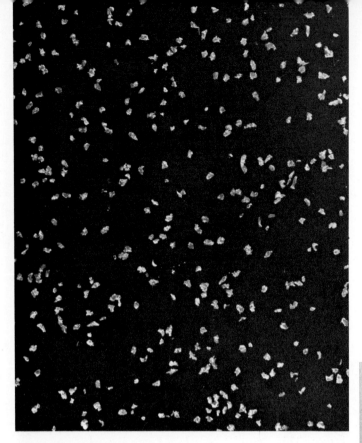

51. DETAIL of hirame nashiji ground used on inside of a lacquer box by Ritsuo.

52. INRO. Dappled horse at a stream surrounded by the Seven Grasses of Autumn. Signed: Toyo. The design is executed in gold, silver, and red hiramakie with fine silver and gold kirigane and inlaid mother-of-pearl on a gold fundame ground. $3\frac{7}{8}'' \times 2\frac{1}{8}'' \times 1\frac{3}{16}''$. 4 cases and lid.

53. DETAIL of inro in Fig. 52, showing kirigane technique used for the design of the flowers surrounding the horse and for part of the saddle. (See Fig. 106 for another detail.)

54. INRO. Clouds and water. Signed: Koma Yasutada. The design is mainly in togidashi on a black ground sprinkled with fine gold powdering (yasuriko). The clouds are in chiriji. $3\frac{5}{8}''\times 2\frac{3}{8}''\times\frac{3}{4}''$. 4 cases and lid.

55. DETAIL of inro in Fig. 54, illustrating chiriji. Note also the surrounding yasuriko ground.

56. INRO. Gama Sennin and toad. Signed: Nagaharu (Joi).
The gourd-shaped metallic insert of Gama Sennin and the
toad was made by the famous Nara metal expert Joi in shibu-
ichi. The ground is gold kirigane. $2\frac{3}{8}'' \times 2\frac{1}{2}'' \times 1''$. 3 cases and
lid.

57. DETAIL of inro in Fig. 56, showing kirigane technique.

58. INRO. Butterflies against chrysanthemum background. Signed: Toyo (with kakihan). The butterflies are done in encrusted mother-of-pearl, gold, shakudo, and tortoise shell. The ground is gold fundame with a design of stylized gold chrysanthemums in hiramakie. $3\frac{1}{8}'' \times 2\frac{3}{4}'' \times \frac{7}{8}''$. 4 cases and lid.

59. INRO. Chinese nobleman on donkey with attendant. Signed: Zeshin. The design is done in low black takamakie on a dull black ground. Note the simulated chips on the edges of the inro and the fine hairline simulated cracks in the ground. $2\frac{1}{2}'' \times 2'' \times \frac{3}{4}''$. 1 case and lid.

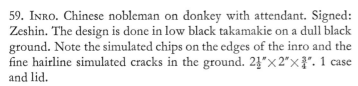

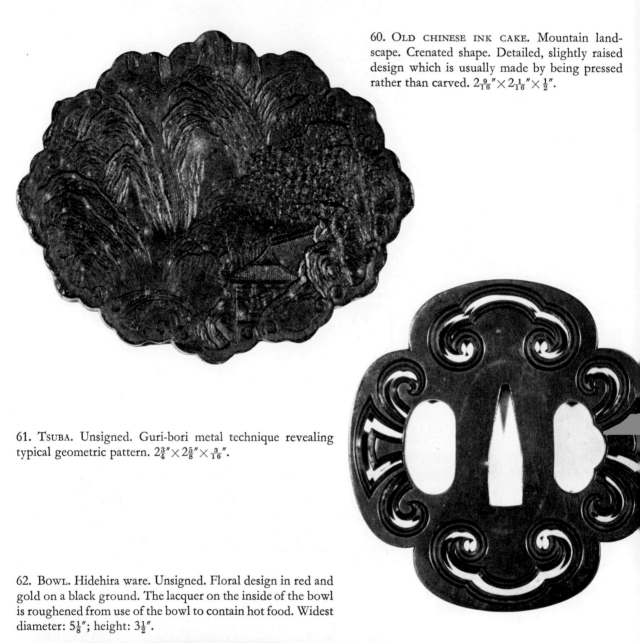

60. OLD CHINESE INK CAKE. Mountain landscape. Crenated shape. Detailed, slightly raised design which is usually made by being pressed rather than carved. $2\frac{9}{16}'' \times 2\frac{1}{16}'' \times \frac{1}{2}''$.

61. TSUBA. Unsigned. Guri-bori metal technique revealing typical geometric pattern. $2\frac{3}{4}'' \times 2\frac{5}{8}'' \times \frac{3}{16}''$.

62. BOWL. Hidehira ware. Unsigned. Floral design in red and gold on a black ground. The lacquer on the inside of the bowl is roughened from use of the bowl to contain hot food. Widest diameter: $5\frac{1}{8}''$; height: $3\frac{1}{2}''$.

63. DETAIL of Kamakura-bori technique, showing geometric design with red surface layer and
underlying black lacquer coat where it is worn
down. Ashikaga period.

64. INRO (tobacco-box shape). Fox. Signed: Zeshin. The entire design is in incised lacquer on a
roiro ground. $2\frac{5}{8}'' \times 2\frac{3}{8}'' \times 1\frac{1}{8}''$. 1 case and lid.

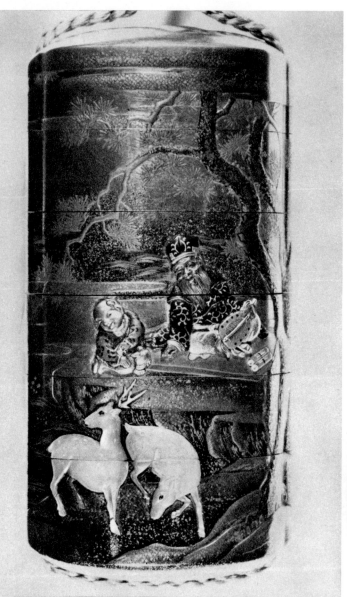

65. INRO. Jurojin, child, and deer. Signed: Shibayama and Kanshosai (lacquer artist). Jurojin and the child are done in metal encrustations of silver, gold, copper, shakudo, and shibuichi. The deer are inlaid mother-of-pearl. The landscape is in gold takamakie and kirigane on a gold ground. 4″×2 1/16″×1 3/8″. 5 cases and lid.

66. INRO. Yamabushi. Signed: Ishiguro Masatsune, with lacquer work by Koma Kyuhaku. The yamabushi is done in encrusted raised metals: shakudo, gold, silver, and copper. The lacquer is gold takamakie on a gold ground. 3″×2 3/8″×1 1/8″. 4 cases and lid.

3 ❖ Lacquer Manufacture and Techniques

Chemical and Physical Properties

Oriental lacquer is not in the Western sense a varnish. A varnish is mainly a gum dissolved in a volatile liquid, such as turpentine, which evaporates, leaving a shiny glaze. Oriental lacquer (except Indian lac, which is the gummy deposit of the insect *Coccus lacca*) comes from the thick sap of a tree called the *urushi (Rhus vernicifera)*, a species of sumac, which when dried, needs thorough polishing to obtain a highly glazed surface. A knowledge of the chemical breakdown and physical reactions of Japanese lacquer gives us a better understanding of its manufacture and durability. Lacquer consists of 60–85% urushic acid $(C_{14}H_{18}O_2)$, a gum (3–6.5%) similar to gum arabic, an albuminoid (1.7–3.5%), a trace of a volatile acid and water (10–34%). The best lacquer is the most transparent, most resistant to solvents and water and that which does not tend to dry up, crumble, or warp with age. The most important process in lacquer manufacture is the slow drying and hardening of lacquer. Lacquer dries best between 68° and 80°F and in the presence of moisture. Chemically the hardening process consists of the albumin acting on the urushic acid, probably as a ferment, with the water acting as a solvent on the albumin so that it can combine with the urushic acid. This probably explains why moisture is actually necessary for liquid lacquer to harden. The gum plays no part in the hardening process but keeps the various components in an emulsion. This hardening of the lacquer is accompanied by the absorption of one atom of hydrogen by one molecule of urushic acid.

$C_{14}H_{18}O_2 + O \rightarrow C_{14}H_{18}O_3$ (oxyurushic acid). Except for concentrated nitric acid, the oxyurushic acid is insoluble in every solvent, even boiling sulphuric acid, and is stable with temperatures below 200°. The gum and albumin, however, are attacked by concentrated acids and alkalis but not by the solvents (alcohol, ether, benzene, ammonia, etc.). Water may cause the gum to swell, and when drying occurs there may occur crumbling and warping, especially in the cheaper lacquer, in which there is more gum. Old lacquer (50–100 years old), through gradual chemical changes in the gum, is therefore not affected by water. In general it is apparent from the preceding chemical discussion, and confirmed by practical application, that the best lacquer has the highest percentage of urushic acid (80–85%), a corresponding low percentage of water (10%), and relatively little gum and albumin. The durability of good, old lacquer is dramatically illustrated in the sinking in 1874 of the French steamer *Nil,* which was carrying back Japanese art objects from the Vienna exposition. Eighteen months later the old lacquer ware was recovered from the ocean and found to be in perfect condition. Chinese lacquer is somewhat inferior to Japanese lacquer because of the lower percentage (55%) of urushic acid and probably also because of the fact that it is softened by mixing with a vegetable oil. Also, Chinese flat lacquer is not made with as many layers of lacquer as are works done by the Japanese artisan.

Preparation of Various Lacquers

As noted, Japanese lacquer comes from the thick sap of a tree called the *urushi.* Originally these trees were planted by order of the government. In ten years a tree grows to about ten feet high and will yield two to three ounces of sap. The trees are tapped between June and October. The spring sap is considered too watery, the midsummer sap being the best in quality. Special tools and methods are used for obtaining the sap. In general, when the tree is two to ten years old it is incised at specific levels, averaging about 25 cuts. Cuts are also made into the branches. The exuding lacquer is scraped into bamboo pots *(go).* The crude thick creamy lacquer called *urushi* is then filtered of impurities through a cloth. When filtered it is called *ki-urushi.* Lacquer taken from different parts of the tree and that taken from older trees have different characteristics. Each type of lacquer so obtained is kept separately, and subsequently each is used for specific purposes. Thus the sap taken from the trunk of very old trees (100–200 years old) produces the best transparent lacquer and is called *suki-urushi.* Similarly, the branch lacquer, or *seshime-urushi,* is highly desired, since when dry it becomes extremely hard. However, it dries more slowly than trunk lacquer.

The excess water in the lacquer is evaporated, paradoxically, by adding small amounts of water. Lacquer will not dry perfectly in the open air, but only in a damp enclosed atmosphere between 68° and 80° F. In drying lacquer the Japanese enclose the object in a damp cupboard, damp press *(muro),* or damp cellar. The press is kept humid by repeated sponging down with water. It may require two to three days for one layer of lacquer to dry and in some cases up to one month for thorough drying. In general, a layer of lacquer is applied to the prepared object, which is dried in the damp press, and then polished. This process is repeated numerous times, employing different types of lacquer, different periods of drying, and different techniques of polishing. This is all done preparatory to the actual process of ornamentation. The following is a partial list of the different types of lacquer, their production, and their uses:

1) middle-coating lacquer *(naka-nuri-urushi)*. Used for middle coats and prepared by thoroughly evaporating good *ki-urushi.*

2) black lacquer *(ro-urushi)*. Prepared from crude or branch lacquer by the addition of a black solution *(haguro)* made by boiling iron filings in strong rice vinegar.

3) inside-line lacquer *(ke-uchi-urushi)*. Made from *shita-maki-urushi* (undercoat lacquer), which in turn is made from *seshime-urushi* and iron oxide. It is kept for months in order to thicken, thereby allowing fine lines to be drawn on raised work. The consistency prevents the lines from spreading and also gives the desired relief.

4) shading lacquer *(kuma-urushi)*. Prepared from *jo-hana-urushi* and lampblack, which lacquer in turn is made by adding small amounts of oil and finishing lacquer. It is used for shading with very delicate lines on flat and raised ware.

5) raising lacquer *(taka-maki-urushi)*. Made by boiling *ro-urushi,* lampblack, and camphor. This lacquer is applied thickly. The camphor renders the lacquer soft, and it dries slowly and evenly. In this way the top layer does not dry first, and subsequent cracking of the top layer does not occur.

6) *ro-se-urushi*. Made from a mixture of *seshime* and *ro-urushi*. It is used as a lacquer base to imbed metallic powders or flakes of gold, silver, or tin.

7) pear-basis lacquer *(nashiji-urushi)*. Transparent lacquer obtained from old trees. It is put over the metallic powderings.

8) *sabi*. Composed of 2 parts burnt clay and $1\frac{1}{2}$ parts *seshime-urushi*. It is used to build up the high relief of *takamakie.*

9) *jinoko*. Composed of 1 part burnt clay and 2 parts *seshime-urushi*.

10) *suki-urushi*. The best crude lacquer, used for colored lacquer.

Lacquer is colored by the addition of various pigments, but no vegetable colors are used, since they are destroyed by the lacquer and will fade. Therefore colors, such as white and purple, are not seen in early lacquer work. In general, colors are used either pulverized as powders or mixed with metallic powders, the design being made by dusting the appropriate powders on the sticky lacquer. In other cases the lacquer itself is colored by mixing it with colored pigments. The lacquer used for this purpose is called *suki-urushi*. Very occasionally special color techniques are used, such as mixing lacquer with lead oxide and oil (see *mitsuda-e,* page 123). The following is a partial list of colored lacquers:

1) black lacquer *(ro-urushi)*. Prepared by mixing lacquer with a black solution obtained by boiling iron filings with vinegar. Lampblack is used in more modern works instead of iron; it is made from pine wood and was not used before the early 18th century. The iron type tends to fade and become brown with age, appearing like tortoise shell.

2) vermilion lacquer *(shu-urushi)*. Made from *ki-urushi* or *suki-urushi*, vermilion, and oil. It is a dull red. For inferior works, red oxide of iron *(benigara)* is used instead of vermilion.

3) browns. These are obtained by mixing various proportions of reds and blacks.

4) chrome-yellow lacquer *(kio*=chrome; *ki-urushi-ji*=yellow lacquer).

5) green lacquer *(sei-shitsu* or *ao-urushi)*. Made by mixing *kio* and Prussian blue *(bero-ai)*.

6) purple powder *(murasaki-ko)*. Made from white lead and magenta roseine *(to-beni)*.

7) white lacquer: silicate powder. (See Jogahana, page 123.)

Along with the above basic colors various metallic powders were used by themselves, in combination or with the above pigments to produce different degrees of shading. Gold, silver, and copper powders were most commonly used.

Preparation of the Core

Lacquered objects usually have a core or structure upon which the lacquer is applied. This core usually consists of wood. However, lacquer may be used to decorate innumerable other types of materials which often require specialized preparatory techniques both to make the lacquer adhere to the object and to render the proper decorative effect. The techniques of lacquering on such materials as metal, ivory, tortoise shell, porcelain, etc., will therefore be described separately. Lacquer was occasionally used for painting and even as decoration on fabrics. In most cases however, the techniques of applying the lacquer, building it up to the desired thickness, and the final application of the pictorial and decorative effects remain the same irrespective of the underlying core.

The wooden core is called *kiji* and is prepared by a specialist, the joiner. The type and thickness of the wood depends upon the object to be manufactured, which might be anything from a large piece of furniture or an entire temple building to a tiny incense box. *Hinoki* (Japanese cypress) is best suited for making boxes, including inro, as it does not warp or split. On the other hand *hinoki* was not usually used for such objects as netsuke because it is soft and tends to wear down. Most sword sheaths were made from *honoki (Magnolia hypoleuca)*, a light wood; carved figures from *himekomatsu* (a species of pine), which does not split; cups and bowls from *sakura* (cherry), which is suitable for lathing; and other woods such as *keyaki* (zelkova) for their ornamental grain. Ornamental woods were either left natural or covered with transparent lacquers to bring out their beautiful color or grain (see "Transparent Lacquer," page 133). Occasionally only parts of such woods were lacquered or they were used for encrustations as practiced by Ritsuo. The wood of the camphor laurel is not suitable for lacquering because its camphor content acts on the lacquer. Woods to be lacquered were very well seasoned, some inro cores being hung up to dry for as long as three years before being lacquered.

The lacquered boxes (including inro) invariably have almost airtight snugly fitting parts, such as a lid or fitted tiers, or boxes enclosed within a parent box. The wooden core was so carefully prepared as to account for the thickness of the subsequent lacquer to be applied and still permit accurate coadaptation of the component parts of the object. And even then, after centuries of use and exposure to varying climates and temperatures, the boxes remain uncracked, unwarped, and perfectly fitting. Such was the extreme care and accuracy involved in the preparation of the wooden core.

The prepared wooden core was then primed and covered with numerous layers of lacquer by a special class of lacquerers called the *nurimono-shi* or *nuri-ya,* and finally the decorative and pictorial work was done by the more highly esteemed lacquer painters, or *makie-shi.* There was even further specialization of lacquerers, such as mother-of-pearl inlayers *(aogai-shi)* and even sword-sheath lacquerers *(saya-shi).* Mother-of-pearl itself was processed and prepared by special craftsmen. Frequently the design itself was done by a noted painter or was copied from a famous painting. Metal artists often combined their talents with those of the lacquerer and supplemented the work with metal encrustations. Metal inro were made by metal artists, and at other times lacquer was applied to a metallic base by the lacquer artist. The combining of talents among specialized Japanese artisans was not uncommon. Many famous painters, such as Korin and Zeshin, were also adept with the handicrafts. The handicrafts were not looked down upon as in China but were even practiced among the patrons of the arts along with painting, poetry, and calligraphy.

Honji : Priming the Core

Having outlined the process in the preparation of the wooden core and the production and use of the various basic lacquers, we are now in a position to understand how the various layers of lacquer are specifically applied to the basic wood. "Real basis" *(honji)* is the term used to denote the best black lacquer on wood. It should be again noted that the "basis" is done by the *nurimono-shi* and is merely preparatory for the lacquer painter, who then takes over to ornament the prepared lacquer base. The same "basis" is used on a lacquer foundation for colored or gold lacquer work. Similarly the same lacquer foundation is used even in raised lacquer work, although less commonly raised lacquer *(takamakie)* may be done on a natural wood base. In general after the lacquer base is applied the design is brought out by repeated dustings of metallic and colored powders associated with repeated applications of lacquer, drying, and polishing. In other cases the design is accomplished by superimposing layers of colored lacquer. Lastly the design may be brought out by inlaying or deeply encrusting various precarved designs made of gold, silver, mother-of-pearl, ivory, pottery, etc.

The steps used in *honji* consists roughly of the following. The wood is primed by adding a layer of *seshime-urushi* and then put in the damp press. Then the channels and joints are covered by means of a spatula with a mixture of *seshime-urushi,* chopped hemp, and rice starch, and the piece is again placed in the press. This layer is now rubbed down, and a layer of *sabi* is applied. After more time in the press the piece is rubbed down again. Then it is covered with hempen cloth *(nuno)* to prevent the wood from cracking and the joints from springing. Following this, several layers of mixtures of lacquer and clay are applied, followed by drying in the damp press each time and polishing each time after the drying process. The true lacquer stages now occur, and the lacquers are applied with a brush of human hair.

First the middle-coat lacquer is applied and then multiple layers of *ro-urushi* (black lacquer), followed by more and more careful polishing with powdered charcoal. The object is finally polished with a mixture of burnt Inari clay reduced to impalpable fine powder, and calcined deerhorn *(tsuno-ko)* is applied with cotton cloth touched with oil. The final coats are of *seshime-urushi* followed by drying and polishing with powdered deer's-horn ashes applied with the finger.

Up to sixty separate steps may be used in applying the basic lacquer layers on the wooden core. The minimal time used for just the damp press is twenty-two days, and sometimes thorough drying of one lacquer layer may take up to one month. A well-prepared lacquer base prevents warping, seals in the wooden resin, and does not allow the slight undulations or irregularities of the wood to show through.

Materials and Techniques of Ornamentation

After the *honji* is completed the lacquer painter commences his work. This consists essentially in transferring a prepared design over the prepared lacquer base and then filling it in according to the method he has chosen. At this point it should be stressed that to the lacquer artist the background is just as essential as the design itself. While in many cases the design is set off on a completely plain black or other colored lacquer background, more often than not the background is enhanced by dusting with various metallic powders and flakes. This technique is extremely important and is called *nashiji,* or pear ground. This technique is also used on the risers and on the inside of the inro cases as well as the insides and bottoms of the majority of lacquer boxes.

The design itself is usually done as follows: after the groundwork is completed the design is drawn on one side of the specially prepared paper with brush and ink. Then, using a fine brush *(neji-fude)* composed of the hair from the back of ship rats, the design is traced on the opposite side of the paper using moist (heated) lacquer. The finished design is then rubbed off onto the lacquered surface using a whalebone spatula. The lines are subsequently dusted with metallic powders and lacquer *(ro-se-urushi).* The entire design is now built up to the desired height or effect by repeated dustings using various types and sizes of brushes and dusting tubes *(tsutsu)* covered with fine gauze mesh. Repeated layers of lacquer followed by drying and repeated grinding down and polishing are also necessary. Similarly, colored lacquer may be superimposed in the same way. By using alternate layers of dustings and coats of lacquer, the design is gradually built up. In this way the artist is actually working in a three-dimensional medium even though the entire thickness of the design through the repeated rubbings may only be 2–3 mm. thick. Similarly, the design may be ultimately constructed as a completely flat surface and still maintain the three-dimensional effect by means of slight shadings in tones and the varying depths in the lacquer in which the dustings are done. It should also be noted that the colors themselves are altered according to the depth in which they are placed in the amber-colored lacquer layers. All of these factors have to be taken into account by the lacquer artist, who must be able to visualize step by step in advance the ultimate complete work, as any error in judgment cannot be rectified by removal or erasure. The additional processes involved in the various lacquer techniques will be described separately.

In metallic dusting the following technical points should be noted: 1) deer's-hair brushes *(menso)* are used for spreading on thick lacquer preparations; 2) *kebo,* or horsehair brushes, of different sizes are used for applying gold dust; 3) white horsehair brushes for drawing coarser outlines, and 4) rat's-hair brushes *(neji-fude)* for drawing finer outlines. These are just some of the brushes used. *Tsutsu,* or dusting tubes, consist of various-sized hollow tubes of bamboo and swan and crane quills, cut at each end at an acute angle and covered at one end with different-gauge gauzes for application of different grades of fineness of the powders. Special sticks *(hirame-fude)* are used to lift tiny scales or squares of metal foil for application to the tacky lacquer surfaces.

Various metals and alloys are used, many of the alloys being indigenous to the Japanese artisan. The metallic powders are also mixed with colored powdered pigments. The following is a partial list of the various metallic dusts. Different shading is obtained according to the amount of gold or silver dust used.

> gold=*kin* or *ogon* (literally, "yellow metal"); *yaki-kin* (literally, "burnt gold" or gold or a brassy color)
>
> silver=*gin*
>
> copper=*akagane* (literally, "red metal")
>
> iron=*tetsu* or *kurogane* (literally, "black metal")
>
> varying shades of "pale" gold:
>
>> *koban-kin* or *koban*=10 parts gold, 2.6 parts silver
>>
>> *jiki-ban*=10 parts gold, 3.1 parts silver
>>
>> *namban*=10 parts gold, 3.6 parts silver
>>
>> *shakudo-fun*=7 parts gold, 3 parts copper (copper tint)
>
> Combinations of metallic powders and pigments are as follows:
>
> *aka-fun* (literally, "red powder")=gold, *koban,* or silver powder with vermilion and charcoal (bronze effect)
>
> *kuro-fun* (literally, "black powder")=gold, *koban,* or silver dust with charcoal
>
> *nezumi-iro-fun* (literally, "gray powder")=silver dust and charcoal in equal portions, with a trace of vermilion
>
> *kuri-iro-fun* (literally, " chestnut-colored powder")=one-half gold dust and one-half powdered camellia charcoal and vermilion
>
> *shu-kin*=an admixture of gold dust and cinnabar

The metals are made in different grades of fineness, different sizes, and different shapes. The first type consists of metal powders: *yasuriko* or *yasuri-fun* (filings or file powders), which are made from pure gold or the lighter-colored *koban-kin* (gold and silver alloy) or pure silver (Figs. 54, 55). They are graded into twelve grades of fineness, from the coarsest *(ara-tsune)* to the finest *(usuji)*. However, an even finer powder called *keshi-fun* is made only out of gold or *koban*. Each of the twelve grades has a different name.

The second type consists of scale dusts, or *hirame* (flat eye), also prepared from gold, silver, and *koban-kin* (Fig. 51). They have eight different sizes, from the largest *(dai-dai-ichi)* to the smallest *(saki)* and are made by flattening metallic filings.

The third group, called *nashiji* (pear ground), consists also of irregular flattened flakes made from pure gold, *koban-kin, jiki-ban, namban,* and pure silver (Fig. 140). They consist of seven degrees of fineness, from the largest flake, called *dai-ichi,* to the finest, called *saki.* In general they are finer than *hirame.* The name *nashiji* comes from *nashi,* a small Japanese pear whose skin has somewhat the aspect of aventurine, and *ji,* which in Japanese means background. *Gyobu nashiji* is a kind of *nashiji* made from 34 parts gold to 35 parts silver. It is quite coarse and requires several coats of lacquer to cover it up sufficiently (Fig. 14).

The fourth group consists of foil *(kana-gai)* cut up into small squares or various-shaped rectangles of gold, *koban,* or silver which are inlaid next to one another according to the decorative pattern. They are made of four different thicknesses (Fig. 53).

The last group consists of scales of mother-of-pearl of different sizes as well as shell-scale powder called *aogai-mijin* (Fig. 77). These scales and powders usually come from the green-blue-reddish iridescent shell called *aogai* (see "Somada," page 127).

All of these various grades of metal and mother-of-pearl are used for composing either the pictorial design or the ornamental background, and the first three groups serve in making up the special ground called *nashiji.*

Classification of Techniques

The entire range and production of the materials used for lacquer work has been briefly outlined. The finished lacquer product consists essentially of three elements: 1) the background, 2) the pictorial design, and 3) the decorative designs (supplementing the pictorial design).

While the same materials and techniques may be used for all of these three elements, special technical effects have been developed peculiar to each element. Thus the pictorial design is often raised in relief by a special technique called *takamakie* which rarely applies to the background. Similarly, the background may be specifically made to simulate iron, a technique which is not usually practiced on the pictorial or decorative designs. On the other hand, pieces of cut foil or mother-of-pearl may be scattered in the background and also used for the pictorial and decorative designs. Similarly, in carved lacquer all of these three elements are involved in the same process. In general, however, while the pictorial and decorative processes make use of similar lacquer techniques, the methods used for background effect in lacquer ware as well as in metal art are often unique.

For the most part, lacquer techniques are named according to the technique used (flat sown picture, lead-oxide painting, etc.), the name of the artist who originated the technique, or the original place of manufacture of a special technique. For example *ji* in Japanese means background and *nashi* is a type of Japanese pear. *Nashiji,* or "pear ground," is therefore a descriptive composite of both of these words referring to a ground appearing like the skin of this Japanese pear. Similarly, *makie* means sown or sprinkled picture, *hira* means flat, and *taka* means raised. *Hiramakie* therefore means "flat sown picture" or a flat lacquer design done by means of sprinkling colored and metallic powders. *Takamakie* is a similar technique in which the sown design is in raised relief. *Me* means aspect or eye and *ishi* means stone. *Ishime* is both a lacquer and a metal technique in which the ground is coarse-textured like a stone. Similarly, *mokume* means "wood eye," the appearance simulating the veins and knots of wood. *Nuri* means coating. Zonsei-nuri is a variety of carved lacquer whose coating is named after the lacquerer Zonsei. Wakasa-nuri is named after the province of Wakasa. *Bori* means carving or chiseling. *Chinkin-bori* literally means sunken gold carving.

Such classification, however, overlaps considerably and is therefore much too confusing. For practical purposes classification may be organized as follows: 1) background techniques, 2) *makie* (sown picture), 3) colored lacquer techniques, 4) lacquer painting, 5) carved lacquer, 6) imbedded lacquer, 7) encrusted lacquer, 8) lacquer imitating or enhancing natural and other materials, and 9) transparent lacquer.

It would be far too confusing to discuss all of the innumerable rare and relatively unimportant lacquer techniques, many of which have already been lost to posterity. From a practical point of view, therefore, only those techniques which are of popular or historical significance will be noted in any detail.

Background Techniques

The background may consist simply of a wooden base with the lacquer design applied directly, or in combination with various encrustations as practiced by the Ritsuo school. Ornamental woods or cherry bark were often so employed. Or the natural grain of the wood might be brought out by covering it with a type of transparent lacquer, often supplemented with colored lacquer designs. Special background techniques were also practiced, such as having the lacquer appear like metal, wood, or pottery. Such techniques are described separately later on in this chapter. Most commonly, the background consisted of a black, gold, or red lacquer. Occasionally other shades were used, including browns as employed by Shunsho and Zeshin. Light browns, including tan, are of relatively recent innovation. Quite often the black lacquer was enhanced with various types of metallic dusts, filings, or pieces of cut metal variously applied as to amount, type, and distribution according to specific techniques, such as *nashiji, hirame,* and *kirigane.* These techniques are described below.

NASHIJI (PEAR GROUND OR AVENTURINE)

The already prepared lacquer base *(honji)* is used, and upon it the *nashiji* flakes are dusted after a layer of *ro-se-urushi* has been applied. Subsequent drying, polishing, and relacquering are repeated. The final three lacquer coats are of Yoshino-urushi, a crude lacquer from Yoshino used for final coatings. The final effect is that of numerous flecks of gold buried at different depths in the transparent yellowish-brown lacquer. This stippled gold Venetian-glass effect is similar to that of the European aventurine lacquer. The range of color from gold to red or brown-red depends upon the depth of the individual gold flecks in the lacquer. Good quality is of even density and appears as if suspended in ice. In general, *nashiji,* especially the common variety, is used for the insides and bottoms of lacquer boxes without any superimposed designs (Fig. 140). In inro it is also used on the insides and risers of the cases. *Gyobu nashiji* is also used for inside decoration on inro. On the other hand, *mura nashiji* is used either as a background effect for the outside pictorial scene or by itself on the inside of lacquered boxes. Varieties of *nashiji* are also done with black or colored lacquer. The following are the numerous types of *nashiji:*

1) *mura nashiji.* The metallic powder forms irregular, more or less dense masses in cloudlike *(mura)* effects. Also known as uneven *nashiji.* There are several variations, including a similar irregular patchy effect called *kasumi nashiji. Mura nashiji* is more artistically effective when dispersed over larger surface areas but is also used in miniature lacquer (Frontispiece, Fig. 13).

2) *kanoko nashiji.* The metallic powder is dispersed in spots resembling the reddish spots on the back of a young deer *(kanoko).*

3) *yasuriko nashiji.* The metallic grains are quite large and very dense *(yasuri*=file, *yasuriko*=filings) and rolled fairly flat. When these heavy filings are strewn very sparingly, it is called *usu-yasuriko nashiji (usu*=thin, not densely spaced). If the background of *yasuriko nashiji* is gold *(kinji)* lacquer, it is also called *ikakeji* (poured-on ground).

4) *gyobu nashiji.* Invented by Gyobu Taro of Edo in the beginning of the 18th century. Consists of large irregular flakes of gold placed alongside of one another irregularly, forming a beautiful mosaic effect of gold. The technique was especially excellent on the inner surfaces of the inro made by the Kajikawa family (Fig. 14).

5) *kin fundame (kin-fun, kin-pun).* Very fine gold powder in black lacquer. *Fundame* (powder ground) consists of fine gold or silver powdered onto the ground or mixed with the lacquer and applied directly with the brush and worked to a soft, dull surface finish. Used as a ground for pictorial designs and also as a plain ground on insides of lacquered articles (Figs. 142, 223).

6) *nashiji ishime.* See page 130.

7) *e-nashiji* (picture *nashiji*). In this case the *nashiji* is used for the design rather than just for the background. Originated in the Momoyama period (Fig. 33).

8) *heijin* (even dust). Background of rough sprinkling of gold dust. Originated in the Heian period.

9) *maki-bokashi* (graduated sprinklings). Spreading metal powder more thinly in some places than in others. Originated in the Heian period.

10) *ikakeji.* Similar to the *heijin* method, but the gold powder is put on more densely. Originated in the Heian period.

11) *chiriji.* A variety of lacquer in which the background of a clear

brown or black lacquer is powdered with fine gold or silver particles and enriched by scattering a few metallic particles. It is therefore a combination of *nashiji* and *oki-hirame* (Fig. 55).

12) *tsuya-keshi* (sheen extinguished). Dull finish, mostly in black, in which the polished lacquer is now purposely dulled by pounding with a hard brush filled with deerhorn powder. Other techniques of dull ground are *fundame* (powder ground), *ishime-nuri,* and *sabiji* (rust ground; Fig. 135). A slightly roughened lacquer surface is known as *kodame chiriji.* One beautiful, subtle style consists of delicate designs of dull black on a highly polished black ground. In general, dull grounds vary in degree of roughness from a smooth, flat mat to a coarse texture similar to the bark of a tree. Similarly, the dull lacquer may be in flat, medium, or high relief. It is most often done in black but also in brown tones and as gold or silver *fundame.* Zeshin's works quite often reveal grounds and also ornamental touches of such coarse texture, the latter usually in low relief. He was also fond of a flat, dull olive-gray ground (Figs. 11, 25).

HIRAME (FLAT EYE)

The two following techniques fall under this heading:

1) *hirame* or *hirame nashiji.* A lacquer technique employing the various irregular flat pieces of *hirame* as with *nashiji.* The particles are dusted into the wet lacquer surface and covered with transparent lacquer. Brilliant little metallic surface points are brought out by polishing. The particles of gold are larger than those used in *nashiji.* In general, this technique, in contrast to *nashiji,* is seen more frequently in the ground of older pieces (Fig. 51). *Nashiji* was more popular during the 19th century, at which time it was often of inferior quality.

2) *oki-hirame.* Relatively large, irregular, flat metallic (invariably gold) pieces are encrusted quite regularly next to one another, giving a rich gold mosaic pattern. This technique was used both on miniature and on larger pieces to produce a strong background effect for a simple central design (Figs. 45, 48, 101, 120, 139, 220). Rarely, the same technique is found using *aogai* (Fig. 15).

KANA-GAI (METALLIC FOIL)

In general, the metallic foil is slightly thicker than the usual gold leaf and is usually used flush with the ground or slightly elevated. Occasionally fairly heavy (thick) pieces are used to accentuate the design, such as indicating an object actually made out of gold rather than for purely ornamental purposes. The following techniques fall under this heading:

1) *kirigane* (cut metal). The metallic foil is cut into small various-sized squares or rectangles. These pieces are inlaid more or less irregularly side by side as a mosaic similar to that of *oki-hirame* or irregularly spaced according to their decorative use (Figs. 56, 57). They may be placed so

that their dimensions gradually decrease. On old lacquer these squares of gold are mixed with squares of silver. Such metallic pieces are also often used in the design itself and are most frequently seen on rocks, on the heights of hills in a landscape, on clouds, on trunks of old trees, etc. (Figs, 53, 94). *Kirigane* is occasionally seen as a *nashiji* ground used mainly on sword hilts, where it is done in very narrow interspersed parallel rectangles. The technique of *kirigane* apparently dates from about the mid-14th century, and we know that it was frequently used by Koami Nagashige (Koami X) during the mid-17th century.

2) *heidatsu* and *hyomon*. Techniques of encrusted design using sheets of gold or silver foil. (See sections on imbedded and encrusted lacquer, pages 126, 127; see also Fig. 16.)

The Pictorial and Decorative Designs

The techniques of background decoration using metallic dustings have been described, as well as the various types of lacquer used for the basis. The methods of using and combining all of these materials into the final pictorial and decorative effects have already been classified. In general, the final design, no matter what technique is used, is either flat or raised to varying reliefs. Flat relief may be effected by level applications of lacquer for the design or by rubbing down, as in *togidashi makie*. Relief may be obtained by building up the design in lacquer or by means of encrustations or by carving out the lacquer *(guri, tsuishu)* or the wooden base itself (Kamakura-bori). Besides using varying degrees of relief, the design itself is brought out by employing numerous techniques, such as the following: 1) repeated metallic dustings, as in *nashiji,* 2) colored lacquers, 3) painting with lacquer solutions, 4) carving into the lacquer, 5) imbedding and encrusting various materials, and 6) combinations of these methods. Each of these techniques is to be described separately.

There are three different basic varieties of the *makie,* or "sown picture" technique: 1) *togidashi,* or rubbed lacquer, 2) *hiramakie,* or flat *makie,* and 3) *takamakie,* or *makie* in relief. These will be explained in detail below.

A second type of lacquer technique is accomplished by cutting the design into the lacquer. Examples are *guri* (crook ring), *tsuishu* (heap red), *tsuikoku* (heap black), and Zonsei.

A third type of lacquer is encrusted lacquer. In this technique the design consists entirely or in part of small or large precarved, relatively heavy pieces of various materials which are encrusted into the prepared lacquer. The material may consist of silver, gold, lead, pewter, metal alloys, mother-of-pearl, coral, ivory, faience, etc., and usually projects to varying heights beyond the level of the lacquer, but may also be imbedded level with the surface of the lacquer. This encrusted type of work was quite often done in conjunction with metal artisans and was also associated with such famous names as Korin, Ritsuo, Shibayama, and Somada.

There are dozens of other varieties of specific types of lacquer ware, some of which are variations of the techniques already mentioned.

Makie (Sown or Sprinkled Picture)

This technique consists essentially of building up the design by repeated alternating applications of thin coats of lacquer followed by metallic dustings and rubbings. The design is therefore gradually applied in layers by dusting rather than being painted on with lacquer. In this way delicate and graduated shadings and a sense of depth may be obtained even when the final surface is completely flat. Various degrees of relief may be obtained by this method by building up specific areas of the design with lacquer rather than applying the lacquer to the entire surface. As previously mentioned, there is no room for any errors in using this technique, since the dustings cannot be removed from the tacky lacquered surface. The artist must visualize in advance the exact order of his dustings, which will bring out the final desired pictorial effect. The art of *makie* is typically and basically of Japanese invention, dating back to the Nara period and ultimately brought to magnificent artistic and technical perfection which no country, including China, has ever been able to imitate successfully.

TOGIDASHI (POLISHING OUT)

The term literally means "to bring out by rubbing" (*togu*=to rub, *dasu*=to bring out). The basis lacquer is prepared up to the first coating of *ro-urushi*. The design is drawn in ink on specially prepared paper and is traced with a rat's-hair brush on the opposite side of the paper with heated moist lacquer. The outlined lacquer design is now rubbed off onto the lacquered surface with a whalebone spatula. The lines are dusted with powdered white whetstone to improve the visibility of the outline, which is then powdered with metallic powders or pulverized colored lacquer before the piece is dried in the damp press. The outlines are now gone over with *ro-se-urushi* and dried, and the gilding or powdering process is repeated. Finally the entire surface is coated with *ro-urushi*, covering the entire design with this black lacquer. The surface is now ground down to the underlying gold (or other) design, and the process is repeated. By this method the design is brought out by the grinding down and has a softened effect at the edges, as in pastel work. The surface is now covered with clear lacquer *(seshime-urushi)* and the product finished as in the previously described *honji* method, the final effect being an absolutely even, polished surface.

In more modern manufacture the design is drawn directly on the object with white lead. *Togidashi* is a very old method and was used as early as

724. It is used in combination with raised lacquer for distant effects, including mists, clouds, and mountaintops; for softly sweeping and curving streams; for leaves fading into the distance, and the like. In some cases the nearer leaves are done in raised lacquer and the more distant ones in *togidashi*. A similar technique, indicating perspective, is used in the metal arts, combining medium and low relief. However, the same effect of perspective can be even more subtly obtained by using various shades and "faintness" of design by employing *togidashi* alone (Figs. 24, 67, 151). There are several varieties of *togidashi*:

1) *iroe togidashi*. This is done in gold, silver, and different-colored lacquers. The families of Shunsho and Shiomi Masanari were especially noted for this technique (Figs. 6, 68, 216).

2) *sumie togidashi*. Here the design is executed only in black lacquer powder, imitating *sumie* ink painting. All shades from black to light gray are obtained, simulating the various washes of *sumie* painting. The background is usually of plain gold or silver. Noted for this technique were Toyo, Hakuho, and Shoryusai (Figs. 20, 22, 209).

3) *shishiai togidashi*. This technique, combining relief *makie* and *togidashi,* was used in the Muromachi period to produce flattened, burnished relief and high relief.

HIRAMAKIE (FLAT SOWN PICTURE)

This is the name given to all gold lacquer which has a flat surface. The design itself is almost level with the background. The outline of the design is transferred to the prepared lacquer basis, as noted in *togidashi*. The spaces are filled in with *shita-maki-urushi* on which gold powder is dusted. The object is dried, and a layer of clear lacquer (Yoshino-urushi) is applied. After drying and polishing, details are drawn with a rat's-hair brush *(neji-fude),* using inside line lacquer *(ke-uchi-urushi)*. After dusting with gold and drying, the clear lacquer is again applied and dried and polished. Final marking and shading is now done with shading lacquer *(jo-hana-urushi)*. In general, the effect in this flat lacquer is obtained through the repeated subtle graduated dustings. In *hiramakie* the outlines (and often the details) of the designs and the background motifs are not actually completely flat but are very slightly raised (Fig. 58).

TAKAMAKIE (LACQUER IN RELIEF, RAISED SOWN PICTURE)

This name identifies all raised gold lacquer, including dusting and inlaying of thin metal or mother-of-pearl flakes (including *kirigane*). Technically the term should be limited to raised lacquer done in *makie,* as the name implies. The technique originated at the end of the Kamakura period (about 1334) and was fully developed under the Ashikaga shogunate in the 15th century. In general, *takamakie* is used for near perspective, including figures, rocks, and trees. At times it reaches almost a sculptural quality, which of course also applies to high encrustations. As previously mentioned, "raising lacquer," which contains camphor, is used in order to produce slow and even drying. This prevents drying of the top layers first as well as subsequent cracking of the top layer.

The ground may be black or any colored lacquer, or of a lacquer imitating some other material, or *nashiji,* or plain wood or metal. The design is transferred from paper, as in all *makie.* A layer of *shita-maki-urushi* (undercoating lacquer) is applied to the portions to be raised as a basis for the raising process. Two layers of Yoshino-nobe-urushi are applied to the design:

1) For slight relief, *taka-maki-urushi* (raising lacquer) is used with fine brushes, dried, ground down, polished, and covered with *seshime-urushi.* The surface is now ready for gilding.

2) For high relief, the design is built up with several coats of *sabi* (clay and *seshime-urushi*) which are applied with the usual drying and grinding process and then coated with Yoshino-nobe-urushi. Then the stages listed above under "slight relief" are gone through before the surface is ready for gilding (Frontispiece).

3) In the gilding processes the *kirigane* is applied first upon a layer of *ro-se-urushi,* and then *hirame* or shell scales are applied separately with a pointed stick *(hirame-fude).* The parts to be gilded with gold dust are now coated with *shita-maki-urushi* (undercoating lacquer) and the powders applied with the *tsutsu.* Repeated dustings are done as necessary. The final details of the design are then done as in *hiramakie* after the application of *shita-maki-urushi*—namely, clear lacquer, inside line lacquer, dusting, shading lacquer, and finally finishing lacquer.

MISCELLANEOUS MAKIE TYPES

In addition to the three basic *makie* types described above, there are a number of variations. These are briefly explained here.

1) *maki-abise.* In this technique, which was used in the Momoyama period, gold dust was heavily heaped onto the raised design.

2) Higashiyama *makie.* Lacquer ware made in the late Muromachi period for Shogun Ashikaga Yoshimasa (1435–90).

3) *jidai makie.* Lacquer products of the Genroku era (1688–1704).

4) *jokei-in makie.* Lacquer ware of the Genroku era named after an appellation of Shogun Tokugawa Tsunayoshi (ruled 1680–1709).

5) *joken-in makie.* Ornamentation of different regular seedings in gold and silver of different tonalities, often found in picnic boxes *(bento-bako)* in which each compartment, tray, or *sake* bottle is decorated with a different geometrical design.

6) Kaga *makie.* Originated in the mid-17th century by the Igarashi family of lacquer artists, who moved from Kyoto to Kaga Province under the patronage of Lord Maeda Toshitsune.

7) *kimetsuke makie.* *Makie* in relief decorated with patterns in gold or silver flakes. The pieces of cut metal flakes are fixed to the design with starch and therefore stand out in relief. The technique was used during the Momoyama period.

8) Kodai-ji *makie.* Lacquer work of the Momoyama period named after Hideyoshi's Kodai-ji temple in Kyoto, which was decorated with lacquer. A technique in which the leaves and stems of plants are outlined in gold lacquer surrounding a *nashiji* filling.

9) Koetsu *makie,* Korin *makie,* etc. Lacquer ware named after individual artists who introduced and popularized a specific lacquer technique.

10) *maki-hanashi.* A Momoyama-period technique in which the gold dustings were left as they were instead of being covered with lacquer and then polished.

Color Techniques

The various colors and pigments used in lacquer ware have already been noted. The pigments may be used either in coloring the lacquer or as pulverized powders; sometimes they are mixed with metallic powders for shading. When used for the production of colored lacquer, the pigments are mixed with *suki-urushi,* the finest crude transparent lacquer. Actually, pure colors are not seen because of the inherent amber hue of the lacquer itself. However, bright, pure colors are not approved of by the Japanese artisan, who prefers more toned-down, delicate, subtle shades. In general, the Chinese used a wider range of colors in their lacquer work, including white, turquoise, yellow, and different shades of green and red. The problem of vegetable colors being destroyed by the lacquer has already been noted. Vivid colors, such as sky blue and crimson, were not produced until the beginning of the 20th century.

Colored lacquered objects are made over the *honji* basis up to the point of application of the *ro-urushi.* The colored lacquer, prepared as noted above, is usually applied in two coats, followed by three coats of transparent lacquer, each step including the drying and polishing processes. The colored lacquer may in turn be embellished with *nashiji* or other ornamental lacquers, encrustations, and designs. The following are special techniques used in colored lacquer work.

TSUGARU-NURI

This type of lacquer, manufactured in the Tsugaru district (Aomori Prefecture) was originally made for the daimyo of Tsugaru. The technique was inaugurated in the late 17th century by Ikeda Gembei, a native of Tsugaru. The final surface is composed of a mottled effect of lacquers of different colors: red, yellow, green, and black (Fig. 69). The base is purposely made hollowed and uneven by means of a paste, such as white of egg and chalk. Successive layers of different colors are then applied to this uneven base, and when it is polished down to a flat surface the mottled effect of the different colors appears. Metallic tints are not used. Occasionally, before the base layer dries, natural foliage (for example, pine needles) and flowers are pressed into the lacquer. When the lacquer has dried, these are removed, and the impressions are covered with successive layers of different-colored lacquer (sometimes gold or silver). When the piece is polished down, the colors of the lacquer reveal the outline of the vegetation. Such pieces, however, are relatively rare.

WAKASA-NURI

This technique originated around the Kyoho era (1716–35). The lacquer is made in Obama (Fukui Prefecture) and is an imitation of Chinese Zonsei. It is made in similar fashion to Tsugaru-nuri, but more colors may be used, including red, green, blue, yellow, and black as well as brown, yellow-gold, and orange lacquers. The last three colors predominated in traditional Wakasa-nuri and at times were the only colors used. In some cases when the foliage impression was used it was filled up with successive layers of colored lacquer and finally with gold or silver leaf (not used in Tsugaru-nuri); then a layer of colored or transparent lacquer was applied, and the surface was ground down until the pattern appeared. This was then covered with successive layers of transparent lacquer until the hollows were filled up. The underlying gold leaf is responsible for the brown-gold *nashiji*-like effect. The overall appearance in this style is a gold-orange-brown ground with more or less angular patterns interspersed with tiny irregular circles of black and yellow (Fig. 70).

YOZAKURA-NURI

Yozakura means "cherry blossoms at night." This lacquer is characterized by a special type of background of black lacquer against which can be seen the contours of the cherry tree, also in black. The effect is achieved by applying to a highly polished black background the design of the flowers of the cherry tree with a mixture of black lacquer and *nashiji-urushi*. After drying, the whole surface is covered with a layer of black lacquer. The cherry-tree design therefore appears as if blended into the night. This lacquer was the specialty of Nakamura Sotetsu of Kyoto (1617–95).

The technique of *kuro-makie* or *urushi-makie* produces a similar style of lacquer utilizing a highly polished black ground with the ornamentation also done in polished black in low relief. This subtle use of lacquer is highly esteemed by the Japanese connoisseur and artisan (Figs. 28, 71, 147). Similar techniques using dark brown or black on dark brown were also developed. The use of all black on inro in imitation of Chinese ink cakes demonstrates the subtleties of black on black, including a rough black ground to imitate chips in the ink cake and a hairline technique to represent fine cracks. Such imitations were quite popular and were made by such renowned artists as Ritsuo and Zeshin (Figs. 59, 60). Dull black lacquer is also known as *sabi-nuri*.

SURI-HAGASHI

Suru means "to rub," and *hagasu* means "to wear off." In this technique, red lacquer is applied over black lacquer, and through usage the red lacquer wears off, revealing the underlying black in irregular spots. Netsuke made in Nara often employ the technique.

NEGORO-NURI

This technique was started by Buddhist priests at the Negoro Temple in the province of Kii (Wakayama Prefecture) in the late 13th century. It is used for the decoration of table utensils in black or red lacquer or, more rarely, red lacquer with a black background. In the latter case, through use, the black background will appear in spots. When their temple was destroyed by Toyotomi Hideyoshi, the priests transported their lacquer industry to Kuroe, in the same province. This old style of lacquer was very popular before the Edo period and was used mainly for moderate-sized utensils like trays, rice bowls, small dining tables, and pitchers. The technique is only rarely seen in miniature lacquer, including inro (Fig. 72), but it was used fairly frequently in netsuke.

YOSHINO-NURI

Yoshino-nuri, named for the Yoshino district of Nara Prefecture, is black lacquer with red lacquer ornamentation. The technique is used especially on cups and bowls.

WHITE LACQUER OF JOGAHANA

This pure-white lacquer is made by dusting with silicate powder. It is named for the place in Etchu Province (Toyama Prefecture) where it was made by the famous lacquer artist Jigoemon Shigeyoshi Ohara (1729–1805).

KOMA-DE

Koma-de is the name for lacquer ware imported into Japan from Southeast Asia during the Momoyama period. Decorated with carved circles of different colors, it was named after the design of the Japanese spinning top. The technique originated in South China and from there was transmitted to Southeast Asia. Lacquer articles decorated in *koma-de* style were imported during the time of the tea master Sen no Rikyu and were much admired by devotees of the tea ceremony.

KIMMA LACQUER

The technique employed for this type of lacquer originated in Siam, where it served for decorating receptacles for a medicine known as *kimma*. In Japan, where it was introduced during the Momoyama period, it is called *tenshitsu*. The base is usually of bamboo in a basket weave. On a ground of blackish red and maroon, designs of fine arabesques, flowers, birds, and animals are hairline-engraved, and the spaces between them are then filled in with a single color or a number of colors (red, blue, yellow, and brown) and polished.

HIDEHIRA OR NAMBU WARE

This type or lacquer is known by two names, the first being the given name of Fujiwara Hidehira, one of the leaders of the powerful Fujiwara branch family in northern Honshu during medieval times, and the second being the name of the district where this family ruled. Lacquer ware in this style usually takes the form of soup bowls and *sake* cups on which plant designs in red or red and gold appear against a black ground (Fig. 62).

FUKIDOME

Fukidome is one of a number of miscellaneous techniques employing colored lacquer. In this type of ware the lacquer is blown onto the basis to produce large irregular blotches, usually of black on a red ground (Fig. 75).

Lacquer Painting

Painting with lacquer is a decorative device used not only for lacquer ware itself but also for other objects such as miniature shrines. Pictures were also painted with lacquer. A number of techniques were developed, but not many of them have survived. The most important ones are discussed here.

KINGIN-E

The literal meaning of *kingin-e* is "gold and silver picture." This technique, of Chinese origin, was used during the Nara period. It consisted of mixing powdered gold *(kin)* or silver *(gin)* with glue and producing a painting with this mixture. The design, however, tended to exfoliate.

KINGIN-DE-GA

In this technique, gold or silver powder was mixed with lacquer and used for painting on a lacquered or a polished wood background. The designs usually consisted of a network of floral arabesques or patterns of stylized animals.

MAKKINRU

This technique, borrowed from the Chinese and used during the Nara period, consisted of painting with a mixture of coarse powdered gold (*makkinru*=powdered gold) and lacquer. When dry, the surface was lacquered and polished. The technique fell into disuse because it was difficult to draw with the thick mixture of lacquer and gold.

JOGAHANA OR GOHANA

Painting in this style is done with lacquers of different colors: green, red, white, brown, and, to a small extent, gold. The lacquers are mixed with oil. The technique is attributed to Jigoemon (1), 15th century, of Jogahana, in Etchu Province (Toyama Prefecture), although Jigoemon apparently learned it from a Chinese artist. It is one of the rarer lacquer-painting techniques. Gold-lacquer Jogahana dates from the 18th century.

MITSUDA-E

In this technique, the painting is done on a lacquer background with a colored solution composed of lacquer, lead oxide, and oil to produce a very light relief. The technique was practiced in both China and Japan, but examples of Japanese *mitsuda-e* are relatively rare. It was first used in Japan during the Asuka period and again in the Momoyama period. The background is usually polished black lacquer. *Mitsuda-e* is considered to be a variety of oil painting.

JOHOJI

Lacquer painting of this type takes its name from the village of Johoji, in the province of Mutsu (Aomori Prefecture), where it was originally made. The technique consists of drawing the design in yellow or green lacquer on a red or black background and embellishing it with cut metal foil. The Ouchi ware of Yamaguchi Prefecture used a similar technique.

YUSHOKU

Yushoku means "oil color." The technique was used in the Nara period and is not clearly understood today. Apparently, after the lacquer had dried, a thin coating of oil was spread over the colored design to prevent fading or flaking.

SHITSUGA

The literal meaning of *shitsuga* is "lacquer painting." The technique was known in China from the time of the Han dynasty (206 B.C. to A.D. 220) and was introduced into Japan in the 7th century. In this method of decoration, the designs are painted on the base with different colors of lacquer.

Carved Lacquer

Carved lacquer, made in imitation of the carved Chinese red-and-black lacquer (in Japanese, *choshitsu*) of the Sung and Yüan dynasties (Pekin, or cinnabar lacquer), was popular in Japan from the 16th through the 18th century and was used for utensils of the tea and incense ceremonies. Other specific techniques of carved lacquer were also adopted from the Chinese, but in general Japanese carved lacquer ware was not as popular as *makie*, nor did it ever reach the technical perfection of *makie*. Carved lacquer, such as *tsuishu, tsuikoku,* and *guri,* was rarely signed. Japanese carved lacquer pieces are usually of moderate or miniature size in comparison to the large Chinese cinnabar furniture. The Chinese tended to use more variety of color in their *choshitsu,* including deep green, light olive green, buff, and brown. Similarly, they quite often carved in a two-color technique, the design on the surface being of one color and the deeper portions of the design being in a different color. The Chinese also occasionally added different types of encrustation to their carved lacquer. The principal Japanese techniques of carved lacquer are described below.

GURI (CROOK RING)

After the basic lacquer layers have been applied, lacquer layers of different colors are added. Thus layers of red lacquer may be alternated with layers of black or yellow. The surface layer is usually a dark reddish brown. As many as forty such layers may be applied. When dry, these layers are deeply cut with a tool in the form of a V. The cuts are made at an angle so that the various layers of lacquer are revealed. The patterns so cut are usually curved, spiral, or geometric (Fig. 73). This method was used essentially on smaller lacquered objects, such as netsuke and inro, but occasionally on larger pieces as well. The technique was adopted from China, where it was practiced before the 8th century. The *guri* technique was also used in Japanese metalwork (Fig. 61).

TSUISHU (HEAP RED)

Tsuishu is a variety of red lacquer in which more than ten coats of lacquer are applied and in which, when the lacquer has dried, the designs are deeply cut in imitation of the Chinese style of *choshitsu* noted above. This technique was introduced into Japan at the end of the 15th century and was originally copied from the Chinese method by a lacquerer named Monnyu.

When the top sculptured layer is black, the lacquer is called *tsuikoku,* or heap black. When several colors are used in superimposing layers or in the same layer (deep green, yellow, red, brown, black), this variety is called *tsuio*. Tsuishu Jirozaemon of Kyoto specialized in this style, as did Tsuishu Yosei (mid-14th century) and his descendants who continued working in this technique into the first half of the 20th century. The name Yosei is a combination of parts of the names of two Chinese *tsuishu* lacquerers whom the Japanese call Yomo and Chosei (Fig. 74)—that is, the "yo" of Yomo and the "sei" of Chosei. The designs of most old Japanese *tsuishu* ware are somewhat in the Chinese classical style, including background ornamentation of key designs or the *asa-no-ha* pattern. This pattern, with its variations, is a geometrical design of a regular arrangement of arcs whose junctions form a repetitive series of stars (Fig. 40).

Choshitsu lacquer is imitated by using a composition of lacquer, ocher, glue, and wheat flour in which the design is often brought out by a stamp. Similar spurious inferior works are made by carving into hard red rubber.

Koka-ryokuyo (red flowers and green leaves) is a variety of *tsuishu* lacquer in red-and-green relief carving. *Hashika-bori* employs the same technique but in shallower engraving.

KAMAKURA-BORI

This variety of Japanese lacquer was inspired by the Chinese Pekin red lacquer. It consists of wood carved in low relief which was covered originally with layers of black and red lacquer and later by other colors. The top layer of red, through usage, is rubbed down, letting the underlying black appear in spots. The wood used is usually from the ginkgo, *ho,* or *katsura* tree. The designs are generally peonies and plum blossoms, broadly treated on a diapered ground *(hana-bishi)*. This technique was originated by Koen around the mid-13th century under the auspices of the regent Hojo Tokimune who ruled in Kamakura from 1215 to 1284, and fell into disuse by the end of the 16th century (Fig. 63). The *chomoku* (literally, "carved wood") technique is similar to that of Kamakura-bori and was used as early as the 10th century for small writing tables.

ZONSEI-NURI

Zonsei-nuri (or Zonsei) is a variety of carved lacquer made in both China and Japan. The Japanese type is named after the 17th-century artist Zonsei, who excelled in lacquer works of different colors. In Chinese Zonsei the colors used are usually green, red, or yellow. Japanese Zonsei also uses red and violet. The technique of carving is similar to that of *tsuishu* lacquer. Sometimes the sculptured design is enriched with engraved details. The designs are mostly in conventional patterns, and the color scheme is irregular and mottled—similar to that of Tsugaru-nuri. When the decoration is carved in layers of red and green lacquer and presents red flowers with green leaves, this special variety is known as *koka-ryokuyo* (red flowers and green leaves).

ZOKOKU-NURI

In Zokoku-nuri the design is sculptured in several layers of red and black lacquer, the method being the same as in *guri* lacquer. The carved-out design is filled up with colored lacquer and rubbed down to a surface like that of *togidashi*. This technique is attributed to the Japanese lacquerer Tamakaji Zokoku (1806–69), of the city of Takamatsu in Shikoku. It is based on the technique of the Siamese lacquer known as *kimma* or *kimma-de*, which was imported by the Japanese in the Momoyama period.

CHINKIN-BORI (SUNKEN GOLD CARVING)

This ancient technique of lacquer engraving originated in China and was also used in metal art. Fine lines are made in a lacquer surface with a steel point or a rat's tooth and then rendered more visible by powdering (usually with gold) or lacquering with a color different from that of the background (Fig. 76). This technique was popular in Nagasaki during the Kyoho era of 1716–35. It is often found on inro with the following signatures: Chin'ei, Chingi, Chinkei, Chokan, and Rinchoken. During the Kansei era (1789–1800), Ninomiya Tohei, a doctor of Edo, was famous for this work and used rats' teeth for his engravings, which were usually of flowers and birds.

SIMPLE INCISED LACQUER

This technique consists of fine superficial carving of figures and ornamental designs in a lacquer surface. The cutting is left untouched. Zeshin quite often used this technique, usually for a small contrasting part of his design and more rarely for the entire design (Figs. 64, 202).

Imbedded Lacquer

In imbedded work the material to be imbedded is sliced into very thin sheets and cut into the desired forms. A layer of lacquer is applied to the ground, and the material is thoroughly cemented. The surrounding ground is then gradually raised to the level of the imbedded material. Further decorations, as described in the discussion of *takamakie* (page 117), are now done. Most commonly used are relatively large sheets of gold and thin sheets of green iridescent mother-of-pearl, such as used by the Somada school. The following are specific techniques of imbedded work.

HYOMON (SHEET DESIGN)

This technique originated in the Nara period. The design is cut out in thin sheets of gold or silver, applied to the lacquer, and then covered with lacquer. The lacquer over the metal-foil design is then rubbed off to bring out the design. The *hyomon* technique enjoyed its greatest popularity in the Nara period.

KANA-GAI (GOLD FOIL)

The *kana-gai* technique employs affixed sheet gold. Designs are cut from thin gold or silver foil and imbedded in the lacquer. The technique was popular during the Muromachi period.

HEIDATSU

Heidatsu is a technique of lacquer ornamentation inaugurated by the artist Hyoman during the second half of the 17th century. It consists of affixing little sheets of gold or silver to form a design on brown, gray, or red lacquer and then covering them with transparent lacquer. If the background itself is gold, the lacquer is known as Owari ware, which features designs of flowers and leaves.

SOMADA

Somada is a generic name for the style created by the Somada family at the beginning of the 18th century. The technique consists of imbedding paper-thin slivers and pieces of iridescent greenish blue *aogai* Ming-style shell, usually on a rich, highly polished lacquer background of deep black. The entire surface is then covered with lacquer and rubbed down to make the mother-of-pearl design level with the lacquer basis. The designs themselves are composed either of an aggregate of these tiny inlays or of larger precarved outlines of part or all of a figure or face. These larger pieces are then engraved with further details, such as facial lines, ornamentation on clothing, and the like (Fig. 78). Early-style Somada was less ornate than later works and was often supplemented by other techniques such as *togidashi* (Fig. 140). Later works were more ornate and usually almost entirely of mother-of-pearl. The Somada artists also occasionally used fine imbedded silver wire, either as pure ornamentation or as outlines for pictorial designs. Very recent (20th century) Somada work has been done by applying a black lacquer ground over a metal base and then imbedding the mother-of-pearl design.

Encrusted Lacquer

In encrusted work the design is transferred from paper to the prepared lacquer, as in all *makie* work. The encrustations, which are usually quite thick, are now shaped and finished by the usual carving, chasing, or engraving. The spaces to be encrusted are sunk through the lacquer into the wooden base, and the encrustations are then cemented in and edged with lacquer. It should be noted that all raised-lacquer work is done before the encrustations are set in, but that enrichment in gold or lacquer on the surface of the encrustations themselves is usually done after they have been imbedded. The height to which the encrustations are raised above the general surface of the object and the thickness and techniques of utilization of the encrustations vary considerably. Thus mother-of-pearl, when used by the Korin school, was usually white and highly raised and of large, simple, purposely crude pieces (Fig. 8). The Shibayama school used moderately raised, intricately carved small pieces of white or tinted mother-of-pearl (Figs. 49, 65, 129), and the Somada school used tiny pieces of flat, very thin iridescent *awabi* shell. In the Somada school the designs were accomplished through the coalescence of the innumerable pieces of colored shell in contrast with the precarved, more sculptural effects of the simple Korin or the elaborate Shibayama school of encrustation. Occasionally, especially as seen in the work of Ritsuo and his school, the encrustations were done on a natural or braided wood ground. This decoration was frequently supplemented by touches of flat or raised lacquer (Figs. 39, 217).

Many materials were used for encrusted work, including—in addition to those mentioned under the specific techniques described below—tortoise shell, ivory, coral, faience, wood, porcelain, malachite, and soapstone. Metallic foil was often put under the translucent tortoise shell to enhance its effect. Richly decorated gold lacquer occasionally had encrustations of pure gold nuggets *(uchikomi)*, most often representing the junctions of tree branches (Fig. 149).

Much of this type of encrusted work, especially in the late 19th century, became commercial and overornate. However, many such masters as Soetsu, Korin, and Ritsuo, as well as the Shibayama school, specialized in this type of lacquer work.

The following are among the more important techniques of encrustation. The materials noted may be encrusted separately or in various combinations.

METALLIC ENCRUSTATION

The metals used include gold, silver, copper, lead, pewter, and alloys such as black *shakudo* and gray-toned *shibuichi* (see "Metal Techniques," pages 135–139). Many inro displaying metalwork were made in conjunction with metal artists, the work usually being signed by both the lacquerer and the metalworker (Figs. 65, 66, 93, 94). Metal wire was occasionally used as an outline for designs—a technique especially characteristic of the Somada school.

MOTHER-OF-PEARL ENCRUSTATION

Mother-of-pearl decoration is known in Japanese as *raden* or *aogai-zaiku* and is the equivalent of the French *laque burgautée*. The word *raden* derives from the Japanese pronunciation of the Chinese character for the shell of the *sazae (Turbo cornutus)* and the word *den,* which means floral decorations in gold or articles decorated with mother-of-pearl. The *raden* technique was used by Chinese as far back as the T'ang dynasty (618–907). Inlaid shell decoration is also called *hanagai.* It was used in Japan from about the 8th century, especially for sword scabbards. The shells used were mainly *omugai* (nautilus), *yakugai* (pearl shell), and *chogai*. From the beginning of the 17th century, *awabi* (sea ear, or *Haliotis japonica*) was used. This shell, also called *aogai*, has a red, green, and blue iridescence and was introduced from China by the lacquerer Chobei about 1620. A variety of *aogai* used in thin sheets was the specialty of the Somada school. In the 19th century, *aogai* decoration became quite popular, and while the works displaying it usually lacked simple artistic taste, they were technically very well executed in extreme detail on a rich black lacquer background. These works are rarely signed (Figs. 80, 83). Occasionally, color or metallic foil is applied under the thin sheets of mother-of-pearl to enhance the final effect. Shell was also used in various-sized scales similar to *hirame* and also as greenish iridescent powder called *aogai-mijin* (Figs. 77, 78).

ZOGAN-NURI

This technique was popularized around 1815, especially in Nagoya. The design is outlined by encrusting gold or silver wire in the soft lacquer. This is then covered with black lacquer and rubbed down as in the *togidashi* technique. The final effect is an imitation of cloisonné enamel.

TAMAGO-NO-MIJIN MAKI

In this technique, pieces of crushed white eggshell are encrusted on the surface of lacquer designs to produce a mosaic pattern. After the lacquer has dried, the entire surface is polished to make the shell flush with the lacquer ground.

Lacquer Imitating or Covering Other Materials

As previously stressed, Japanese artists were fond of imitating natural materials like wood as well as manufactured materials like pottery, iron, and bronze. The Japanese appreciate an object not only visually but also texturally. They love not only perfection but also imperfection. Thus the rough texture of pottery was often much more highly esteemed than that of a perfectly glazed piece of porcelain. Defects in purposefully crude glazes as well as imperfections in nature, such as knotholes in wood, were similarly incorporated into artistic concepts. Such aesthetic ideals were expressed in lacquer ware as well as in other handicrafts.

In imitating nature, lacquer ware was made to imitate wood, or a transparent lacquer was applied over a natural wood to bring out the grain (see "Transparent Lacquer," pages 133–134). At other times the bark of a tree or the textural appearance and feel of crude iron, rough pottery, or pebbly leather (Figs. 12, 79) would be imitated. Quite often the background was subtly made, using such effects to enhance the pictorial element. Lacquer ware was made simulating an old broken black ink cake or even depicting the patina of old bronze. At other times a unique effect was produced by lacquering a natural material, such as cherry bark, sharkskin, braided bamboo, and Raku pottery.

Similarly, metal artists imitated and portrayed materials of nature, such as rain, earth, and wood. Netsuke artists quite often took delight in imitating such objects as old worm-eaten or rotted wood, papier-mâché toys, or a dried-up piece of fruit. Even Japanese dolls were so cleverly made to simulate porcelain, wood, or papier-mâché that the actual material could only be detected by touch.

LACQUER IMITATING TEXTURE AND NATURAL MATERIALS

1) *mokume* (wood grain). The *mokume* lacquer technique imitates the grain and knots of natural wood by dusting fairly broad, sinuous gold or silver lacquer bands on black lacquer. A similar, more realistic technique was done in brown on a black background (Figs. 13, 48). In general, lacquer is made to imitate not only the grain in wood but also various types of woods and barks.

2) *takemozo-nuri*. Lacquer imitating the surface and grain of bamboo. This technique was a specialty of the lacquerer Hashimoto Ichizo (1817–82).

3) *shitan-nuri*. Lacquer imitating sandalwood *(shitan)*. A dense layer of vermilion lacquer is applied, and then small parallel interrupted lines are drawn before the lacquer is dry. The entire surface is then covered with black lacquer and carefully polished. This type of lacquer is rare.

4) *matsukawa-nuri*. Lacquer imitating the bark of an old pine tree. The lacquer is built up in successive layers, somewhat in the *guri* style.

5) *zogan-nuri*. Lacquer imitating cloisonné enamel (see "Encrusted Lacquer," page 129).

6) *sabiji*. Lacquer imitating the surface of old metal, generally iron. It has a rusty, finely pitted, dull ground appearance. The lacquerer Ritsuo was quite famous for his imitations of old metal grounds, even old bronze. Occasionally, purely for decorative purposes, *tsuba* and *kozuka* were made entirely of lacquer simulating the various types of metals and metal grounds (Fig. 85). Quite often large lacquer storage boxes were decorated in *takamakie* with such imitation *tsuba,* which gave the appearance of actual *tsuba* imbedded into the lacquer ground. The term for dull black lacquer is *sabi-nuri*.

7) *nashiji ishime* or *ishime-nuri* (*ishi*=stone; *me*=aspect). Unpolished background in lacquer (or metal) which imitates to some extent the rough skin of the Japanese pear *(nashi)*. When the surface is slightly roughened, it is known as *kodame chiriji*.

8) *nunome*. Lacquer imitating cloth.

LACQUER COVERING OTHER MATERIALS

1) cloth. Lacquer was used along with mother-of-pearl and metallic

foil for decorative effects on garments. Hempen cloth, as previously noted, was used over a wooden core in some forms of lacquer ware. A similar technique was used by the Chinese, except for *fouchou* lacquer, for which silk cloth was used. The *dakkatsu kanshitsu,* or dry-hollow-lacquer technique, was used for large sculpture in the Nara period. It was adapted from the Chinese Han-dynasty technique of *chia-chu,* in which multiple layers of lacquered hemp cloth were applied over a light frame of wood or clay. In the similar dry-lacquer technique of *mokushin kanshitsu,* also used in the Nara period, the lacquer was modeled over a crude solid-wood core (Fig. 81). In the lacquered-cloth technique, a fairly thin, coarse, grill-like cloth is covered with a thin layer of red lacquer, permitting the outlines of the material to be seen in slight relief (Fig. 86).

2) cord. Cord was frequently imitated in lacquer, wood, and metal or occasionally lacquered, as in *saya-maki* (*saya*=scabbard; *maki*=winding), in which the scabbard of an old type of Japanese sword was wound with cord and then lacquered.

3) *same-nuri.* The *same* is a species of shark, and *same-nuri* is the technique of lacquering sharkskin. Good-quality sharkskin is characterized by relatively large, brilliant white nodules. The nodules are filed down evenly and then coated with black or brown lacquer and finally highly polished. Sometimes the skin is dyed with a color like indigo, and the interstices between the bumps are filled with *sabi.* This technique, in which the nodules are surrounded with a halo of indigo, is called *ai-same* (*ai*=indigo). *Same-nuri* is seen mainly on sword hilts but also occasionally on inro and other miniature lacquered articles.

4) hide or leather *(kawa).* Hide or leather has often been used—particularly by earlier lacquer artists—as a basis for lacquer, since it is lighter and thinner than wood. It is first softened in water and then fashioned into the proper shape and lacquered. This technique dates back to the 8th century and was especially popular in the Nara period. Both heavy and thin hides were used, including those of such animals as the cow, the deer, the wild boar, and the dog.

5) ivory. Ivory netsuke and other miniature articles, such as inro and *kobako,* were occasionally ornamented with lacquer designs. During the late 19th century many poor-quality commercial inro were made of ivory and decorated with numerous detailed inlays of mother-of-pearl, horn, metal, etc., in Shibayama style. In general, most of these carved, lacquered, and encrusted ivory works were of relatively late date (Fig. 82).

6) metal. The metal ground is prepared by repeated firings of crude lacquer on the metal in intense heat so as to make the lacquer adhere to the smooth surface. Subsequent processes are similar to those used on wood grounds. Lacquering on a metal ground is of late date and often includes Somada-style mother-of-pearl inlay. Lacquer artists, like Jokasai, occasionally did lacquer ornamentation on *tsuba* or *kozuka* (Fig. 87). The

close similarities between miniature lacquer and metalwork have been noted. Thus *guri* and *mokume* techniques have their parallel in metal art. Similarly, metal artists often worked in conjunction with lacquer artists, making metal inlays on lacquer pieces, especially inro. The metal artist Omori Teruhide (1730–98) was famous for his metal *nashiji* ground. This consists of tiny flakes of gold imbedded in a metal ground to simulate lacquer *nashiji* (Fig. 88). In general, however, lacquering on a metal ground was relatively uncommon.

7) paper. Lacquering on paper or silk *(urushi-e)* was an ancient technique which was revived by Zeshin in some of his paintings and sketchbooks. The technique is quite difficult. Browns and blacks predominated, with touches of reds and greens (Fig. 123). In the papier-mâché technique, sheets of paper are pasted together with starch, lacquer, and mashed unripe persimmons to form a plastic material from which various forms are molded and then decorated. This technique was often used in making Japanese dolls. Still another technique employing paper is Ikkan-bari, named for a Chinese artist (in Japanese, Hirai Ikkan) who came to Kyoto in the Kan'ei era (1624–43). He made objects for the tea ceremony in wood covered with lacquered paper or composed entirely of lacquered paper.

8) pottery. Lacquer was occasionally applied over pottery, a technique dating back to the Momoyama period and used more often by the Chinese than the Japanese. (Lacquer does not adhere to a glazed surface—for example, to porcelain.) An example of the lacquer-over-pottery technique is seen in Horaku-yaki, also known as Toyosuke-raku, which is a technique invented by Oki Toyosuke (d. 1858) of Owari (Aichi Prefecture). Toyosuke applied lacquer to unglazed earthenware and decorated it with gold lacquer.

9) tortoise shell, amber, horn, etc. Lacquer is applied on these materials for decorative effects, especially in toilet articles, such as ladies' combs, in which tortoise shell *(bekko)* was often used (Fig. 145). Carved tortoise-shell inlays were commonly used in miniature lacquer. The tortoise shell itself was sometimes further decorated with lacquer, and occasionally gold metal foil was placed under it to give a better color effect through this semitransparent material.

10) tree bark. The actual bark of a tree, especially cherry bark, was often covered with a transparent lacquer. Further decoration was then most often done by using *hiramakie* and encrustations, the cherry bark itself being an effective and colorful ground (Fig. 124).

11) natural wood. Transparent lacquer was used to bring out the grain of the underlying natural wood. Quite often the lacquer was applied over a wooden basket weave (Fig. 125). This basket-weave design was also popular in the metal arts. Painting in lacquer on a background of natural wood (Fig. 89) is called *kiji* (*ki*=wood; *ji*=background) *makie*.

12) fungus *(kinoko)*. The fungus not only played a significant symbolic

role in Japanese culture but was also used as a food and as a base for lacquer ornamentation. Symbolically, the fungus is an emblem of longevity, the *jui,* or scepter, being in fungus shape. There is a branching tree fungus, *Boletus versicolor,* known as *saru-no-koshikake* (monkey stool), which is very beautiful, brightly colored, and often very large. Its border shows two to three growth rings. It is very porous, basically brownish in color, and quite durable when dried. This fungus is hollowed out and made into utensils such as plates and has occasionally been used as a basis for lacquering. Inro were sometimes made from it and were usually ornamented with metal encrustations or, more rarely, with lacquer (Fig. 126).

Transparent Lacquer

Transparent lacquer is used mainly to reveal the grain of the underlying wood. Only the most important types and techniques are described in this section.

KIJIRO-NURI

This is the finest of the transparent-lacquer techniques. A hard fancy wood, such as *shitan* (sandalwood), ebony, or *karin* (Chinese quince), is carefully polished. It is then primed with Yoshino-urushi, covered with a layer of *sabi* (clay and *seshime-urushi*), and dried in the damp press. This process fills up the pores of the wood. The entire layer of *sabi* is then ground off, along with most of the first layer of Yoshino-urushi, down to the wood grain. After this, numerous coatings, dryings, and polishings of *nashiji-urushi* and Yoshino-urushi are done. Various coloring matters are used, including gamboge gum, *beni,* yellow vegetable juices, Cape jasmine *(kuchinashi),* pitch *(kasu),* and cinnabar. When the colored lacquer is rubbed on, it is called *suri-urushi* (rubbed *urushi*), and when it shows the underlying wood grain, it is called *kimedashi.*

SHUNKEI-NURI

This type of transparent lacquer, which is also known as Aka Shunkei (Red Shunkei), was invented around the end of the 14th century by the lacquerer Shunkei, of Sakai (Izumi Province). The technique consists of first applying a layer of Yoshino-urushi and then one of *shu-urushi* (*shoki-urushi* and oil), drying the piece, and then rubbing it. The color produced by this process is a red-brown which tends to become lighter with age.

HIDA SHUNKEI

This technique was commonly used in the city of Takayama in Hida Province (the present Gifu Prefecture) for the manufacture of tea-ceremony articles, particularly during the Kan'ei era (1624–43). It is said to have been inaugurated by the lacquerer Narita Sanzaemon, who lived in Takayama at that time. As the name implies, Hida Shunkei is a variant of the Shunkei lacquer described above.

NOSHIRO SHUNKEI

Another Shunkei variant, similar to Hida Shunkei and often called Hida Noshiro, was originated by the Hida lacquerer Yamauchi Sankuro in Noshiro (Akita Prefecture) in the late 17th century. This lacquer, of a clear yellow and very transparent, is extremely rare. The type was later imitated in various parts of the country (Fig. 127).

Three other types of transparent lacquer deserve brief mention here: the Awano Shunkei of Ibaraki Prefecture, the Ukitsu-nuri of Nagoya, and the Sugara-nuri originally made at Fuchu in Sugara. Ukitsu-nuri is a type of Shunkei-nuri made by the lacquerer Ukitsu around the middle of the 19th century. In making Sugara-nuri, different kinds of wood were joined together and then covered with lacquer to enhance the underlying variety of grains.

Miscellaneous Technical Terms

It will be worthwhile at this point to define a number of miscellaneous terms relating chiefly to decorative techniques.

1) *daimyo-nuri*. This term is used to designate specially decorated lacquer ware used mainly as household utensils by the families of feudal lords. The background is a brilliant black, and the decoration is usually an entanglement of vines and conventional foliage. Sometimes the family crest appears.

2) *hakeme*. The literal meaning of *hakeme* is "brush marks," and lacquer of this type imitates a variety of Korean pottery in which the glaze is streaked with the strong marks of a brush.

3) *iji-iji-nuri*. This special lacquer decoration, consisting of a faint network of finely executed designs, was originated by the lacquerer Kondo Doshi in the 17th century.

4) Ichimatsu. Decoration in a checkerboard pattern takes its name from the Edo-period Kabuki actor Ichimatsu, who popularized a kimono pattern of small black and white squares.

5) *nuri*. The literal meaning of *nuri* is "coating," and this term refers to a visible layer of lacquer on an object. Thus *shu-nuri* means a background of red lacquer.

6) *roiro*. The term *roiro,* which literally means "wax color," is used to designate the best-quality, highly polished deep-black lacquer.

7) *seigai-ha*. Also called Kanshichi-nami, this is a stylized lacquer wave design originated by the artist Seigai Kanshichi in the early 18th century and later revived by Zeshin (Figs. 11, 25).

Metal Techniques

It has already been noted how closely the metal arts paralleled lacquer art historically as well as in technique and ornamentation. It will be worthwhile here to take a closer look at Japanese metalwork *(kanamono)* in its relation to miniature lacquer.

The production of sword furniture is to the Japanese a miniature art form which equals that of miniature lacquer work in artistic creativity. This art form was developed independently by a special class of artisans *(soken-shi)*. It was this class of artisans rather than the sword-blade forgers who occasionally made or ornamented lacquered objects, especially inro, in conjunction with the lacquer artist. Specifically many inro were made entirely of metal by these metal artists (Fig. 114), but more frequently they combined their talents with those of the lacquer artist and encrusted part of the design in metal into the lacquered surface (Figs. 65, 66, 93, 94). Therefore a basic understanding of the major metal techniques is indispensable in order to fully appreciate these magnificent metal encrustations. The all-metal inro usually consisted of a background of gray *shibuichi* with designs produced by various types of chiseling and detailed metal encrustations of gold, silver, and alloys such as *shakudo*. The majority of these inro were of the sheath type, the inner compartments usually being of silver. Such inro were usually of a relatively late commercial type. The lacquered, encrusted variety usually consisted of a gold-lacquered ground whose design employed a combination of *hiramakie* and *takamakie* along with small metal encrustations. These encrustations were usually of figures or animals done in minute detail in relatively high relief and using gold, silver, copper, and various alloys for color effect. Such encrustations appear similar to *menuki,* which were used for decorative purposes on the sword handle. Well-known lacquer artists, such as Jokasai, often used this kind of metal encrustations (Figs. 93, 94). The Kajikawa school often worked in conjunction with metal artists for their inro decoration. Metal encrustation, at first judiciously used, came into more and more lavish use by the mid-19th century, reflecting the beginning of the commercial market for lacquer products. This trend was typified by the less artistic works of the Shibayama school. Here, basically, the entire design consisted of technically perfect, multiple, overcrowded, gaudy, minute encrustations not only of metal but also of ivory, coral, mother-of-pearl, malachite, and the like. It should be noted that during this period, along with the disbandment of the samurai class, the wearing of swords was prohibited, leaving metal artists literally without jobs. They were forced to turn to other outlets, such as metal *okimono, kagamibuta* netsuke, and metal encrustations on lacquered pieces.

The Japanese metal artist was highly esteemed, and there developed many schools of metal carving devoted to making sword guards and smaller sword furniture, such as the *kozuka, menuki, fuchi-kashira,* and *kogai.* The metal artist was well acquainted with the five basic metals *(gokin)* of iron, copper, silver, gold, and tin (or lead). Besides these metals the Japanese developed specific alloys to enhance decorative effects. Furthermore, both the primary metals and the alloys were subjected to specific methods of staining in order to produce patinas and colors of varying shades. Finally, as in the lacquer industry, specific nuances were developed by means of chiseling, hammering, incising, onlaying, and inlaying. Through such methods tremendous artistic variety could be obtained both in the pictorial design and in the background effects. Iron *(tetsu)* and bronze *(karakane)* were rarely used on inro. The Japanese preferred using gold and gold alloys for yellow coloring. Instead of brass *(shinchu)* an alloy called *sentoku* (yellow bronze) was commonly used. This consisted mainly of copper (73% copper, 13% zinc, 8% tin, 6% lead) and, when chemically treated, gave a flecked gold appearance similar to *nashiji.* It is pale yellowish brown in color.

Copper *(akagane* or *do)* and its alloys were frequently used for decorative effects on inro. Various types of chemical baths were used to bring out different-colored patinas. Such baths varied with the school and the artist, there being no definite formula. Vinegar, copper sulfate, various clays, and plant roots were used in varying proportions. Occasionally the metal was covered with a paste instead of using a chemical bath. The processes were repeated many times, sometimes involving a period of months, to obtain the desired effect. The patina also varied considerably in depth from a superficial stain to one deeply ingrained into the depth of the surface metal. By such methods copper would appear green *(seido),* vary in red from a deep coral to a light vermilion, or reveal varying shades of brown. A special lobster-red patina is known as *suaka.* By adding lead to the copper a violet copper *(shido)* was obtained. The two commonest and most beautiful Japanese alloys were made of copper. They are known as *shakudo* (literally, "red copper") and *shibuichi* (literally, "one part in four"—that is, one part silver, by weight, to three of copper). *Shakudo* consists of 94–97% copper, 3.7–4.9% gold, and 1.5–2.9% silver. By boiling this alloy in a chemical bath of copper sulfate, verdigris, and other ingredients, a rich black patina with a violaceous sheen is obtained. This alloy is quite malleable and takes an excellent polish. A minimum of 3% gold is necessary to get a satisfactory rich patina, and as much as 5–6% was used in better works, giving a much deeper black effect. The famous Goto school of metal artists developed a beautiful dark black violaceous *shakudo.* This color was used as a background or in the design itself and occasionally to produce an effect of *sumie* painting. *Shibuichi* consists of 50–70% copper and 30–50% silver, the best patina being found where the silver content is greatest. By boiling this alloy in a chemical bath, a rich gray patina with a silvery luster is developed. It should be noted that this alloy also contains a small quantity of gold (0.08–0.12%). *Shibuichi,* like *shakudo,* is used either for the background or in the decorative design.

Gold *(kin)* was used either in relatively pure form or as an alloy in *shakudo* or as pale gold *(koban-kin, jiki-ban,* etc.) by adding varying amounts of silver. The netsuke artist Tokoku used such a gold-silver alloy as a thin encrusted plaque for his signature.

Silver *(gin)* was used either by itself or as an alloy with copper *(shibuichi)* or gold. It was also used for the metallic rims on lacquer boxes, especially after the 18th century. Tin and lead were used fairly frequently by old inro artists for encrustations, especially by the Korin school. Tin was occasionally used as a cheap substitute for gold dustings in lacquering but was also used by excellent artists for alloys, especially pewter *(byakuro).* These alloys gradually take on a decorative mottled patina. Pewter (tin and lead) was also used for the metallic rims on older lacquer boxes, as was silver on 18th- and 19th-century works. These metal rims are called *okiguchi.* Pewter, with its coarse texture, was often used by the Korin impressionistic school as large crude inlays designed to give a masculine effect. Thus it might be used impressionistically as the coarse chitinous body of a crab. *Nigurome (chin-sho)* consists mainly of copper with small amounts of lead and tin, giving a dull red appearance with a dull gray overcast. *Sawari (kyodo)* consists mainly of copper with the addition of about 25% tin, giving a grayish color. *Shirome* (white solder) also has a grayish color and consists essentially of copper with the addition of lead, arsenic, antimony, tin, and silver.

Many specific metal techniques are used to gain the desired effects in these various metals and alloys. The early metalwork tended to be simple but artistic, using iron alone. Ultimately, as with lacquer work, techniques became more and more numerous and gaudy and thus more ornamental than utilitarian and aesthetic. Metal techniques can be roughly classified into the following nine groups:

1) casting: *iru*
2) repoussé or embossing: *uchidashi* or *uchiage*
3) onlaying, gilding: *kin-kise, gin-kise* (gold and silver gilding)
4) turning: *rokuro-zaiku*
5) chasing: *horu, horiage*
6) chiseling, engraving: *hori (-bori)*
7) inlaying, encrusting, damascening: *zogan*
8) specific background techniques: *nanako* and *ishime*
9) special techniques, including enameling: *shippo*

It is not necessary to discuss all of these techniques, which play no direct part in lacquer art. However, mention should be made of those methods which have their counterparts in lacquer techniques. As does the lacquer artist, the metal artist has his own set of tools. He actually uses about 250 cutting and graving instruments. The expert can even judge and recognize the chisel marks of individual metal artists as accurately as the brush strokes of the painter or the distinctive style of the lacquerer.

KE-BORI

This technique consists of hairline chasing by means of knifelike chisels. The lines are of uniform thickness and depth. The technique is similar to the *ke-bori* lacquer technique, in which the lines are done by means of a fine rat's tooth.

SPECIFIC BACKGROUND TECHNIQUES

As in lacquer work, background plays a considerable part in the overall decorative effect. In metalwork a shiny, bright surface is considered vulgar. The use of subtle, toned-down color gradations by means of specially produced patinas has already been noted. The grounds in metalwork are usually of gold, *shakudo,* or *shibuichi.* Furthermore, these grounds are secondarily decorated by being broken up into hammered, chiseled, or engraved patterns known collectively as *nanako* and *ishime.* While *nanako* is specifically a metal technique, varieties of *ishime* have their counterparts in lacquer art.

Nanako (fish-roe ground) consists of filling the background with almost microscopically perfect, evenly placed dots, producing a finely granular surface. The diameter of the dots may be one-third of a millimeter, and it usually takes three blows to produce each dot. They are usually done on a *shakudo* background, as typically practiced by the famous Goto school of artists. Occasionally, technicians specialized only in making these dots. There are also various rarer forms of *nanako.*

In *ishime* (stone ground) the background is broken up into various irregular rough surfaces so as to produce an appearance of stone (*ishi=* stone; *me*=aspect, look). There are several varieties of *ishime* corresponding to similar-looking lacquer background designs. One of these is *nashiji-ishime,* in which the surface imitates the skin of the *nashi,* or Japanese pear. Several other types of *ishime,* as in lacquer work, imitate the texture of natural and manufactured materials, such as matting, basket weaves, tree bark, and the like. *Yasurime,* a subclassification of *ishime,* includes such background techniques as *nekogaki* (cat scratches) and *shigure* (rainstorm).

MISCELLANEOUS SPECIAL TECHNIQUES

Here again there are several metal techniques which have parallels in lacquer art. These will be discussed quite briefly.

1) *mokumehada.* The surface decoration imitates the grain of wood or shows undulating lines like those of rippling water. The lines are brought out by hammering wires of different hardness into sheets. After repeated

folding, the final effect is produced by a corroding bath in which the softer lines are more heavily attacked.

2) *mokume* (veins of wood). This effect is obtained by a thin lamina of reddish copper plus dark black-green *shakudo* hammered and folded in, thus welding it into a flat surface, so that an undulating and occasionally marbleized effect is produced, simulating the veins and knots of wood. The equivalent appearance in lacquer work has already been described.

3) *guri-bori*. This technique simulates *guri* lacquer. Alternating layers of different-colored metals are welded and then deeply cut on a slant to bring out the colors. The commonest types are alternating layers of copper and *shakudo* (Figs. 61, 73).

4) *togidashi-zogan*. An onlay of *shibuichi* is covered with a design of thin *aokin* (silver-gold) and finally with a thin layer of silver, revealing a faint golden design through the silver. The entire surface is then polished down to reveal all three layers. This gives a feeling of depth and is used in designs of fish swimming in water, etc. Its similarity to lacquer *togidashi* is apparent.

5) *shippo* (enameling). No discussion of metalwork would be complete without mentioning enameling. Enameling was occasionally applied to *kagamibuta* and sword furniture but rarely to inro (Fig. 128). The decoration is first sketched with white lead. The *cloison*s are made to conform to the design, glued down, and then soldered to the groundwork. The enamel, which is pulverized and then made into a paste, is placed in the cells. The material is dried and then fired. The enamel is rubbed down (as in lacquer work), but because of shrinking, with resultant pitting and cracking, the entire process must be repeated, usually four times. In poor works the defects are filled in with a vegetable wax *(ro)*. Good quality is also determined by subtle color gradations. Occasionally the enamel is painted over with different colors and then burnt in. Incidentally, the same enameling technique is applied to ceramic ware, except that solder is not used and at other times lacquer is used for filling the cells instead of enamel, as in the encrusted lacquer called *zogan-nuri*. The famous Hirata family decorated inro with translucent cloisonné enamels, such inro being rare and highly esteemed. They did characteristically fine work, including delicate metal inlays of decorative floral designs and typical fine whorls of inlaid gold wire.

67. INRO. Rosei's dream. Signed: Iizuka Kanshosai. This side of the inro illustrates the dream sequence, showing the nori-mono and the long, trailing retinue of retainers, with the design gradually fading in the distance through the clever use of togidashi technique, all on a roiro ground. The adjacent trees and foliage are done in hiramakie, takamakie, and mother-of-pearl encrustations. $3\frac{3}{8}'' \times 2\frac{1}{2}'' \times 1\frac{1}{16}''$. 4 cases and lid.

68. INRO. Manzai dancer. Signed: Moei. The inro, which pictures a strolling comic dancer holding a drum, is done in togidashi in olive green, silver, red, black, and gold on a roiro ground. $3\frac{1}{16}'' \times 2\frac{1}{2}'' \times 1''$. 4 cases and lid.

69. DETAIL of writing box, showing Tsugaru-nuri ground. Note the marbleized pattern of red, black, and light green. The box is decorated with a design of a sumie ink-cake inro in black takamakie.

70. KOBAKO with overhanging lid. Unsigned. Typical mottled orange, gold, and black Wakasa-nuri lacquer technique, decorated with various types of leaves in low gold takamakie. $3'' \times 3\frac{1}{8}'' \times 2\frac{1}{2}''$. 2 cases and lid.

71. INRO. Spring wildflowers. Signed: Tatsuke Takamasu. The finely raised designs of the flowers, along with ferns and a butterfly, are done in black on a roiro ground which is beginning to turn tortoise-shell brown from age. $2\frac{7}{8}'' \times 2\frac{1}{8}'' \times \frac{7}{8}''$. 4 cases and lid.

72. INRO. Scepter and fly whisk. Signed: Koma Kansai. The design is in gold takamakie on an imitation nunome ground superimposed over a Negoro ground. $3\frac{1}{4}'' \times 1\frac{3}{4}'' \times 1''$. 4 cases and lid.

73. NETSUKE. Carved guri manju. Unsigned. The geometric pattern is carved to reveal eleven alternating layers of colored lacquer. 1″ square.

74. KOGO. Karashishi. Signed: Yosei. Carved tsuishu lacquer with design in relief. Ground and ball in asa-no-ha pattern. $2\frac{1}{4}″ \times 2\frac{1}{4}″ \times \frac{5}{8}″$.

75. DETAIL of fukidome lacquer technique on an inro. The design of the shishi is of encrusted silver in high relief.

76. INRO. Samurai. Unsigned. The inro is done entirely in gold chinkin-bori technique on a black ground. The design is surrounded by a diaper, also in chinkin-bori, of asa-no-ha pattern. $3\frac{3}{4}'' \times 2'' \times 1\frac{1}{8}''$. 5 cases and lid.

77. DETAIL of inro displaying powder technique known as e-nashiji.

78. INRO. Boys' Festival. Signed: Somada Hisamitsu. The design is done in flat encrusted aogai, silver, and gold along with gyobu-style aogai and aogai powderings. $3\frac{3}{4}'' \times 2'' \times 1\frac{1}{4}''$. 5 cases and lid. (See Fig. 105 for inro with cases separated.)

79. INRO. Lotus flower and leaves. Unsigned. Lacquer inro in
the shape of a purse, simulating the coarse texture of leather.
The design is in gold takamakie and encrusted metal. $2\frac{3}{4}''\times$
$2\frac{1}{4}''\times1''$. 3 cases and lid.

80. INRO. Jurojin and deer. Unsigned. Somada school. Design in tiny, intricately carved pieces of iridescent aogai and
gold leaf on a roiro ground. $4\frac{1}{4}''\times2\frac{1}{4}''\times1\frac{3}{8}''$. 4 cases and lid.
(See Fig. 83 for detail and Fig. 138 for opposite side.)

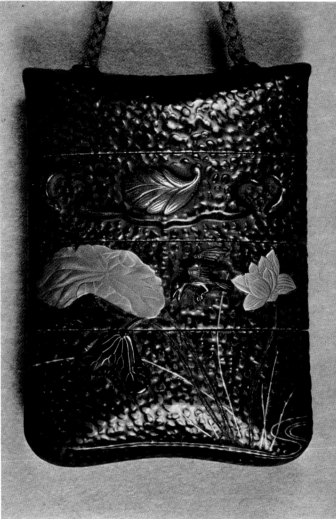

81. DETAIL of kobon by netsuke artist Kyusai, showing carved kanshitsu technique simulating bodaiju (bo tree).

82. KOJUBAKO. Dragonfly and butterflies. Unsigned. Mid-19th century. Insects in black, red, silver, and gold takamakie on ivory ground. Edges of box are encrusted in aogai mosaic. $4\frac{1}{4}'' \times 2\frac{1}{2}'' \times 1\frac{1}{4}''$. (See also Fig. 158.)

83. DETAIL of inro in Fig. 80, showing intricate inlay work as typified by the deer.

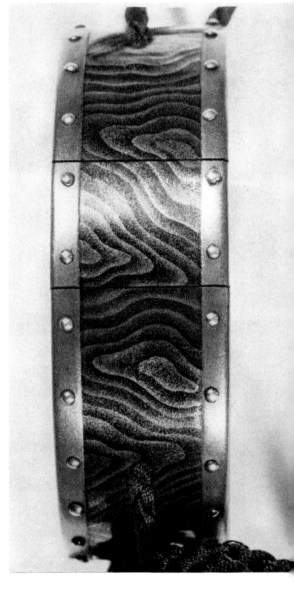

84. DETAIL of side of an inro, showing typical mokume technique in black and gold.

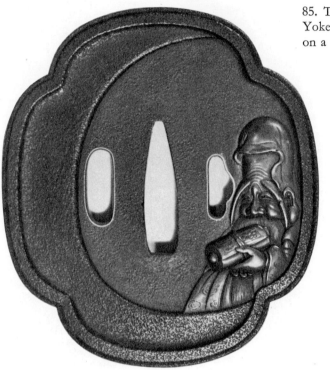

85. TSUBA. Lacquer. Jurojin holding a scroll. Signed: Yokei. The deity is in high takamakie imitating shibuichi on a sabiji ground simulating iron. $3\frac{1}{2}'' \times 3\frac{1}{8}'' \times \frac{3}{8}''$.

86. KOBAKO. Geometric design. Unsigned. Ashikaga period. Sides of box reveal pressed-cloth technique in red lacquer. Remainder of design consists of alternating silver and black lacquer squares. $3'' \times 2\frac{1}{2}'' \times 2\frac{1}{16}''$.

87. KOZUKA. Chrysanthemums and leaves. Signed: Jokasai. Lacquer design done in takamakie in black, gold, and red. Ground lacquered in black sabiji imitating shakudo. $3\frac{13}{16}'' \times \frac{9}{16}'' \times \frac{3}{16}''$.

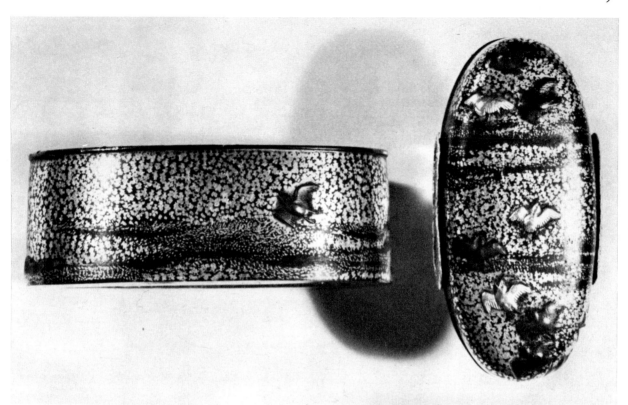

88. FUCHI-KASHIRA. Birds and clouds. Signed: Omori Teruhide. The clouds are done in tiny flecks of embedded gold simulating lacquer nashiji. $1\frac{3}{8}'' \times \frac{3}{4}''$.

89. INRO. Herons. Signed: Koma Kansai. A small inro with a Korin design of two herons in low takamakie on a plain wood ground. This small size inro was used by little girls during the Girls' Festival celebration. $1\frac{5}{8}'' \times 1\frac{3}{8}'' \times \frac{3}{8}''$. 1 case and lid.

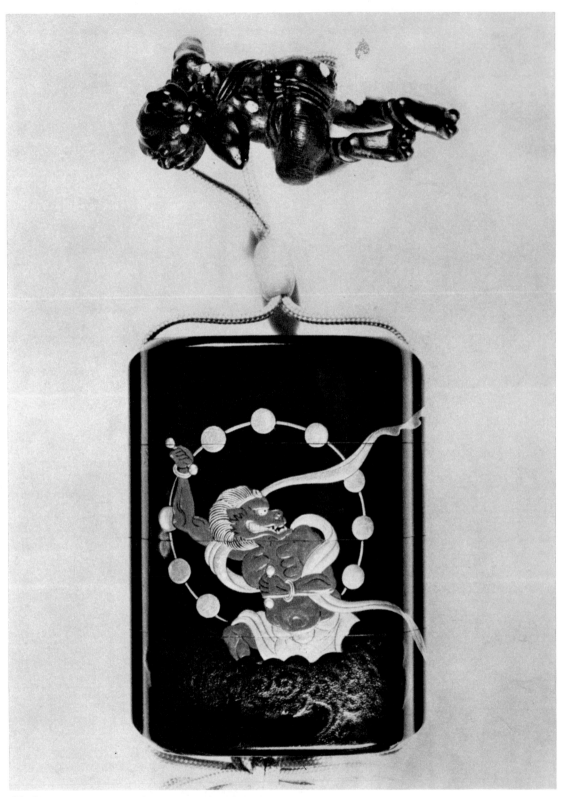

90. Inro. Raiden, god of thunder. Signed: Zeshin. Netsuke. Oni being stoned. Unsigned. Ivory ojime.
The god of thunder is done in red lacquer in slight relief, the drums in gold takamakie, and the clouds
in rough black hiramakie. Roiro ground. $2\frac{1}{2}'' \times 1\frac{7}{8}'' \times \frac{5}{8}''$. 3 cases and lid.

91. INRO of Fig. 90 with cases opened, showing risers.

92. INRO of Fig. 90 with lid and first case tilted, showing shoulders, himotoshi, and inner surfaces of lid and case.

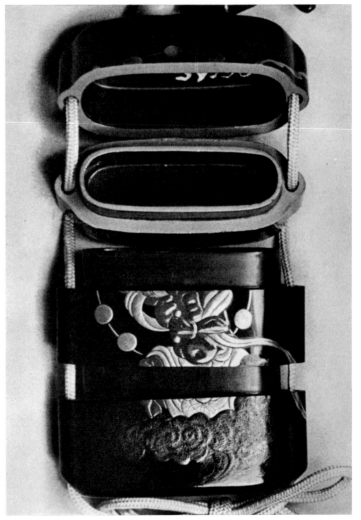

93. INRO. Lizard and tree. Signed: Joka (lacquer artist) and Yokoya Hidekiyo (metal artist). The lizard is in shakudo. The rocks and the tree are done in gold takamakie, with details in fine gold kirigane. The stream is in togidashi. Three of the leaves are made of encrusted aogai, with the veins outlined in gold hiramakie. Roiro ground. $3\frac{3}{8}'' \times 2\frac{3}{4}'' \times \frac{7}{8}''$. 4 cases and lid.

94. DETAIL of inro in Fig. 93, showing metal lizard.

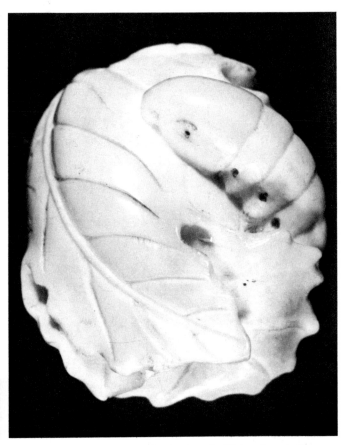

95. OJIME. Caterpillar on leaf. Signed: Kaigyokusai. Ivory. $\frac{11}{16}''$ in greatest diameter.

96. INRO. Design of character for "treasure." Unsigned. Round inro employing external metal rings in place of cord channels. Design augmented on perimeter by irregular-shaped ceramic inlays on rough dark-brown ground. $2\frac{7}{8}''$ in diameter; $\frac{3}{4}''$ in thickness. 3 cases and lid.

97. INRO. Pheasant and autumn flowers. Signed: Kanshosai (To-yo). Pheasant in red, black, and gold low takamakie; foliage in gold and silver takamakie. The ground is a fine gold yasuriko. $3\frac{5}{16}'' \times 2\frac{13}{16}'' \times 1\frac{3}{16}''$. 4 cases and lid.

98. INRO of Fig. 97 with cases opened, showing the internal cord channels. Inside of cases is in nashiji.

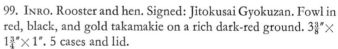

99. INRO. Rooster and hen. Signed: Jitokusai Gyokuzan. Fowl in red, black, and gold takamakie on a rich dark-red ground. $3\frac{3}{8}'' \times 1\frac{3}{4}'' \times 1''$. 5 cases and lid.

100. INRO of Fig. 99 with cases opened, showing external cord channels. Inside of cases is in gyobu nashiji.

101. SAYA INRO. Temple guardian and fence. Unsigned. Deity done in slightly raised red lacquer on a gold oki-hirame ground. Sheath done in red lacquer with the fence in gold lacquer and decorated with the names of famous lacquer artists. $3\frac{3}{8}'' \times 2\frac{9}{16}'' \times 1\frac{1}{4}''$. 4 cases, lid, and sheath.

102. INRO of Fig. 101, showing the sheath separated from the inro cases.

103. INRO. Symbols of happy marriage. Signed: Kochosai. Inro in shape of three folding fans with design in takamakie, hira-makie, togidashi, and kirigane in red, silver, gold, and black on a gold ground. This inro was probably made for a bride to use at her wedding ceremony. $3\frac{1}{2}''\times 2\frac{3}{4}''\times\frac{3}{4}''$. 2 cases and lid.

104. INRO. Turtle. Signed: Keido. An inro of carved wood done in a highly realistic manner. $3\frac{1}{4}''\times 2\frac{1}{4}''\times 1\frac{1}{4}''$. 3 cases and lid.

105. Inro of Fig. 78 with cases separated, showing different geometric and floral designs on each of the risers in aogai and silver and gold foil.

106. Detail of inro in Fig. 52, showing inside of one case and a tiny box within the case having a strip of inlaid silver upon which can be inscribed the name of the medicine which it contains.

107. INRO. Examples of four different-sized inro, the smallest ($1'' \times \frac{3}{4}''$ $\times \frac{3}{8}''$) being a toy and the largest ($4\frac{5}{8}'' \times 3\frac{5}{8}'' \times \frac{7}{8}''$) an actor's inro. The toy inro is unsigned; the second is signed Koma Kansai; the third, Tai-shin; and the largest, Taisai.

108. INRO. Hobgoblins and *go* players. Signed: Yoyusai. A "lobster-shaped" inro illustrating a famous story and decorated with fanciful creatures in colorful togidashi and e-nashiji on a roiro ground. The *go* players are in low takamakie. $3\frac{5}{8}'' \times 2\frac{3}{16}'' \times 1\frac{1}{8}''$. 4 cases and lid.

109. INRO. Dragon. Unsigned. A typical example of an early inro in both shape and subject matter. The design is in silver and gold taka-makie on a black ground. $3\frac{7}{8}'' \times 1\frac{1}{2}'' \times \frac{7}{8}''$. 5 cases and lid.

110. INRO. Fighting cocks. Signed: Seishi. The cocks are in gold and red takamakie on a roiro ground. $3\frac{1}{8}'' \times 3'' \times \frac{3}{4}''$. 3 cases and lid.

111. INRO. Peacock and peahen. Signed: Kajikawa. Design in gold takamakie, togidashi, and aogai, utilizing hyomon and kirigane techniques on gold ground. $3\frac{3}{4}'' \times 1\frac{7}{8}'' \times 1\frac{5}{8}''$. 5 cases and lid.

112. INRO. The warrior Ujigawa Senjin. Signed: Shunsui. Design in togidashi, hiramakie, and takamakie in red, silver, and gold on a roiro ground. $3\frac{1}{16}'' \times 2\frac{1}{4}'' \times 1''$. 5 cases and lid.

113. DETAIL of inro in Fig. 112. Note the elaborate attention to minute detail as in the rendering of the links in the armor.

114. INRO. Bird and moon. Signed: Goto Shinjo. Metal inro of shibuichi with a simple artistic design of an inlaid silver moon and a gold bird flying over a small stream. Interior in silver. $2\frac{7}{8}'' \times 1\frac{5}{8}'' \times \frac{5}{8}''$. 4 cases and lid.

115. INRO. Quail and flowers. Signed: Shibayama. Typical late Shibayama style of minute precarved pieces of mother-of-pearl and diverse colorful materials encrusted into ivory. $3\frac{1}{4}'' \times 2\frac{1}{4}'' \times \frac{7}{8}''$. 4 cases and lid.

116. INRO. Dwarf pine tree. Signed: Koma Yasutada. Design in gold and silver togidashi on a black ground. $3'' \times 2\frac{3}{8}'' \times 1\frac{1}{8}''$. 4 cases and lid.

117. INRO. Crow and moon. Signed: Koma Kansai. The crow, in black hiramakie, is flying toward a silver moon, while the overhanging clouds are done in mura nashiji—all on a light-brown ground. This simple design contrasts sharply with the risers and insides of the cases and lid, which are highly ornamented with colorful flowers in flat inlaid aogai and gold foil. $3'' \times 2\frac{5}{8}'' \times \frac{7}{8}''$. 3 cases and lid.

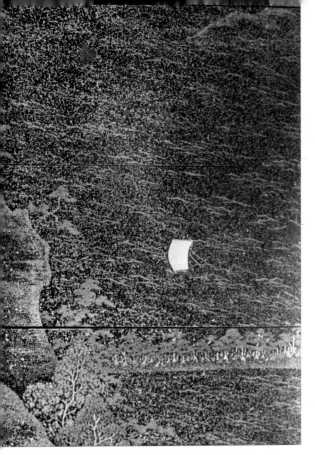

118. DETAIL of inro in Fig. 134, showing sails. The sail in the foreground is in gleaming white mother-of-pearl, and two tiny distant sails are in silver togidashi.

119. INRO. The Seven Sages of the Bamboo Grove. Signed: Shiomi Masanari. The sages are done in silver and gold takamakie and the bamboo leaves in different tones of gold togidashi, giving excellent perspective. Black ground. $2\frac{7}{8}'' \times 2\frac{5}{8}'' \times \frac{7}{8}''$. 3 cases and lid.

120. DETAIL of top corner of inro in Fig. 119, showing how the bamboo-leaf design flows over the top surface of the lid. Note the gold oki-hirame technique on the outside of the external cord channels.

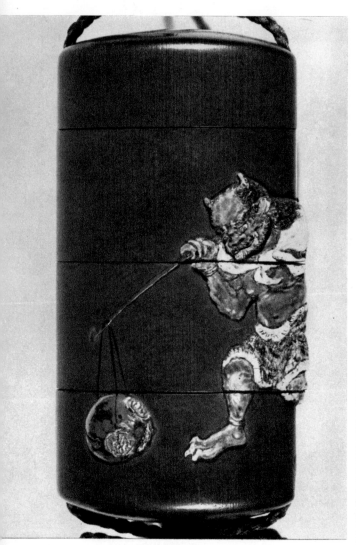

121. INRO. Oni and mokugyo. Unsigned. Late 18th century. Style of Hanzan. The oni is in raised inlaid green, white, yellow, and blue pottery, and the mokugyo is in red and black simulating Negoro-nuri lacquer. Plain wood ground. 3⅝″×2″×⅞″. 3 cases and lid.

122. OPPOSITE SIDE of inro in Fig. 121, revealing the completion of the design flowing over from the major side of the inro. The oni is also carrying a large temple bell which is in beautiful black ceramic inlay imitating an iron ground.

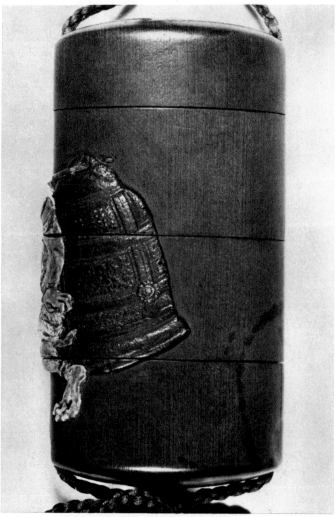

123. DETAIL from a book of lacquer paintings illustrating well-known Japanese landscapes. Signed: Zeshin, at the age of eighty-four. This page depicts two deer in Nara Park and is done in shades of black and brown lacquer on paper. $3\frac{11}{16}'' \times 2\frac{15}{16}''$.

124. INRO. Ghost. Signed: Hanzan. The ghost is done in gold takamakie, the rocks and leaves in encrusted pewter, aogai, and colored pottery. The design is on a beautiful mottled cherry-bark ground in shades of brown and red-brown. $3\frac{1}{4}'' \times 1\frac{7}{8}'' \times 1\frac{1}{8}''$. 3 cases and lid.

125. INRO. Snakes. Signed: Gyokuzan. Two snakes in high taka-makie, one in gold and the other in brown on a red-lacquered basket-weave ground. $2\frac{7}{8}'' \times 2\frac{1}{8}'' \times 1''$. 4 cases and lid.

126. INRO. The story of Jo and Uba. Un-signed. The design is done in medium-relief takamakie and encrusted aogai shell on a plain brown fungus ground. Note the groove for the cord on the bottom surface of the inro. $3\frac{3}{8}'' \times 2\frac{1}{4}'' \times \frac{3}{4}''$. 1 case and lid.

127. DETAIL of small lacquer sweetmeat tray by Zeshin illustrating Noshiro Shunkei technique. Design of eggplants in corner of plate in low takamakie on brilliant transparent yellow Shunkei ground.

128. INRO. Butterflies. Unsigned. The butterflies are done in gold and red takamakie and in raised, encrusted, transparent colored cloisonné. The ground is a geometric pattern in gold and silver togidashi. $3\frac{3}{4}'' \times 2\frac{1}{8}'' \times 1\frac{1}{4}''$. 4 cases and lid.

129. INRO. Frogs fighting grasshoppers. Unsigned. Late Shibayama school.
Pouch shape with decoration in inlaid mother-of-pearl, gold, silver, and ivory
in minute detail on a gold ground. $2\frac{3}{4}'' \times 4\frac{1}{2}'' \times 1\frac{1}{4}''$. 3 cases and lid.

4 ❖ Miniature Lacquer Art Forms

The Inro

As with most objects of Japanese art, the miniature lacquer objects were primarily designed for utilitarian purposes and only secondarily did they become ornamental objets d'art. Of all the lacquered articles which we consider as miniature, by far the most popular and most important is the inro. The inro is a highly decorative small lacquer box worn by the Japanese people primarily from the 17th to the 19th century. This object, measuring approximately 3½″ by 2″ by 1″ deep, divided into several hollow sections, was worn suspended by a silken cord which ran under the sash. At the other end of the cord was attached an ornamental ivory or wood sculpture called a netsuke, which rested on the sash, suspending the inro and preventing it from falling (Figs. 90–92).

The great popularity of such a receptacle arose from the peculiar characteristics of the Japanese style of dress. The Japanese kimono is essentially a robe with long wide sleeves. It is crossed from left to right and is held closed by being tied at the waist with a sash called an obi. Both men and women wore essentially the same basic garment. The obi has been in use since ancient times, although it was not at all like the elaborate and beautiful wide sash worn by women today. Indeed during the Fujiwara period (897–1185) the obi was merely a narrow sash of no significance and was worn beneath the outer clothing, where it was never seen. Following the Muromachi period (1392–1573) ladies began to wear their obi over their outer garment. This custom continued through the Momoyama period (1573–1615), when a braided obi with tassels at either end was first introduced into fashion, with, however, little popularity. It was during the Edo period (1615–1868) that the obi became fully accepted as an important part of the national dress. During the Kyoho era (1716–36) of the Edo period, the obi for women developed into an exceedingly wide, highly ornamental, and exceptionally beautiful and important item of women's apparel. The obi was also worn by men, and although the decorative design became more elaborate throughout the years, the obi never became as wide or as elaborate as that of the women. Since this type of clothing provided no pockets, small items were carried either in the deep, wide sleeves or were tucked into the folds of the kimono or were simply tucked under the sash. However, it was apparent that a more secure means of carrying seals, ink pastes, medicines, and other similar items would be much more ideal, and it was from this need that the use of the inro became popular. The inro was hung from the sash or obi by silken cords which were attached to the inro, the cord being slipped under the obi and held in place above it by another Japanese miniature art form, the netsuke. The netsuke, which is basically a form of artistic sculptured button or toggle, rested above the sash and thus prevented the inro from slipping or falling. In order to hold the inro cases closed, a small pierced bead called an *ojime* (*o*=cord; *shimeru*=to tighten) is threaded on the silk cord between the inro itself and the netsuke. By sliding the ojime toward the netsuke the tension is taken off the cord and the inro cases may be opened. In order to close the boxes and hold them secure the process is reversed (Figs. 90, 91). Once it has been put in place, the netsuke, having bulk, is unable to slide under the obi, and the inro therefore cannot fall. Ojime are made of as many different kinds of materials as are netsuke. Often we find that all three—netsuke, ojime, and inro—are made to match, and occasionally they are executed by the same artist. It should be noted that the Japanese are such master craftsmen that even the slide fastener, the ojime, is executed with the greatest care and attention. Most frequently used, however, are beads of coral, which according to an old superstition "will split into pieces in the presence of poison and thus issue a warning that the medicines within the inro cases are unsafe." Crystal, jade, or other semiprecious stones, which may vary in size and shape, and by their very simplicity and lack of decoration are designed to set off and compliment their component parts, are also frequently used. In general the approximate size of the ojime varies from about $\frac{1}{4}''$ to $\frac{1}{2}''$ in diameter. They may be made from various metals, woods, ivory, nuts, or ceramics. The metal ojime often have minute designs and figures done by chiseling, onlaying, inlaying, and quite frequently by openwork. They were done most often in pure gold or silver, but the various alloys and patinas were also used. They were often made by famous sword-furniture artists. Similarly, many ojime were carved from wood, ivory, and small nuts by well-known netsuke artists and are often executed in sculptural form. Figure 95 illustrates such a sculptural ojime of a caterpillar on a leaf designed in a ball-shaped form in ivory by the famous 19th-century netsuke artist Kaigyokusai. Fairly frequently, ojime were made of porcelain or pottery by well-known ceramic artists or correspondingly of lacquer by lacquer artists. In general then, ojime designs are done either in graphic or sculptural forms. Their shapes vary from the usual bead shape to rounded oval and rectangular or shapes representative of the subject matter, such as a monkey or Daruma. Many Japanese art connoisseurs specialize in collecting these gems of extremely minute craftsmanship.

No discussion of the inro could be complete without acquiring some knowledge of its inner construction and how it is made. Let us first examine the basic anatomy of an inro. The top and bottom surfaces are called *joge,* and these may be perfectly flat or may vary in degree of convexity. The inro itself is divided into a series of boxes, each fitting snugly in layers, one on top of the other, these boxes being referred to as cases. When describing an inro it is spoken of as consisting of a specific number of cases and a lid, the topmost section called *futa,* or lid, never being considered as a case since it cannot be used as a receptacle for herbs, medicines, etc. Extending upward from each case is a thin lip, called a riser, which fits into the bottom of the case above (Fig. 91). The inside of the cases, where the medicines were carried, consists of the inner surfaces of the risers and is usually oval or rectangular. The small flat surface which can be seen encircling the upper edge of each case where it fits against the case above is called the shoulder (Fig. 92). The primary areas for decoration consist of the outer front and back surfaces. These also vary in shape and do not necessarily match the shape of the risers or the inner surface.

There are many inro which consist of but one case and a lid. These two-section inro were most likely used for carrying seals. Frequently they are subdivided within, and these inner trays were used for the black or red ink paste *(inniku)* used for stamping impressions on documents. These two-section inro were also used to carry other items, such as small shrines *(zushi)* or religious images, which fitted inside the case and could be safely carried along with the traveler in this manner to be taken out and used for worship whenever it was so desired (Fig. 34).

Some inro are made entirely of wood, ivory, or metal, particularly silver, *shakudo,* and *shibuichi.* These, however, are relatively rare and generally date from the 19th century, the great majority being made of many coats of lacquer applied over a wooden, leather, or wood and leather core. Other materials have sometimes been used, particularly in the later art periods, such as cloisonné, sharkskin, cherry bark, stiffened woven basketwork, glass, tortoise shell, crystal, soapstone, and even, as noted, the very light, porous, spongy fungus called *reishi.* Even less suitable for carrying medicines, because of the difficulty of an airtight fit as well as being materials too fragile for use and wear, are porcelain, faience, and pottery, which though rare and ill-suited for inro were nevertheless occasionally used. These last several items are more artistic in value than practical.

The inner core or frame of the inro itself was composed of tiers of cases, made usually of specially seasoned *hinoki* wood. The core was prepared by a special group of artists called *inro-shi*. This wood, found growing in large quantities all over the country, especially in Mino and Owari, resists both drying and dampness. It is very elastic and easily worked and is virtually warp-proof. It also allows for a fine finish. These wooden frames were invariably covered by numerous layers of lacquer, each being thoroughly dried and polished before the next coat was applied, until layer upon layer of lacquer was built up. Frequently 30 or more such processes were employed in this preparation. Each time after the lacquer was applied the piece was dried in the damp press for a number of days, and then the lacquer was carefully polished, as natural lacquer is not shiny. This tedious, important, painstaking groundwork was done by a lacquer artisan called a *nurimono-shi* and usually required a minimum of a month or more to complete. Upon completion of the work of the *nurimono-shi* the object was turned over to the lacquer artist, or *makie-shi,* for decoration.

In general the design was accomplished by one of four methods: 1) addition of lacquer into which the design was carved; 2) addition of layers of lacquer with gold dustings, raised lacquering, etc.; 3) addition of lacquer, using colored lacquer for the design; 4) addition of layers of lacquer and the encrustation of metal, ivory, mother-of-pearl, and other materials. These various techniques have already been discussed at great length and in detail in Chapter 3.

In preparing the core of the inro, pieces of the *hinoki* wood were molded into shape and glued together with great care, and as much attention was given to the preparation of the inside of the box as was given to the outside. Thinner slivers of wood were used for the lips, which would ultimately form the risers. The *nurimono-shi* had to take care to leave ample room for the innumerable applications of lacquer layers which would follow his preparatory work. The cases must ultimately fit together with complete accuracy in order to maintain an airtight compartment in which to keep the medicines which would be carried in it. However, the lacquer artist would apply as many coats to the risers and to the inside of the cases as he would to the outside surfaces. It was imperative, therefore, that enough leeway be allowed for his decoration while still making a strong riser without too much give, in order to insure proper fit and an airtight compartment.

Possibly the earliest method of preparing the frame or core was that of applying strips of strong leather fitted over a wooden frame, using thinner leather strips for the risers and reinforced wood for the top and bottom. This combination of leather and wood was probably the most commonly used method in earliest times, but it soon gave way to the faster and relatively simpler method of using only wood. There were some artisans who produced cores made almost entirely of lacquer applied over specially prepared cloth or paper. These, however, were rare.

One of the most important tests of quality of an inro is the way in which the cases fit together. In good-quality work the cases will be tight enough to keep the objects within in perfect condition—that is, to prevent moisture and air from deteriorating the pills and powders which inro were designed to carry. The cases should stay closed with normal handling and with all movements of the body to which they are normally subjected while being worn. At the same time they should permit opening with a gentle pulling pressure of the fingers. Extreme caution was exercised so that the wood used for the core was so well seasoned that even over hundreds of years there would be no warping, splitting, or cracking.

As previously stated, upon completion of the core the *nurimono-shi*'s work was done, and the article was given to the *makie-shi* for artistic decoration. When examining an inro of good quality, perhaps the last thing to catch one's eye will be the divisions between the cases. The design is applied so masterfully that these separations are almost invisible, and yet upon light pressure the inro will separate into five or six pieces. The design itself is never bound by the area of an individual case. Rather it flows over the broken and unbroken surfaces alike without paying heed to these divisions. Two main techniques of decoration were employed in order to give this appearance. The finishing of the interior surface was done first. The artist applied the lacquer in layers of either *nashiji* or colored lacquer which would either complement or correspond to the ultimate finished outer surfaces. One method was to coat the surface of each case where it fitted against the case above with a thin wax and then tightly clamp the entire inro body together. Once this was done, the artist proceeded to apply his decorative background lacquer, drying and polishing each layer in turn before applying the next. Inlays of pewter, mother-of-pearl, pottery, and the like were cut out and placed on the surface in accordance with the design. After the entire decorative process had been completed, the artist, or occasionally a specialist in this particular process, warmed the inro over a fire, thus melting the wax between the cases and making the divisions faintly visible. Then with a sharp blade he cut through the lacquer, following the original separation lines. Occasionally some damage would be done in the separation process, and this would be repaired and retouched, at times causing a slight variation in color.

The other far more time-consuming but perhaps more technically desirable method was as follows: Again with wax, the segments were glued together, but after each thin layer of lacquer had been applied, dried, and polished, the cases were separated, the waxy film was removed, and each case was finished off before proceeding to the next decorative step. This procedure was repeated for each successive step until the decoration was complete. Of course this second method was far more tedious and required much more time. Great care had to be taken to remove the entire film of wax before applying the next coat so that, when finished, the boxes retained their precision fit. This method was superior in that it assured evenness of layers and uniformity of color on the finished article.

In order to accommodate the silken cord which is attached to all inro, they are provided with cord channels called *himotoshi*. Most likely the earliest cord channels were merely little metal rings or tubes attached to the outside of the cases through which the cord was threaded (Fig. 96). With further development, two distinct styles of cord channels were adopted. In the first of these the channels were concealed within the body of the inro, the cord running usually just on the outer edge and to either side of the risers and emerging at the top and bottom of the inro. These are called internal channels and generally have no bearing on the overall shape of the inro (Figs. 97, 98). The second style employed external channels. These were executed in the form of tubes which projected slightly from either side of the body of the inro on the outer surface. Here again, the cord itself is only visible as it emerges from the *joge* on either end; however, the channels affect the overall outside shape of the inro and are incorporated into its basic design (Figs. 99, 100). Another variety considered as having external channels is the *saya* inro, *saya* meaning sheath. The lid and cases are slipped within a more or less solid outer casing or sheath, which may be made of the same or of an entirely different material. The Japanese name of *otoshi,* or dropper, is assigned to them. The sheath itself may be merely a frame—that is, with the front and back surfaces mostly cut open so as to enable the design on the inner cases to show through (Figs. 101, 102). In this type of sheath inro the sheath is usually made of the same material as are the cases. Another type has irregular openings which may blend in with the design on the *otoshi* and may enhance the decoration by being of a contrasting material. The third variation consists of a solid sheath having openings at the top and bottom in order to enable one to push the cases up and drop them back within. It should be noted that with these sheath inro no highly raised decoration could be used on the cases, since the sheath would not fit snugly and the decorations on the inner cases would tend to rub off. However, the cases will always be fully decorated in low relief and especially *togidashi* or, as in the case of silver or other metal, will be incised or engraved. Frequently, particularly with metal inro, the sheath will be pierced with openwork, one purpose being that this type of decoration has the advantage of making the inro lighter in weight, a consideration to be taken into account with this heavy material.

Often the inro lacquer artist was aided in his decorative art by the very shape of the object he chose to decorate. For example, when decorating an inro to portray a bag of rice, the lacquer artist started with his basic form in the shape of a bag (Fig. 212). Daruma, a favorite subject in Japanese art, was created on an inro whose basic outline was that of his body shape. As previously noted, another favorite and often seen design was that of a cake of *sumi,* the solid Chinese ink used by painters. Here again the general form of the inro coincides with the design it bears. Figure 103 depicts an inro in the form of three fans, each with separate decoration depicting omens of good luck, longevity, and marital fidelity. It is supposed that this inro was specially made to be presented to a bride as a wedding gift. Another example is that of an inro in the form of a turtle which the artist has created in wood and carved to resemble a realistic tortoise (Fig. 104). Sometimes entire inro, although these are probably from later periods, were intricately carved from one piece of wood or ivory.

In inro decoration, as in all Japanese lacquer art, all sides and parts of an object were finished. That is to say, no part of the object was left undecorated, whether this decoration was an intricate design or merely a continuation of a rich deep background color. The insides of the cases were no exception to this rule. Indeed it is on the inside of the boxes that we often find examples of excellent *nashiji* or outstanding colored lacquer, and particularly red, black, or a matte gold are to be found on earlier works. *Chinkin-bori* in waves and flowers will be found decorating the risers, and artists often used a diaper pattern between the cases, many times a different detailed design between different cases (Fig. 105). Frequently the diaper patterns were used not only for their own value to add to the overall design but also to outline and bring out a part of the design. Highly intricate diapers are seen covering the tops and bottoms of inro as well as running along the cord risers and thus endowing these purely practical channels with an artistic element all their own (Fig. 10).

We have already discussed the *himotoshi,* or cord passers, and have described in great detail the internal and external channels which are provided for the cord. Let us now turn our attention for a moment to the cord itself. The cord is always made of fine soft strands of colored silk braided into ropes of various thicknesses. It should fit the inro channels snugly to allow easy movement of the cases when separated but not so tightly as to produce undue tension, nor so loosely as to allow slipping. The color of the cord varied with the taste of the individual wearer. It was chosen on the basis of personal taste, governed either by superstition, family or clan color, or tradition, rather than in an attempt to merely complement or offset the inro. Almost all colors are seen, although shades of purple, brown, and green appear to be the most dominant colors, with white rarely found. The cord passes through the ojime above the inro and is knotted out of sight through the two holes provided for this purpose in the netsuke. Enough length is permitted so that the inro hangs down about 3 to 4 inches below the obi. The cord beneath the inro is tied into a many-looped bow. It might be noted that the cord, being one continuous piece below the inro, presents an interesting problem in tying a bow. A great deal of practice is required to shorten and adjust the cord to the desired length and then fasten it into a graceful bow so as to balance in the center of the inro with all loops of equal length. The cord is approximately 56 inches long. Wider triple-looped bows are made for the broader, more bulky inro, and frequently only a double loop is used for smaller more delicate inro. There are some early inro which have a groove running along the bottom into which the cord fits, and it may be that this type was meant to be used without the cord being fashioned into a bow (Fig. 126). Undoubtedly the early inro were used without an ojime. Since the exact and tightly fitting cases of good quality inro do not really require any external tension on them to keep them closed, the ojime was most likely added in order to permit the inro to hang more gracefully, as more of a decorative appendage rather than a necessary one. The ojime also serves the purpose of allowing enough slack in the cord so that it is unnecessary to open and retie the bow on the cord each time the inro is opened.

Care is taken that the component parts of the inro—that is, the netsuke and ojime—be in perfect harmony. In this respect color of the wood or material used for the netsuke carving is not the deciding factor. Rather it is the subject matter which must be considered. Also, metal netsuke are to be avoided with delicate wood or lacquer inro as they might dent and damage the inro if they were to accidently bump against it. The netsuke should be strong enough to support the inro; thus a light wooden or lacquer netsuke would not be suitable for a heavy metal inro, but it should never be heavy enough to cause possible damage. Many netsuke artists provided their netsuke with reinforced ivory or jade cord runners with this thought of support in mind, no detail being too small for consideration by the expert Japanese craftsmen and technicians.

Despite the elaborate and beautiful decoration and the almost effeminate nature of the inro, it is doubtful that they were worn very much by women, by virtue of the very large obi which was part of women's clothing. There are some existing inro which are said to be "sleeve inro" and which do not have channels or runners for cords to attach them to a sash, and we can speculate that perhaps these were carried mostly by women. Probably only in early times when the costume of the women was far less elaborate, the obi consisting of merely a narrow silk sash or a simple cord which knotted to hold the kimono closed, did women use the typical form of inro. During the Tokugawa period (1615–1868) the size of the obi increased greatly, becoming wider and longer and encircling the body serveral times, reaching from breast to hip, or approximately 9″ to 10″ wide, hugging the body snugly, and ending with a very large bow in the back. This style of corsetlike woman's obi would practically make it impossible and indeed extremely uncomfortable to suspend an inro from it. Therefore when inro were worn they were suspended from the thin braided cord called *obijime* which is worn over the obi. Furthermore, although Japanese women undoubtedly enjoyed sugar pellets, pastilles, and other small candies, these always had distinctive boxes of their own and were not carried in inro. Perfume, when used, which was fairly seldom, was carried in tiny gourd-shaped bottles within the folds of the dress. The most frequently used scents were sandal, musk, some herbs, dried flowers, fragrant woods, and stick incense, which was kept in special incense boxes called *kyara-bako*. For the most part, scents were applied to the clothes themselves through various techniques, instead of to the body directly. Although authorities differ on this question, it is most probable that the custom of wearing inro, while not restricted to men, was certainly more common with them.

While children did not regularly wear inro, it was the custom on some festive occasions for them to do so. We therefore find small-size inro with suitable youthful designs which were undoubtedly intended to be used by a child. There are some tiny replicas of inro, far too small to be of any practical value, which were meant merely as toys or as part of the costume for a doll. Even these tiny objects, however, were executed with great care and by skillful artists (Fig. 107).

It should also be mentioned that inro were not carried by Buddhist priests, since the very teachings of their religious doctrines forbade them the use and self-indulgence of any decorative article of dress. Also their religion taught of the healing of illness through spiritual faith and meditation rather than by medicine or drugs.

It is generally agreed that although lacquer ornamentation was practiced in Japan from the 7th and 8th centuries onward, it was not until the end of the 16th century, in about 1585, that people generally adopted the custom of wearing inro. Few countries are able to boast of an art form which is indigenous to their particular civilization. The Orient, however, is unquestionably credited as the founder and leader in the field of artistic lacquer ware. A form of lacquer art to develop and indeed remain characteristic only of Japan was the inro.

The word "inro" means literally seal case (*in*=seal; *ro*=case) and was first introduced in the latter part of the 16th century. There were no restrictions as to the size or shape in which inro were made. In general, however, the inro are rectangular in shape, flat, and in cross section elliptical. They are divided into several sections usually consisting of from three to five cases. As an average the overall height is between 3″ and 3⅛″, the depth about 1″, and the width between 1¾″ to 2¾″. Inro of unusually large size are to be found, and these are said to have been worn by actors or wrestlers (Fig. 107). As the name implies, the inro was originally made to hold a seal and stamping pad or colored ink paste with which to make an impression. At the beginning of the Tokugawa period, about 1603, all legal papers had to bear the seal of the head of the family regardless of whether they concerned him or another member of his household. In early times, the people of the lower classes were unable to write and would make a mark: a cross, a circle, an impression with the palm of the hand, the thumb, or some other similar identifying mark. During the 17th century the better educated upper classes were not only well acquainted with the art of writing but had fully adopted the use of an individual *kakihan,* which literally means a written seal. This was formed by the combination of some characters selected more or less at their pleasure to form a sort of monogram. Indeed, the use of the *kakihan* became more or less mandatory, and it had to be registered at government offices.

Since the majority of the lower classes were unable to write, they were allowed the use of a *jitsuin,* or seal. The *jitsuin* was an inscription or any word, character, name, or phrase which was engraved on the smooth surface of some solid substance, such as a ring or a netsuke, or of any other object which would be neat and portable. The engraved face of this seal would vary in style and design in accordance with the taste of the user, insofar as size, shape, material, and style of calligraphy were concerned. A great deal of attention was also given to the appearance of the rest of the seal itself. Once again, its form reflected the taste of its owner, great emphasis being put on its ease of handling and general shape and decoration. Here again, a utilitarian object becomes decorative under the influence of Japanese aesthetics and through the work of skilled craftsmen. The ink for stamping the impression was generally black, red being reserved for use by government officials. Later this rule was relaxed, however, and all colors of ink gradually came into use, red and black still remaining the most predominant by far. The inro was made originally to hold the ink paste or stamping pad and at times even the seal itself, although probably the netsuke served more commonly as the seal.

The earliest seal cases were originally used toward the end of the 15th century as a part of the decoration in the *tokonoma,* the alcove recess which is such an important place in every Japanese home. These early boxes, probably first imported from China, were usually round or square and consisted of a nest of boxes, one set on top of the next, having from two to five divisions. At this time also, there is record of a receptacle to hold medicines called *yakuro, yaku* meaning medicine, *ro* meaning case. This was generally a covered bowl-shaped object and also constituted part of the *tokonoma* display. Both objects were distinguished by the tightness of fit of the tiers of boxes and the cover, which thus protected the commodities contained within. Neither object was portable, and they were not originally intended to be carried about on the person.

It was during the Keicho era (1596–1614) that the portable type of inro became popular. Undoubtedly, centuries before the appearance of the inro, Japanese hunters carried other personal belongings attached to their swords or suspended from their sashes. These objects or girdle pendants were called *sagemono* or *koshisage* and were also held in place by means of a primitive form of netsuke. Probably the earliest such pendant was a tinder box called *hiuchi-bukuro*. This was a small baglike receptacle used to carry flint and tinder for use by the traveler or hunter to light fires. Mention of such a device is found in the records as early as the 8th century. Later, small pouches to be used for carrying money, amulets, and other personal items were introduced, and these were called *kinchaku*. Little is known about the size and shape of these early pouches, but most likely they were made of some kind of soft material, cloth, leather, or brocade, tied at the top and thus forming a bag in which to hold small articles. Reference is also made to the use of such materials as horn, bone, bamboo, and wood, but these probably came somewhat later. There have been many other *sagemono*, such as *kiseru-zutsu*, the tobacco pouch and pipe, popular since the 17th century; the *tabako-ire*, or tobacco pouch, usually of leather or brocade; the *yatate*, or portable writing case and brush; and the *bokuto*, or wooden dummy sword, usually carried by physicians as an indication of their profession but also worn by others who, not belonging to the samurai class, were forbidden to carry arms. It is interesting to note that occasionally these "dummy" swords actually housed concealed weapons. Among the many other *sagemono* were the *hyotan*, a type of gourd from which to drink; the *hashi-ire*, a case to carry chopsticks; *kagi*, a bunch of keys, and the *kaishi-ire*, which contained paper used as napkins for the tea ceremony—to mention just a few. Frequently combinations of *sagemono* were worn. In other words, along with the inro, which was usually worn suspended from the sash and hanging over the right hip and slightly to the rear, such items as the *kinchaku* and *tabako-ire* would be suspended over the left hip. Inro differed from the pouches in that they were divided into several compartments and were suitable for holding several different items, keeping each one separate. Although the inro was most likely first used for carrying the seal and ink, it gradually became most popular for transporting various medicines. Because it was divided into several individual cases, the inro was extremely useful in that medicines and powders could be separately housed without danger of becoming mixed. The idea of patent medicine was introduced into Japan from China. From the time of their introduction the Japanese were greatly enthusiastic about patent medicines and would never travel about without carrying an abundant supply of dried roots, herbs, and leaves, which were prepared by steeping in hot water which was drained off and drunk. The patent-medicine industry had its start in Japan in about 1650 in what is now Toyama Prefecture. It was sponsored by great interest on the part of the daimyo Prince Seiho Maeda and soon flourished and became a prosperous industry, as it remains to this day. There were no patent medicines in liquid form; they were rather in the form of pills, powders, pellets, pastes, and pastilles. With the growth of the industry and the rise of interest, people began to carry such items as myrrh, musk, ginseng, cinnamon, licorice, roots, and herbs in the portable inro. The lacquer and the tight-fitting cases combined to keep the drugs fresh and in good condition. Sometimes found inscribed on the individual inro compartments are the names of particular items or medicines meant to be stored within each division, or there remain traces of powders or pastes inside the compartments. Similarly, traces of red or black stamp paste can occasionally be found. There are inro in which, within each case, fits a small covered box to hold the medicine. The example shown in Figure 110 has a strip of silver on the top of each tiny container on which to inscribe the nature of its contents.

The earliest inro were undoubtedly made of either red or black lacquer, many with encrusted mosaics of large pieces of *raden* and *aogai* shell designs, in rich color. This method was introduced from China. Early decoration was more in a stylized pattern, generally of dragons or other mythological subjects, stiff, formal landscapes or court scenes, or stylized floral or crest designs. Early inro decoration was simple, often portraying a single wisteria vine or a design consisting of written characters for longevity and good luck. During the Momoyama period, from the late 16th to the early 17th century, art reflected the rise of culture among the people. Exceedingly popular with the nobility and upper classes were inro whose subject matter was derived from a line of poetry. Indeed being able to identify a poem thus portrayed in the lacquer was a sign of learning and culture and became somewhat of a game among the people. Somewhat later the *chonin,* or townspeople, merchants, and craftsmen were awakened to the delights of the handicraft arts which had previously belonged mainly to the nobility and samurai classes. They encouraged freshness and a tendency toward more elaborateness in the crafts. There was a general breaking away from stiff and formal subjects and from the traditions still favored by the court and the nobility, and there began a rise in interest in secular and everyday life which was reflected in all art forms. The upper classes and nobility had gradually become almost effeminate in their artistic taste, and it was not until this time that inro exhibiting greater strength of design and decoration were encouraged and accepted. So it was that inro began to portray the interests of the general public, and household and lucky gods, sages, Noh dancers, animals, insects, nature in all forms, and other everyday scenes became frequent and popular inro decoration.

The Edo (Tokugawa) period (1615–1868) saw the greatest advance in artistic development, and during this time, particularly in the Genroku era (1688–1704), inro art flourished. During this longest peaceful period in Japan's history, the artist was able as never before to move freely about the country, spreading his talents among the people. Gradually the subdued art sponsored by the nobility became more and more lavish as inro were adopted and worn by merchants, tradesmen, actors, wrestlers, and artisans. Inro were widely used not only by the people of the large cities but by those of the *chonin* classes from the provinces as well, and by members of the shogunate, daimyo, village heads, doctors, and the samurai who had previously been the most frequent wearers of inro. People displayed the inro on their person in such a way as to easily attract attention. They became more lavish and ornate. The wealthy people had many and would choose the one best suited to enhance their costume for the day. It was worn with civil dress, occasionally with armor, and always on festive occasions, although not with court costume. It became fashionable in those days, even as now, to collect inro, and this hobby was in vogue among the wealthy classes during the Tokugawa period. Frequently special chests were designed and executed by outstanding lacquer artists and were used to store a collection of inro. Similarly these artists executed lacquer stands on which inro were hung and displayed in the *tokonoma*. These chests and stands often bore the family crest as part of their lacquer design.

Inro became an indication of the wearer's taste, a means of displaying his refinement and artistic taste as well as his affluence. Gradually this initially utilitarian box developed into a primarily decorative appendage, meant to be seen and appreciated rather than to hold anything within it.

Inro were actually used for a relatively short period of time extending from late in the 16th century through the middle of the 19th century. During this time they varied in style in accordance with the fashion and tastes of the people. It is difficult to assign with any great certainty a specific design or shape to any one era. In general, however, there were a few outstanding trends. Insofar as shape is concerned, inro vary greatly, as seen from a cross section, from circular to flat oblong, from square to rectangular. There seem to have been preferences for different shapes during various eras and in different areas. There is the round shape—in Japanese, *marugata*—or flat shape, *hiragata*. The round shape can vary from nearly a complete circle, although this is somewhat rare, to the more frequently appearing thick ellipse. The flat shape, or *hiragata,* varies to the other extreme from a blunted or rounded end of oval shape to a thin, slender ellipse. Less popular, although still seen, are square-shaped sections. Each inro has its own individual shape, and rarely will two be found to have identical cross sections and body shapes. They usually do, however, conform to one of many general classifications. Most likely the rather long, cylindrical inro with fewer and deeper cases was common in the 18th century because of its practical, yet artistic, shape for utilitarian and decorative purposes at that time. One of the earliest shapes to become fashionable was the tall, narrow, cylindrical shape. In cross section it appears as a thick oval. This had external channels, or perhaps even rings with flat or slightly convex *joge,* and was in vogue early in the 17th century. One interesting shape, as occasionally seen on sword handles, is the "lobster" shape, in which the outer edges of the cases are made in a series of definite convex arcs similar to the top shell of a lobster. The external surfaces of these cases are also slightly convex (Fig. 108).

During the rule of the Tokugawa shogun Yoshimune (1716–45) a thick, squat, horizontal-shaped inro was introduced. In cross section this appears as a thick oval. The *joge* was flat, and the cord channels were external. This shape, which had a rather clumsy appearance, did not remain popular for long. Originally made at Edo, there appeared also during the first part of the 17th century a narrow oval shape with flat *joge* and external cord channels. A type known as *kobangata* (the *koban* being a gold oval-shaped coin) soon became popular. This had internal channels and rounded *joge* and in cross section was oval, with rounded edges. Another type very similar to this was introduced probably during the Genroku era (1688–1704). This is known as the Edo inro, having met with great popularity in Edo during the early 18th century. Its decoration is usually done in one tint of gold.

The *chajin,* or tea masters, generally adopted an inro known as *maru-cha-ire-no-gata,* which means literally the shape of a round pottery tea caddy. The tea-master type exemplified the simplicity and subdued nature of the tea ceremony in its coloring and its decoration.

An oval-shape inro with flat or bluntly rounded ends, having flat *joge* and internal channels, was introduced before the middle of the 18th century. This shape was preferred for decoration by many of the family of Koma artists (Figs. 54, 116, 136, 215).

For the most part, the inro artists were not restricted by, and gave but little attention to, the shape of the article upon which they worked. They did not seem to have any particular preference and did not confine their work to any one shape only. Indeed, the large variety of body shapes seemed to give added impetus for varying the decorative designs. The more rounded, longer, more cylindrical shapes are generally to be found in earlier inro (Fig. 109), while a flatter, larger size was in greater abundance during the late Meiji era (Fig. 110).

Concerning inro decoration and artistic design, this too underwent certain changes. Chinese influences were still strongly seen in the lacquer work until the end of the 16th century. The works of Aogai Chobei in mosaic decoration with mother-of-pearl were popular during this time. Also the techniques utilizing carved red and black lacquer, again directly influenced by the Chinese artists, were common, as was *chinkin-bori* work. In general a minimal amount of detail of design was portrayed on these early inro. Subject matter was generally simple, consisting mainly of mythological creatures, such as dragons, and designs illustrating poetry or various aspects of nature. With the appearance of Koetsu in the early 17th century, artists broke away from the Chinese decorative style, and, following his direction, a new trend in an almost impressionistic sense was adopted (Fig. 8). He introduced broad and simple inlays to obtain such effects. The newly risen samurai class, however, was greatly in favor of the richer and more ornate type of inro which were beginning to be made, rather than the previous subdued, subtle designs favored by the nobility. This period also saw the rise of other great artists, such as Korin and his large, crude-appearing, almost abstract designs, as well as the beginning of the Kajikawa (Fig. 111) and Koma families with their finely executed gold-lacquer and magnificent *togidashi* techniques. Gorgeous and lavish designs in powdered gold were encouraged, stressing the decorative element (Figs. 112, 113). The Genroku era (1688–1704) is often felt to be the peak of perfection in lacquer-art design and decoration. Designs tended to be simple and placed so as to make use of blank spaces as an integral part of the overall picture. During this era the people lived extravagantly and enjoyed the utmost in luxury.

The mid-Edo period (1681–1764) saw the rise of the *chonin* classes, who tended to appreciate more lavish designs and encouraged artists to become more decorative and profuse in their use of gold. However, many of the great lacquerers were still under the employ of the shogunate, and they gave their attention to producing such work as pleased their patrons, and much emphasis was still given to technical skill and perfection of quality rather than to ornate decoration.

The late Edo period (1765–1868) was marked by a decline in the overall quality of lacquer work. As inro began to be used by all classes with greater frequency, taste on the whole began to decline. We find coarser, more elaborately decorated, gaudier, flashier work. Inro of many different materials, such as carved ivory, pottery, and faience, began to appear. Displays of technical skill on inro became predominant; designs consisting of works displaying microscopic details were common, while less work was created displaying simplicity and larger overall patterns. About this time also, artisans began to use shortcuts in working with lacquer. Great attention was given to making the outside of the article beautiful while at the same time less care was given to the finish of the inside, revealing a tendency toward quantity with less attention to quality both in the overall work and in the materials employed.

Generally speaking, the type and quality of *nashiji* which the artist used on the inside of the inro is an indication of its age. Earlier works, especially those of the Kajikawa school, show larger *nashiji*, which is called *gyobu* (Fig. 14). Toward the middle of the Edo period it became slightly smaller in size, a type known as *hirame*, while toward the close of the period it became much smaller and more finely ground. Frequently the older inro artists used plain flat matte gold *(fundame)* or red lacquer for the inside of the cases, but this too was abandoned in later works in favor of *nashiji*.

Although encrustations of work with various materials was not new, with the appearance of Shibayama in the lacquer field, great impetus was given to this type of work, particularly in the late 18th and in the 19th centuries. It became fashionable to employ carvings of ivory, colored soapstone, shell, coral, and metal to form the figures depicted. During the late 18th century the use of gold ground was increasingly common. The detailed, technically perfect encrustation work is characteristic of the early 19th-century inro (Fig. 129). At this time pictures created by the use of colored lacquer in various styles were less frequently seen.

Metal inro were made mainly during the late 18th and 19th centuries, most often commercially, but frequently by famous artists and their schools (Fig. 114). As noted, the inro were either encrusted with *menuki*-like metalwork or were made entirely of metal. Such famous artists included Joi, Yasuchika, Hamano Masayuki, and Somin. Along with the Nara and Hamano schools were the equally famous schools of Ishiguro, Shoami, Yanagawa, Hirata, and Yokoya. Many individual metal artists who made inro are listed separately from page 395.

Similarly, netsuke artists carved inro in wood and ivory, and occasionally in tortoise shell or horn. Among such well-known artists are Garaku, Gyokuzan, Issan, Jugyoku, Kaigyokusai, Masakazu, Masanao, Sukenaga, and Tokoku (Figs. 164, 230). Ichimuken Nanka, who made *manju* etched with minute maps of Japan, did similar work on ivory inro in such calligraphic detail that, for example, all of the names of the fifty-three stations on the Tokaido are legible. Most of the better ivory inro were carved or engraved. Many ornate ivory inro were made for export purposes during the late 19th century and usually consisted of technically and artistically poorly done designs in Shibayama style, whose inlaid pieces readily tend to dislodge from the ivory base (Fig. 115).

Finally, ceramic inro were occasionally made by such famous artists as Kenya, Kenzan, and Hoki Toyosuke. The latter artist covered unglazed pottery with lacquer. Ceramic inro, however, were impractical, as they tended to be fragile and could not be made sufficiently airtight to preserve the medicines which they were meant to contain. Besides ceramic inro, ceramic inlays on wood or lacquer grounds were executed by Ritsuo and his school (Figs. 121, 122, 124, 204, 217).

It was during the late 18th century that color prints rapidly became popular. These *ukiyo-e*, or "pictures of the floating world," portrayed actors and theatrical scenes, courtesans and the vicissitudes of their lives (Figs. 2, 43, 225), and scenes from the lives of the commoners, as in Hiroshige's *Fifty-three Stations on the Tokaido* (Fig. 151). The contemporary lacquer artists readily adopted these currently fashionable secular themes. As time progressed, more and more gold-lacquer inro became popular, and the decorations of shell, mother-of-pearl, metal, and other materials became more elaborate. A new style with emphasis on microscopic detail, using almost exclusively iridescent blue-green *awabi*-shell ornamentation and covering almost the entire surface, became more popular. This was known as Somada work in deference to its creator and the greatest exponent of this style. Gorgeously lacquered inro lavishly adorned with powdered gold were also in vogue. The luxury and extravagance of the people and of the times was indeed being reflected in their art. Toward the latter part of the Edo period, foreign trade was resumed and inro were produced as an export item. The workmanship, while retaining a high level of craftsmanship, became increasingly elaborate, perhaps because this was felt to be what was required to satisfy Western taste. Early in the 19th century, a wallet which was carried in the folds of the kimono became popular, and the wearing of inro became less fashionable. The samurai class ceased to exist after the Restoration of 1868, and inro, which had previously been worn by the samurai on all formal occasions, fell into gradual disuse. Over the next few years, Western dress and customs became popular, and inro production ceased as the majority of the people gradually discarded the traditional kimono.

One of the most difficult questions to answer is just what makes some inro better than others. Why are some to be considered as masterpieces while others are only adequate or fair? Of course, as with any art form, personal taste is of primary consideration. However, there are some general objective qualifications which also must be kept in mind. In old inro and lacquer ware, one of the prime goals of the lacquer artist was to produce a substantial object which, while being not only utilitarian and artistic was also hard and durable, would resist damage from extremes of temperature, both hot and cold, would not be harmed by climatic factors, would acquire a brilliant polish, and in general would last, technically, forever. In order to achieve these goals, great lengths of time were required as well as endless patience combined with skill, artistic talent, and the use of the finest first-quality materials. The finest lac available was also the slowest drying lacquer, each layer requiring many days in which to dry thoroughly. Sometimes a fine lacquer object was the product of one or two years' work. Special attention was given to the lacquer priming and groundwork, usually of black or gold. In all cases fine lacquer should not show any irregularities or brush marks on the finished polished surface. No underlying undulations of the wooden core should be visible. Sometimes, as a result of inferior work, part of the wooden core or the grain of the hemp cloth covering it can be seen. Every part of the object, whether the inside or the outer surfaces, should show finished, polished work. In many instances, in fact, the most beautiful portion of the design will be found on a most inconspicuous part of the object, such as on the inside of the article. This is rarely the case with inro, however, because of their limited size and shape, but is frequently true of other miniature pieces, such as *kobako,* in which the most delicate work is often applied to the inside of the cover of the box. This is done in order to protect the more delicate work, or perhaps the artist wishes this design to be an inspiration to the one who opens and uses the box. In either case this is a distinctive quality of Japanese lacquer work (Figs. 9, 29, 130, 131). Many of the Japanese lacquer boxes displayed extremely simple designs on the outside but were augmented by much more ornate designs on the inner surfaces. Philosophical reasoning for such ornamentation is that the outside reflects the more simple, stoic, sublimated exterior of the Japanese people but that the interior represents their more truly complex nature and feelings. From an artistic point of view the exteriors reflect the simple, unencumbered, esoteric Zen influence and the interior the basic love of the Japanese artisan for decorative ornamentation and technical craftsmanship.

The inro artist painted his picture with layer upon layer of lacquer, using sprinklings of metallic powders and filings and various colors of lacquer, each layer being dried and polished before the application of the next layer. It is remarkable indeed when one views the end result to ponder the foresight and planning required to produce the minute detailed pictures in lacquer that decorate inro. It was essential that the various materials, the metallic powders and filings, the various colored lacquers, the inlays of mother-of-pearl, metal, ivory, and shell be applied in such an order as to produce tiny variations and shadings which were only obtained after a succession of innumerable further applications of lacquer, drying, and polishing processes, to ultimately produce the desired design. Thus the artist had not only to be able to visualize the end product; he had also to be able to break it down step by step and apply the proper materials in such a sequence as would respond to subsequent steps and culminate in the finished picture. As stated, these pictures painted in lacquer were painted in layers rather than all at once. The *makie-shi* knew that a certain number of coats of lacquer, when applied over the metal filings, dried, and polished would make the filings appear to assume different colors depending upon the depth and the level at which they were applied, how deeply imbedded they were, and how thick the subsequent layers of lacquer would be, as well as the initial color and purity of the filings. In order to make these colors appear he had to apply his powderings at the proper level and depth to cultivate the desired gradation of color and effect. It might be said that he was painting in a three-dimensional manner —the conventional height and width, with the addition of depth as the third dimension.

By virtue of the medium itself, no mistakes could be made, for they would be uncorrectable. Because of the stickiness of the lacquer, it is an extremely difficult material with which to work. It is hard to imagine anything more difficult than drawing a fine, thin line on a soft gummy surface. Once the metallic powderings or filings have been imbedded in the surface of the lacquer and dried, hardened, and covered with endless subsequent coats of the same material, they cannot be removed or covered up.

The one color for the ground, even when the entire surface is to be ultimately covered in gold, red, brown, or any other color, is black. There were two methods of preparing this black, one by mixing acetate of iron with the lacquer and the other by adding lampblack to the lacquer. The first and probably the older method was nearly always used by Tsuchida Soetsu. It is an excellent test of age, for while originally the acetate black radiates a deep translucent color, with time it becomes a rich brownish, almost tortoise-shell color in appearance (Fig. 71). The opaque lampblack, however, has a deep inky color which never changes. Fine-quality black lacquer has always been highly valued. It is called *roiro* and at times is referred to as "daimyo lacquer." It should have a rich, velvety, deep tone, perfectly flat, unmarred surface, hard luxurious polish, and high luster. The luxurious, deep, mirrorlike surface quite often found on the black ground used by the Somada artists is undoubtedly the lampblack variety. Poor work is lusterless and shallow and shows unevenness and brushmarks.

It is very useful to compare old and new gold-lacquer work. In the fine-quality old work, the gold grounds have the appearance of almost being a metallic surface. It has a rich and uniform tone and texture. These qualities improve with age. Inferior-quality gold grounds are often cloudy or uneven and mottled in appearance. Unfortunately age will only increase these defects instead of mellowing and softening them. Part of this comes from using poor-quality gold powder, and frequently it is due to incomplete or hasty preparation and the substitution of other materials, such as tin powders and filings, for pure gold. The fullest luster of gold and other metallic powders and filings is brought out only by repeated polishings. The gold used for decoration prior to the end of the 18th century was practically pure, appearing as a golden-orange hue and never changing in color. However, among less dedicated artists it became the practice to dilute the pure gold and mix it with other less expensive metals, such as copper, tin, or bronze, resulting in a lighter yellowish tint. These alloys had the advantage of being less costly and also required less time and work through fewer polishing processes to give them a finished appearance, but they also lacked the rich luster of the finer-quality gold. An outstanding example of the excellence to be achieved in gold grounds can be seen in the works of Korin, who is famous for his gold-lacquer work.

As a school the Kajikawa were outstanding for their gold lacquer work as well as for the sharpness and clarity of their *nashiji*, grounds which they used almost exclusively for their risers and the linings of inro. *Nashiji* is prepared by sifting the metallic powders onto a layer of moist, transparent lacquer which is then permitted to dry, after which it is polished and subsequent layers are added in the same manner. Little spaces are left between the metallic flakes, and the finest quality is that in which a fine, granulated, evenly distributed surface of rich color is visible through the transparent layers of lacquer. In older *nashiji*, because of the hardening of the lacquer beneath the metallic flecks, these flecks appear pitted and granular as distinguished from the completely smooth surface seen in relatively modern *nashiji*. In *nashiji* the dimensions of the grain, its color and clarity, which varies with its depth, the purity of the metal, the richness of the patina, the evenness with which the grains are distributed, as well as the artistic effect which the finished product presents, all should be considered. Poor quality is dull, lusterless, and lacking in depth and variety. It is interesting to note that Japanese *nashiji* is always polished, whereas the similar type of Chinese groundwork is never polished. Later *nashiji* is finer in grain than earlier works but often lacks the above-mentioned desired qualities.

Fine lacquer work should display strength of line, accuracy of technical detail and execution, delicacy of finish, grace of conception, transparency and perfection of surface, clarity and artistry of design, and a sparkling, vital quality, combined with subtlety and gradations of tones, which are produced by the building up of the pattern through layer upon subsequent layer of lacquer. In poor-quality work, lines, instead of being sharp and clear, may spread and run together. These lines tend to be thick or beaded, blurry, and unsteady in inferior work instead of fine, even, steady, and sharp. In some instances, it has been said that in order to obtain these thin, hairline, fine, sharp lines the lacquer artist would move the object he was decorating rather than move the brush with which he was working. We must always bear in mind the enormous technical difficulties encountered arising from the intrinsic difficulties of working with the sticky, slowly drying resinous material itself. Occasionally, particularly in poor-quality work, because of the fluid consistency of the lacquer, two lines flow together and the lines spread and blur. Many fine artists overcome this difficulty by using lacquer of a special consistency for drawing fine lines. The good artist technically knows how to get the most out of the material with which he works and has full control over it. Add to this the tremendous obstacles encountered in working on such a small, irregularly shaped, uneven, concave or convex surface as that of an inro, as opposed to a large flat area with no corners or angles, and one cannot help but feel the greatest admiration for the lacquer artist. In general, then, the lacquer artist has to be endowed with the artistic ability of the painter combined with the technical skill necessary for working with his difficult medium. Mere ability to copy objects or pure technical skill alone does not suffice.

Often the works of the master craftsmen may appear deceptively simple. However, these craftsmen are so skillful and such masters of the use of their materials that frequently their skill is hidden beneath the quiet beauty of the finished article. Figure 132, for example, depicts two fireflies hovering near a blossoming flower. Upon closer scrutiny we find that the artist has imbedded three separate tiny pieces of iridescent red, yellow, and green shell, each measuring less than $1/16$ of an inch, in the tail of each firefly and has surrounded this with gold powderings to indicate the glow of light being emitted from the tail (Fig. 133). Another example is seen in Figure 116, which shows snow falling upon a dwarfed tree growing in a large urn. Note how the artist Koma Yasutada has indicated the falling snowflakes by the use of rather large, irregular flecks of silver dust distributed unevenly over the entire surface.

The inro, because of its size and shape, presented many problems to the lacquer artist. First of all, he was limited to an exceedingly small area, and therefore he had to be selective in his design. He had to create an illusion and through suggestion complete the picture without sacrificing the idea that he wished to portray. For instance, an entire seascape on an area measuring but a few inches would be impractical and hardly suitable. Figure 134 shows an excellent example of selective representation, or foreshortening. Here we see a single sail floating in the distance on a vast body of water. The artist, Shiomi Masanari, has used tones of gold in *togidashi* technique to create the background picture. In order to draw attention to the sail, he has made it of inlaid mother-of-pearl as if the sun were gleaming on the distant sail so that it immediately catches our eye (Fig. 118). Another example of this principle is seen in Figure 117. Here the artist portrays birds soaring through the sky by simply portraying a single bird headed toward a part of the moon, which the artist places at the very top edge of the inro and permits to flow over the side. He surrounds this with a few gold sprinklings to indicate clouds. And yet, with these few representative images, he has fully created the entire scene. As these examples show, great planning and ingenuity are important as well as artistic handling in order to make the condensed representative design create the illusion of the whole. These examples of foreshortening illustrate the clever portrayal of the immensity of space and the beauty, grandeur, and awesomeness of nature and show how this concept can be aptly depicted on the small, confined area of an inro. Indeed, one need only be an excellent craftsman to portray in complete detail an entire landscape, whereas one must be both a craftsman and an artist in order to create the illusion of an entire picture by the use of only a few well-chosen representative details.

Placement of the subject matter was given attention and thought and was handled with great care and planning. The entire external surface area was used for the artist's pictorial design. This was accomplished in one of three ways. Frequently there was only one major design which was eccentrically placed on the main surface area, tended to flow over the sides of the inro, and usually terminated on a portion of the opposite side (Figs. 121, 122). Frequently parts of the design flowed over the top and bottom surfaces as well (Figs. 191, 120). This sense of continuity of design is typical of Japanese art in general. A second method was to tell a story on both sides of the inro. One side depicts the major allusion to the story while the reverse side illustrates some secondary phase (Figs. 67, 166). Finally, if the main design simply represented an object of nature, or a religious symbol, the opposite side would have a complementary symbolic design (Figs. 80, 138). Thus an inro with a picture of a crane, symbolic of longevity, might have a pine tree, also symbolizing longevity, on its complementary side. In a similar fashion the netsuke should be symbolically in keeping with the motif on the inro.

The Japanese artist loves asymmetry, and this is apparent in all his art mediums. It is a predilection that is sometimes carried to extremes (Fig. 29). He will place his subject design not necessarily in the center of his decorative field but more readily off to one side and will continue the object by permitting it to flow around the sides or over the top of the lid. Through this technique he tends to visually enlarge the decorative field. Although all surfaces are fully decorated and finished, most usually one side can easily be determined as being the front. Often the reverse side is used merely to finish the design as it flows around from the front. This is also true, although less frequently, of the top and bottom surfaces as well. Artistically the inro did not lend itself well to depicting a whole picture. This has been a severe criticism of the inro artist in the late Edo period. One reason for the overdecoration and overelaborateness of the inro at that time was the tendency to leave nothing to the imagination but rather to display in great detail an entire idea or picture, thereby revealing the artist's technical skill rather than his artistic taste.

Because of the various techniques and individualistic approach of each artist, the same subject matter, which is often repeated, tends never to be exactly alike and thus each time still has a fresh appeal. For example, a very popular art motif is the pine tree. This tree, symbolic of good luck, long life, strength, and durability, is portrayed very frequently. Each lacquer artist or lacquer school has its own individual style and distinctive use of materials, but the basic motif always emerges completely recognizable. In studying the following examples (Figs. 135–139) we must also bear in mind the technique of foreshortening or selective representation and the other previously noted aesthetics of Japanese art.

In the first example (Fig. 135), the pine saplings are portrayed in a distinctive manner typical of the style of the school of Ritsuo. Here the rough bark of the tree is represented by an inlay of coarse old pewter, adding great strength and artistic genius. The tips of the small branches are highlighted by inlays of pink and green mother-of-pearl shell while the pine needles themselves are executed in gold lacquer. The coarse rust-colored background simulating pottery completes the picture, and the entire object has a feeling of strength and vitality.

Figure 136 again portrays the pine tree but here the resemblance ends. This artist, Koma Kyuhaku, worked in a much more delicate manner and used a completely different technique. Here again a portion of the gnarled pine tree is portrayed, combining strength and delicacy, both effects being obtained by the *togidashi* technique, using shades of gold and red against a rich black background. The small reddish-gold leaves change color from gold to red depending on the direction of the light, which is a characteristic of the work of the Koma school. The angularity and strength of the branches are brought out in soft sweeping curves, and the extreme delicacy of the pine needles is portrayed by tiny sharp lines of gold lacquer which taper to pinpoint fineness. In this instance the grace of the trunk and its twisted branches is made to suggest growth and movement.

The next inro, in Figure 137, is much more masculine and powerful in effect. Here the artist, using gold *takamakie* in high relief, portrays a pine tree in a rainstorm. The heavy gold lacquer of the trunk and branches is powerful and gives a feeling of easily being able to weather the storm. Artistically the tree is given great strength through highly raised lacquer with sharply cut angles setting off the gnarled trunk, thick branches, coarsely striated bark, and prominent knotholes. The intensity of the wind and the storm is indicated by the oblique angles of the rain streaks and the exaggerated size of the pine needles being blown in the same direction as the rain, as well as the exaggerated twisting of the upper branches of the tree. The thick roots groping downward and extending off the bottom of the inro intensify the feeling of strength and stability.

The next example, Figure 138, is a typical example of fine-quality work of the Somada school. The outline of the irregular old tree trunk is executed by means of a large thin plaque of relatively white mother-of-pearl with the details added by fine engraving. Each of the profuse pine needles is elaborately depicted in a regular conventionalized pattern of minute pieces of individually inlaid greenish *aogai* shell. The highly intricate and magnificent technical skill which is displayed only serves to heighten the overall effect. On the whole, however, the entire picture, while strikingly beautiful at first glance, loses much of its artistic element by its excessive detail.

The final example, Figure 139, is executed by Kajikawa Bunryusai. Here the pine tree is almost impressionistically portrayed. It appears out of the background almost as if a section of the rich *oki-hirame* had been removed and we saw behind it parts of the tree. Only a small segment of the trunk and one delicate branch, not even attached to the tree, are visible. The trunk, however, is thick and masculine, its wavy outline suggesting the thick bark, although the artist has left the trunk in completely flat gold lacquer, entirely devoid of any carving or decoration. The overall picture is one of subtle beauty, serenity, and grace.

These are but five examples of how an artist will handle similar subject matter in his own individual style. In all of these examples one should note not only the style of presentation but also the method of foreshortening, the asymmetrical placement of the object, and the ingenuity of utilizing the small, confined, difficult shape of the inro to its best artistic advantage.

We have discussed in detail the difference between good and poor lacquer work from the point of view of craftsmanship, including technique and ingenious methods of presenting subject matter. Of equal importance are the criteria distinguishing good from bad aesthetics and design as noted in Chapter 1 and including the canons of Japanese art. Here there is more subjective leeway on the part of the observer, there being relatively little in regard to technical ability. Thus the individual appeal of a design may range anywhere from the more stylized conventionalized formal Chinese designs to the typically more graceful, soft, delicate Japanese motifs. For example, when the draperies of a robe are done in good taste in Chinese style, they may appear somewhat formal and even stiff in comparison with some Japanese standards. Yet the overall effect is graceful and regal, with simple, powerfully executed, eloquent lines, and never stiff, weak, or ungainly. On the other hand a gown may be depicted in a much more decorative, graceful, flowing Japanese fashion and still be just as effective and well done without being insipid or inarticulate. The style, therefore, may vary considerably and yet be of either good or bad quality. Similarly, a lacquer piece may be very simple in appearance, or even impressionistic in style but still maintain its majesty with great power of suggestion. On the other hand, when a simple design is done poorly it actually becomes crude, but when done by a master, purposeful oversimplification adds strength, as exemplified by the work of the Korin school. At the other extreme a work can be detailed and naturalistic and yet maintain an overall beautiful decorative effect, balance, and charm. If poorly done, the same work becomes just overornate photographic craftsmanship with lack of imagination. Thus both extremes of style, the simplest and the most detailed, may be either great works of art or badly done and completely ineffective.

Fine lacquer in accordance with the above qualities is indeed exceedingly costly. It demands not only great technical and artistic skill but also endless hours of work and exceedingly expensive materials. During such times as the mid-Edo period, when most artists were employed by the shoguns and daimyo, their time was relatively unimportant in that it was the quality of their work which supported them, not the quantity. This is no longer the case. In modern work the need arises to produce greater numbers of articles more rapidly, using cheaper materials. Unfortunately some concessions have to be made in order to meet these needs, and this often results in work of poorer quality, technically and artistically. The larger and more showy articles so popular during the late Edo period often utilize coarser gold leaf and powderings and consequently require less time. Cost of living, wages, materials, and similar expenses have made it necessary for lacquer artists to seek short cuts by which to cut down on the number of their processes and reduce their overhead by shortening the hundreds of hours formerly spent on a single work. While the modern lacquer artists have not necessarily lost their skill, which is often demonstrated through their many fine duplications of the works of the old masters, and though there are still a few outstanding craftsmen who are closely adhering to the old standards, they are of necessity rare. In the majority of late works artistic treatment and durability have had to be sacrificed in order to meet economic factors. Primarily the methods of overcoming these factors have been twofold: by reducing the time required to complete an object and by resorting to less costly and poorer-quality materials. The introduction of varying quantities of catalytic agents, such as oil and iron oxide, into the lacquer, which enables it to dry much more rapidly and also allows it to be worked more easily, is one means of dealing with the situation. However, the oil tends to dry out and evaporate after a while, and the surface hardens and contracts, which often causes the object to warp, tarnish, fade, blister, or crack as months or years go by. Also the wood used for the inner core is not allowed sufficient time to season well, and after a while this too splits or warps. The only sure test of modern lacquer is time, which alone will show whether proper materials and care have been used in its manufacture.

Finally attention should be given to the artistic design as well as to the technical aspects of lacquer work. At the height of their excellence, inro designs were rich, elegant, and refined. Simplicity, gentility, subtlety, and refinement in conception as well as execution are characteristic qualities of Japanese art. Japanese lacquer artists intent only on producing the finest in taste and elegance frequently adopted designs and paintings from well-known masters. The use of blank space as part of their decorative pattern, and their excellent and masterful characteristic asymmetrical arrangement of their pictures was unsurpassed. The rise of the modern realistic painters afforded great impetus to *togidashi* work. Shunsho, an outstanding master of *togidashi*, as well as some of the Koma family, often used only browns and golds to create magnificent landscapes in this technique. Other artists, such as Toyo, simulated *sumie* pictures on gold grounds, creating a singularly striking effect in only black and gold (Figs. 22, 209). Other variations, such as leaving portions of the design to appear dull or unpolished in order to create a hazy or dreamlike effect, attest to the endless creative abilities of the lacquer artists.

Familiarity with the styles of the outstanding artists, including signature characteristics or methods of signing (or not signing) their work, such as inlaid mother-of-pearl plaques for members of the Shibayama family, or hairline engraving in the lacquer by Zeshin, or a red lacquer seal in the shape of an urn by members of the Kajikawa family, while not infallible criteria, will still offer some protection from forgeries. Further attention should be given to the coloring of the decoration to attempt to determine if these pigments were used during the time when the artist worked and if the materials are those which that artist was known to have employed. Also the color of the signature should match any similar color which was used for the decoration. It is very important to keep in mind that many fine artists were in the employ of the shogunate and the daimyo and were therefore forbidden to sign their works. For this reason we often find many inro of the highest quality without any signature. It cannot be emphasized too strongly that an unsigned object does not indicate an inferior work and that the absence of a signature does not negate its quality and value. A superior piece of lacquer work maintains its importance whether it bears a signature or not. However, often an unscrupulous dealer or collector will attempt to elevate the status of such an object by adding to it the signature of a renowned artist, this addition often being made many years after the completion of the article. Bear in mind that any object which bears the signature of an artist who did not work in the manner in which the lacquer piece is executed is in all probability a forgery, such signature most likely having been added at a later date. It is not important that an object be signed, but should it be signed, it is important that it be truly a piece made by the artist whose name it bears. For this reason it is important to become familiar with the various styles of the outstanding artists. In general, inlays of pewter and lead represent older techniques, whereas inlaid work using tinted ivory, soapstone, or mother-of-pearl is more modern. The colors of the more modern works are sharper and brighter and tend to be somewhat gaudier, while older lacquer is usually decorated in more subdued tones, is more symbolic in nature, and, in very early works, often still retains Chinese-influenced stylized geometric patterns and motifs. In more modern work subject matter is more commonplace and banal and is likely to be executed in minute detail, often to the point of overdecoration.

The Japanese people regarded their inro and other lacquer art objects with such great admiration that when the pieces were not actually being used or displayed they would be carefully placed in special silk or brocade bags and stored away out of harm. Most people, certainly those of the nobility and upper classes, possessed several inro which were worn according to costume or occasion. Thus a much more subdued type would be used while partaking of the tea ceremony and a more resplendent one for festive occasions. It is an indication of this great care that so many inro today dating from the 17th and 18th centuries are still in perfect condition, as well as being a testimonial to the workmanship itself.

The same respect and attention should be given to the inro today. Care must be taken in handling the inro so that the ojime or netsuke does not strike and damage it. The cords should be held tightly with one hand while closing the cases to avoid kinking and forcing the cords into their channels. The lacquer surface should be handled as little as possible and should be wiped clean and dry after handling.

In general lacquer resists hot liquids, alcohol, ether, turpentine, and even most acids. It is affected mainly by rapid temperature changes and light. Dry heat causes splitting and warping of the wood. It also causes the encrustations, especially mother-of-pearl, to become loose and detached. Excess humidity and sulphides in the air may cause oxidation of metallic encrustations, especially lead, silver, and silver alloys, which tend to darken and tarnish when exposed to the open air. Direct light, especially sunlight, fades the gold lacquer and the *nashiji* and gives black lacquer a grayish tint. Bright light also tends to decompose lacquer, causing it to lose its gloss and become parched in appearance. As has been noted, old black lacquer made from iron filings naturally tends to turn brown. Pewter assumes a pretty mottled patina with age. The sweat of the finger tips and even the moisture of one's breath may stain and tarnish metallic surfaces. Lacquer can also be damaged by water, especially the modern lacquer, through absorption of the water by the lacquer. When finger marks are left on lacquer too long they may become difficult to remove. Fine works of art in general should be handled with a soft material and stored and wrapped in well fitting boxes. If on display, they should be kept in glass cases, protected from strong light and dust, with a container of water in the case to prevent undue drying. Even then it is advisable that no item be kept on display for any protracted period of time but be rotated and properly stored.

Even with great care and attention, occasional damage will be found on lacquer ware. Any repairs should only be undertaken by experts in the field of lacquer. Great harm can be done by allowing untrained hands to attempt to remedy the damage.

There will be occasions when the beauty of a piece of art is hidden under layers of dust which accumulate over periods of time. In order to return the piece to its full glory careful cleaning may be done as follows: old wax and dirt may be removed by gentle rubbing with a soft damp lint-free cotton cloth, rather than with silk, which is too hard and may scratch. Tarnished silver dustings may then be brightened by gently rubbing the surface with a small amount of powdered hartshorn applied to the pulp of the finger. The black tarnish will readily come off on the finger. The entire surface is then gently rubbed with a small amount of vegetable oil, preferably rapeseed oil, also using the finger tips. Finally the excess oil is removed by rubbing with either a soft cotton cloth or with white flannel. Certain finishes, however, are best left alone—for example, *fundame,* which has a purposely dull, nonglossy appearance. Also extreme care must be taken while rubbing with cloth any article having inlaid pieces, as the fine pieces tend to catch on the cloth and become detached. Inlays are handled separately according to the material involved. Ivory may be cleaned with soap and water and then gently rubbed with the fingers to bring back the gloss. Silver and gold may be cleaned with bicarbonate powder moistened with water. This paste, however, tends to remove the patina on copper inlays. Wood is brightened by the application of a thin coat of a solution of beeswax and turpentine. The wax is allowed to dry and the wood is then briskly rubbed with cotton or brushed with a soft badger brush. Small encrustations are best cleaned by using cotton-tipped toothpicks. The beautiful patina on pewter should of course be left alone. Finally, careful wrapping of the lacquer object in special "silvercloth" bags plus the use of an airtight box will further protect the object and prevent recurrence of any tarnishing.

The general shape of the inro—that is, a series of separate tiered cases—was adopted for use in other larger lacquer pieces. This new design was readily used for many household articles, and *jubako* (nests of boxes) became popular for holding various cooked foodstuffs, cakes, and sweets. During the relatively luxurious Edo period outdoor parties were fashionable, and the fitted picnic boxes were another adaptation of the basic inro design. On these occasions *jubako* were used to hold an assortment of picnic or holiday delicacies.

Other Miniature Forms

It should be understood that the term miniature as applied to miniature lacquer art does not just apply to the minuteness of the workmanship. Many of the relatively larger pieces of lacquer, such as the writing box *(suzuri-bako)*, have just as much minute detailed work. It is basically the small surface area that defines the word miniature along with the concomitant adaptation and condensation of ornamentation and design. Arbitrarily we are assigning the term miniature to any lacquered object whose primary surface area is 36 square inches or less as meeting all of the above criteria. A 5"×7" or a 4"×9" object would therefore be considered to be miniature, as would an object measuring 6"×6". Thus the long lacquered pipe cases are to be classified as miniature. In fact, such elongated shapes tax the ingenuity of the lacquer artist in regard to difficulty of design and placement of subject matter far more than does a more symmetrically shaped object. Some of the larger lacquered objects sometimes contain smaller lacquered articles and boxes which fall within the category of miniature lacquer art. Similarly, there were considerable variations in size of some of the larger boxes and articles, so that on occasion a larger form would fall into the classification of miniature. In general the most popular and most frequently signed miniature lacquer art form was the inro. Of equal importance are the *kogo* and the *kobako*, used for storage of incense. These works were used for the highly formal Zen-influenced tea ceremony and reflected the typical quiet, simple, aesthetic taste of their users. They remain as examples of the epitome of subdued Japanese taste. The *natsume*, or tea caddy, used during the summer and the *sakazuki*, or *sake* cup, round out the major and most important examples of miniature lacquer art. There are numerous other objects, such as combs, incense burners, pipe cases, and lacquered netsuke, which are often of considerable interest to collectors of miniature Japanese lacquer art.

The following is a classification of the above lacquered articles, their origin, a brief description, and their uses. It will be seen that all of these objects were basically utilitarian, used either for the incense or the tea ceremony, as various specific storage boxes, or as food and household utensils. However, in typical Japanese fashion, each and every one of these tiny articles, whatever the relatively insignificant role they played, was usually an exquisite work of art. A simple decorative comb was very often lavished with months of work by a lacquer artisan, reflecting as much care and work as a major piece of art. The Japanese even prepared and presented their food in an aesthetic manner, and the food was artistically placed on beautiful lacquered trays and plates so as to be pleasing to the eye. The dishes themselves, along with their beautiful stands, were similarly aesthetically pleasing. Such was the appreciation of beauty of even commonplace everyday articles. We can readily understand, therefore, the extravagance and stress placed on the aesthetic perfection of the lacquered articles found in the more highly developed aristocratic pastimes, such as the tea and incense ceremonies.

Lacquered Objects (Nuri-mono)

Practically every type of object was lacquered, from a tiny netsuke to almost an entire temple. However, most of the decorative lacquered articles of interest to collectors consist of relatively small utilitarian objects (such as inro, fans, and writing boxes), storage boxes (for toilet articles, shells, papers, etc.), eating utensils (bowls, cups, trays), and small household furniture (tables, screens). Within the scope of this book on miniature lacquer art details will be given only in regard to true miniature lacquer forms of artistic significance. The following is a partial list of the articles, their corresponding Japanese names, and their approximate sizes and usual shapes, both of which often varied considerably with each individual object.

UTILITARIAN OBJECTS

1) Clothing was occasionally decorated with lacquer, mother-of-pearl, and metallic foil.

2) Lacquered toilet accessories included brushes, combs, mirror stands,

toilet boxes, and the smaller traveling toilet boxes. Toilet boxes *(te-bako)* were often articles of extreme artistry but not of miniature size. Combs *(sashi-gushi)*, however, were of miniature size. They were cut and shaped by special classes of artisans and were made of tortoise shell *(bekko)*, ivory, wood, or horn. They were often gorgeously lacquered on the surfaces above the teeth, and frequently, in typical Japanese fashion, the design sweeps over the teeth. The best wood basis for the combs was the reddish brown *tsuge* (boxwood) and the tough, fine-grained camellia wood. Japanese women did not wear any jewelry beyond the combs (Fig. 145) and the ornamented hairpins known as *kanzashi*. They did use cosmetics such as *oshiroi*, or face-whitening, and lip rouge. The combs measured about $2'' \times 4'' \times \frac{1}{4}''$. Women spent relatively large sums of money on their cosmetic accessories, and great stress was placed upon the elegance of their coiffures.

3) Fans were in common use by the entire populace. The framework of the folding fan *(ogi)* was often lacquered in fine detail.

4) Medicine boxes (inro) and netsuke have been discussed in great detail elsewhere in this book.

5) Tobacco articles came into vogue after the introduction of tobacco by the Portuguese. They included pipes *(kiseru)*, pipe sheaths *(kiseru-zutsu)*, tobacco boxes *(tonkotsu* or *tabako-ire)*, and tobacco cabinets *(tabako-bon* or *tabako-dansu)*. The Japanese pipe has a tiny bowl and a relatively long, thin stem. It is usually made of metal but occasionally is of lacquered wood. The pipe sheaths are usually more decorative. They consist of two tubes which fit snugly into each other, enclosing the pipe. They are made of carved ivory, horn, metal, or lacquered wood (Fig. 147). The tobacco box was used as an alternative to the tobacco pouch and is usually slightly rectangular in shape with a small lid on top. It is about the size of an inro, being slightly wider and deeper, and is usually made of wood, which is often lacquered. Tobacco boxes differ from inro in that they are not divided into a series of cases but consist merely of one deep case and a lid. The tobacco cabinet measures about $8'' \times 10'' \times 5''$ and has drawers for the tobacco. Its top surface contains a receptacle for ashes *(hibachi)* and hooks for the pipes. Most of the lacquered tobacco articles are of relatively late date (19th century) and are somewhat commercial in taste and design. However, many carved pipe sheaths were executed by well-known netsuke artists and inlaid by expert metal artists, while lacquered pipe sheaths and tobacco boxes were made by such famous lacquer artists as Shibata Zeshin and Koma Kansai (Fig. 146).

6) Of extreme importance to the lacquer collector are the writing sets and implements. These consist essentially of the low writing stand *(bundai)* and the relatively large writing box *(ryoshi-bunko* or *ryoshi-bako)* which often accompanies the true writing box, or *suzuri-bako* (box for the inkstone). The *ryoshi-bunko* is a fairly large deep box used to hold the writing

utensils, papers, and sometimes manuscripts. The *suzuri-bako,* reflecting the importance of calligraphy in the Orient, are often great works of art but do not fall within the province of miniature lacquer art. They are usually squarish or rectangular in shape and comparatively flat, measuring approximately $9'' \times 8'' \times 2''$. They often display extremely minute workmanship and strong overall designs compatible with their relatively large size. The insides of their covers are often more detailed and exquisite in taste and decoration than the outside design. This reverse side of the cover is called the *mikaeshi.* The writing tools include a knife, an awl-like instrument for punching holes through sheaves of paper in order to bind them together in the manner of old-style Japanese books, two brushes, the inkstone, and a small metal receptacle for holding water. The water container *(mizu-ire)* is often done by a well-known metal artist or occasionally decorated with lacquer (Fig. 148). The accessories (knife, brushes, and paper punch) have elongated pencil-shaped handles and are of plain or ornamental lacquer complementing the overall decorative design. Slightly smaller writing boxes, approximately 7 to 8 inches in maximum length, were used by women, including court ladies (Fig. 149). Most of the *suzuri-bako* were not signed, as they were often made for a local daimyo and the signing of such a commissioned article would have been disrespectful and in poor taste. However, they were more frequently signed than the various storage boxes listed below, which were almost never signed.

STORAGE BOXES AND TRAYS

The Japanese have always been particularly fond of various types of highly specialized storage boxes, including those especially made for works of art. Such art objects were usually wrapped in valuable silk brocades (often imported) and enclosed in lacquered boxes, themselves often works of art. Most of these boxes, however, are not of miniature size. They are of innumerable varieties and range from such items as special large boxes for storing Gigaku masks to boxes made in the form of a sleeping dog *(inu-bako)* and used as a charm to insure safe delivery during childbirth. Boxes with drawers *(inro-dansu)* were used for storing inro, *tsuba,* and other accessories. Such boxes, frequently made for the daimyo, were usually decorated with the family crest of the owner. Lacquer trays were also made in considerable variety. Several of the important types of boxes and trays are described below.

1) Lacquered boxes were made to contain the articles used for various games, especially the aesthetic pastimes of the feudal-period aristocracy. These included the *goki,* or box for holding the stones for the game of *go;* the poetry-game *(uta-awase)* box, which is called the *uta-bako* and includes a tray and a lower drawer for the inkstand and inkstone; the shell box *(kai-oke)* used for the gilded or painted shells in the ancient game of *kai-awase,* or shell matching; and a special box to hold the cards for the popular

game of *uta-garuta* (poem cards). These boxes are in general 6 inches or more on a side and therefore do not fall into the classification of miniature lacquer art.

2) Miscellaneous relatively large boxes of significance to the lacquer collector include the letter box (*fubako* or *fumi-bako; fumi*=letter), a long rectangular box (approximately 2–3″×9″×4″) used for carrying letters or messages and tied with heavy silk cords attached to two metal rings; the scroll box *(karabitsu* or *karahitsu),* an oblong four-legged Chinese-style chest made to hold sacred Buddhist scrolls in temples; ceremonial document boxes; needle boxes *(hari-bako);* string boxes *(ito-bako)* to hold the strings used for musical instruments, and the more important oblong sutra boxes used for holding Buddhist sutras.

3) Various trays made of lacquer include scroll trays *(juku-bon),* on which decorative scrolls *(kakemono)* were placed; rectangular or square trays *(midare-bako)* used by servants for placing clothing or other items for their masters' use; and special trays used for eating during the tea and incense ceremonies (Figs. 141, 154).

EATING UTENSILS

Eating utensils were usually made of thin light wood lacquered in black or red. Red lacquer, however, was considered more aristocratic. In 1546 General Takeda Shingen rewarded his bravest warriors by serving them their food in red-lacquered utensils while the others ate from black ones. Bowls and cups were made of woods which were easily turned on the lathe, such as *keyaki* (zelkova) and *sakura* (cherry). Special decorated eating utensils were used for the New Year's celebration. Articles such as picnic boxes and *sake* cups were also highly decorated.

Among the most important of the lacquered eating utensils were the *sake* cups *(sakazuki).* They come singly or in sets of up to 20 cups, accurately fitted together by stacking one within another. They are shaped as moderately shallow round bowls about 4″ in diameter and 1–1½″ high, with short, narrow, round bases called *itodo* (Fig. 150). They were made with an extremely thin wood core, usually *keyaki,* and strengthened with lacquer. The top layer is invariably in red lacquer and is decorated in *hiramakie* or *takamakie* and less often in *togidashi.* The decorative designs are primarily done on the inner surface of the bowls, with secondary ornamentation on the sides and bottoms of the cups, even extending over the round base. The cups were sometimes signed by the lacquer artist. The subject matter was invariably of pleasant connotation, including nature subjects, famous places, sea life, birds, or flowers. Only rarely were there portrayed subjects associated with war. *Sake* is the popular traditional Japanese rice wine, usually drunk warm and used socially at various festivals, weddings, and Shinto religious rituals. *Sake*-drinking games were also favorite Japanese pastimes.

Other eating utensils, although not miniature in size, included the lacquered *sake* pitcher *(choshi)* used to hold *toso* (sweet *sake*) for the New Year's celebration; stands for *sake* bottles and cups; and numerous boxes, bowls, pitchers, and trays of varying sizes. These include such articles as nests of food trays *(jubako)*, usually square-shaped and used with a large tray and large dishes for the New Year's celebration; the meal tray *(zen)*; a tray with legs used at formal dinners *(honzen)*; serving trays *(bon)*, and sweetmeat boxes *(kashiki* or *kashi-bako)*. The last of these were of miniature proportions (3″×4″×5″ or larger) and held cakes or sweetmeats (Fig. 151). When made in sets of two or three, they included a cover and were called *ju-kashi-bako*. The picnic or lunch box *(bento-bako)* is also quite well known. It is actually a small cabinet, approximately 12″×14″×6″ which holds boxes, trays, *sake* cups, and a *sake* bottle. Most of these boxes date from the 19th or 20th century and are occasionally made by well-known lacquer artists.

HOUSEHOLD FURNITURE AND ACCESSORIES

The traditional Japanese house was practically devoid of furniture. Household articles were stored in closets. Since sitting, eating, and sleeping were done on the *tatami* floor mats, there was no need for chairs, couches, or beds, and only low dining tables were used. There were, however, some utilitarian objects in the Japanese house, and these were frequently decorated with beautiful designs executed in lacquer. Most of these articles, except for a small cabinet *(kodansu)*, do not come under the heading of miniature lacquer and therefore will be mentioned only briefly to give an idea of the important role played by lacquered articles in the typical Japanese household.

There were various-sized lacquer cabinets like the *tana,* with its short legs and both open and closed shelves; the *keshodai,* or cosmetic cabinet; and the *tansu,* a chest with numerous drawers. A smaller version of the *tansu* is known as the *kodansu,* a miniature form of which is one of the traditional accessories of the Girls' Festival, or Hina Matsuri (Fig. 140). Many of the larger lacquered boxes and stands had beautiful carved metal fittings of silver and gold. Miscellaneous lacquered furniture included the *kendai,* or slanted stand for holding books or mirrors; the nonfolding decorative screen, or *tsuitate;* the *bundai* or *kadai,* which is a low table used for writing or for holding various objects; the container or stand for the *hibachi* (charcoal brazier), which is occasionally lacquered or decorated with inlaid mother-of-pearl, and such articles as hanging flower vases *(tsuri-bana-ike)* and flower stands *(kadai)*. Other lacquered articles included the sword rack *(katana-kake)*, which is an open rack on which several swords were placed horizontally at different levels, and beautifully decorated horse trappings *(bagu)*.

Still other lacquered pieces included the sword sheath *(saya)* made of *hinoki* (cypress) wood, with the handle covered with sharkskin, and the large *norimono,* or enclosed, highly decorated portable chair used to carry the daimyo. There is also the *zushi,* a miniature portable shrine made of wood, carved on the inside and often simply decorated with lacquer on the outside (Fig. 152). It was frequently made of sandalwood. On the inside of the *zushi* is carved a god in low relief which is often highlighted with gold dusting. There were even fanciful lacquered cages for holding such insects as fireflies and crickets.

OBJECTS FOR THE TEA CEREMONY

The tea ceremony, which played such an important role in the aesthetic thinking of the aristocracy of feudal Japan, gave great impetus to the development of pottery and lacquered utensils employed in its performance. A similar impetus arose from the incense ceremony, which will be discussed in the next section.

The tea ceremony *(cha-no-yu)* is thought to have originated in Japan in the 9th century, although it did not become important until the 13th century. It was practiced originally by Zen priests without any particular ritual. Later, in the 13th century, it was used by the priest Eisai as a religious ceremony in association with ancestor worship. It soon developed into an aesthetic cult and was advanced by the shogun Ashikaga Yoshimasa and the military dictators Nobunaga and Hideyoshi. During the rule of Hideyoshi the famous tea master Sen no Rikyu reorganized the rules associated with the ceremony, and out of these the following basic formalized order of performance evolved.

Briefly, the tea ceremony may be divided into three parts. 1) The invited guests enter the garden pavilion for quiet contemplation of nature and then enter the house. They admire the objects in the *tokonoma:* the specially prepared flower arrangement and the *kakemono.* The host then starts the fire and sprinkles incense on it to mask its odor. The guests each in turn admire the incense box, and then they return to the garden. 2) The guests return to the house, eat, and discuss philosophical problems, after which they again return to the garden while the host cleans up, hangs up a new *kakemono,* and changes the flowers. 3) The guests return to the house, and the host brings in all the tea utensils, which are examined and admired for their artistic values. The host then makes a thick tea especially prepared from a powder. During the tea serving the master comments upon the age and artistic qualities of the ceremonial articles. There is even a special lacquered document tray which holds the authentication papers and a description of the valuable utensils used for the ceremony (Fig. 141).

The entire tea ceremony reflects the simplicity and the meditative, cultural, and aesthetic values of the Zen religion along with the quiet beauty of nature, which is reflected in the simple evergreen garden. It was only natural that these principles of austerity, simplicity, and unpretentiousness associated with the tea ceremony be reflected in the associated art forms. Stress was placed on actual crudity and defects (these articles were appropriately called *sabi-mono*, or rusty things), especially in the crude rough-textured pottery, exaggerated almost to a fault. However, this trend when applied to lacquer ware luckily resulted in magnificent simplicity and effectiveness of design along with subdued color effects and the development of rich deep black lacquer. There were slight differences between the winter and summer tea ceremonies. In the winter the incense used was in tablet form *(neriko)*, and the incense box was of earthenware or porcelain. In the summer the incense in its natural form was used and was kept in lacquered or carved wooden boxes known as *kogo* and *kobako*. The tea caddy in the winter was made of pottery *(cha-ire)*, but in the summer the lacquered *natsume* was used. The *natsume*, the *kogo*, and the *kobako* comprise three of the best-quality miniature lacquered art forms along with the inro and the *sake* cup. The following are the lacquered articles used in the tea ceremony: the *cha-dansu*, a lacquered cabinet, occasionally miniature in size, used for holding the tea utensils, including the counters, scoreboard, trays, tea caddy, tea bowl *(chawan)*, and whisk *(chasen)*. Such cabinets were used for drawing lots for order of precedence in connection with the tea and incense ceremonies, flower arrangement parties, and the like. The *satsu-bako* is a box with a tray for holding the tea-ceremony utensils. It usually measures about 5″×7″×4″. There are also lacquered bowls (3″×4″) and lacquered stands (4″×6″) for the bowls *(chawan)* used in the tea ceremony, as well as sets of sweetmeat trays (Fig. 154). Of greater significance is the *natsume*, or tea caddy. Its shape was allegedly adopted by a maker of tea-ceremony utensils, Haneda Goro, during the second half of the 15th century. It is approximately cylindrical, being on the average 3″ high and 2½″ in diameter, with the bottom slightly more rounded than the top cover and tapering slightly toward the bottom (Fig. 153). It is made of *kiri (Paulownia imperialis)*, a light, odorless wood, and is usually unsigned. It is similar in shape to the Japanese date, which is also called *natsume* and is an elliptical olive-sized stone fruit *(Zizyphus vulgaris)*. Figure 154 represents one cake plate of a set of five made by Shibata Zeshin for use in the tea ceremony.

OBJECTS FOR THE INCENSE CEREMONY

Before discussing the different types of lacquered accessories used in burning incense, a brief outline of the types, uses, and significance of incense is of considerable importance. The burning of incense *(kodo)* in Japan is widespread for both religious and secular purposes. It was originally introduced into China from India during the later Han period. Incense was first introduced into Japan from Korea in A.D. 551 for Buddhist religious purposes, its burning symbolizing the purifying effect of flame. It is used in ceremonies for the dead to protect the departed soul from evil spirits and is also employed against evil powers responsible for diseases. Incense bags were hung up to drive away evil spirits and even as a protection against lightning. Incense played an important part in Buddhist rites but was not used in the Shinto religion. In the Buddhist religion incense was used to please the gods by wafting one's prayers via the incense smoke, and at Buddhist rituals it was used as an ointment of purification on the hands of the priest and in powder form was sprinkled about the room. Incense is burned before large shrines, tiny home shrines, wayside idols, and graves. Special incense was even used to conjure up visions of departed souls (*hangon-ko*=spirit-recalling incense). Besides being used for religious and superstitious reasons it was used purely for secular reasons for its aromatic qualities, as well as in the tea and incense ceremonies for its mind-calming qualities. It was used to render a pleasant aroma to the home and even steamed to give fragrance to clothing or to scent the warrior's helmet.

By the 7th century, 24 varieties of incense were known, and later Yoshi-masa noted 130 different varieties, which were soon expanded to 200. The various Japanese incenses are usually vegetable forms (leaves, berries, roots, seeds, resins, and gums) and specifically include aloes, cloves, sandalwood, spikenard, musk, camphor, olibanum, cinnamon, and laurel. Occasionally materials such as amber were used. Ten different schools of the art of mixing incense developed, and various incense compounds included ten or more ingredients. There were also many expensive imported varieties. Incense was made in various forms but not in the liquid perfume with which the Western world is familiar. The least expensive form is the *senko,* or "joss-sticks," which are solid pencil-shaped sticks 8″–9″ long. These are lit directly from a flame and burn rather slowly (for about 40 minutes). Other more expensive varieties consist of wood spicules of varying sizes, coarse sawdust, or pills and are burned with charcoal in special small braziers *(koro)* which are placed on wooden or lacquered stands and often form part of the display in the *tokonoma*. The small tablets and the powders were kept in special paper folders and they in turn in special beautifully lacquered boxes *(kogo* and *kobako)*.

Of considerable importance in the development of an interest in incense and its accompanying utensils was an aristocratic game called *ko-awase,* or incense matching. The game essentially consists of the ability to guess the names of incenses by their aroma given off while burning. There are many specific rules and variations to this game which include a thorough knowledge of Japanese literature and poetry. For example, the incense used was of the powdered or pastille variety. Sometimes the incenses used were mixed or compounded. The incenses had such fanciful names as plum, pine, snow, and moon or were also given names alluding to the seasons, such as maple leaf (autumn) or first snow, or names suggesting love, such as "sweet face," or were named after famous places. This game in its simplest form was called "10 varieties of incense" *(jisshu-ko)* and consisted of separating each of three different incenses into four packs along with a single pack of the incense which was brought by the guests and was known only as "guest incense." This then made 13 packs. One pack of each of the three incenses was named in turn by the host and then burned, except for the guest incense, which was not burned. There now remained 10 packs for the beginning of the game. Each pack was now burned in no given order and without being named, and the person who was able to correctly name the greatest number of scents won the game. Variations of the game consisted in burning compound incenses as well, making recognition even more difficult. Since the windows and doors were all closed tightly at the beginning of the game, the game became progressively more difficult because of the mixture of scents in the room. Another popular variation was naming the incense by means of erudite allusions to the name of the perfume through a literary phrase or part of a poem, or of spontaneously composing a poem as a means of identifying the burning incense. The most applicable and aesthetic answer won the game. Great stress was placed on esotericism and reconditeness. While this aristocratic game has completely gone out of fashion since the Meiji period, it has still left us with the beautiful lacquer, metal, and porcelain accessories used in the game. These accessories are kept in the *kodana,* or small cabinet housing all the equipment for the incense ceremony and often a writing box as well. This equipment includes the *jisshu kobako,* a box containing the following paraphernalia: counters, marking boards, a book, a measure, a brazier *(koro),* incense boxes *(kogo),* bags of incense, scrapers, knives, feather brush, ruler, scoops, pincers, mallet and chisel, silver stand to hold these utensils, a cylindrical lacquered box to hold the written guesses *(fudazutsu),* and an incense tray *(kobon).* Such complete sets are extremely rare.

Of interest to the art of miniature lacquer were the *hitori koro,* or box for hot charcoal, and especially the *kogo* and *kobako.* The *hitori koro* is a squat, flat-bottomed miniature form, usually of bronze or pottery but occasionally lacquered and lined with silver or copper. It has a decorative cover of open metalwork (Fig. 155). A piece of charcoal is taken from the *hitori koro* and placed in a celadon *koro.* Then a piece of talc *(gin-yo)* is heated in the charcoal in the celadon *koro,* and finally the incense is put on the talc in order to burn more slowly.

The *kogo,* or incense box, was made as early as the emperor Konoe's reign (1142–55), when a decree was issued regulating the amounts of materials to be used for a box of certain size. Early *kogo* were of simple cylindrical shape with pewter or silver rims, and only later did more ornate forms and ornamentation appear. Incense boxes all fall into the sphere of miniature lacquer art, and they exhibit the height of the lacquerer's art to perfection. Occasionally they are made of pottery and more rarely of metal (Figs. 156, 157). In the main they are tiny objects of utmost perfection.

They are basically flat shaped, with a cover, the inside of the cover often having an even more beautifully ornamented design than the outside. They are done in flat or raised lacquer or in *togidashi,* or in flat or raised encrustations (Fig. 142), or in carved lacquer (Fig. 74). The slightly deeper ones contain two to four perfectly fitting smaller boxes with matched lacquer designs (Fig. 158). There is often a circular hole in the bottom of the larger box to facilitate removal of the snugly fitting enclosed smaller inner boxes. Occasionally there is enclosed also a small perfectly fitting beautifully decorated shallow tray (Fig. 159). Single boxes are usually under 1″ deep and tend to be round or square, but many other fanciful forms exist, including quatrefoil, diamond-shaped, fan-shaped, shell-shaped, etc. The slightly larger boxes which contain the smaller sets of boxes have more leeway for odd shapes, including double or single fan shapes, four-lobed, birdcage-shaped, etc. In general, these incense boxes are not signed but were executed through the ages by the best of lacquer artists, reflecting the taste of the aristocracy for whom they were made. Relatively few over-ornate, gaudy, or commercial ones are to be found—in comparison, for example, with inro, for which the use was more plebeian and widespread. The following is a classification of the incense containers:

1) Sets of boxes for containing incense

a) *kojubako.* About $2\frac{1}{2}″ \times 4″ \times 2\frac{1}{2}″$. Usually contains two to four smaller boxes and has a cover and occasionally a tray (Figs. 158, 160).

b) *jukogo.* Similar to the above but made in three divisions, the upper for talc squares, the middle for the incense, and the lower box lined with metal to hold the ashes. Occasionally also encloses a tray.

2) Single boxes for incense

a) *kogo.* Very shallow box, less than 1″ high, with a cover about equal in depth to the lower part. Approximately $\frac{1}{2}″ \times 2\frac{1}{2}″ \times 2″$ to 3″ in diameter (Figs. 29, 74, 130, 142, 169, 205).

b) *kobako.* Differs from the above in that it is deeper and larger and more flexible in its dimensions, which are usually about $3″ \times 4″ \times 3″$. There is no sharp dividing line separating the *kogo* from the *kobako.*

c) *kyara-bako.* Similar type of miniature box containing scented woods for burning as incense. The pieces of wood are larger than the pellets and powders, which are kept in stiff jeweled paper containers.

d) *tsutsu.* Lacquered or carved wooden tubes to hold the incense sticks *(senko).* In general, these tend to be less elaborate.

Finally, any discussion of lacquered articles would be incomplete without mentioning the beautiful lacquered paintings of the renowned artist Shibata Zeshin. While he occasionally painted larger *kakemono* with lacquer, he is justly best remembered for this technique in his whimsical miniature lacquer sketches of nature, which were usually mounted into book form (Fig. 123).

130. Kogo. Flower clusters. Unsigned. The outside cover shows a few gold and silver flowers artistically dispersed over an incised geometric pattern on a gold ground. 3"×3"×1".

131. Inside of lid of kogo in Fig. 130, showing an intricate colorful design of bright-orange plum blossoms in togidashi on a roiro ground. Note that the design typically flows over the sides of the box.

132. INRO. Iris and fireflies. Unsigned. Attributed to Shunsho. Design in togidashi on a dark-brown ground, showing two fireflies hovering over an iris flower by a stream. $3\frac{7}{8}'' \times 2\frac{1}{16}'' \times 1\frac{1}{4}''$. 4 cases and lid.

133. DETAIL of inro in Fig. 132, showing firefly.

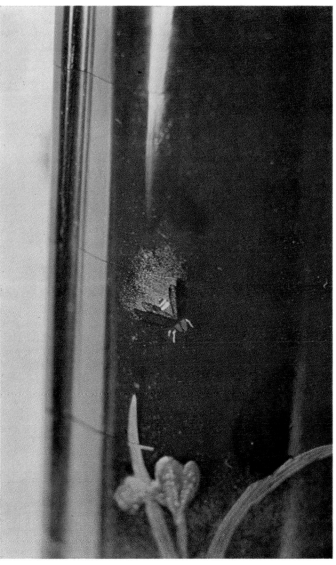

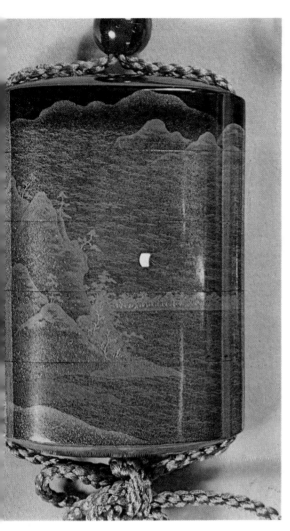

134. INRO. Pine grove of Miho. Signed: Shiomi Masanari. Seascape in gold togidashi on a roiro ground. $3\frac{3}{8}'' \times 2\frac{3}{8}'' \times \frac{7}{8}''$. 4 cases and lid. (See Fig. 118 for detail.)

135. INRO. Pine saplings. Unsigned. Attributed to Ritsuo. Note the beautiful coarse-textured brown ground simulating Raku pottery. $2\frac{1}{8}'' \times 1\frac{7}{8}'' \times \frac{11}{16}''$. 1 case and lid.

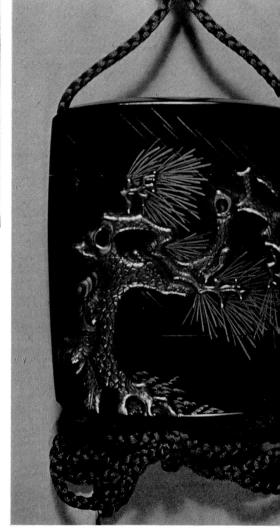

136. INRO. Pine tree and lespedeza branches. Signed: Koma Kyu-haku. The entire design is in reddish-gold togidashi on a roiro ground. Note the typical shape of the Koma-school inro. $3\frac{7}{8}''\times 2\frac{3}{8}''\times\frac{3}{4}''$. 4 cases and lid. (See Fig. 224 for opposite side.)

137. INRO. Pine tree in rainstorm. Unsigned. $3\frac{5}{16}''\times 2\frac{3}{4}''\times 1''$. 3 cases and lid.

138. INRO. Old pine tree. Unsigned. Somada school. $4\frac{1}{4}'' \times 2\frac{1}{4}'' \times 1\frac{3}{8}''$. 4 cases and lid. (See Figs. 80 and 83 for opposite side and detail.)

139. INRO. Pine tree. Signed: Kajikawa Bunryusai. An example of the oki-hirame technique of encrusted gold flakes. $3\frac{1}{4}'' \times 2\frac{1}{4}'' \times \frac{3}{4}''$. 4 cases and lid.

140. KODANSU. Peony design with butterfly. Unsigned. Old-style Somada work. The butterfly, leaves, and flowers are done in aogai and colored togidashi, the clouds in mura nashiji on a black ground. The scenes on the various sides of the kodansu are augmented by irregular patches of inlaid flat tiny pieces of gold and aogai in a geometric design. The inside of the door is done in fine nashiji. $3\frac{3}{4}'' \times 3\frac{3}{8}'' \times 4\frac{7}{8}''$. Three drawers, with a tray in the top drawer.

141. DOCUMENT TRAY. Moon and rabbit. Signed: Shibata Zeshin. The moon is executed in matte light gray, the rabbit in coarsely textured dark gray, and the ground in simulated teakwood in a reddish-brown color. $7\frac{1}{8}'' \times 4\frac{7}{8}'' \times \frac{5}{16}''$.

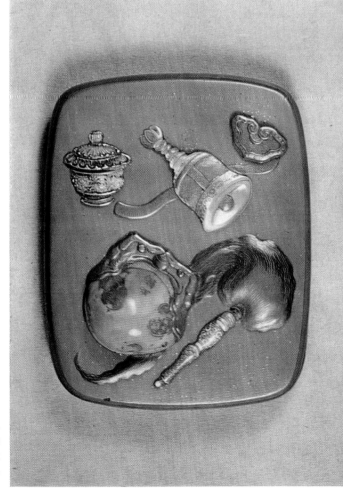

142. KOGO. Buddhist emblems. Signed: Gyokurin. Koma school, about 1800. A flat, rectangular-shaped kogo in gold fundame upon which are high encrustations of various materials depicting Buddhist emblems, including a hand bell, jui, mokugyo, and hossu. The rims are in silver covered with gold. $3\frac{1}{4}'' \times 2\frac{3}{4}'' \times \frac{1}{2}''$.

143. Kogo. Chrysanthemums. Signed: Shirayama Shosai. The design of stylized chrysanthemums is done in minutely inlaid silver and gold kirigane and red and gold lacquer on a gold fundame ground. Diameter: $3\frac{1}{16}$″; height: 1″.

144. Netsuke. Lobster. Signed: Toyo. Hako manju netsuke in lacquer. Lobster in rough red takamakie on a gold ground. $1\frac{1}{4}$″ high.

145. KOGAI (hair ornament) and matching sashi-gushi (ornamental comb). Flowers and insects. Signed: Masamitsu. The design of butterflies, dragonflies, and flowers is done in silver, gold, and aogai on a gray ground over tortoise shell. Kogai: 6″ long and $\frac{3}{8}$″ at widest diameter. Sashi-gushi: $3\frac{13}{16}$″ × $1\frac{1}{2}$″ × $\frac{3}{16}$″.

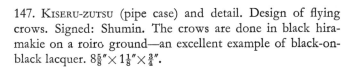

146. TABAKO-IRE. Design of rabbit and grasses. Signed: Zeshin. Typical Zeshin style in subject matter, design, and background. The rabbit is simply executed in roiro, the grasses and rocks in a rough black ground. A few twigs are finely incised, and the background is done in a semipolished tea-green color. Plain wooden lid. $2\frac{3}{4}$″ × $3\frac{1}{2}$″ × $1\frac{1}{16}$″. 1 case and lid.

147. KISERU-ZUTSU (pipe case) and detail. Design of flying crows. Signed: Shumin. The crows are done in black hira-makie on a roiro ground—an excellent example of black-on-black lacquer. $8\frac{5}{8}$″ × $1\frac{1}{8}$″ × $\frac{3}{4}$″.

148. DETAIL of suzuri-bako, showing mizu-ire. Sleeping cat. Unsigned. The cat is done in black and gold lacquer with a gyobu ground. The water container itself is in silver. Mizu-ire: $1'' \times 1\frac{3}{8}'' \times \frac{1}{2}''$.

149. SUZURI-BAKO. Sacred Bridge at Nikko. Unsigned. Attributed to Ogawa Shomin. Part of the bridge is in encrusted heavy gold foil. The stones in the river are in raised aogai and nuggets of solid gold and shakudo. The cypress, pine, maple, and oak trees are in hiramakie and takamakie. In order to give a misty effect, the distant mountains are purposely done in tones of gold togidashi. The ground is black, with fine yasuriko filings, and the rims of the box are in silver. $6\frac{13}{16}'' \times 6\frac{1}{8}'' \times 1\frac{1}{2}''$.

150. SAKAZUKI. Falcon. Unsigned. Two views of a *sake* cup, illustrating its typical shape. The design of the falcon is in low gold takamakie with aogai ornamentation on a red ground. Widest diameter: 5″.

151. KASHI-BAKO. Scene at Shono (one of the fifty-three stations on the Tokaido). Unsigned. The entire scene is done in togidashi. The farmers and their umbrellas are in red, gold, and black, while the distant mountains are depicted in shades of black against a silver background. The heart-shaped design is outlined by narrow strips of aogai, and the ground of the rest of the box is in hirame nashiji on a black ground. Diameter: $5\frac{3}{8}$″; height: $2\frac{5}{16}$″.

152. ZUSHI. Unsigned. The outside of the lid shows a design of lotus petals in gold and silver on a black ground. Inside is a carved wooden Buddha on a lotus throne. Diameter: 2⅝″; height: 1″.

153. NATSUME. Design of tsukushi (horse-tail grass). Korin style. Late 18th century. The tsukushi is in gold and black lacquer and colorful inlaid mother-of-pearl on a gold fundame ground. Diameter: 2⅝″; height: 2¹³⁄₁₆″.

154. SWEETMEAT TRAY. Mount Fuji. Signed: Zeshin. One of a set of five trays. The top of the mountain is in silver hiramakie, and the bottom is a rough, flat black-textured lacquer. The ground is dark brown. $4\frac{7}{8}'' \times 6\frac{1}{2}''$.

155. HITORI KORO. Moon and reeds. Unsigned. Silver and gold hiramakie on a black ground. Cover in silver openwork. Diameter: $3''$; height: $3\frac{3}{4}''$.

156. METAL KOGO. Pine trees and clouds. Signed: Shoami Katsuyoshi. Impressionistic pine trees in shakudo and clouds in gold flecks simulating lacquer nashiji. Shibuichi ground. Such an almost oversimplified design is more likely to be found on metalwork than in the more pictorial lacquer arts. Diameter: $3\frac{1}{16}''$; height: $1\frac{3}{16}''$. (See also Fig. 157.)

157. INSIDE OF LID of kogo in Fig. 156. Flying birds executed in shakudo. The clouds simulate nashiji, as on the cover. Shibuichi ground.

158. INSIDE OF IVORY KOJUBAKO of Fig. 82, revealing three small boxes with overall matching zigzag design. The flowers are done in tiny pieces of gold and aogai on a yasuriko ground. The geometric-patterned half of the design consists of gold kirigane.

159. KOBAKO. Autumn flowers and grasses. Unsigned. Early 19th century. Fan shape. Cover design in togidashi, hiramakie, takamakie, and gold oki-hirame on a black ground. The tray has a design of butterflies on a gold ground. Radius: $1\frac{5}{8}''$; length: $4''$; height: $1\frac{5}{16}''$.

160. KoJUBAKO (closed and open).
Daikoku and rats. Unsigned. Somada school. Design of Daikoku, rice
bale filled with sacred jewels, and rats
in aogai and silver and gold foil. The
kojubako contains seven separate
round boxes, each decorated in Somada style with a different Buddhist
symbol. The entire box has a roiro
ground. Diameter: 4″; height: $1\frac{1}{16}$″.

5 · The Netsuke as an Art Form

THE COMPANION OF THE INRO, THE NETSUKE, REPRESENTS A fascinating, unique phase of Japanese art and craftsmanship. In general the netsuke is made of wood, ivory, or lacquer, measures $1''$–$2\frac{1}{2}''$, and is usually in the form of a miniature three-dimensional carved figure or sometimes that of a flattened glyptic button or box. Since the Japanese kimono had no pockets, all portable objects were held suspended from the sash by means of this small toggle. Hence the derivation of the word netsuke (the "u" is silent), which means literally root *(ne),* and attached or hung *(tsuke).* The netsuke, which started as a crude piece of wood or shell, was eventually transformed into a fully developed aesthetic and highly sculptured art form perpetuated by specialized craftsmen, the *netsuke-shi.* Thus what was originally a crude utilitarian object, in typical Japanese fashion ultimately became a highly decorative ornamental object. Since the netsuke was universally worn by all classes of people during the era in Japanese history when Japan was virtually isolated from all foreign influences, it developed in an unfettered manner representative of the indigenous tastes and values of a complete cross section of the Japanese populace. Different techniques of carving, involving varied materials combined with an endless range of subject matter, gave the netsuke artist free rein to express his aesthetic and technical skills. The early netsuke carver of the 18th century was often primarily a lacquer, metal, or Buddhist-image artist, who made netsuke as a hobby or side job. By the early 19th century, because of the increasing demand for netsuke, the true netsuke artist evolved, stressing basically the three-dimensional sculptural figure form. Further specialization developed, so that an artist or school often used not only a certain technique of carving but also special materials and subject matter. Thus Bunshojo, a female netsuke artist (1764–1839) specialized in carving spiders in wild-boar tusk and Asahi Gyokuzan (1843–1923) was well known for his skulls carved in ivory.

From the foregoing it can be surmised that the netsuke, so indigenous to Japan, truly represents the aesthetic values, the customs, and mores, as well as the religious and symbolic thinking of the various strata of the Japanese populace.

History of the Netsuke

As we have noted, the netsuke is basically indigenous to Japan, its only counterpart elsewhere being the metal Hungarian netsuke. Similarly, while early Japanese netsuke were often Chinese in origin, they were actually small Chinese objects that were converted into netsuke form by making two holes in them.

The netsuke was used not only in conjunction with the inro but also to carry many types of small suspended objects called *sagemono*. In its earliest form (15th century) it was probably used for suspending keys and consisted of a simple toggle, such as a shell or a piece of wood. By the end of the 16th century, a gourd *(hyotan)* was used as a netsuke. The use of ivory seals *(to-bori),* an old Chinese custom, came into vogue, and by the outset of the Tokugawa period (1615) all legal papers had to bear the seal of the head of the family. Thus the seal netsuke *(ingyo)* developed. This at first consisted of Chinese imports which were converted into netsuke by making holes in them for the cord. Other small Chinese objects were also imported for use as netsuke. The *manju* (button netsuke), made of wood, probably preceded the true figure netsuke, which was not developed until early in the 17th century. By the end of the 17th century, the netsuke had evolved into its true sculptural form and was used with the purse *(kinchaku)* and the inro. With the advent of the inro the lacquer artists made lacquered netsuke in *manju* shape, the first being attributed to Hon'ami Koetsu (1558–1637). While the inro was originally used as a seal box to carry the red paste *(inniku),* its use soon became more widespread for carrying patent medicines. Since the Japanese kimono had no pockets, all the *sagemono* were carried by means of netsuke and by various classes of people. This created a greater demand for netsuke than for the inro itself, which was used primarily by the nobility and the samurai. Among the various *sagemono* were the portable writing kit *(yatate)* with its brush *(fude)* and ink *(sumi),* the flint-and-tinder box *(hiuchi-bukuro),* the gourd-shaped perfume flask *(nioibin),* lunch bags, amulet cases, cosmetic boxes, snuff bottles, and water bottles, as well as objects related to the occupation of the wearer. A carved piece of so-called unicorn horn (part of a whale jaw) was popularly used as a netsuke, as it was thought to have medical qualities, and scrapings from it were swallowed to allay fever.

Netsuke may be divided artistically and historically into three periods, the early, middle, and modern. However, this division is purely arbitrary. Basically the earliest period consists of the development of the netsuke into its true sculptural figure form from its inception. This extends approximately from the 15th century to 1764. The second period consists of the golden age of netsuke, with its evolution as an independent, unique art form developed by netsuke artists and their schools. The third period extends until the Meiji era (1868–1912), and marks its extreme popularization and beginning commercialization. We might add a fourth period extending from 1868 until the present time, when netsuke are being made basically for commercial purposes as small *okimono,* since the change in dress to Western style obviated their use as a utilitarian object. *Okimono* are basically nonutilitarian sculptured objects of art and were made expressly for the Western market after the Meiji era. They are usually of various-sized realistically carved ivory or wood figures.

EARLY PERIOD

The earliest figure netsuke probably originated in Kyoto and were simple, crudely cut, quite elongated, and rarely signed. They represented conventionalized subjects and both legendary and historical figures as well as foreigners, such as Koreans, Hollanders, and Chinese. The first netsuke sculptor about whom we have any significant information was Nonoguchi Ryuho (1595–1669). He specialized in *hina ningyo* (*hina* dolls). As mentioned, lacquer artists during this period, including Hon'ami Koetsu and Kajikawa Kyujiro, also made netsuke. In the early stage of netsuke development, during the 17th century, netsuke were made as a side job by architectural sculptors, shrine and Buddhist image carvers, metalworkers, *ramma* (openwork panel) carvers, mask makers, wooden doll carvers, makers of musical instruments, joiners, dentists, and, as previously mentioned, lacquer and inro artists. They were also made as an artistic pastime (along with the other arts, such as painting and composing poetry) by noblemen and samurai.

In the early 17th century, the Japanese musical instrument, the *samisen,* became popular. The plectrum *(bachi)* was made of ivory, and triangular remnants of the tusk were used for making netsuke, although this material was usually of inferior quality. However, ivory was not commonly used until the late 18th century, at which time it started to be imported from India by way of China and Korea. The first well-known carver in ivory was Ogasawara Issai (late 18th century). The sculptors of Buddhist images, who used mainly wood, similarly carved netsuke in wood. The Nara doll carvers also carved wooden netsuke which they brightly colored. They often used a faceted type of carving called *itto-bori.* The carvers of Noh masks developed the miniature mask netsuke. The earliest mask netsuke were attributed to either Deme Eiman (died 1705) or Akamasa or Akamatsu. This famous Deme school of mask carvers flourished during the last part of the 17th century, the most famous being Deme Uman (Sukemitsu), who worked for the shogun in Edo, and Deme Joman (Takamitsu). Both carved mask netsuke solely in wood. Their works are usually signed.

Metalworkers chiseled the metal disks for the buttonlike netsuke called *kagamibuta*. This type probably preceded the figure netsuke. Yokoya Somin (1669–1733), a metal carver of Edo, engraved *kagamibuta* during this era. The end of this era included such famous artists as the lacquerer and painter Ogata Korin (1658–1716) and the lacquerer and ceramist Ogawa Ritsuo (1663–1747), both of whom occasionally made netsuke.

MIDDLE PERIOD

The second period of netsuke carving (1764–1868) saw the development of the netsuke into its true miniature sculptured figure form. The beginning of this period was dominated by Yoshimura Shuzan (Mitsuoki), who received the title of *hogen*. He carved in *saishiki* technique (*hinoki* wood figures decorated with water colors), using a powerful, expressive, and yet simple realistic style. His works are all unsigned and are recognizable only by his individual style (Fig. 170). The transition between crude carving of stereotyped subject matter, such as Buddhist gods and mythological animals, now gave way to a wider range of subject matter to include Chinese and Japanese historical figures and quadruped animals. However, it was not until the advent of tobacco, introduced by the Portuguese at the end of the 16th century, that the netsuke ultimately found its greatest and most universal use. During the succeeding two centuries, the netsuke was used to suspend the tobacco pouch and pipe case. Usually the inro was worn over the right hip and the tobacco articles were suspended over the left hip. With the popularization of the netsuke in the 18th century there developed a separate class of netsuke artisans (*netsuke-shi*) who in the main worked commercially for money rather than being subsidized by local daimyo, the court or the shogunate. As in the case of other Japanese art forms, netsuke schools and families were founded during the 18th century. There thereby developed four main centers of netsuke carving: Osaka, Kyoto, Edo (Tokyo), and Nagoya; also, to a lesser extent, netsuke were made in the provinces. Yoshimura Shuzan was the founder of the Osaka school. Hogen Hara Shugetsu worked in Osaka and Edo in the mid-18th century. The most famous artists in Kyoto during the 18th century were Masanao, who carved animals, especially in ivory, and Tomotada (Izumiya Shichiemon), an independent carver of Kyoto who also carved animals in wood and ivory and who was famous for his recumbent oxen. The most famous 18th-century netsuke carver of Edo was Miwa I (Hiromori Yukan). He carved in uncolored cherry wood *(sakura)*. He never carved ivory netsuke, but he was the first artist to reinforce the cord holes with dyed ivory (light green) or horn. His works were original, powerful, expressive, and yet simple (Fig. 171). The Deme netsuke mask school also worked in Edo from the 17th century to the late 19th century, among the most famous being Deme Uman and Deme Joman of the 18th century (Fig. 172). It might be mentioned that Hogen Shugetsu was responsible for many Edo schools of netsuke carving. The Shibayama school of inlaid lacquer work (including netsuke) was also founded in Edo by Shibayama I late in the 18th century. Finally the well-known *kagamibuta* metal school was established in Edo by Yokoya Somin in the late 17th century. The most famous 18th-century Nagoya artist was Tametaka (Kiemon Kita), who originated *uki-bori,* or relief carving, which consists essentially in carving out the designs of clothing, etc., in slight relief (Fig. 173). From the provinces rose other outstanding artists, among whom were Tanaka Minko (1735–1816), originally a Buddhist-image carver. He carved in wood, used metal for the eyes of animals, and used clever contrivances, such as moving parts in his netsuke figures. His works were bold and lifelike (Fig. 174). No less famous was Ogasawara Issai from Wakayama, who carved in ivory and whale tooth. His works were executed in minute detail (Fig. 175). Toyomasa (1773–1856), a seal carver from Tamba, made original minutely carved wooden netsuke with inlaid eyes of translucent horn (Fig. 176). Finally there was Shimizu Tomiharu (1733–1810) of Iwami, who carved animals and insects using mainly ebony wood and wild-boar tusk (Fig. 177).

LATE PERIOD

In general the great netsuke artists of the late 18th century and early 19th century carved their subjects relatively "crudely"; they expressed strength and originality with a minimum of detail. By the end of the 19th century artistic feeling had given way to flashy craftsmanship and minuteness of detail. Realism became more photographic than expressive of the artist's concept of his subject matter.

As mentioned, with the advent of smoking the netsuke came into great demand mainly by the lower classes and the merchant class, since the samurai were forbidden to smoke in public. The netsuke, because of its widespread use, became much more commonplace than the inro, and consequently both the subject matter and the style of carving were made to express the plebeian taste of its users. This explains why the netsuke artist was not considered to be on as high a plane as the Japanese painters, lacquerers, or metalworkers. Nevertheless, some netsuke artists did, as in the other arts, obtain honorary titles, such as *hogen,* and a few were commissioned by feudal lords and the imperial house. With the total popularization of the netsuke, along with other Japanese arts, such as the woodblock print, the subject matter became correspondingly varied. Since there were no restrictions imposed by the taste of patrons, conventionalism gave way to complete artistic liberty both in form and in expression as well as in subject matter. Besides historical and mythological subjects, all forms of nature were depicted, including animal, insect, and plant life. Mythological and historical figures gave way to subjects of everyday Japanese living, not usually seen in the lacquer arts. Often subtle or broad humor, occasionally with decided erotic overtones, was reflected in animal and human portrayal. Special netsuke forms were made for use as ashtrays, telescopes, sundials, and even abacuses. The demand for art by the newly rich merchant class resulted in increased lavishness and detail in netsuke and inro. Shibayama-style lacquer netsuke and netsuke figures with more and more detailed carving and inlaid work flourished. While this resulted in increasingly fine technical perfection, it simultaneously caused a debasement of the strong, simple, sculptural qualities of earlier carvings. The rounded feel of the original practical, utilitarian netsuke gave way to a visually ornate miniature type of *okimono* (Fig. 178). By the end of the 19th century, the great demand for netsuke by the lower classes, coupled with increased export demand as "trinkets," resulted in the mass-production of a tremendous number of cheap, poorly carved, and poorly stained commercial products including lathe-turned *manju*. The final blows to the art of netsuke carving were the introduction of Western dress, the abandonment of the inro, the abolishment of the samurai class, and the replacement of the pipe and the tobacco pouch by the cigarette. The metal artists, who were virtually without jobs after the wearing of swords was officially forbidden, turned to mass-production of *kagamibuta* netsuke. The use of the netsuke as a utilitarian object ceased. Yet a few excellent netsuke artists continued to practice their profession, and a few are still working to this very day. However, the main barrier is economic. During the 18th century and in the early 19th century netsuke were often carved as an artistic hobby or side job, or they were made at the request of the feudal lords. Under this system, which applied to all forms of Japanese art, quantity gave precedence to quality, and the problem of time played no part. A netsuke artist might spend a few months or even a year to perfect a single piece. Students spent years studying under their masters. Most of the great netsuke carvers were conversant with other Japanese art forms, such as painting, Buddhist-image carving, mask carving, or metal and lacquer work. With the abandonment of the feudal system, increased commercialization, inflation, and the Westernization of Japanese thinking and customs, the laborious aesthetic forms of Japanese art, such as the metal arts, lacquer work, and netsuke carving, have for the most part come to an end.

General Characteristics and Construction

Netsuke may be classified according to their various basic forms or shapes along with various techniques of carving. There are, however, certain basic techniques and qualities about a good netsuke which all the various forms have in common. The netsuke figure, whatever its form, had to meet certain basic utilitarian purposes as well as aesthetic ideals. Both of these values were incorporated into the final product.

The most common form is the figure carving *(kata-bori)*, which is essentially a three-dimensional miniature sculpture. This contrasts with the two other basic forms, the *manju* and the *kagamibuta,* which are flattened forms of relatively graphic effect. Netsuke usually measure about 1″ to 2½″ in greatest diameter, except for some of the older netsuke and the elongated *sashi,* or sash netsuke. They invariably have two small holes *(himotoshi)* in them for the passage of the silk cord from the suspended *sagemono.* One hole is usually larger than the other, especially in the older netsuke, to accommodate the knot. These holes are made in an unobtrusive part of the netsuke, such as the back and especially the bottom. The holes had to be so placed and constructed as not only to be unobtrusive but also to secure the netsuke with its most artistic surface in full view. The holes were often strengthened by encircling them with a round encrusted strip of ivory, horn, or jade. Quite often the carved natural openings in the figure itself were used for the cord passages instead of making separate holes. The netsuke as well as the *himotoshi* had to be strong enough to support the weight of the *sagemono.* Thus, except for encrustations or when diverse materials were combined, the netsuke was invariably carved out of a single piece of material. While this gave greater strength to the netsuke it also added to the technical difficulty. From an artistic point of view "one-piece carving" was usually given variety of effect either by incorporating into the design the natural variations of the color or grain of the material used or by employing different staining and carving techniques on the material. Thus one single piece of material might be purposely made to appear as if composed of various materials or seemingly joined pieces of the same material. Figure 179 represents a series of old metal coins loosely tied together with a coarse piece of twine which appears to pass through the central openings of the coins. The twine is in natural light-beige color and is carved to simulate strands of woven coarse twine. The coins are stained darker brown and appear polished and even partially worn as if from use. Yet on close scrutiny we see that the entire work is composed of a single piece of wood! Occasionally this design is so contrived that one of the inner coins can be rotated and twisted around on the "twine."

The netsuke figures from a utilitarian point of view were so carved as to avoid any sharp prominent edges that might catch on the clothing or, if too attenuated, might readily break off. Furthermore, the netsuke was often purposely carved to be slightly flatter on its unseen surface, and its cord passages, as noted, were so arranged that the netsuke would be securely held, exposing its major artistic surface. In spite of these factors, the netsuke, in typical Japanese fashion, was carved with equal care and detail on all sides. This included the undercutting and inner recesses, the back, bottom, and all parts hidden from view while the netsuke was being worn. A good-quality netsuke therefore appears perfectly balanced and well carved from any angle. The true sculptural figure netsuke basically has six surface areas: front, back, two sides, top, and bottom. As is true of many other Japanese art forms, the netsuke looks equally effective on closer examination with the aid of a magnifying lens. It is then that the facial expressions, the power, and the motion, along with the minute craftsmanship, further come to light. Such observation also reveals the style of carving. The usual carving is exceptionally smooth, so that no cut marks can be noted, except perhaps for some of the deeper interstices or when purposely done to increase the power and effectiveness of the stroke. This smoothness is amazing, considering that no manufactured abrasives like pumice or carborundum were used by the netsuke artists. Woods were carefully carved and then rubbed down with wet aspera leaves and finally with silk. Further polish and patina were obtained through constant use and from the oil of the skin through handling. Hardwoods as well as ivory lend themselves to detailed carving. In the case of ivory it was polished with pulverized hartshorn. Both ivory and woods were often stained with various acids and berry juices. Technical perfection of carving was stressed by such artists as Kaigyokusai Masatsugu (1813–92), especially in his later works (Figs. 18, 180). However, the earlier artists did not stress details and technical perfection of carving but preferred to obtain their artistic effects through a minimum of details. This basic simplicity, using bold, powerful strokes, and combining imagination with remarkable skill, forms the basic creed of Japanese art. The power of a carving is often lost through detail and overornateness. At the other extreme is the rough carving technique called *itto-bori,* in which the cuts appear as large facets. This technique was used in the colored light wood netsuke previously noted as Nara *ningyo* and in the Uji *ningyo* netsuke representing tea pickers. This "one-stroke" carving is a relatively uncommon technique which reveals the dexterity of the artist in completing a netsuke figure with a minimum number of bold, sharp strokes. The final articles, however, are somewhat crude and impressionistic in appearance (Fig. 181).

One unique characteristic in the construction of the figure netsuke is their perfect balance, physically as well as artistically. Netsuke figures are invariably carved so that they will stand upright perfectly balanced, even, for example, if the subject is standing leaning forward on the tips of the toes of one foot. Yet at the same time they are so constructed as to reveal the main pictorial surface in proper perspective when in use above the sash as a toggle. The netsuke was even constructed so as to give a rounded, comfortable "feel" in the palm of the hand. This artistic stress on the sense of touch and texture is reflected in other Japanese art forms, as in the satisfactory "feel" of the rough texture of the "crude" pottery used in the tea ceremony. Many carvings were therefore often purposely constructed compactly and oval in shape so as to fit snugly into the palm while concomitantly, from a utilitarian point of view, they served as more durable and comfortable toggles (Fig. 176). A very rounded netsuke is uncomfortable and tends to move around and slip instead of lying flat against the body. It might be said that this oval technique tends, from a Western point of view, to detract from true three-dimensional sculptural carving. However, the two-dimensional effect typical of Oriental art is in reality a more subtle form insofar as the slight variations in relief or encrustations or in depth of carving actually render a most subtle three-dimensional effect. Such effects are also achieved in the lacquer and metal arts through low, medium, and high relief and encrustations, along with varying degrees in the depths of chiseling and carving.

The Japanese often took artistic license when it came to the problems of proportions in netsuke subjects. The very size of the netsuke in most cases did not permit accurate proportion as, for instance, in the figure of a man standing alongside of an elephant. Yet in such cases the artistic effect is no more impaired than when the Japanese painter purposely makes the beautiful leaves of a tree proportionately larger than the trunk or surrounding objects. At other times an object is purposely made smaller or larger to enhance its artistic effect or bring out the underlying symbolic meaning. Artistic license is usually, however, softened by combination with proportional realistic detail, so that the overall effect is quite pleasing to the eye. In fact, from a purely aesthetic point of view such artistic license enhances the work. Figure 182 reveals such an example of simple artistic license done with typical Japanese aestheticism. The netsuke represents a frog perched on top of a dried persimmon. The frog is actually disproportionately larger than the persimmon. On the other hand, both the frog and the persimmon are artistically perfectly conceived. The overall oval shape is excellent for that of a netsuke. From a technical point of view the color and the polish of the wood, along with the minuteness of carving from all angles, are irreproachable. The realistic details, such as the lighter-colored pit seen through a defect in the fruit, are typical of keen observation of nature. The frog itself is not only accurate in detail but also goes one step further in appearing realistically alive and tensed as if ready to jump. Incidentally, the natural variations in the color of the wood (yew) have entered into the design of the netsuke, which is typical of the work of this artist, Matsuda Sukenaga (early 19th century).

In general, then, the netsuke comprises a perfect balance between that of a miniature sculptural piece of art and that of a practical utilitarian object.

Forms and Shapes

This section describes the netsuke according to its particular form or shape as well as to the utilitarian purpose for which it was sometimes made

—that is, a purpose additional to the basic one of serving as a toggle to hold the inro. "Trick" netsuke are also included here.

KATA-BORI NETSUKE

The *kata-bori* netsuke is a figure carving and includes various types of dolls. This class of netsuke can be subdivided into various categories according to the style and specific techniques used.

1) *saishiki-bori* (*saishiki*=painting; *bori*=carving). Water-color-painted figures. The most famous carver in this style, using old *hinoki* wood, was Yoshimura Shuzan, late 18th century. This style is contrasted with *su-bori* (*su*=without ornament), or unpainted netsuke.

2) *ningyo* netsuke (*ningyo*=doll or puppet). These are usually small doll-like figures in light *hinoki* or tea wood, painted in water colors and often carved in crude faceted style or *itto-bori* (Fig. 168). These netsuke were originally carved by dollmakers who made *hina ningyo* (small dolls). The following five types of *ningyo* netsuke are particularly worth mentioning:

a) Nara *ningyo*. Netsuke made by the doll carvers of Nara in Nara-bori style, which consists of decorating carved *hinoki* wood with colors. The netsuke usually represent Noh dancers. Okano Shoju IX and Morikawa Toen were well known for these carvings.

b) Uji *ningyo*. Colored doll netsuke of old tea wood originated by Kamibayashi Gyuka of the famous Uji tea-growing district in the mid-19th century. The netsuke usually represent women who pick tea leaves.

c) Asakusa *ningyo*. Netsuke originated by Fukushima Chikayuki of Asakusa in the 19th century. They usually represent Noh dancers.

d) Hida *ningyo*. Carved figures originated by Matsuda Sukenaga (early 19th century) of Hida, who replaced coloring by using the natural color of yew wood.

e) Negoro *ningyo*. Figures covered with lacquer in the Negoro-nuri technique. They were made especially by the 18th-century artist Sokyu and are extremely rare.

FLAT SHAPES

The second most common form of netsuke after the *kata-bori* is the flattened buttonlike shape. These netsuke are usually about $1\frac{1}{2}''$ in diameter but were occasionally made much larger for wrestlers. Most often they were made entirely of ivory or lacquer or of a shallow round bowl of ivory or wood covered with a carved metal lid. The carvings are basically two-dimensional, in flat or low relief or in an openwork pattern. They are therefore not true three-dimensional sculptural pieces. They are further classified into specific types, the *manju* (named for a kind of Japanese bun), the *hako* (little boxes), the *kagamibuta* (literally, "mirror lid"), and the *ryusa* (named for a netsuke carver). These types are briefly discussed here.

1) *manju*. Named after a Japanese cake or bun of similar shape. The

manju is round and consists of either one piece or of two equal accurately fitting, slightly convex, flat, hollow halves (Fig. 35). The cord passes through a ringlike elevation on the inside of one half and out through a hole in the other half. The older pieces were usually made of lacquer by inro artists. The more modern ones (19th century) were often made of ivory and were of the solid variety. Some schools and artists excelled in *manju* netsuke—for example, Hakuunsai (early 19th century).

2) *hako* (little box). A small square or rectangular hollow-box *manju,* usually made of lacquer. The hollow *manju* were often used as receptacles (Fig. 144). Also known as *kaku,* or angular netsuke. The *hako,* as well as the *manju,* were occasionally made of wood, metal, or ceramics. All forms of decorative techniques were used, including all the techniques for lacquer, ivory, plaited metal, etc.

3) *kagamibuta*. The *kagamibuta* consists of a shallow round bowl of ivory or wood covered with a flat metal lid. This metal disk was carved by the metal-sword-furniture artists *(soken-shi)* and was either chiseled or engraved, hammered out (embossed) into designs in low or medium relief, or encrusted with various metals and alloys (Fig. 184). Occasionally the disk was made entirely of gold. Sometimes the bowl itself was also carved, but more often it was left undecorated. The cord passes from under the surface of the metal lid through a half ring projecting from the under surface of the metal disk. Occasionally lacquer artists imitated the *kagamibuta,* doing it entirely in lacquer. Most of the *kagamibuta* netsuke were done after the middle of the 19th century and stemmed from the disuse and final banishment of the sword, which left the metal artists seeking other means of employment. Among the well-known metal artists who excelled in *kagamibuta* were Temmin (early 19th century) and his pupil Shuraku. Yokoya Somin (1669–1733) and Sugiura Joi (mid-18th century) were well-known earlier metal artists who made excellent *kagamibuta*. Issai Tomei (1817–70) and Kano Natsuo (1828–98), famous metal artists of the late 19th century, occasionally made *kagamibuta*.

4) *ryusa*. A type of one-piece *manju* named after Ryusa (mid-18th century), who also made ashtray netsuke. Like the *manju,* it is hollowed out on a lathe, and its surfaces are then carved into an openwork of arabesques, birds, or flowers. *Ryusa* are usually made of ivory, which is often enhanced by metal encrustations. Less commonly, they are made of wood (Fig. 185).

SPECIAL UTILITARIAN FORMS

Netsuke were also made for specific purposes rather than just as utilitarian toggles or for decorative effect. For example, they served as seals or ashtrays and some were even used for medicinal purposes. The most important of these utilitarian forms are described here.

1) *ingyo,* or seal netsuke. One of the earliest types of netsuke imitating the Chinese seals (*to-bori,* or foreign carving) imported at the end of the

16th century during Hideyoshi's invasion of Korea. They were square in shape, made of ivory or occasionally of wood, and were used in conjunction with the inro, in which the colored ink paste was kept. They were never signed. The early Chinese ones were usually made of stone and were converted into netsuke by making holes in them through which to pass the cords.

2) "medicinal" netsuke. "Unicorn horn" (actually the upper jawbone of a narwhal), which resembles ivory, was used for medicinal purposes. Scrapings were taken from the uncarved portions of narwhal netsuke to allay fever. Similarly, deerhorn was used as an antidote for snakebite.

3) *hiuchi,* or "lighter" netsuke. A functional flint-and-steel netsuke made in metal-box form or in the shape of a miniature European blunderbuss in wood and metal. Used as a lighter for pipes.

4) *suigara-ake.* A small ashtray netsuke used in conjunction with tobacco pouches. It was made of metal. The *suigara-ake* netsuke was a specialty of Ryusa (mid-18th century).

5) *fudekake* (brush rest) netsuke. This type of netsuke, which was in the form of a reclining human figure, served as a rest for a writing brush. The form was copied from that of the reclining nude female figure used by Chinese doctors to assist their modest women patients in indicating the area of their ailments without having to disrobe.

6) *soroban* netsuke. Abacus netsuke made of wood, ivory, or metal.

7) miscellaneous utilitarian netsuke. These include the *hidokei* (sundial), *to-megane* (telescope), *kunizu* (map of Japan, usually etched in black on ivory *manju*), *shokudai* (candlestick), and similar items. Most of these utilitarian netsuke have no artistic beauty, even though they may be cleverly contrived.

MISCELLANEOUS FORMS

Three other general categories of netsuke according to form are grouped together here for the sake of convenience. They are the *sashi,* the *ichiraku,* and the *nioibin.* The *sashi* is an elongated rod-shaped piece of carved wood or ivory worn thrust through the sash (Fig. 183). *Ichiraku* designates a basketwork netsuke of metal or rattan in the shape of a box, a gourd, and the like. The *nioibin* is a perfume-bottle netsuke in gourd shape.

TRICK NETSUKE

Still another category of netsuke forms is that of the "trick" netsuke. These feature ingenious contrivances in the carving—for example, movable parts. Thus a doll netsuke may be so delicately balanced that the eyes and the tongue move almost perpetually at the slightest movement of the doll. Old Japanese dolls were often made in similar fashion. The *okiagari* netsuke is usually a Daruma which readily rights itself when knocked down, since it has a cleverly weighted base. It resembles the popular

Daruma toy. Symbolically, this represents struggle and final success. Other cleverly constructed netsuke often represent the *karashishi* with a marble ball in its mouth, the ball being larger than the mouth opening, or a fruit with loose seeds or a worm in it. Tilting the netsuke only partly extrudes the seeds or the worm, which are larger than the opening through which they appear and therefore cannot be removed from or fall out of the netsuke. Occasionally such netsuke are made for purely humorous effect (Fig. 186).

MASK NETSUKE

One more important form of netsuke is that of the mask. Netsuke simulating the masks of the Noh drama were originated by the Deme school. The early ones made by Deme Uman and Deme Joman were of wood and were usually signed. Ivory was also used for netsuke of the mask type. Kano Tessai (1845–1925) made netsuke copied from old masks, even simulating the flakes of color of the old peeling paint.

Materials

The majority of netsuke, especially the early ones, were made of wood. A close second, however, was ivory, which became more and more popular after its importation during the 18th century. Wood, however, remains unsurpassed in its warmth, color, detail, and flexibility of carving—especially such hard, close-grained woods as boxwood. Wood could also be readily stained, painted, lacquered, or inlaid in Shibayama style with innumerable decorative materials, such as ivory, coral, jade, mother-of-pearl, tortoise shell, etc. Numerous other materials were used for netsuke, such as horn, metal, lacquer, ceramics, bone, amber, walnuts, peach stones, sea pine, "crane's skull" (Malayan hornbill), etc. Occasionally a natural object was used, such as an animal skull or a gourd. Such objects were often lacquered.

WOOD

The netsuke artists used an infinite variety of woods, usually indigenous but also occasionally imported. Such woods were chosen for their color, durability, grain, hardness, and ease of carving, among other factors. Quite often they were stained brown with the juice of the *kuchinashi* berry, dyed black (as with Chinese sandalwood), painted with water color, or covered with lacquer. The painted and lacquered netsuke were usually made from a light wood, such as *hinoki, honoki, kiri,* and *keyaki.* Identification of the woods is made more difficult by the fact that they developed a softer, more lustrous, darker patina with age and use. In his book *The Industries of Japan,* Rein describes the more useful Japanese woods as consisting of 38 families, which include 146 species. While each species has certain characteristics in common, each subspecies may differ as to strength, grain, color, and porosity. The difficult problem of identification of the various woods used for netsuke thus becomes apparent.

Certain schools favored materials, or even specific woods, and many individual artists as well favored particular types of wood. Knowledge of such preferences is occasionally helpful in the identification of an unsigned work. Thus Miwa I often used heavy imported Chinese ebony, which sinks in water, and this may be used as a test of authenticity. Along the same lines, Miwa I never carved in ivory.

Wood carving is called *ki-no-horimono* (*ki*=wood; *hori*=carving; *mono*= thing or object). Soft wood, such as *hinoki* (Japanese cypress), favored by Buddhist-image carvers, was used early but tended to be discarded because it readily wore down. However, for this very reason, *hinoki* was used by the famous netsuke artist Shuzan. His figures were relatively long, in accordance with the early style of netsuke, and were painted in many colors. With use, parts of the colors wore off, ultimately giving the striking mottled patina for which his works are famous. Similar techniques were used by the Nara doll netsuke carvers. Sukenaga carved from Hida pine and used the natural variations in the color of the wood for artistic effect rather than staining the wood.

The practice of encrusting wood with different materials or of making different parts of a netsuke from different materials became more popular in the mid-19th century and was perfected by such renowned artists as Dosho and Tokoku (Fig. 161). Thus a human figure might be composed of a wood torso, an ivory face and hands, and embellished with coral and jade beads, gold earrings, and a silver hat. Such craftsmanship, however, did not always compare favorably with the purposefully simple, seemingly crude, and yet powerfully expressive, artistic, and utilitarian works of earlier masters done in plain wood. In general old wood carvings were also relatively large and long and were unsigned. As noted, old wood develops a rich patina through age, becoming browner, harder, and smoother through constant use and handling. The oils of the skin contribute to the polish; in fact, the best way to bring out the luster of an old wooden netsuke is to rub it with the fingers or with a turpentine-diluted solution of beeswax and then polish it with a soft brush or cloth. While many old wooden netsuke show little wear, having been carefully preserved as art objects, the majority show evidence of considerable wear, so that the relief carving as well as the signature may be almost completely obliterated. Similarly, the cord channels *(himotoshi)* reveal evidence of wear. The cord channels of the older netsuke were larger; furthermore, one hole was made larger than the other to accommodate the knot of the cord. The more modern works have two equal, relatively smaller holes. The wooden cord channels of older works up to the late 18th century were unlined.

The following is a list of woods most commonly used for netsuke carving as well as for other art work in which wood is utilized, including lacquer art:

1) *chanoki* (tea wood). Hard, light, light ash-colored. Used for tea-doll netsuke, which were usually painted and were originated by the 19th-century artist Rakushiken.

2) *Chosen-matsu* (Korean pine). Red and yellow wood with marked streaks. Used by the early Hida school.

3) *hinoki* (Japanese cypress). Light, soft, whitish. Used by Buddhist-image carvers and early netsuke carvers, especially Shuzan. Tended to wear down. Very resistant to water. Often lacquered, as were other light woods. Also used for painted Nara doll netsuke by the Okano family and for bent work. It is the best wood for making lacquered boxes, since it does not warp.

4) *ho* (Japanese cucumber tree). Whitish.

5) *honoki* (magnolia family). Soft, elastic, light, with fine, even grain. Often lacquered. Used for sword-sheath work and cabinetwork. Varieties include a fine striped Owari *masa-honoki*.

6) *ichii* (yew). Red, tough, fine-grained. Used by the Hida school and especially by Sukenaga, employing the natural color variations of the wood to enhance the effect of the netsuke.

7) *isu (Distylium racemosum)*. Dark-brown and red shades. Heavy, tough, fine-grained, with small pores.

8) *jinko* (eaglewood). Imported.

9) *kaede* (a type of maple). Light-colored, pinkish, fine-grained.

10) *kaki* (persimmon). Yellowish, with black heartwood. Small to large unevenly scattered pores. Used by Minko and also by Tadanari (mid-19th century), who carved gargoyles in wood. Also used for joinery work.

11) *(kaki) shitan* (red sandalwood). Rarely used. Fragrant. Dark-reddish mahogany-colored. Was stained black. The sandalwoods of the tropical monsoon regions were used by Matsuda Kaneyuki (mid-19th century). See *shitan-nuri,* page 130.

12) *kashi* (oak). Evergreen oak. Tough, elastic.

13) *keyaki (Planera japonica)*. Used by joiners. Does not split or warp. Has a great number of small pores. Resists both moisture and dryness. Used for trays, bowls, furniture. Like oak, but lighter. Parallel fibers. Includes varieties with fine-curved knots. A hard-grained ornamental wood of excellent quality.

14) *kiri* (paulownia, or empress tree: *Paulownia imperialis*). The best variety has a brilliant luster. Light, very porous, gray-white to light brown, strong, soft, odorless. Does not warp. Often lacquered. Used for small furniture and boxes, including the *natsume*.

15) *kokutan* (ebony). Hard, heavy. Becomes black at the core when old. Good for *sukashi* work. Miwa used Chinese ebony, which sinks in water. Imported from China and India. Same family as *kaki* wood. Kamman (late

18th century) carved frogs from ebony. Also used by Tomiharu (1733–1810).

16) *kusu* (*Cinnamomum camphora,* or camphor wood). Light brown to dark red. Many varieties. Moderately porous.

17) *kuwa* (Japanese mulberry). Yellowish, durable. Used by joiners for furniture. Dark-colored variety imported from China *(to-kuwa)*.

18) *sakura* (*Prunus pseudo-cerasus,* or cherry wood). Reddish, fine-grained. Used by Nagoya school. First employed by Miwa. Also used for wood-cuts. Excellent for furniture, especially *yama-zakura,* a reddish-brown variety.

19) *sendan (Melia japonica).* This type of wood includes *tama-moku sendan.* Dark knots on yellowish base. Used for furniture, boxes, timber.

20) *setsu* or *yusura-ume (Prunus tomentosa).* Heavy, close-grained, reddish. Used by Ikkan (mid-19th century) of Nagoya.

21) *sugi* (Japanese cedar, *Cryptomeria japonica*). Reddish brown; also a white variety. Easy to work, but brittle and soft. Used for housing construction and bent work. Includes *yaku-sugi,* which has fine brown-flame-colored fibers.

22) *tabu (Cinnamomum pedunculatum).* Includes *tama-tabu,* which is the best variety, with curved knots and light-yellow color. Used for furniture, joinery.

23) *tagayasan* (ironwood). A Chinese wood. Striped, veined, hard-grained. Dark brown. A hard and heavy wood.

24) *take* (bamboo). Irregular speckled brown spots in cross section. (Smoked bamboo=*iyo.*) Used by Gyokkin (1817–80), Ikko (late 18th century), Kyusai (1879–1938), and Yasuchika (1670–1744). Bamboo workers made it into baskets, boxes, scabbards, screens, vases, etc.

25) *tsuge* (boxwood). Hard, fine-grained, yellowish, with very fine pores. Takes a good polish. Most commonly used wood for netsuke.

26) *tochinoki* (Japanese horse chestnut). Hardwood. Bokugyoku (early 19th century) made netsuke of chestnut wood as a hobby. Used for lathe-work (such as bowls) and joinery.

27) *umi-matsu* (petrified underwater sea pine). A type of coral. Blackish with patches of golden brown. Frequently used by carvers of the Iwami school.

IVORY AND ALLIED SUBSTANCES

Ivory was second in popularity among netsuke carvers, especially by the late 18th century, when it began to be imported from India by way of China. Ogasawara Issai (late 18th century) was one of the first and most famous carvers who used ivory. Ivory carving is called *zoge-no-horimono* (*zoge*=ivory; *hori*=carving; *mono*=thing, object). Ivory lends itself to detailed carving, being hard and close-grained. Occasionally the artist took into account the natural whorls of the grain in his artistic creation. At first ivory was difficult to obtain and was specially cut to avoid any waste. The result was the roughly triangular, relatively elongated figures seen in early ivory netsuke carvings. These triangular carvings were known as *sankaku-bori*. The hard-grained core of the tusk was used for the front of the carvings. As ivory gets older, it darkens to a yellow-brown patina, but the parts exposed to the light tend to retain their original whiteness. Some artists liked pure white ivory while others, like Ryukei (early 19th century), studied and practiced tinting the ivory. A yellowish or brownish stain was obtained by using the juice of the gardenia *(kuchinashi)* berry, while outlines were etched brown-black with iron sulfate or nitric acid. Green staining was obtained by the use of copper vitriol. Modern ivory carving is often characterized by poor staining techniques. The ivory was polished to varying degrees with pulverized hartshorn. Ivory tends to dry out and split with age, the presence of moisture being a deterrent factor to this process. Further splitting is prevented by bridging with a tiny wedge of metal placed across the progressing split. Cleaning may be done with soap and water, drying and rubbing briskly with a silk cloth. Ivory was used also for encrustation into wood netsuke or in combination with wood by pegging it into the wood. Such joining is so perfect as to be invisible to the untrained eye. There were numerous well-known ivory carvers, including Nagai Rantei (Fig. 187) and Ogasawara Issai (both late 18th century), Kaigyokusai Masatsugu (1815–92), Yamaguchi Tomochika (1800–73), and Asahi Gyokuzan (1843–1923). Various types of ivory were used, including the spirally grooved narwhal tusk, the partly iridescent spermwhale tooth, and the wild-boar tusk. The latter two were used by the Iwami school. Specifically, Ogasawara Issai carved in ivory and whale tusk, and Kamman (late 18th century, of the Iwami school) carved lobsters out of boar's tusk. Bunshojo (1764–1838) and Tomiharu (1723–1811) both carved in tooth. Inferior ivories include walrus, with its semitransparent core, and hippopotamus tusk, with even, concentric lines and dead-white color.

Bone was also used and is recognized by its relative lightness and porosity in comparison to ivory. The more dense thighbone of domestic animals was usually used. Gemmin and Tsuzen (19th century) both carved in bone. The identity of some ivory-like specimens remains an enigma since even fossil-like bone and ivory remnants were used.

Horn was often used, especially deerhorn, but also rhinoceros, buffalo, antelope, and oxhorn. Horn was also used for encrustation. Buffalo horn, however, was often worm-eaten. Rhinoceros horn was also used for medicinal purposes, especially the opaque or black varieties. However, for artistic purposes the more translucent forms of yellow amber or gold color veined with black were used. Shogetsu (mid-19th century) and Ryukoku (mid-19th century) carved in deerhorn. The best known deerhorn carver was Kokusai (mid-19th century). Pipe cases were also often made from this material. Oxhorn was also often used (black or clear amber color) by Komin and the Iwami school. Typical of the netsuke of Toyomasa were figures with eyes inlaid with translucent horn.

Tortoise shell (*bekko; bekko-zaiku*=tortoise-shell work) was occasionally used, usually for inlay work. Its translucent golden brown is easily recognizable. As noted earlier, in lacquer ware its effect was heightened by inlaying over gold foil. Garaku (mid-19th century) often used tortoise shell. Occasionally crane "skull" (Malayan hornbill, or *honen*) was used, the color being a waxy snow white with fine hairlines and reddish sides. The red was often used to represent the hair of a divinity or monster. Ono Ryomin (late 19th century) occasionally carved in this material.

VEGETABLE, MINERAL, AND OTHER MATERIALS

Various nuts were often carved into netsuke, the commonest being the walnut *(kurumi)* and, less often, the coconut *(yashi-no-mi)*, the betel nut *(binroji)* from the ivory palm, and the palm nut *(korozo)*. Damson *(sumomo)* and peach *(momo)* stones were occasionally used. Kurokawa Masahide (mid-18th century) carved both walnut and coconut. Hidemasa and Shoju (both early 19th century) also carved walnut, the latter carving mostly Daruma figures.

Minerals were more often used as inlay work on netsuke than for netsuke carving itself. The Shibayama-school artists, as well as Kagei Dosho (1828–84) and Suzuki Tokoku (mid-19th century), were famous for such inlaid work. Inlays of this type included metals and metal alloys, ivory, tortoise shell, malachite (known as peacock stone, or *kujaku-seki*), mother-of-pearl *(raden)*, coral *(sangoju)*, enamel *(shippo)*, marble *(dairiseki)*, jade *(gyoku)*, soapstone *(roseki*, or "wax stone"), etc. Very rarely, netsuke were made entirely of stone, quartz, jade, or soapstone. Amber netsuke are also occasionally seen.

Occasionally, natural objects were converted into netsuke—for example, the head, skull, or paw of a small animal. These were usually covered with lacquer. Gourds were also used as netsuke and, again, were usually lacquered. Coral netsuke were made by such artists as Gensai (mid-19th century).

LACQUER

Some of the earliest netsuke were made by lacquer inro artists in conjunction with their inro. The lacquer was usually applied over light wood, such as *hinoki, honoki,* or *kiri*. These lightweight lacquered netsuke were ideal for inro since they were least likely to damage the inro should they strike it. On the other hand, they were not particularly strong, nor did they wear well. The most common type of lacquered netsuke is the *manju,* which entailed basically graphic lacquer techniques rather than true sculpture. However, the very small surface area of the *manju* is generally inadequate for any significant pictorial design. At most a simple animal or bird or a few flowers or leaves could be properly displayed. At other times the design was purely ornamental, exhibiting a few key designs or diaper patterns. The work was usually done in flat or slightly raised *makie* or by encrustation, especially in later works of the Somada and Shibayama schools (Fig. 35). *Togidashi manju* are quite rare, the surface area again being too small for such pictorial work. Fairly common are *tsuishu* and *guri* netsuke in *manju* shape. Small *tsuishu* carving was more suitable for square or round, flat, graphic netsuke. On the other hand, a similar type of graphic work, as seen in the *kagamibuta,* was readily done by the metal artists. Here the surface area was essentially the same as that of the smaller sword furniture, and tiny metal chiseling, embossing, and encrustations could be readily done on the flat metal disks of the *kagamibuta.* Occasionally figure netsuke were carved by a netsuke artist which were later embellished by a lacquer artist. In many such instances the signature of both the netsuke and the lacquer artist can be found on the netsuke (Fig. 162). Such lacquered figure netsuke were occasionally done by the Koma and Kajikawa schools. Even less commonly the entire figure would be covered with *tsuishu* lacquer and the finer details then carved (Fig. 163). Sometimes the figure is coated with Negoro-nuri, or in minute encrustations along with lacquer in Shibayama style. Rarely we find *kanshitsu* technique. In general when lacquering and inlay work was done for ornamental purposes it was done over ivory figures, and when the object was to be completely lacquered it was done over a light wood base. Once in a while interesting lacquer techniques were used, such as lacquer imitating pottery, as seen in Figure 188. Lacquer was also used over such objects as animal paws and skulls, which occasionally served as netsuke. Negoro *ningyo* netsuke were wooden doll or figure subjects lacquered in the Negoro-nuri technique. As mentioned earlier, lacquered netsuke, both figure and *manju* types, were made by the Kajikawa and Koma schools. Ogawa Ritsuo also made netsuke encrusted with pottery. Shibata Zeshin and his followers frequently made lacquered netsuke, usually in conjunction with their inro. Iizuka Toyo, Hara Yoyusai, and Nakayama Komin were other lacquer artists who occasionally executed lacquer netsuke (Fig. 144). *Tsuishu*-lacquered netsuke were made by Roshu (early 19th century) and by Zokoku (1806–69).

METAL

Metal was often used as inlay work on wood or ivory netsuke. This was done either by the netsuke artist, as in the case of Tokoku, or by the metal artist in conjunction with the netsuke artist. The most common form of metal netsuke was the *kagamibuta.* With the abolition of wearing of swords and of the samurai class in 1877 by the government, the metal artists sought other artistic outlets, such as the production of *okimono,* metal netsuke, and especially *kagamibuta* netsuke.

Less common are netsuke made completely of metal. Such heavy netsuke, from a practical point of view, were more likely to damage the
accompanying lacquer inro and were used therefore mainly in conjunction
with metal inro. The earliest ones were made in iron by the Myochin
family (the most famous family of armorers) during the 17th and 18th
centuries, usually in the form of helmets, saddles, stirrups, and gourds.
Ashtray netsuke were made of metal; Ihei (Toshimaya) made such netsuke
in the mid-18th century from woven silver or copper wire. This basket-
weave pattern was a popular form of box netsuke, both in metal and in
wood. Kyubei (mid-18th century) made ashtray netsuke from individual
wax molds. Ryusa (mid-18th century) acquired a high reputation as a
maker of ashtray netsuke. The famous metal artist Kano Natsuo (1828–90)
also occasionally made metal netsuke (Fig. 189), as well as netsuke in the
kagamibuta style.

Finally, it might be noted that metal artists occasionally carved netsuke
out of materials other than metal, such as wood. Such carvings often show
rather sharp and deep cut marks, the metal artist being unaccustomed to
the relatively soft wood.

CERAMICS

Ceramic netsuke were relatively uncommon but were sometimes made
as a hobby by such well-known ceramic artists as Ritsuo and Hanzan
(Fig. 190). The majority of ceramic netsuke were the white Hirado ware,
the dark-brown Bizen ware, and Raku, Kyo (made in Kyoto), Kutani, and
Banko wares. Other artists noted for their ceramic netsuke were Eiraku
Hozen (1794–1853), Ninnami Dohachi (1783–1855), and Miura Kenya
(1825–89), who made netsuke in the style of Kenzan. The ceramic netsuke
were usually figure netsuke, but are occasionally seen as the disks of *kagamibuta*.

In general, earthenware and porcelain netsuke are relatively crude in
comparison to wood and ivory netsuke. It should also be mentioned that
ceramics are a poor material for netsuke, being too fragile to withstand
much wear and handling.

Subject Matter

The subject matter of netsuke was governed by the taste of netsuke pur-
chasers. This involved not only netsuke for the inro of the nobility and
samurai but also those for the vast majority, who used them with tobacco
pouches and other *sagemono* worn by all classes, as well as those for the more
ostentatious taste of the rising wealthy merchant class. The tremendous
demand resulted in an outpouring of netsuke of all types and quality. Netsuke were ready-made or made to the order of the taste of the individual
purchaser. In general they were made on a commercial basis by the *netsuke-*

shi beyond the influence of the aristocratic patrons of the other fine arts. The netsuke art form therefore developed unfettered by tradition and revealed complete artistic and technical license in form, expression, and subject matter. The subject matter, which had originally been limited to seals, mythological animals, and Buddhist subjects, now completely opened its doors to represent practically every type of animate and inanimate object as well as commonplace scenes and objects typical of everyday Japanese life. No topic, no matter how seemingly insignificant, escaped the eye of the *netsuke-shi*. Animal representation was exceptionally common and included not only large quadrupeds but also monkeys, dogs, birds, rats, snakes, toads, and all forms of fish and insect life. Many artists and their schools specialized in portraying animal life, or even a specific animal or insect. Thus the Masanao school favored toads, while the well-known artist Okatomo (mid-18th century) specialized in carving quail with millet seeds. The animals were usually depicted in quite a realistic manner, but as in other forms of Japanese art, they also suggested historical, mythological, symbolic, and occasionally humorous meanings. Such allusions were often subtle and quite fragmentary, to the delight of the Japanese connoisseur, who took pleasure in being able to recognize such erudite aesthetic inferences. However, it must be presumed that the netsuke artist often carved an object simply as a work of art not necessarily in conjunction with any symbolic significance. Yet the portrayal of such a form must not only be technically accurate but must even go beyond this to be considered a work of art. For example, a frog must appear to be lifelike, ready to hop, and the tiger must look intensely fierce. The inner spiritual qualities of the portrayed object must be revealed rather than mere physical accuracy. The story is often told of the famous artist Okyo, who quietly studied and then painted a boar which he found asleep in the bushes. The painting was carefully examined by a friend who noted that the boar lacked spirit and appeared lifeless. Not satisfied with his work, Okyo returned to the same spot where he had previously seen the boar, and to his surprise he found that the boar was in reality dead!

A common netsuke subject is the toad *(gama),* a favorite subject of the Masanao school. To the Occidental such a carving may simply represent a warty-looking amphibian. To the Japanese however, the toad is symbolic of many things because of the various Chinese and Japanese folk tales associated with it. Thus the toad represents the lure of money, as once a three-legged poisonous toad was caught by the means of suspending gold coins on the end of a fishhook. The toad's skin often exudes a poisonous vapor. Toads, like other animals, are associated with certain gods and mythological figures, including the Gama Sennin (of Taoist origin). The toad may also have benevolent characteristics, such as being able to draw down the clouds and cause needed rain. Hence the toad is also a symbol of spring. A common portrayal of the toad in netsuke art shows him sitting on an old broken well bucket. To the Oriental this symbolizes the transience of things on earth, since the toad is now sitting on a bucket which used to constantly endanger him in his abode, the well.

Certain animals, such as the tiger and the elephant, were portrayed unrealistically. This was simply because they were not indigenous to Japan and were copied after Chinese models. Highly stylized and conventionalized Chinese motifs and designs, such as the crane, rocks, waves, and trees, were often similarly depicted in Japanese painting, but not as a rule in netsuke art, where realism played a predominant role. Mythological animals, such as the dragon or *kirin,* were popular subjects of netsuke, as were such fabulous creatures as the *kappa, tengu,* and *kudan* (Fig. 191). These mythological animals, except for the dragon, were rarely depicted on lacquer. Nature was represented not only by animals but also by various insects as well as vegetable subjects. Such still-life subjects were quite frequently depicted and revealed the artist's keen observation of nature. Because of the limited physical scope of the netsuke form, landscapes were rarely depicted. On the other hand, even the minutest aspects of nature lent themselves to netsuke portrayal, which included practically anything from a rotted tree trunk to a cluster of gourds (Fig. 192). Artists like Gambun (early 19th century) took delight in carving in minutest realistic detail decayed and rotted plant life being infested with small creeping insects (Fig. 193). Occasionally such nature subjects were portrayed in abstract or impressionistic form, while still maintaining classical beauty and artistic simplification of the object (Fig. 194). As previously noted, impressionism is seen in other forms of Japanese art, such as the works of the Korin lacquer school, but never in Chinese art. The closest comparable form in Chinese art would be the stylized conventionalization of animal and plant forms rather than true impressionism. The human subject was perfectly represented in its every motion of anger, fear, sorrow, and joy. Yet Japanese art, unlike Occidental art, rarely depicted the nude form. Scientific anatomical knowledge was limited until the arrival of Dutch medical and anatomy books at the beginning of the 19th century. The human body was not aesthetically venerated but, according to Buddhist teachings, was transient and unclean. This also accounts for the meticulous cleanliness of the Japanese and also for the ancient custom of moving out of a house which had been contaminated by a dead body. This latter custom, associated with the realization of the transience of life, is partly responsible for the development of the domestic architecture of Japan along the lines of insubstantial and impermanent abodes. On the other hand, great stress was placed on movement—of the flowing robes and of the posture of the arms, fingers, legs, and torso. We have seen how the stiff Chinese Buddhist robes and the impassive almost stereotyped facial expressions were altered by the Japanese artist, who stressed movement, expression, and individuality. We have also seen how such portrayals ultimately became exaggerated in the Japanese drama and in the Japanese wood-block print. The plebeian netsuke art similarly followed this trend, and the human form now revealed in miniature what the powerful huge Nara sculptural images and grotesque Noh masks formerly expressed. Thus, along with the emotionally expressive bodies and dynamic free-flowing robes, we see correspondingly accurate and often exaggerated facial expressions. These powerful grimaces are enhanced by associated bone outlines and muscular contractions of the adjacent undraped parts of the neck, chest, shoulders, forearms, and lower legs. In more detailed work minute expressive furrows and facial lines can be seen in the netsuke upon using a magnifying lens. Such powerful expressive delineations are typical of the works of the early netsuke artists, who used a minimum of necessary detail to obtain such effects (Fig. 195). Later realistic carvings have much more anatomical detail and accuracy but often lack the strength of these earlier works.

The Japanese love of the grotesque was given full rein in depicting fabulous animals as well as skulls, snakes entwined through skulls, skeletons, etc. (Fig. 187). These skulls and skeletons incidentally reveal that the Japanese artisan actually did have considerable and accurate anatomical knowledge. Along with the grotesque, fear, horror, and various whimsical expressions in exaggerated form were commonly seen in human figure netsuke.

Humor and satire complete the cycle of human emotions and were favorite subjects for the *netsuke-shi*. Such subject matter was uncommon in the more serious aristocratic lacquer work. Scenes from everyday life provided the majority of humorous subject matter, such as a man with tongue in cheek plucking a hair from his chin, a woman picking fleas from her kimono (Fig. 196), or a monkey half-seriously studying an inro with a hand lens. The range of humor extended from the most subtle to the more ribald, erotic, and phallic. However, even the erotic scenes are usually presented in a rather subtle manner. Less commonly, historical and mythological subject matter and even venerated gods were at times satirized. The latter case is understandable because many of the Japanese gods were *kami,* or spirits, of former humans on earth who reached nirvana or heaven, through honorable religious devotion on earth. This in a way parallels the large pantheon of gentle, almost human ancient Greek gods, who were also delicately satirized by their own people. Thus the figure of Ono no Komachi, the highly respected poetess, seated on an old log, may be seen replaced by a monkey seated on a similar type of log. Ofuku, a goddess, is often represented in a humorous or erotic manner. Incidentally the very configuration of Ofuku's face has interesting philosophical and symbolic significance. Her protruding forehead means that woman should not aspire beyond reasonable bounds. Similarly, her protruding cheek-bones indicate that she should not go to the other extreme and look down

(Fig. 197). This philosophy embodies the Japanese concept of the ideal woman.

Many other fields of subject matter are covered in netsuke art. Combinations of subject matter are quite common, such specific combinations invariably having definite symbolic significance. Combinations of animals may represent the night and corresponding day hours, as each two-hour period is represented by a different specific animal. The same applies to the animals of the zodiac and animals representing the various seasons as well as the astrological field. Most gods are associated with specific animals in mythology and folklore. Similarly, combinations of animals are common because of their similar symbolic meaning or presence together in folk tales. The principle of the male and the female, the positive and the negative, applies to a somewhat lesser degree in netsuke than in other forms of Japanese art, such as painting.

Animals and figures are often used to depict some fragmentary scene of a myth or folk tale. Such allusions can only be recognized by being thoroughly familiar with this tremendous wealth of folklore, including legends of great heroes of the past. Every possible field was fit subject matter for netsuke, including articles representing the tea ceremony, Buddhist symbols, fairy tales, good and evil spirits, Noh masks and Noh actors, Kabuki dancers, *sumo* wrestling, children, household pets, toys, dolls, games, gods both Shinto and Buddhist (including the Seven Gods of Good Fortune), the Twenty-four Filial Paragons, *sennin* (revered hermits), *ronin* (lordless samurai), and military heroes, such as Yoritomo and Yoshitsune.

Finally, it should be noted that the Japanese insistence on historical accuracy and symbolic compatibilities in grouping subject matter apply to netsuke work as well as to other forms of Japanese art. However, more often than not, because of the small size of the netsuke, the subjects portrayed were usually single or in groups of two or three.

Netsuke Artists

No discussion of netsuke could be complete without some mention of the netsuke artists. While many netsuke were made by metal, lacquer, ceramic, and other artists as a side line, individual great netsuke artists flourished along with their followers and descendants. These men took great pride in their work and spent many months and even over a year in some cases in designing and carving a single netsuke. A student often studied for as long as ten years under his master before he was allowed to use part or all of the master's or the school's name. Some netsuke artists were known for their style, their subject matter, or the materials which they used. The greatest confusion exists in interpreting signatures on netsuke. Some of the older artists did not sign their names or did so only rarely; in other cases all the descendants and many followers of a master used the identical signature, along with many which are pure forgeries. The use of art names, or occasionally just a seal, as well as abbreviations of the inscribed names, adds to the confusion. The problem of authenticity is therefore considerable in collecting netsuke. Some artists had favorite designs for netsuke which they copied either identically or with sundry variations (Fig. 198). Thus it must not be presumed that more or less identical pieces by an artist are necessarily copies or forgeries. However, popular artists have been copied along with their favorite subjects throughout the centuries and even during the life of the master, so that even age itself is not an infallible criterion of authenticity. The age of a netsuke only eliminates the possibility of its being a late copy, so that one has to rely as well upon the quality and style of carving of the artist, the type and quality of the materials with which he worked, along with the authenticity of the calligraphy of the signature. Occasionally a separate box was made for the netsuke which was authenticated by the artist, his students, or family, and which may even include the names of its various prior owners and the dates of their ownership. In general, however, a netsuke is best chosen for its artistic qualities, interesting subject matter, excellence of execution, and only secondarily for its signature alone.

Netsuke artists and schools flourished mainly in Edo, Kyoto, Osaka, and Nagoya and to a lesser extent in the provinces. Many of the schools consisted of descendants of netsuke carvers who were often adopted sons of the master. Such adoption was used for adept pupils of the master in order to perpetuate the family name. In other instances the pupils, after years of apprenticeship, might be rewarded with part or all of the master's name. These schools of carving revealed certain similar characteristics, especially when students copied their teacher's works both out of deference to him and for training purposes. On the other hand, each netsuke carver, especially the more renowned ones, ultimately developed his own particular style, technique, materials, and subject matter. For example the Owari (Nagoya) school usually used wood, especially cherry wood, rather than ivory or other materials. They realistically carved simple animal and plant forms. They were known for a style of carving called *uki-bori,* or carving in fine relief, such as for the designs on clothing and raised ridges on plant life. The signatures were also rendered in *uki-bori.* Even the frame about the signature was characteristic, being rectangular in shape. On the other hand, each major artist of the Owari school had his own individual traits and techniques. Thus Hogen Tadayoshi used light wood which he stained darker in parts, and he carved mainly fish, shells, and animals, whereas Ikkan used mainly *setsu* wood and was noted for his sleeping *shojo* and mice.

It is not within the scope of this chapter to list some 1,300 netsuke artists who have been adequately dealt with in specific books on netsuke art. The following is an abbreviated commentary on the outstanding schools of netsuke carving in relation to the cities and provinces in which they developed and worked, their historical and chronological development along with a brief description of some of the most outstanding netsuke artists and their pupils. Finally it should be stressed that many of the most magnificent old carved netsuke were unsigned and were done by some unknown artist or perhaps by an outstanding artist who simply did not sign his work. In the latter case we can only state that the netsuke is done in the style of that particular artist or his school.

OSAKA

Osaka was a famous city for netsuke carvers, the earliest and most famous being Hogen Yoshimura Shuzan, who worked during the first part of the 18th century. The founder of the later (19th century) Osaka school was Garaku I (late 18th century), whose most famous follower was Doraku (mid-19th century), who carved in ivory and often used inlaid materials. From the same school also was Shukosai Anraku (early 19th century), who carved human figures and animals in ivory, and Wada (Kokeisai) Sansho (1871–1936), who carved mainly in wood, usually revealing a distinct style of carving and of humor. Two famous late-Osaka artists were Ohara Mitsuhiro (1810–75) and Kaigyokusai Masatsugu (1813–92). Mitsuhiro studied by practicing on discarded ivory scraps from his master, who made *samisen* plectrums. He did realistic carving of figures, animals, and plant life. His signature was accompanied by a written seal. Masatsugu used only the finest quality wood and ivory, often employing the natural holes in his figures for the cord runners. He made sketches from life before doing his carving. His early works were done in the simple, strong style of the old master carvers, but his late works became extremely realistic, detailed, and refined and consisted mainly of animals carved in ivory. He signed his works with three different pen names and *kakihan* at different ages. He taught himself carving and studied under no particular master. Although he made mostly netsuke he also occasionally carved inro, *okimono,* and pipe cases. There are often seen many forgeries of his late-style detailed ivory carvings of animal life, including many executed by his own pupils. His real works, however, are unsurpassed (Fig. 18), and the animals appear vital and alive when viewed from any direction because of his careful planning and the magnificent execution of his carving.

KYOTO

The three outstanding netsuke artists of Kyoto during the 18th century were Yoshinaga or Koyoken, Masanao, and Tomotada. The well-known Masanao of Kyoto should not be confused with the Masanao school of Yamada. The former carved in both ivory and wood, making simple and yet realistic figures and animals. His favorite subject was the toy sparrow. His signature is engraved and characteristically surrounded by an engraved oval. Tomotada did minute wood and ivory carving, especially of recumbent oxen, for which he was renowned. He was often imitated even in his own lifetime. The most famous of his pupils was Yamaguchi Okatomo who carved in ivory and in wood, his favorite subject (and often copied) being quails with millet seeds. In the 19th century the most famous netsuke artists of Kyoto were Kagetoshi (also associated with Nagoya), Horaku, and Hogen Nagai Rantei. Kagetoshi and Horaku were probably of the same school and carved minute landscapes with tiny foliage and figures in *sukashi-bori* (openwork). Rantei carved mainly in ivory, making figures and animals that were usually simple and yet quite powerful.

OWARI

From Nagoya, the chief town of Owari, came many renowned netsuke artists. Kita Tametaka (mid-18th century) was the originator of *uki-bori,* or fine-relief carving. He carved in wood. He was an independent carver and was frequently copied. Tadatoshi (late 18th century) and his school also carved in *uki-bori* style, using cherry wood. He made figures, birds, beasts, and fish. His signature was in relief. His best pupil was Hogen Tadayoshi (mid-19th century) who did similar style carving in wood. Ikkan carved about the same time. He was a priest. He used *setsu* wood and was famous for his sleeping *shojo* and mouse netsuke, many of which were copied.

MISCELLANEOUS PROVINCES

From the province of Ise was Tanaka Minko (1735–1816), who was in the service of Lord Todo. He stressed expression rather than realism and used metal eyes for his animal figures. He carved mainly fruit and animals and rarely people. He used contrivances such as rotating eyes. He often signed with a *kakihan*. He was also a very good painter and carver of Buddhist images. He carved only in wood, and his works were often copied. One of his well-known pupils was Kokei.

Another netsuke master from Ise was Miyake Masanao of Yamada, whose followers continued the art up to the 20th century. The favorite subject matter of this school was small animal life, such as frogs, fish, and snakes, done in wood. They are all realistically carved, the earlier ones being simpler and more artistic.

From Gifu in Mino Province was Kano Tomokazu (early 19th century), who carved animals, especially monkeys and tortoises, in boxwood. His works are strong and realistic.

From Takayama in Hida Province was Matsuda Sukenaga (early 19th century), who used the natural colors of yew wood to enhance his carvings. He was very fond of carving frogs, which he depicted in a humorous manner (Fig. 182). He was the founder of the Hida *itto-bori* school, but later he used a more polished and realistic style. He occasionally carved inro (Fig. 230).

From Wakayama was Ogasawara Issai (late 18th century), who did minute carving in ivory and whale tooth. His works were rarely signed.

From Tamba was Naito Toyomasa (1773–1856), who was a seal engraver but who made netsuke as a side line. He carved only in wood and used inlaid translucent horn for the eyes of his netsuke.

The last well-known school from the provinces was that in Iwami Province founded by Shimizu Tomiharu (1733–1810). He was originally a priest. He usually carved small animal and plant life in wood, often employing ebony (Fig. 177). The details of his works were often done in extremely fine *uki-bori,* giving a realistic and yet soft, simple artistic touch to his works. He signed in extremely fine *ke-bori* characters or in fine *uki-bori.* He also carved in boar's tooth and signed these works in fine *ke-bori* characters. His many pupils and followers also signed their works in a similar manner.

TOKYO

The most famous of the 18th-century netsuke carvers from Tokyo were Miwa I (Hiromori) and Hogen Shugetsu I. As previously noted, Miwa I carved only in wood, including cherry wood and sandalwood, and lined the cord holes with dyed ivory or horn. His carvings were powerfully done in the style of grotesque caricatures and were quite original in design. His works were signed with a *kakihan,* often on the soles of the feet of his figures. There were four generations who used the name Miwa. The later artists, while using the same type of woods and subject matter, carved in a more refined, polished, and detailed manner.

Shugetsu I was an outstanding painter of the Kano school and held the title of *hogen.* He made mask netsuke, especially of Ofuku. He used a written seal. His art name was repeated for four generations up into the late 19th century. Associated with this school was Minkoku I, a master netsuke artist skilled in both wood and ivory carving. He was also followed for four generations.

The Deme netsuke mask carvers also worked in Tokyo during the 18th century, the most famous artists being Deme Joman and his son Deme Uman, both of whom were extensively copied.

Another well-known artist of Tokyo was Ryusa, who worked for the shogun. He made ashtray netsuke and was the originator of the *ryusa* netsuke (Fig. 185).

During the 19th century the famous Yamaguchi Tomochika (1800–73) of the Tomotada school in Kyoto moved to Tokyo and founded the largest of all netsuke schools. His art name was Chikuyosai. He used ivory and carved figures, birds, beasts, and skulls. He executed unique designs, often after Hokusai's caricature style. He was followed by three generations who used the same name.

Jikan Gambun (early 19th century), who originally worked in Kyoto, later moved to Tokyo. He made netsuke and pipe sheaths, his favorite subjects being minute realistic ants or snails crawling over decaying wood or fungi. The woods were usually bamboo and ebony, and the snails and insects were done in a variety of inlaid materials including metal, ivory, mother-of-pearl, and pottery (Fig. 193).

Two other well-known 19th-century Tokyo netsuke artists were Ozaki Kokusai (Koku) and Suzuki Tokoku. The former carved humorous atypical animal figures in deerhorn, using interesting designs and shapes, his favorite being deerhorn *sashi* netsuke caricaturing various animals. His works are usually signed with a characteristically engraved scroll-like seal of "Koku." Tokoku (mid-19th century) was an expert in carving and combining in minute detail various materials which were perfectly inlaid into his wooden netsuke, such as tiny multicolored beads, fine gold earrings, etc. (Fig. 161). He studied by himself. His signature exists as an inlaid rectangular plaque of a gold-silver alloy. Three generations of artists used the same name.

Another well-known Tokyo school was the Shibayama lacquer school, who did their typical detailed inlay work on inro and to a lesser extent on netsuke.

Since Tokyo has become the economic and cultural hub of Japan during the present century, the modern schools of netsuke carving have developed in this city. Note should first be made of five netsuke artists all of whom were known as sculptors and who worked in Tokyo during the late 19th and early 20th centuries. The first was Takahashi Houn (b. 1824), who established his own school at Kanda, Tokyo. He was given the title of *hogen* for his carving of Buddhist images. He was the teacher of Takamura Toun (1847–1910), who was also granted the title of *hogen* for his carvings of Buddhist images. Toun in turn was the teacher of Takamura Koun (1852–1934), who became one of the greatest wood carvers of his time and was appointed professor of the Tokyo Academy of Fine Arts. Along with this school was Ishikawa Komei (1852–1913), who, while basically a sculptor, also carved ivory *okimono,* tobacco-pipe sheaths, and occasionally ivory netsuke. He also studied painting under Kano Sosen. Another famous contemporary sculptor was Asahi Gyokuzan (1843–1923), who was especially noted for his realistic skull netsuke. He was originally a priest and was appointed along with Komei as a professor in the Tokyo Academy of Fine Arts.

The last famous school of netsuke artists of the 19th century in Tokyo was founded by Yamada Hojitsu (d. 1872). He worked for the shogun and had many followers. Hojitsu did detailed realistic carving in both wood and ivory. Miyazaki Joso (1855–1910) carved netsuke as well as tobacco-pipe sheaths and worked for the imperial household. Among Joso's pupils were Soko and Gyokuso, whose followers are the present-day remaining netsuke artists of Japan. Both were born in 1879, the former carving mainly in wood and the latter mainly in ivory. Their carvings, typical of the Hojitsu school, are minute, detailed, and realistic. While beautifully done, they lack the simple powerful strength and elegance of the earlier netsuke artists. Ouchi Sosui (b. 1911), the eldest son of Gyokuso, was a pupil of Soko and at present is the best known living netsuke artist carving primarily in wood. Shoko, of the same school, is another excellent present-day artist who does similar-style realistic carving.

Finally it must be realized that while each school had certain characteristics, the individual netsuke artists also had their own characteristics of design, carving, and use of materials. Such knowledge ultimately determines the authenticity of a netsuke. Even an authentic signature is not foolproof, for occasionally the master signed his name to one of his pupil's works, even though much more frequently the student out of deference signed his master's name to his own work. Many artists have certain recognizable characteristics. Thus Sukenaga's frogs have typical smooth bulbous enlargements on the tips of their toes (Fig. 182). Similarly, Kaigyokusai's animals have perfectly parallel, extremely fine-carved lines for their hair. Even more characteristic are the artistic lifelike smoothed-out inner surfaces of the ears of his animals (Figs. 18, 180) as compared to the relatively short, unfinished, stiff ears of forgeries bearing his name.

Evaluation and Forming a Collection

Evaluation of a netsuke depends on many factors. The most important is the artistic quality of the work. Excellence of technical craftsmanship in itself does not constitute a work of art. However, in rounding out a collection many secondary factors come into consideration, such as the age of the netsuke and the different styles of carving, as well as unusual examples of subject matter or materials. Typical carvings of famous artists should be sought, realizing of course, that many artists did not always sign their pieces and many were copied by their students as a means of learning their craft, and many were just actually forged. Finally, good examples of carvings of unusual materials such as horn, nut, or amber should round out the collection. Many collectors find pleasure in gathering examples of specific subject matter, such as frogs or monkeys.

In judging the quality and age of a netsuke certain negative as well as positive factors must be kept in mind. We have already discussed the balance, shape, quality, and strength of the carvings. However, there are certain other fine points and incongruities that must be kept in mind, especially in judging copies or forgeries. When a piece is signed, it is best to compare the calligraphy with that of a known authentic piece by the same artist. The piece should be carved in the style of the artist whose signature it bears. Thus a detailed netsuke signed Miwa is most probably by Miwa III or it is a forgery, since Miwa I did crude though powerful carving. The material should be carefully examined also. If the netsuke is allegedly old but has two equal-size cord holes which show no evidence of wear, we can well question the authenticity. One should always carefully examine the netsuke to see if the ivory actually is old or if it has been stained so as to appear old. Usually the exposed portions are bleached relatively whiter than the unexposed surfaces, which tend to turn a mellow yellow-brown with age. Often the ivory is too dark through having been crudely overstained. It should be noted whether the artist worked with the material which is signed with his name. Care should be taken to see if the carving is well done on all surfaces, including the bottom, as no good artist would leave any part more crudely carved than the rest. Similarly, on poorer carvings the artist has not thoroughly thought out his overall design, so that part of the carving may be disproportionately flattened because he cut the original material inadequately or used a poor-quality scrap of wood or ivory. It is also important to determine if the overall artistic details are carefully worked out, such as the balance of the figure, including its general proportions. For example, are the joints of the body done weakly or with full depth and sweep? Similarly, the fine details should be well done and in accordance with the style of the artist. The netsuke should be even more effective when seen under the magnifying lens, in evaluating technical skill and facial expression. Are the finer lines such as the hair on an animal done clearly, neatly, and evenly, or are they poorly scratched in short strokes, uneven and carelessly crossing one another? Are the ears, toes, and nails carefully done along with the under-cuttings? In general we should first study the carving as a whole to establish in our own mind what the artist has attempted to create and whether he has carried out this interpretation. The netsuke should be carefully studied from all directions. Placing it on a table and slowly turning it is a good way of judging it from all angles. Then, having examined and established its gross configuration, we should study it in detail.

Keeping all these factors in mind, in the long run, the ultimate choice is dependent upon the individual taste of the collector abetted by his knowledge of Japanese artistic ideals and the particular styles which most appeal to him. He should, however, always remember that his taste in netsuke as well as in lacquer art often continues to grow and change as his knowledge and appreciation mature.

161. NETSUKE. Rakan coming out of a scroll. Signed: Suzuki Tokoku (with seal). Cherry wood. Eyes, whisk, and roller of scroll in inlaid ivory; earrings in gold. $1\frac{3}{16}''$ high.

162. NETSUKE. Shojo dancer. Signed: Jugyoku (carver) and Koma Kansai (lacquer artist). Lacquered wood. Hair in red tsuishu; mask in tinted ivory; hands, feet, and fan in ivory. $1\frac{9}{16}''$ high.

163. NETSUKE. Shojo dancer. Unsigned. Style of Matsuki Hokei. Finely carved red tsuishu lacquer over light wood foundation. 1⅞″ high.

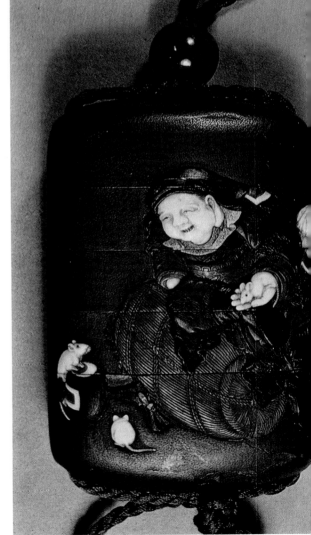

164. INRO. Daikoku and rats. Signed: Tokoku (with seal). Design done in inlaid ivory, gold, tinted ivory, tsuishu, and various woods on a coarse gray lacquer ground. 3¼″ × 2⅜″ × 1 1/16″. 4 cases and lid.

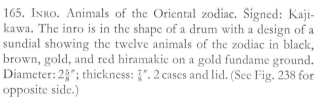

165. INRO. Animals of the Oriental zodiac. Signed: Kajikawa. The inro is in the shape of a drum with a design of a
sundial showing the twelve animals of the zodiac in black,
brown, gold, and red hiramakie on a gold fundame ground.
Diameter: $2\frac{5}{8}''$; thickness: $\frac{7}{8}''$. 2 cases and lid. (See Fig. 238 for
opposite side.)

166. OPPOSITE SIDE of inro in Fig. 67. Design executed in
red, silver, and gold takamakie, augmented by togidashi,
fine kirigane, and inlaid mother-of-pearl on a black ground.

167. INRO. Chrysanthemums. Signed: Shiomi Masanari. Flowers and leaves in gold togidashi on a roiro ground. $3\frac{1}{8}'' \times 2\frac{3}{8}'' \times \frac{7}{8}''$. 4 cases and lid.

168. NETSUKE. Woman holding basket. Signed: Gyuka I. Painted tea wood. Uji ningyo (tea picker) netsuke using itto-bori technique and water-color painting on light tea wood. $1\frac{9}{16}''$ high.

169. KOGO. Butterflies. Unsigned. Early 18th century. Two stylized butterflies in aogai, with details in gold lacquer on a fine yasuriko ground. The perimeter of the lid is red basket weave along with geometric-patterned inlaid mother-of-pearl. Octagonal shape. Diameter: 3"; height: $1\frac{1}{16}$".

170. NETSUKE. Skeleton and grave post. Unsigned. Attributed to Shuzan. Authenticated by Tokyo National Museum. Hinoki (cypress) wood with mottled water-color (mostly white) patina. $5\frac{1}{4}$" high.

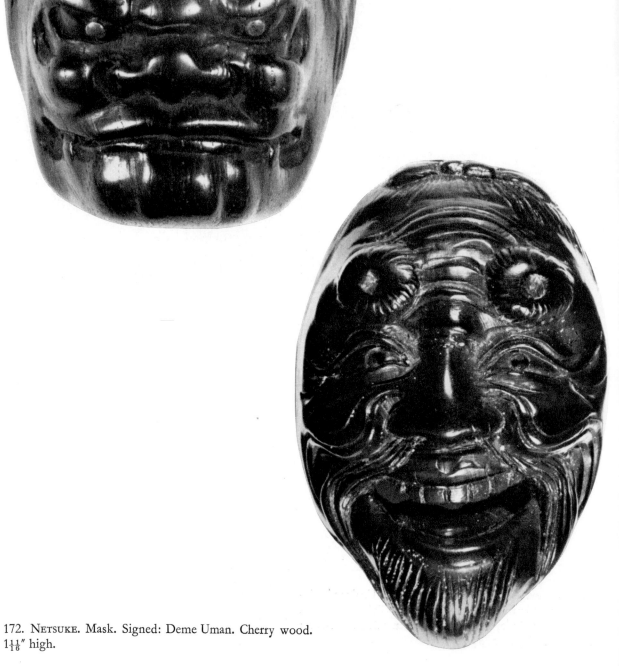

171. NETSUKE. Mask. Unsigned. Attributed to Miwa I. Chinese ebony with silver eyes. 1⅝″ high.

172. NETSUKE. Mask. Signed: Deme Uman. Cherry wood. 1¹¹⁄₁₆″ high.

173. NETSUKE. Recumbent ox. Signed: Tametaka. Wood. 2$\frac{3}{16}$" long.

174. NETSUKE. Recumbent ox. Signed: Minko. Ebony, with eyes of inlaid gold. Note the combination of simplicity and strength in this carving. 1$\frac{9}{16}$" long.

175. NETSUKE. Karashishi and ball. Signed: Ogasawara Issai of Kii Province. Ivory. Carvings by this artist are rarely signed. 1$\frac{3}{8}$" long.

176. NETSUKE. Bird breaking out of shell. Signed: Naito Toyomasa. Wood. Note the perfect oval netsuke shape. 1¾″ long.

177. NETSUKE. Snail on furled leaf. Signed (in fine uki-bori): "Carved by Tomiharu Seiyodo Kaaigawa Iwami." Ebony. Note the fine uki-bori technique typical of the Iwami school. 2⅛″ long.

178. NETSUKE. Oxherd and ox. Signed: Sosui. Boxwood. 1⅝″ long.

179. NETSUKE. Old-style pierced coins tied with twine. Signed: Morita Soko. Wood. 1⅜″ long.

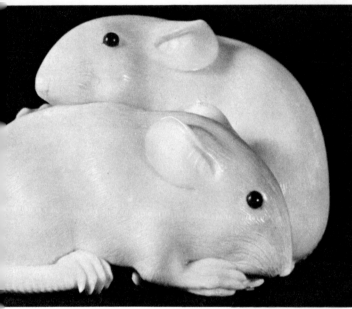

180. NETSUKE. Two mice nibbling on nuts. Signed: Kaigyokusai. Ivory, with inlaid hornbill eyes. 1⅝″ long.

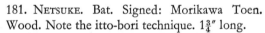

181. NETSUKE. Bat. Signed: Morikawa Toen. Wood. Note the itto-bori technique. 1¾″ long.

182. NETSUKE AND DETAIL. Frog on dried persimmon. Signed: Matsuda Sukenaga. Yew wood. 1⅝" long. Lower photo shows toes of frog.

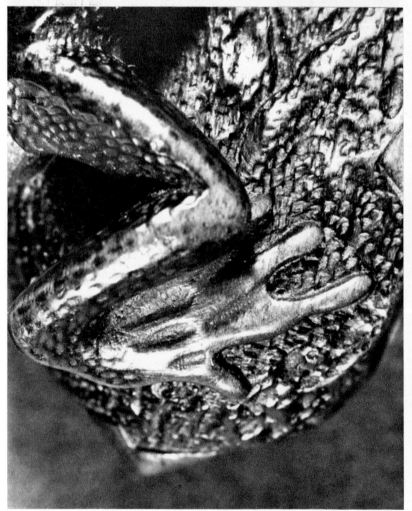

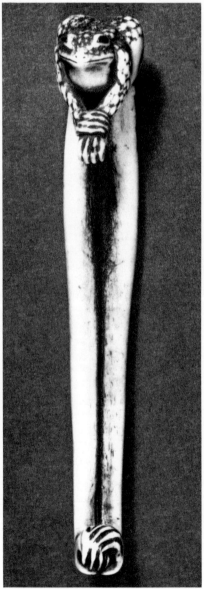

183. NETSUKE (sashi form). Humorous form of frog with elongated legs. Signed with seal of Koku (Kokusai). Deerhorn. 4¾" long.

184. NETSUKE (kagamibuta). Millet design. Signed: Ginshotei Tomei. This well-known metal artist (1817–70) of the Goto Ichijo school was famous for this design. The millet grains are done in minute gold encrustations. Diameter: $1\frac{5}{8}''$.

185. NETSUKE (ryusa form). Maple leaves. Signed: Morita Soko. Wood. $1\frac{3}{4}''$ long.

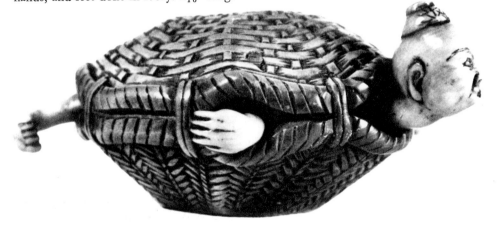

186. NETSUKE. Man at a party pretending to be a turtle, using two wicker baskets and wearing a *sake* cup on his head. Signed: Wada Sansho. Wood, with movable head, hands, and feet done in ivory. $2\frac{5}{16}''$ long.

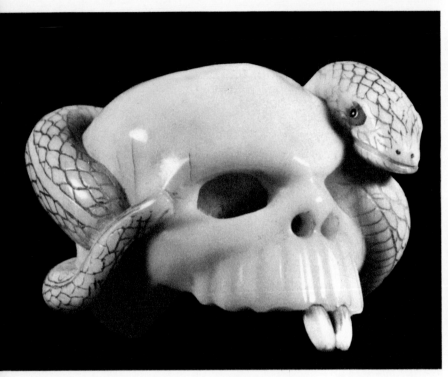

187. NETSUKE. Snake on a skull. Signed: Nagai Rantei. Marine ivory. Note the highly polished finish and the powerful, stark simplicity of design. 1⅛" high.

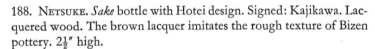

188. NETSUKE. *Sake* bottle with Hotei design. Signed: Kajikawa. Lacquered wood. The brown lacquer imitates the rough texture of Bizen pottery. 2½" high.

189. NETSUKE. Mandarin duck. Signed: Kano Natsuo. Gold. 1¾" long.

190. Netsuke (kagamibuta). Daruma. Signed with seal of Ogawa Haritsu (Ritsuo). Pottery. Diameter: $1\frac{9}{16}''$.

191. Netsuke. Kudan. Unsigned. Wood. A rarely portrayed mythological animal. $1\frac{3}{4}''$ high.

192. Netsuke. Cluster of small gourds. Signed: Gyokuso. Cherry wood. $1\frac{7}{8}''$ long.

193. NETSUKE AND DETAIL. Mushroom, snail, and ants. Signed: Gambun. Wood, with snail in marine ivory and ants in metal. 1¾″ long. Detail (lower left) shows ants.

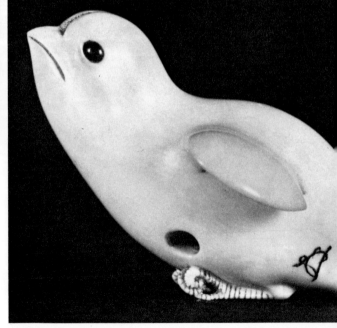

194. NETSUKE. Impressionistic bird. Signed with kakihan of Mitsuhiro. Highly polished ivory. 1⅝″ long.

195. DETAIL of a figure netsuke. Oni. Unsigned. Wood. The powerful expression of the demon's face is notable.

196. NETSUKE. Woman picking fleas from her kimono. Signed: Tokoku. Wood. 1⅜″ high.

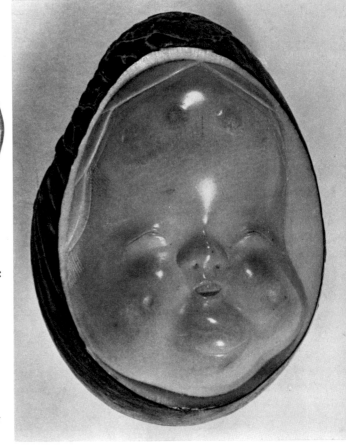

197. NETSUKE. Mask of Okame. Signed: Shoun. African ivory nut. 2″ high.

198. PAIR OF NETSUKE. Vendors
blowing gluten. Signed: Kyoku-
sai. Wood. Each 1⅞″ high.

199. INRO. Shoki and oni. Signed:
Nagaharu (Joi). The design consists
of an inlaid silver fan-shaped plaque
upon which is chiseled the figure
of Shoki. The oni is in inlaid copper
and gold, and the ground is fine
gold kiriganc. 2⅜″×2½″×1″. 3 cases
and lid.

200. INRO (two views). Sansukumi (snake, snail, and frog).
Signed: Jokasai. The design is done in silver, gold, black, and
red takamakie on a green ground. $3\frac{1}{2}'' \times 2\frac{1}{8}'' \times 1\frac{1}{8}''$. 6 cases and
lid.

201. INRO. Pine branches. Unsigned. Black persimmon wood. The design is of conventionalized pine branches against a background carved to simulate pine bark. $3\frac{3}{8}'' \times 2\frac{1}{4}'' \times 1\frac{3}{16}''$. 3 cases and lid.

202. INRO (tobacco-box shape). Bird and young ferns. Signed: Zeshin. The bird is etched in the lacquer, and the ferns are done in rough hiramakie on a rough gray ground. $1\frac{5}{8}'' \times 1\frac{5}{8}'' \times 1\frac{3}{16}''$. 1 case and wooden lid.

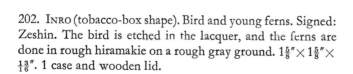

203. INRO. Peony and leaves. Signed: Kajikawa Toshihide. The peony is in raised, encrusted white mother-of-pearl and the leaves in solid-gold encrustations and gold lacquer over aogai encrustations. Part of the branches are in encrusted coral on a dark-brown ground. $3\frac{5}{8}'' \times 2\frac{1}{4}'' \times \frac{3}{4}''$. 4 cases and lid.

204. INRO. Buddhist emblems: stylized lotus flower and scepter. Signed: Ritsuo. The lotus is done in green and white pottery, and the scepter is in red lacquer. Rich brown lacquer ground. $2\frac{1}{2}'' \times 2\frac{5}{8}'' \times 1''$. 2 cases and lid.

205. Kogo. Plum blossoms. Signed: Shuran. Intricately carved tsuishu of plum blossoms and part of tree trunk. Diameter: 2⅞″; height: ⅞″.

206. Inro. Ants on oak leaves. Signed: Hasegawa. The ants are inlaid in gold, shakudo, and pewter. The leaves are in rough black and red hiramakie on a polished wood ground which is carved to emphasize the grain of the wood. The cord channels are lacquered to simulate bamboo. 3″ × 2⅜″ × ¾″. 4 cases and lid.

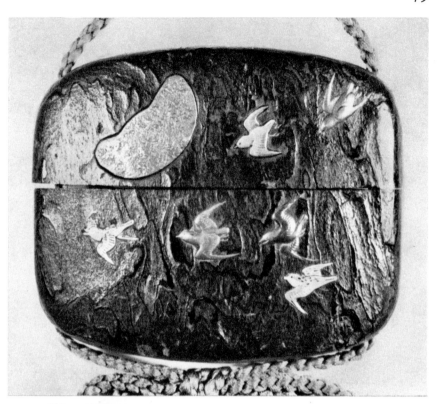

207. INRO. Plovers. Signed: Toyo, at the age of sixty-one. The plovers, slightly conventionalized, are done in pottery, mother-of-pearl, and silver and gold takamakie. The half-moon is done in pewter, and the ground is of pine bark. $2\frac{9}{16}'' \times 3\frac{1}{8}'' \times 1\frac{3}{16}''$. 1 case and lid.

208. INRO. Badger. Signed: Kozan (Shohosai). The badger is done in pottery and the foliage in brown and gold takamakie. The roiro ground is turning brown with age. $2\frac{3}{8}'' \times 2\frac{1}{4}'' \times \frac{7}{8}''$. 4 cases and lid.

209. INRO. The Blind Men and the Elephant. Signed: Toyo. Most of the design illustrating the famous story is in black and silver togidashi on a gold fundame ground. $3\frac{1}{8}'' \times 2\frac{5}{16}'' \times 1\frac{3}{16}''$. 3 cases and lid.

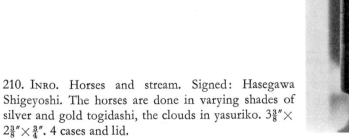

210. INRO. Horses and stream. Signed: Hasegawa Shigeyoshi. The horses are done in varying shades of silver and gold togidashi, the clouds in yasuriko. $3\frac{3}{8}'' \times 2\frac{3}{8}'' \times \frac{3}{4}''$. 4 cases and lid.

211. INRO (tobacco-box shape). Snake attacking a crane. Signed: Koma Kansai. The snake and the crane are done in takamakie simulating metal. The ground is coarsely carved natural wood. $2\frac{5}{8}'' \times 3'' \times 1\frac{3}{8}''$. 1 case and lid.

212. INRO. Rat on a rice bag. Signed: Jokasai. The rat is in gold and black takamakie on a gold fundame ground. The inro itself is in the shape of a rice bag. $3\frac{3}{8}'' \times 2\frac{1}{2}'' \times 1\frac{1}{8}''$. 4 cases and lid.

213. INRO AND NETSUKE. Tiger in bamboo grove. Signed: Koma Kansai. The design of the inro is mainly in low takamakie, with the tiger in gold and silver on a gold ground. The manju netsuke matches the style of the inro. Inro: $2\frac{7}{8}'' \times 3\frac{1}{16}'' \times \frac{7}{8}''$. 3 cases and lid.

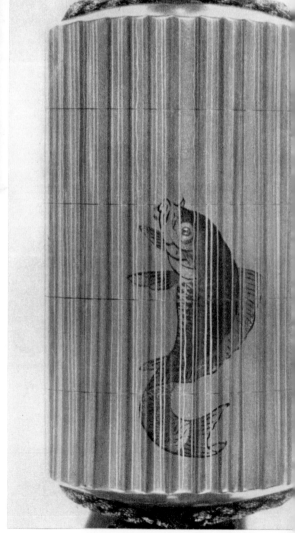

214. INRO. Carp ascending a waterfall. Signed: Toju. The carp is in black togidashi on a gold fundame ground, which is deeply fluted to give the impression of falling water in a three-dimensional effect. $2\frac{3}{4}'' \times 1\frac{9}{16}'' \times 1\frac{5}{16}''$. 4 cases and lid.

6 ❖ Subject Matter of Lacquer Art

General Considerations

Subject matter in Japanese lacquer art is merely a reflection of all the closely integrated influences that contributed, over the centuries, to molding the thinking, mores, and customs of its people. Japanese art did not consist of a self-perpetuating independent form of culture. It was not "art for art's sake" but was basically a utilitarian form of culture paralleling the Japanese social way of life. Both art and the Japanese social structure consisted of a complex of integrated influences, such as religion, nature, cosmology, mythology, folklore, fairy tales, and stories of military and other famous heroes. These influences, which formed the core of the subject matter of Japanese art, not only blended and overlapped one another but were in themselves the composite picture of an amalgamation of further influences. For example the Japanese cosmology and gods of the sun, moon, and water were figments of the imagination and were endowed with supernatural powers. Many mythological tales were associated with them. As a result of Shinto beliefs and concomitant ancestor worship famous emperors, priests, and military heroes also became gods. They too were ultimately attributed with supernatural powers and became associated with imaginative folklore and mythological tales. Fact became blended with fiction, and the natural with the supernatural. These reciprocal influences of mythology, superstition, religion, and philosophical thinking similarly applied to every facet of nature, both animate and inanimate. The early Japanese religion recognized anything awesome or unusual as having "spirit" *(kami)*, whether it be animate or inanimate. With the advent of Buddhism these superstitions and feelings were intellectualized according to the concept of transmigration. In essence, this states that all things on earth possessed "spirit," and after death one would change into any of these forms—human, animal, insect, or even inanimate. This was further developed into the belief (probably Shinto) that demons could change into various animals or could possess one's own spirit. The ultimate result was the development of symbolic thinking, each creature on earth reflecting various human and supernatural characteristics. This concept of nature secondarily influenced religion and custom. Shrines were built to appease the animals (animal cults) and thereby drive out the demons from one's body. Similarly, all forms of nature were revered and became the favorite subject of Japanese art. As a result of this concept of nature and transmigration, meat was not eaten by Buddhists and no living creatures were harmed because of religious fears and, in some instances, legal punishment.

There were other reasons for the development of this web of inter-related religious, superstitious, moral, ethical, and timely political codes. Many of the adopted religions, such as Confucianism and Zen Buddhism, stressed social, cultural, and ethical concepts even more than religious dogma. Similarly, the emperors used Shintoism as a political scheme to enhance their power by stressing, through ancestor worship, their direct descent through the sun goddess. Seemingly simple Japanese customs evolved from pagan superstitions, religious ideas, and Chinese philosophical concepts. Thus the Japanese custom of cleanliness stems from the purification rites of the old Shinto religion. Uncleanliness was also related to menstruation, childbirth, and death. Families often moved from houses defiled by death, and this custom may well relate to the development of the flimsy, temporary type of Japanese architecture.

The problem of the integrating influences on Japanese art and life becomes even more involved when one realizes that each of these influences in itself was evolved from a composite complex of prior influences! Such was the case in Japanese religion. The original pagan superstitions gradually evolved into Shintoism. This in turn was combined with various Chinese religions and philosophies. Many of the Chinese religions had originated from Indian Buddhism and were secondarily influenced with their own concepts. Finally the Japanese themselves altered this combined religion into innumerable sects, each with its corresponding tenets. There were other reasons for changes in religions, based on the changing Japanese social and economic standards. Originally Japanese society was divided into clans practicing a simple agricultural economy. The system of the early clan gods was, from a practical point of view, ideal under this economy. However, with the development of the family household unit of society and the specialization of the Japanese economy into specific crafts, there arose a demand for specific household gods, who were often adopted in accordance with the occupation of the head of the household—such as Ebisu being chosen by the fisherman. Thus many original clan and Shinto gods with certain physical, mental, and moral attributes, under the influence of Buddhism as well as the changing economy, soon developed new attributes propitious to the times. Therefore as a result of other religious influences these household gods evolved as combinations of the original Shinto gods with Buddhist, Chinese, and Brahmanic gods.

The Japanese lacquer artist's interpretation of subject matter is not simply just realistic or impressionistic but reflects complicated symbolic influences. Thus in order to fully comprehend the subject matter in Japanese art it is not sufficient just to be familiar with the Japanese mythology and folklore that the artist is portraying, which in itself is voluminous. It is also essential to go two steps further. The first is to acquire a thorough knowledge of the symbolism reflected in the subject matter. The second is to comprehend the reasons behind the symbolism. These reasons lie in a thorough understanding of the origin and development of Japanese religions, philosophies, mores, and customs. The constant blending and gradual alteration of early religions and ethical concepts make it at times almost impossible to accurately establish the origin of certain customs or symbolic representations. On the other hand, it must be surmised that the artisan himself was often ignorant of much of the long-forgotten symbolic and ethnic origins of his subject matter, and would ply his art simply for its decorative and aesthetic values. In many instances, however, to complicate matters further, the Japanese artist not only portrayed complex iconography and the artistic concepts of his day but also took pride in presenting such symbolism or historical allusions in most recondite ways.

A good example of the various influences on symbolic and abstract thinking is the artist's representation of the quail *(uzura)*, which symbolizes 1) martial spirit, 2) poverty, 3) autumn, 4) divinity, and 5) Fukakusa (a suburb of Kyoto). The meanings behind these symbolic allusions are different in each case. Thus, according to Japanese custom, the quail was used as a fighting bird and hence represented the martial spirit. The keen Japanese observation of nature (which was given its impetus through Zen Buddhism) takes note of the ragged appearance of the bird—hence its symbolic reference to poverty. Similarly, the bird is associated with the millet plant, thus typifying autumn. Superstition and mythology related that the quail changed into a pheasant and again into the revered *ho-o*, or phoenix—hence its symbolism of divinity. Finally, when the quail is seen in the grass, it represents Fukakusa, since *fuka* means "hatching" and *kusa* means "grass," and in this play on words we have an example of Japanese humor. It should be noted that on occasion the symbolic meaning of a subject may simply derive from a word's having two meanings. Thus the pine tree symbolizes longevity because of its other name, *chitose*, which means "1,000 years." Similarly the word "four" *(shi)* is considered unlucky because it is pronounced the same as the word for death.

Specifically, subject matter in Japanese lacquer art was related to artistic portrayal of interest to the Japanese artist and his patrons. This naturally was in turn related to religious and cultural backgrounds and aesthetic influences. Early lacquer art essentially reflected Chinese and Buddhist influence, including formalized religious and mythological subject matter and ornamental designs of patterns and arabesques in Chinese fashion. With the introduction of Zen Buddhism various aspects of nature were portrayed in "simple Zen style." Artistic concepts stressed the artist's own individual feeling of his subject matter. Both subject matter and ornamentation became more typically Japanese. By the 18th century all of the arts became increasingly refined, especially lacquer techniques, and were given further stimulus through the new patrons of the arts, the military class. By the 19th century, with the popularization of the arts among the merchant and lower classes, the subject matter turned to more commonplace everyday portrayals of Japanese life, often associated with humorous and ribald overtones. Such influences predominated especially in netsuke art. However, lacquer ware, a more costly art form, still reflected the more aesthetic taste of its primarily aristocratic patrons. The majority of inro and other miniature lacquer art forms therefore consisted of simple, subtle portrayals of nature suitably altered for the small surface area to be ornamented.

Definite differences exist in the type and extent of subject matter in lacquer as compared to the other arts. There are even further basic differences inherent in the miniature form of lacquer art. In sculptural miniature art such as seen in the netsuke, single figures predominated without any background decoration. Here the subject matter was much more variegated and commonplace because of the extensive use of the netsuke by the general populace. In painting, the large flat surface area provided the artist with an ideal means for more extensive pictorial scenes, including complete landscapes. In miniature lacquer art the small irregular surface area aesthetically necessitated the use of ingenious foreshortening requiring abbreviated pictorial scenes and yet still creating the entire image. As the inro gradually came to be worn as an object of display, its decorative elements developed much more fastidiously than most of the other arts. But since lacquer art was so expensive it was not only highly valued but also fostered mainly by the nobility, the shogunate, and the local daimyo. It therefore reflected, subjectwise, the more elegant and conservative tastes of these more highly cultured and wealthy patrons. Careful analysis reveals that approximately 80% of the subject matter on inro of the late 18th century and early 19th century centered about nature, particularly abbreviated landscape scenes, plant life, and birds, along with various types of supplementary decorative background effects and design. To a lesser extent other types of subject matter were presented and consisted of animate aspects of nature, such as animals, fish and insects, gods, allusions to mythological and folk tales, and purely ornamental designs, along with decorative abstractions. The latter were invariably symbolic in nature, such as calligraphy, religious symbols, family crests, etc. One would rarely find a frivolous or humorous subject on an old inro in distinct contrast, for example, to the more plebeian arts of netsuke or woodblock prints. Similarly, netsuke subject matter involved subjects befitting sculptural qualities while lacquer art necessitated a basic pictorial element with occasional secondary sculptural effects obtained by the use of *takamakie* and raised inlays. Again, in netsuke art as distinguished from lacquer art, various schools as well as individual artists specialized much more in the use of specific materials, in the carving of very specific subject matter, and in characteristic styles of carving. Thus Masanao more or less specialized in portraying frogs in wood and Gambun in inlaying tiny metallic ants on rotted wooden mushrooms. Such specialization was not as often seen in miniature lacquer art, although occasionally we see artists who tended to repeat their favorite designs—for example, Shiomi Masanari with his bulls in *togidashi* and Shibata Zeshin with his wave design and small plant and animal life. Similarly, the Koma school tended to use a typically shaped inro, and the Kajikawa school typically lined their inro with *gyobu nashiji*. Finally we might note that military heroes and famous battle scenes were less frequently depicted in lacquer art in contrast to miniature metal sword furnishings, in which these subjects naturally predominated.

From a technical point of view the liberal use of color and the innumerable lacquer techniques gave lacquer artists an extremely varied and unique range of ways in which to pictorially portray their subject matter along with the use of raised lacquer and encrustations to add soft sculptural effects.

It is with these factors in mind that we present subject matter along with its symbolic content, while placing the greatest emphasis upon the subjects that were most commonly portrayed by the lacquer artist.

Cosmology, Mythology, Gods, and Religions

Japanese cosmology is fully recorded in the *Kojiki* (Record of Ancient Matters), which was compiled in A.D. 711. There was no written language existing in Japan before this time until the adoption of the Chinese ideographs, and so the ancient Japanese mythology, customs, folklore, and superstitions were handed down by word of mouth. Since there had already been intercourse with China and Buddhism for about a hundred years, Chinese mythological and folklore influence had already penetrated Japan.

According to the *Kojiki,* chaos originally consisted of water with a layer of mud. There first arose the five original celestial beings and then the seven generations of celestial spirits ending with the Male Who Invites (Izanagi) and the Female Who Invites (Izanami). Izanagi thrusts his spear into chaos and pulls up some mud which forms the island of Onokomo-jima, and some muddy drippings from the spear form the stars. Subsequently Izanagi and Izanami give birth to the remaining islands of

Japan and to the gods of nature representing water, wind, trees, etc. One of their sons was Ebisu, the only true Shinto household god. Izanami finally gives birth to the god of fire (Kagatsuchi), and she dies from the burns. She is visited in the lower world by her disconsolate spouse, who, when he returns to the upper world, bathes in order to purify himself from his contact with Hades. (This concept of purification by washing permeates Shintoism.) While he is washing his left eye, the Heavenly Shining Goddess, Amaterasu Omikami, arises; by washing his right eye he causes the Moon Ruler, Tsukiyomi, to appear; and by washing his nose he brings forth the Valiant Swift Impetuous Hero, Takehaya Susano-o, the god of storms. Because of Susano-o's bad behavior Amaterasu hides in a cave, thereby causing complete darkness. A mirror and a precious stone are hung on a *sakaki* tree obtained by Ame no Koyane (a celestial being) and midst raucous laughter by the gods, Ame no Uzume does a dance to music. The sun goddess appears out of curiosity and is prevented from returning to her cave by a strung-out hempen cord, and so light is returned to the world.

Other mythological descendants arise from Amaterasu and Susano-o. Ninigi, the sun goddess's grandson, receives the precious stone, and sword, and the mirror (which constitute the sacred regalia) and marries the goddess of the land in Satsuma. According to the legend their grandchild was Jimmu Tenno, the first emperor of Japan, who ruled from 660 to 585 B.C. in Yamato and who inherited the sacred regalia. The story further states that Susano-o's fifth-generation descendant was Onamuchi, whose descendants, in turn, were the priests of Izumo, while the descendants of Ame no Koyane were the Fujiwara clan.

The Japanese concepts of god and the supernatural, along with their ideas of purification, formed the crux of their Shinto religion. The word *kami,* or spirit, can be loosely used to mean god. Under the ancient clan system the clan chieftain was also the spiritual leader. When he died, his spirit was worshiped as a god. This type of clan-*kami* worship is then essentially a form of ancestor worship. Clan-*kami* worship naturally evolved into true ancestor worship in the form of household ancestor worship after the clan system of society fell into disuse. This indoctrination of clan and ancestor worship paralleled the ancestor worship of the emperor, who claimed to be of divine descent and therefore demanded overall domination and idolatry of his people. He was in essence a divine representative on earth, forming a link between heaven and his people. This concept was used by the emperors as a hereditary political expediency. The Japanese concept of *kami* therefore did not sharply divide natural from supernatural, or man from god. Thus famous emperors and military heroes were also deified and had temples built in their honor. The Japanese religion consists of a pantheon of benign, almost human figures similar to that of the ancient Greek religion. The Japanese system of ancestor worship was later abetted by Confucianism, which stressed continuation of the family line, a necessary factor in keeping up the continuity of ancestor worship. However, Shintoism did not profess any moral, ethical, or social codes. There was no concept of a hereafter or its relation to obligations in life. The only concrete Shinto ideas were related to purification and *kami* possession of one's body. Its dogma stated that the body was essentially unclean and was contaminated by birth and death. Expiation was done by prayer to the gods and certain acts of purification, such as bathing and symbolic washing of the mouth. There was also fear of possession of one's body by evil spirits. These spirits enter the body of a person, usually as some animal, and then demand worship for themselves as those animals. Hence the origin of different shrines and cults, such as the fox cult. This idea of spirits entering people, and of animals and the natural elements having "spirit" and subsequent relation to nature and animal worship, appears in a different form under Buddhist philosophy, namely that of transcendentalism and the universal spirit of the all-loving god. Fear or awe of nature or anything unusual probably even antedated Shintoism or any concepts of *kami* or gods. Thus the worship of mountains and the use of simple amulets as a means of appeasement in ancient pre-Shinto Japan.

In the Taoist (Chinese, 7th century B.C.) scheme of cosmology we already find highly intellectualized metaphysical concepts which are not unlike George Berkeley's philosophy of the early 18th century and which parallel the equally ancient Hindu and Yoga philosophies. According to Taoism, chaos originally consisted of nothing, from which there arose substances consisting of *yang* and *yin* (in Japanese, *yo* and *in*), the male and the female principles. (These two principles are often depicted in art as two comma-shaped objects, one light and one dark, one reversed from the other, and both encircled as an ornamental conventionalized pattern.) This origin of substance from nothing is not contradictory, as it is explained that light, hearing, and color are also so-called substances coming from invisible sources, or nothing. These philosophical concepts developed by the Indian and Chinese metaphysical religions laid the foundation for a nihilistic philosophy of life on earth, stressing the transient and unreal life on earth in contrast to the permanent true spiritual life found upon attaining nirvana (heaven) after death. This theory, along with transcendentalism, forms the basic elements of Buddhist philosophy. Thus Buddha was a means of final emancipation of the human soul by means of transmigration and the final union with the universal Soul. Each object on earth—animate or inanimate—possessed this Buddha-elect spirit. In the process of transmigration one's spirit and body might be those of an animal or insect. Hence the Buddhists abstinence from eating meat and their reverence for all forms of living creatures. This close union of man and nature was further stressed by Zen Buddhism. It was only by meditating on nature and by living a simple ascetic life that one could reach final enlightenment from the transience of this false earthly life. This stoic philosophy readily appealed to the samurai class. The religious and physical closeness which the Japanese had with nature naturally resulted in its extremely popular portrayal in their art. Similarly, the various spirits with which objects of nature were endowed, such as longevity, happiness, valor, strength, etc., all contributed to the symbolic representation of nature.

The various Buddhist sects basically stressed the same metaphysical concepts concerning religion and the universe. Their main difference was their professed means of attaining salvation (nirvana). Some sects disdained the pantheonic system and complicated rituals, stressing the individual's right to heaven through his own effort. While some sects stressed extreme asceticism and constant meditation and a series of transmigrations to obtain nirvana, other sects simplified matters so that salvation could be obtained by merely repeating the name of their god. Each of these different systems (sects) appealed to different segments of Japanese society—the more intellectual forms to the aristocracy, the Zen sect to the military, and the simple repetitive religious utterances to the common folk.

With the advent of Buddhism in Japan it was found expedient to incorporate the firmly entrenched Shinto gods into this religious system. This resulted in dual Shinto-Buddhism or Ryobu-Shinto. The Shinto gods were considered as *gongen,* or temporary manifestations of Buddha, or as saints *(bosatsu)* of the highest grade before attaining true Buddhahood. The Shinto gods were given new Chinese Buddhist names, and even the old Shinto liturgies and popular festivals were incorporated into the Buddhist scheme. Along with this conglomeration were elements of absorbed Brahman and Taoist gods and concepts, and even new gods were created.

An example to illustrate this dualism, complexity, and evolution of Japanese gods is the Japanese goddess Kannon, the goddess of mercy. She was originally the Indian male Buddhist god Avalokitesvera, the spiritual son of Amida, representing mercy. There are forty different forms and varieties of portraying this god, each with corresponding symbolic allusions. The eleven-headed form represents the story of his head splitting into pieces with grief from watching the wretched condition of humanity—a Lamaistic conception. Another form, Sengan-senju Kannon, represents the 1,000 eyes *(sengan)* to pity and the 1,000 arms *(senju)* to save. In China this god, in female form, is quite popular and is the patroness of young women and children. Her feminine form exists because of confusion with the legend of her Chinese origin, which represents her as the merciful daughter of an emperor of the Chou dynasty (1122–225 B.C.). In Japan her full name is Kanzeon Daibosatsu, and she is one of the 75 Bodhisattvas. As in China, she exists in a female form. However, her Indian drapery and Aryan features are replaced by Japanese features and draperies. The thousand-armed Kannon in Ryobu-Shinto has her identified with Kuni-satsuchi (second generation of celestial spirits) and the eleven-faced form with Izanami. Various Japanese legends are associated with Kannon which include her incarnation into various people, such as Chujo Hime, the daughter of Fujiwara no Toyonari (A.D. 704–65) and Doryo, a hermit of the 15th century, and even Prince Shotoku.

Only those gods who are significantly represented in lacquer art will be noted, including their origins, symbolic meanings, and characteristic portrayals in lacquer art. These gods include basically Kannon (who has already been noted), the Seven Lucky Household Gods, Daruma, and Uzume.

The Seven Lucky Gods (Shichi Fukujin)

No group of mythological beings are as frequently portrayed in Japanese lacquer and other art forms or are as beloved by the people of all classes as the Seven Lucky Gods, or the Household Gods.

Rather than being deities in the true sense of the word, the Shichi Fukujin, as they are called, represent the seven basic elements of worldly happiness as interpreted in the daily desires of the Japanese people. Thus there is no religious significance or any particular sect associated with the Household Gods. They are not worshiped as idols; there is no particular ritual to be followed, no penance to pay, no self-denial or punishment imposed by the gods. Out of every man's desire for worldly comforts and everyday pleasures grew this little group, which encompasses gods of longevity, wealth, ability, daily food, strength, love and beauty, learning and achievement. Each household chooses to honor those gods that represent the things which they desire most on earth. Generally these number between two and four within each family group, and rarely is the god of longevity excluded from the choice. These worldly deities are worshiped at home, not in temples, and are purely to provide for the comforts of this world.

At New Year's time particularly, the little Household Gods are frequently represented in a group, for, according to legend, on New Year's Eve the *takarabune,* or treasure ship, comes into port carrying the Shichi Fukujin as passengers and the *takaramono* or *shippo,* the seven precious things, as cargo.

In art these gods are frequently represented either singly or in groups, and each is easily distinguished. They are often treated in a humorous manner. They are Benten, Bishamon, Daikoku, Ebisu, Fukurokuju, Hotei, and Jurojin.

BENTEN

The only female among the Seven Lucky Gods, Benten (sometimes called Benzai-ten), is reputed to have her origins as the Hindu goddess

Sarasvati, the wife of Brahma. She represents the cultural talents and is the Japanese goddess of knowledge, eloquence, wisdom, motherhood, education, beauty, talent, poetry, music, and the fine arts. Women particularly worship her for her feminine qualities. She is also goddess of the wealth of the sea. Her messenger is a dragon or a white snake, as it is related that she first appeared in Japan on the day of the snake and one of her first deeds was to quell the destructive dragon who was ravishing the island of Enoshima—by marrying it.

She is usually represented seated, often upon the back of a dragon, carrying in her hands either a *biwa* (lute) upon which she plays or a sacred jewel and a key. When seen among the other seven gods, she is represented as the musician of the group. She often wears a small crown upon her head and is dressed in a long flowing robe.

BISHAMON

Possibly the least frequently portrayed member of the seven gods, Bishamon is representative of masculinity, strength, power, and martial spirit. He is occasionally portrayed conquering an *oni* as a representative symbol of overcoming evil spirits. Furthermore, he is said to have originally been one of the protectors of Buddha and of Buddhism. For these reasons he is portrayed clothed in full armor and always carries a spear in his right hand and a pagoda (with varying symbolic explanations) in his left hand. He is the patron of soldiers and was a great favorite with the samurai, who looked to his image as a source of inspiration.

In legend he is one of the four guardians of the heavens and represents the north quarter, which was his realm. His messenger is the centipede.

DAIKOKU

Daikoku is the god of wealth and prosperity. He was originally an Indian god called Mahakala or Big Blackface One. The Indian priests would rub his body with oil and burn incense at his feet, which caused a dark discoloration of his wooden body and face, and it was thus he acquired his Indian name.

In Japan Daikoku, along with Ebisu, is often placed in the kitchen, where he insures plentiful food and where he gradually becomes covered with soot; so he is occasionally represented in Japanese art with a darkened face.

The messenger of this jovial god and one of his important attributes is the rat. He is rarely seen without at least one or two of these animals at his feet. There are several explanations for this choice of messenger, one being that rats multiply quickly and thus are a good omen of the riches that Daikoku brings. Another explanation is that rats eat rice, so they must always be carefully watched, and this serves as a constant reminder to watch over and guard one's wealth lest it gradually be depleted.

Daikoku is portrayed wearing a lavish loose-fitting long jacket over his plump body. On his head is a soft cap with a high crown on which is often drawn the sacred jewel. His feet are encased in high loose-fitting boots. He stands upon or is next to one or more bales of rice. The rice bales are of course representative of prosperity, since rice has always been a staple food and in the feudal days, especially, was used in lieu of money as payment and was representative of a man's wealth. Daikoku carries in his hand his precious mallet, from which he is said to produce his riches. Upon the mallet is drawn either the *tama* (precious jewel) or the *tomoe* (a representation of *in* and *yo,* whence all things come). On his back or by his side is a large sack which is said to contain the *takaramono,* or precious things.

Daikoku is frequently represented in Japanese lacquer art and is by far one of the most popular of the household deities (Figs. 160, 164).

EBISU

The only lucky household god of pure Shinto origin, Ebisu is reputed to be the son of Izanagi and Izanami, the creators of the universe. He was, however, a disappointment to his parents, and at the age of three he was placed in a woven wicker boatlike cradle and set adrift upon the sea, where it was expected that he would perish. Instead, however, he conquered the elements, survived, and flourished. He is highly esteemed as the god of the fisherman and of daily food and is often seen along with Daikoku as a kitchen deity.

His messenger is the *tai* (sea bream), and he is portrayed in a great variety of activities revolving about this fish. He is dressed in the clothes of a fisherman and often carries in his hand a fishing pole and a woven basket. He is short and chubby and usually has a beard.

Ebisu is the only one of the Seven Lucky Gods who is strictly of Japanese mythological origin, and he is one of the most popular Japanese gods, although he is not too frequently portrayed in the lacquer arts.

FUKUROKUJU

This member of the group is purely of Taoist origin, and some authorities feel that he is actually a personification of the legendary Taoist sage Lao-tzu himself.

He is the god of good fortune, wisdom, prosperity, and longevity, and his name is made up of ideograms relating to his symbolic significance. Thus *fuku*=luck and happiness, *roku*=wealth and prosperity, and *ju*=longevity. He is also the god of wisdom and learning. In many ways he closely resembles Jurojin, another of the Seven Lucky Gods.

He is frequently represented in art and is always portrayed as a short, elderly, scholarly man with a great elongated head which is indicative of his many years of study and his resulting wisdom. In a humorous manner he is occasionally depicted attempting to remove a fly or other annoying insect which is perched on top of his long bald head and which is just out of his arm's reach. In one hand he usually carries a staff, or *jui,* the Chinese scepter, while in the other he carries a fan, which is a symbol of power, or he will be holding or reading from an ancient scroll, again attesting to his intellectual superiority. Nearby will be his messenger, usually a crane or a long-tailed tortoise, the popular symbols of longevity. His overall appearance is that of dignity, serenity, and wisdom.

HOTEI

The fat, jovial, carefree Hotei is possibly the most frequently portrayed and certainly one of the most beloved of the Seven Lucky Household Gods. His origin is uncertain and he has mixed attributes of Taoist, Buddhist, and Chinese background.

He is above all the Santa Claus of Japan, the patron saint of children, whom he loves as dearly as they love him. The name Hotei means hempen sack or cloth bag, an accessory that he always carries with him and that is said to contain all his worldly possessions (which are few) and above all an endless quantity of wondrous toys for the children. Occasionally, however, his huge sack is seen to contain the *takaramono.* He is always portrayed as an undignified, merry, bald, grossly obese man with a huge, round, often naked belly and a smiling face free from all worry and care. He is frequently surrounded by happy children who sprawl over him and his large bulging cloth bag anxiously trying to get to the treasures within. He is always thought of as the god of happiness and good things and exemplifies constant good nature and contentment.

JUROJIN

The god of longevity and wisdom among the Household Gods is Jurojin, who many authorities believe was originally the same deity as Fukurokuju but was added to the Shichi Fukujin as an individual being in order to bring the members of the group to the lucky number of seven.

In art there is a definite close resemblance between the two, although Jurojin tends to be depicted in a more dignified and solemn manner. He is portrayed as an old man with a long beard dressed in the fashion of a Chinese scholar. His head, although at times elongated to call attention to his wisdom, is rarely as long as that of Fukurokuju. On his head he often wears a small hat which frequently bears the emblem of the sun on the front. He carries a fan and a long staff from which hang the ancient scrolls, further attesting to his wisdom and said by some authorities to contain the dates of birth and death of all people. The possession of this vital information also attests to his powers as the god of longevity. His messenger is usually a deer, although he may also be portrayed, as is Fukurokuju, surrounded by any of the well-known symbols of longevity, such as the crane, the tortoise, or the plum, pine, or bamboo plants (Fig. 80). His physical and symbolic resemblance to Fukurokuju is so close that the two are frequently mistaken for each other.

Daruma (Bodhidharma)

Daruma is the Japanese name for the Indian Bodhidharma, a Buddhist priest (d. A.D. 529). He was born in Southern India in the early 6th century and from India went as a missionary to China in 520 and thence to Korea and Japan. It is said that he went to Korea by water by means of a rush leaf. It is to Daruma that the introduction of the Zen sect of Buddhism in China is attributed. He taught the doctrine of contemplation, or Zen, which in Sanskrit is *dhyana,* or meditation or spiritual enlightenment and wisdom through concentration. Owing to his extreme piousness, he is supposed to have been seated in prayer and devout meditation, with legs crossed, neither moving nor speaking for nine successive years, with his face turned toward the wall of a monastery on Mount Su. During this long period of motionless meditation his legs withered away. He cut off his own eyelids for shame after having fallen asleep, and where he cast them on the ground the tea plant arose to help holy men keep their vigil.

In Japanese art he is usually caricatured and is seen very frequently in netsuke art though only occasionally in lacquer art (Fig. 31). He is depicted with a roundish body with the red cloak of his order about his body. His legs are absent and occasionally his arms as well. He is usually yawning or stretching with arms over his head as if coming back to consciousness after a long sleep. His lidless eyes are wide open, and there is a scowl on his face. He carries a priest's fly whisk in his hand. He is usually portrayed humorously in netsuke art and sometimes even as a female, since what female could resist the temptation to talk for nine years! Toy Daruma are quite popular in Japan and are armless and legless and have round weighted bottoms. When tipped over, they will immediately right themselves and are therefore called *okiagari-koboshi*—that is, a bonze who can easily get up —signifying the spirit to fight against failure.

Uzume, Okame, or Otafuku

Uzume (Dread Female), also known as Okame or Otafuku (Big Breasts), is a primitive Shinto goddess whose full name is Ame no Uzume no Mikoto, or goddess of mirth. She is commonly represented in Japanese art, most often in netsuke, less frequently in lacquer, and usually in a humorous or erotic vein. Her artistic presentation is fairly characteristic. She has a round face with plump, puffed-out cheeks, an always smiling countenance, a small heart-shaped mouth, and small eyes with shaven eyebrows. High on her forehead, in accordance with an ancient court custom, two imperial ornamental black spots. She has a protruding forehead covered on top and at the sides by streaming straight black hair brought over the temples in two wide, flat bands and occasionally tied behind into a bun (Fig. 197). She has a plump, rounded body and wears the dress of a court lady. She often carries a bamboo branch and *gohei*.

The religious *kagura* court dance performed by the priestesses in Shinto shrines is the dance of Uzume, which originated with the *sarume,* the girl monkey dancers, since Uzume is their reputed ancestress.

It was Uzume whose erotic dance and song before the cave enticed the sun goddess to emerge from her retirement, thus giving back sunshine to the darkened world. Uzume represents the chief lady official of the palace and is also prayed to for long life and protection from evil and plays a prominent role in old Japanese phallic ceremonies.

One of the commonest forms of portrayals, mainly in netsuke art, shows her smiling and erotically stroking the elongated nose of the god Saruta Hiko no Mikoto or of a long-nosed *tengu.* The former is an allusion to her captivating this god, who opposed the progress of Ninigi no Mikoto from heaven to earth.

Heroes, Demigods, Legends, and Folklore

We have seen the influence of ancestor worship in ancient Japan and the religious, symbolic and philosophic tendencies which neglect to distinguish animate from inanimate, truth from fiction, and natural from supernatural. Along with these factors there was word-of-mouth folklore amalgamated with adopted Buddhist and Chinese mythology and folk tales. It is therefore no wonder that many Japanese literary and military heroes have been readily endowed with numerous supernatural traits, just as readily as Japanese gods have been endowed with human attributes. Such fanciful thinking is difficult to grasp and appreciate by the Occidental mind, which has been materialistically and scientifically oriented with limited interest in tradition and folklore. In Japanese folklore, then, heroes may be considered as demigods endowed with supernatural powers, just as the emperors were considered as the descendants of the Shinto gods. The majority of Japanese folklore consists of purely imaginary beings, mythological animals, and fairy tales, usually associated with moral or philosophical concepts or of a purely adventurous nature.

Among the highly revered personages of nonmilitary nature are the Six Famous Poets, the Seven Sages, the Twenty-four Filial Paragons, and the *sennin.*

Poetry was always popular in Japan, including poetic contests known as *uta-awase.* It was stressed by the court and the military and consisted mainly of short odes, lyrical and ideational in character and invariably describing or lauding some aspect of nature. While certain forms existed, there was no rhyme or weighing of syllables. In April and May when the wisteria is in full bloom, Japanese people of all classes honor the plants along public paths by improvising short poems about them which are written on slips of paper and attached to the most beautiful branches of the flowers. The Six Famous Poets are quite popular subjects in Japanese lacquer art, which reveals them in their beautifully flowing, colorful court robes and hats. This group is known under the name of Rokkasen, representing the six *(roku)* most celebrated poets *(kasen)* who lived in Japan during the 9th century. Their names are as follows: nobleman Ariwara no Narihara, nobleman Bunya no Yasuhide, Buddhist priest Kisen Hoshi, court lady Ono no Komachi, nobleman Otomo no Kuronushi, and Buddhist priest Sojo Henjo. This list is occasionally varied to include the two famous 8th-century poets Kakinomoto Hitomaro and Yamabe no Akahito and the equally famous nobleman of the 10th century Ki no Tsurayuki. There are also the lesser known group of 36 poets known collectively as the Sanjurokkasen. The most famous of all the poets from a romantic and sentimental point of view and by far the most commonly depicted in Japanese art, especially in lacquer and netsuke, is Ono no Komachi. She lived in the 9th century and was a beauty as well as a famous poetess. She was allegedly of noble birth, but there exists no evidence of whether she actually existed or was a purely legendary figure. In either case she was also very proud and vain and ultimately aged and grew to spinsterhood an old and ugly shriveled hag, representing the Buddhist adage that all is vanity. In lacquer art she is usually depicted as a beautiful court lady with long flowing black hair, seated or in a semireclining position. In netsuke art she is usually shown seated on a *sotoba*, or wooden grave post, as an ugly old hag with old tattered clothes wearing a worn-out straw hat.

The Seven Worthies (Sages) of the Bamboo Grove (Chikurin Shichi Kenjin) were seven learned men of the 3rd century who were occupied with music, reading, and conversation and whose meetings were held in a grove of bamboo trees. Their philosophy was that human happiness consisted of emancipation from cares and worries and unrestrained indulgence in wine. This subject is quite commonly portrayed in Japanese lacquer art (Fig. 119).

The Twenty-four Filial Paragons (Nijushiko) are persons from Chinese lore famous for acts of devotion toward their parents involving self-sacrifice, for which they were in most cases properly rewarded. Such rigid devotion stems from Confucian philosophy specifying the duties of members of a family toward one another, which philosophy was later incorporated by the imperial court into a similar type of allegiance of Japanese subjects toward the emperor. References to one or another of these 24 tales are occasionally seen in Japanese lacquer. Other examples of filial piety are occasionally portrayed in Japanese lacquer art. One of these is taken from the story of Yoro-no-taki, a waterfall in the province of Mino.

According to this legend, a woodcutter named Kosagi was so poor that he could not continue to provide *sake* for his aged parents. He is usually pictured about to fill his gourd with water from this waterfall when the gods, as a reward for his filial piety, convert the water into wine.

The *sennin* or *rishi* are hermits who, according to Taoist teachings, attained immortality through meditation and asceticism. There are literally hundreds of them, a few of whom are commonly depicted in lacquer and netsuke art. They attained magical powers, practiced alchemy, including brewing the elixir of life, and lived alone in the mountains and caves. They lived five or eight centuries, after which they were often borne away into the sky by a cloud, a dragon, or a phoenix. There also existed eight female *sennin*. Physically the *sennin* are depicted in human form, having large ears, wearing a coat made of leaves over a simple Chinese dress, and carrying a knotted and crooked staff. They usually have fairly long beards and are often accompanied by transcendent animals. The famous netsuke artist Shuzan was noted for his powerful carving of *sennin*. In lacquer art, along with netsuke art, specific *sennin,* such as Gama Sennin, Kanzan, Jittoku, and Kinko, are most popular. The most popular in lacquer art is Gama Sennin. He lived in the mountains with a large white toad *(gama)* with three legs (one behind and two in front) for a companion. He is also called Kosensei and has flat, ugly features, no hair on his face—not even eyebrows—and a skin covered with protuberances (Figs. 56, 57).

The Rakan (Arhats) are some 500 in number but are limited to 16 by Japanese artists and worshipers. They are perfected saints of Buddhism who have conquered all human passions but are still humans with supernatural powers. They are depicted in Japanese art with halos around shaven heads, long eyebrows, elongated earlobes, often with earrings, and a Buddhist cloak hung over one shoulder, leaving the other shoulder bare.

Rosei's Dream

This legend is quite commonly depicted in lacquer art, especially on inro, being also a favorite subject of the lacquer artist Toyo. It depicts the tale of Rosei, who set out to see the Chinese emperor, who was in need of counselors. On his way he met the Sennin Lu Kung and complained to him about his poverty. The *sennin* thereupon gave him a magic pillow upon which he fell asleep. He then dreamed, according to the legend, that he attained a high position with the emperor and that an enemy invited him to his house in order to boil him in his bath. He awoke only to find that the steaming food being brought by the innkeeper had awakened him, and he then realized the transitory nature of earthly possessions and the vanity of human greatness. In lacquer inro Rosei's dream pictures him reclining on a pillow with a fan held over his sleeping face, while the opposite side of the inro reveals his dream, portraying a procession of retainers coming to fetch him with a court palanquin. His fan is usually made of thin translucent mother-of-pearl, so that the underlying face can be visualized, and the dream sequence is usually done in *togidashi,* with the end of the procession of retainers fading in the distance. This technique renders a beautiful dreamlike effect as well as excellent perspective (Figs. 67, 166).

Military heroes and famous battle scenes are naturally extremely popular subjects in Japanese sword furnishings and occur with some regularity in netsuke art, but are relatively rare in Japanese lacquer art (Figs. 14, 112, 113). Thus such heroes as Yoshitsune and Yoritomo are rarely seen in lacquer art.

Various Deities, Demons, and Ghosts

This rather loose classification encompasses a particular sphere of Japanese art expression depicting the fierce and horrific in a very dynamic, imaginative, and rather exaggerated way. A typical example would be a huge forbidding god with powerful rippling muscles and wildly thrashing robes. Such a figure is much more adaptable to the sculptural arts than to lacquer work. These subjects, in comparison to benevolent gods and spirits, only occasionally appear in lacquer art. They are often portrayed in *takamakie* and in encrustations engendering a subtle sculptural quality.

Among such fierce gods are the guardian Fudo, Emma the King of Hell, the god of wind Futen, the god of thunder Raiden, and Nio, the two keepers of the temple gates. Miscellaneous frightening subjects include the commonly portrayed devil-imp, the *oni,* often in association with Shoki the Demon Queller, and the more rarely portrayed ghosts and various hobgoblins associated with specific mythological tales and legends. In general, demons are portrayed in Japanese art, as distinguished from humans, in vivid colors, such as red or green, to add to their infernal appearance. While such figures often have fanglike teeth, they never have cloven hoofs or tails.

FUDO

Fudo (Acala the Immovable) is one of the five great kings who protect the Buddhist world. While he usually incorporates the terrifying aspects of Buddhism, he is actually a huge figure with a fierce expression whose function is to deter the evildoer. His head is covered with thick black hair in long pigtails held by several cords and falling over his left shoulder. He has two short fanglike teeth. He sits or stands on "an adamantine rock of self realization" and is surrounded by the "flames of the power of intellect." He holds in his left hand the rope to restrain one's passions or to bind the guilty and in the other hand the sword which cuts through the darkness of ignorance or deters the evildoer. He is usually accompanied by his two chief attendants the *doji* Seitaka and Kongara. Fudo is the god of wisdom and one of the eight patrons of life in Japanese astrology. He is also considered as the patron of waterfalls and is occasionally represented in a grotto next to a waterfall. He is erroneously considered as the god of fire.

EMMA-O

Emma-o or Emma-ten is the king of hell, one of the Twelve Deva Kings, and in Japanese Buddhist art is represented quite differently from the original Indian form. He is usually seated on the ground cross-legged, looking slightly downward. He has a very fierce expression, a red face, large eyes, an open mouth (often with sharp canine teeth), frowning brows, and a bristling beard. He wears a crown resembling a judge's hat of black and gold with the character "king" written on it. On the top of his crown project three lobes, the center one in black, the one on the left representing the moon, and the one on the right the sun. Projecting sidewise from the crown are two scepter-shaped objects. In his right hand he holds his *shaku,* or regal wand (Frontispiece). He is occasionally associated with the mirror of Harikyo and the scales or *go* (deeds), as souls are judged by their reflections in the mirror. He is sometimes accompanied by the "evil woman," the keeper of the Japanese River Styx.

FUTEN

Futen (Fujin), the god of wind *(kaze no kami),* is one of the Twelve Deva Kings and is of Brahmistic origin (Vasu or Vasava) but is presented quite differently in Japanese art. He has a devil-like head with sharp protruding canine teeth, pointed ears, three clawlike fingers on each hand and two claws and a big toe on each foot. Grasped in each hand are the open ends of a large inflated bag which is blowing over his head and from which the winds escape. He is usually standing on some conventionalized storm clouds. He occasionally wears a leopard skin and is sometimes shown with Raiden, the god of thunder.

RAIDEN

Raiden, the god of thunder, is also called Raijin and Kaminari-sama. He is represented as a devil-like figure with a red face, two small goatlike horns protruding from his forehead, and two claws on each foot. He is often riding on a storm cloud. He is surrounded in back by a circle or semicircle of eight drums which are held together in the form of a wheel. He holds in each hand double-headed drumsticks with which to beat the drums to send forth the peals of thunder (Fig. 90). Occasionally he is represented resting and enjoying a smoke of tobacco, suggesting calm weather. Swallowing of a few beans at the first peal of thunder protects against lightning during the year. The Japanese child also, according to superstition, always keeps his belly covered for fear that the god of thunder will steal his navel, since children's navels are something of which he is quite fond.

NIO

Nio (or Nio Kongo), the two keepers of the temple gates, are of inferior position in the Buddhist pantheon, but they originally represented the two great Brahmanic gods Brahma and Indra. The word Nio is derived from *ni,* meaning two, and *o,* meaning large. These gods are placed on either side of the entrance to a temple to guard it from evil spirits. They are standing figures of huge powerful proportions, large rippling muscles, and frowning, menacing expressions (Fig. 32). They are dressed in loincloths and a scarf loosely flowing overhead and attached at either end to the waist. The god on the right represents Indra and is the red Deva with open mouth ready to pronounce the Sanskrit vowel "ah," thus symbolizing the male *yo (yang)* principle inviting in the good. He holds in one hand the *tokko,* a scepter symbolizing the power of prayer. The god on the left in green is Brahma. His compressed lips are ready to pronounce the syllable "um" representing the female *in (yin)* principle for shutting out evil.

ONI

The *oni,* or devils, were originally Shinto in origin and represented personified diseases which could be exorcised by means of the peach. Most of the modern ideas relating to them, however, are derived from Buddhist sources. They are fierce-looking and yet are to be considered more like humanized pranksters or imps than true malignant devils. They are usually portrayed in Japanese art in a humorous fashion. They are not only popular in netsuke art and in the art of small sword furnishings but are also depicted fairly frequently in lacquer art, especially in the relatively more modern works of Shibayama style. The *oni* have large square heads with one or two little horns protruding from the forehead, a large mouth extending from ear to ear, sharp canine fangs, and large fierce eyes with bristling eyebrows. Their skin color is usually red, green, or blue. Their bodies are human-shaped and they occasionally wear girdles of tiger skin. Their feet usually consist of two claws and their hands of three claws, but they often have human fingers as well. They are expelled from the household on the first day of spring under the lunar calendar in a special ceremony called *oni yara* or *tsuina.* The ceremony consists of a special incantation and the throwing of roasted black beans, of which *oni* have a tremendous fear. Holly and the dried head of a sardine are also talismans against *oni* and their tricks. In Japanese art the *oni* is frequently found hiding in a tree trunk or under a box or a hat or even in a well. In netsuke art *oni* are commonly depicted fearfully crouching under the hail of the beans striking their backs. *Oni* occasionally enter monkhood by repenting and having their horns sawed off and are then depicted often as temple guardians beating the temple gong. *Oni* also appear in many legendary tales and in Noh plays. They are frequently portrayed in association with Shoki the Demon Queller (Fig. 199).

SHOKI

Shoki the Demon Queller dates back to the T'ang dynasty, his Chinese name being Chung Kuei. Legend relates that he was buried with high honors by the emperor for honorably committing suicide after having failed in the imperial examinations. His spirit, in gratitude, vowed to expel the demons from China forever. He is represented in Japanese art as a fierce giant, usually with a long flowing beard, brandishing a large double-edged sword and clothed in a Chinese court-style robe. He is most often associated with an *oni* who is often humorously teasing him or hiding under an object, often Shoki's own hat.

GHOSTS AND GOBLINS

Ghosts *(yurei)* or the spirits of dead people were first depicted in Japanese art by the painter Maruyama Okyo (1733–95) at the request of the shogun and since then have become popular art subjects. Pictorially they have long straight hair, often long snakelike necks, terrifying white faces with a haggard look, hands raised to the breast with fingers limply pointing downward, and bodies and dresses tapering below the waist into nothingness, since Japanese ghosts have no legs or feet (Fig. 124). Some ghosts are benign, representing deceased loved ones reappearing on earth, but many are of the more fearful type, most commonly a wronged person taking revenge by appearing as a ghost. *Bakemono,* or ghostly goblins, are various-shaped ugly ghouls associated with various specific myths and folk tales (Fig. 108). Some animals such as foxes assume goblin manifestations, and spiders after dark become goblins.

The Zodiac (Junishi)

The zodiac is a division of the heavens (stars) into constellations. Each of the 28 Chinese constellations consists of a group of stars which is represented by a different animal and a different element. The elements consist of wood, metal, earth, sun, moon, fire, and water. Furthermore, the zodiac is divided into four quadrants, the dragon presiding over the eastern quarter of the first seven constellations, the phoenix over the second seven constellations or southern quarter, the tiger over the western, and the tortoise over the northern quarter.

The old Japanese year according to the lunar calendar (which is still followed in rural areas) is divided into 12 months or moons. The first day

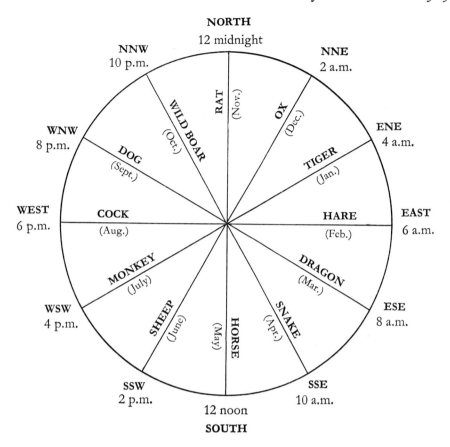

ORIENTAL ZODIAC

of each month corresponds to the new moon and the fifteenth day to the full moon. The lunar months have 29 or 30 days, and since these 12 months do not equal one solar year, one month is repeated every third year so as not to interfere with the dates for the seasons, solstices, or equinox. The lunar months have no names but are identified by numbers one through twelve and by means of the 12 zodiac animals. Each animal is related to a specific month. The end of our month of January marks the beginning of the Japanese first month. In fact, no accurate numerical comparison can be made, as the Japanese lunar New Year varies each year according to our calendar from January 16 to February 19. Incidentally, everybody becomes one year older on New Year's Day irrespective of his date of birth. Each Japanese year is named according to one of the twelve zodiac animals and one of the celestial stems or elements. These elements are five in number, being wood, fire, earth, metal, and water. They are further subdivided into positive and negative, such as wood positive and wood negative, making a total of 10 stems. The 12 animals run in the same sequence year by year as do the 10 stems, and therefore every 60 years the same cycle is repeated, as the common denominator for both 12 and 10 is 60. Thus the year 1910 is represented by the dog and is metal positive; the year 1911 is the boar and is metal negative. The year 1912 is the rat and is water positive; the year 1913 is the ox and is water negative. Thus each year for 12 years is represented by a different zodiac animal, and the sequence is repeated. The stems are similarly repeated. The year 1970 completed the cycle and returned to the dog and metal positive as in 1910. Figure 165 shows an inro illustrating the 12 zodiac animals.

Each of the same 12 zodiac animals is also representative of a specific month, a specific time (hour), and a specific point of the compass. It should be noted that the old Japanese hour was equivalent to two of our hours and was counted backward from 9 o'clock to 4 o'clock, there being no 1, 2, or 3 o'clock. Sunrise and sunset were always called 6 o'clock throughout the year. The Japanese 9 o'clock is equivalent to our 12 a.m. and 12 p.m., 8 o'clock being our 2 a.m. and 2 p.m., 7 o'clock being equal to our 4 a.m. and 4 p.m., 6 o'clock to our 6 a.m. and 6 p.m., 5 o'clock to our 8 a.m. and 8 p.m. and 4 o'clock to our 10 a.m. and 10 a.m. Specifically, for example, the rat represents our 11 a.m. to 1 p.m. (the hour of the rat or our 12 midnight and the Japanese 9 o'clock), November, and the north direction. The twelve-part diagram on the preceding page summarizes all of these factors, using Western time.

It should be noted that in view of the strong Oriental beliefs in the power of nature and the universe and their influence on time and people, the various elements of the zodiac were closely correlated with fortune-telling as good or evil spirits affecting every day life. The five directions, each of the zodiac animals, the sun and moon, negative and positive years, the five elements, and even corresponding numbers and colors all held symbolic good and bad influences. Thus there were propitious as well as bad days for weddings, building, sewing, repairing, planting, and even funerals. Similarly, a man born under a certain element, star, color, or animal year, had best marry a woman born under a compatible element and year as well as in accordance with certain lucky ages. Japanese fortune-tellers use nine stars, each with an associated color, including white, black, blue, green, yellow, red, and purple. These stars and colors run in specific daily order as well as according to the year, much as do the animals of the zodiac. Thus 1910 represents #9 purple star, 1911 #8 white star, 1912 #7 red star, 1913 #6 white star, etc.

The Japanese years and eras are historically or chronologically divided into the names of the reigning emperors as well as the *nengo,* or year names. There were usually two or more year names under each emperor, each year name extending from one to as many as 44 years. Finally the Japanese numerically count our year 1 as equivalent to the reign of their first emperor, beginning in 660 B.C. They therefore add 660 to our calendar year, so that our year 1900 is equivalent to the Japanese year 2560.

Since the zodiac animals and the five elements exerted such an important symbolic influence on Japanese life, it is no wonder that they were portrayed with considerable frequency in Japanese art, including lacquer ware. The animals were often depicted according to their month or season along with corresponding symbolic grasses, trees, and vegetation. Occasionally two seemingly symbolically incongruous animals are seen on a lacquer piece. Their strange combination can usually be explained, however, by their relationship through the zodiac, such as the combination of the monkey and the tiger, which corresponds to the hours of 4 a.m. and 4 p.m.

Frequently a lacquer artist made a series of twelve inro, each representing a different month as symbolized in the zodiac. These sets were done by many renowned artists, such as Zeshin, Ritsuo, and Koma Kansai.

An understanding of the Japanese zodiac is also often necessary for interpreting the signed age of lacquer and netsuke pieces. Such recorded ages may note the month, the zodiac animal year, and even the *nengo*. Thus if the calligraphy states the 3rd of Ansei, the year would be 1856, since Ansei started in 1854. However if the writing only states Ansei, the year of the dragon, we would have to refer to the Ansei period and then see which zodiac year corresponded to the dragon, which again would prove to be 1856. This year, according to the zodiac calendar, is a fire positive year and #9 purple star.

Of course it must be noted that in this present age the ancient Japanese calendar and zodiac calendar is, for all practical purposes, no longer in use. However, an understanding of the nature of the zodiac calendar is a necessity in order to determine the ages of works of art which were almost entirely signed in accordance with this ancient calendar.

Each of the 12 animals of the zodiac has intricate and specific symbolic significance. This is discussed in detail further on in this chapter under the heading of "Animals," where each is discussed in alphabetical order.

Nature

By far the commonest subject portrayed in Japanese art is nature. This consists of both realistic and aesthetic depiction of animals, birds, and insects as well as inanimate forms, such as an entire landscape or its composite parts down to a single leaf or blade of grass. The influence of the seasons on nature and the ethereal aspects of clouds, mists, and winds were particularly stressed. Nature had always been regarded with awe and as being endowed with "spirit" from early paganism to primitive Shintoism. With the advent of Buddhism and the philosophy of transmigration, the influence of nature became increasingly predominant. All forms of nature, both animate and inanimate, were considered to be endowed with "spirit" and ran the gamut of human and even superhuman attributes. According to Shinto concept, this "spirit" represented *kami,* and in Buddhist philosophy the "spirit" represented the reincarnation of the soul of Buddha or a stage of transmigration of man's soul on his way to ultimate nirvana. Thus, according to his deeds in earthly life, man would either elevate himself or revert to lower animal or plant forms toward his ultimate goal: the nihilistic union of his soul with the universal soul of Buddha. Therefore basically through religious beliefs, and abetted and expanded by mythology, superstition, folklore, and actual physical appearance, each animal, insect, and plant form was considered to be endowed with certain characteristics and influences. Thus there evolved the extensive symbolism seen in Japanese nature and life and therefore in the art forms.

Furthermore, according to Shinto beliefs, nature was under the control of various gods, such as the god of thunder, the god of wind, the god of the moon, and the god of agriculture. Such gods were, by practical expediency, incorporated into the Buddhist pantheon as representing different aspects of the Almighty Buddha. The close link between religion and nature reached its peak of development with the advent of Zen Buddhism, which stressed the importance of meditating in the presence of nature. Under Chinese and Buddhist influence nature was portrayed as a spiritual, awe-inspiring, symbolic representation of the universe which could only be expressed artistically through the contemplative soul of the inspired artist. This resulted, especially in Japanese art, in considerable abstract realism, impressionism, and individualism. With the advent in the 19th century of the realistic school of painting and the popularization of the arts, nature portrayal became much more realistic, photographic, and accurately detailed, often losing the inspired artistic simplicity and aesthetic strength of earlier works.

Specifically, animals were not only endowed with human qualities but, according to Shinto belief, could possess one's body as a demon. This was usually done by an offended "spirit" who would assume the form of an animal and thereby enter the body of the person to be possessed. As previously noted, to placate these spirits, animal cults arose. In general, then, in life as well as in death, gods and spirits could assume animal forms and also animals could assume human and godlike forms or even other animal forms. Such tales are extremely common in mythology and folklore. Certain animals were associated with certain gods by acting in the capacity of transporting the god or by being symbolically compatible with the god, or by being associated with the god in folklore or mythology. Certain combinations of animals or animals and plants were portrayed together for similar reasons. It should also be noted that a bird or a fish was just as capable of transporting an individual or god as a horse or an ox. Thus to the Japanese mind there is not the sharp distinction between man and god *(kami),* animals or plants and human attributes, fact and fiction, or natural and supernatural. Hence food is offered to dead ancestors and to gods as well as to the living. Animals, besides being possessed with human qualities, were also endowed with physical, mental, and emotional supernatural qualities or were entirely mythological in character. Thus evolved the nine-tailed fox, the turtle with the long tail, and the purely mythological and fabulous creatures, such as the *kirin,* the phoenix, and the purely Japanese *tengu* and *kappa.* Finally, animals were also used in association with the zodiac, including symbolic representation of the hour, day, season, and year. Along with these concepts arose superstitious customs concerning the appropriate or propitious times to act according to the zodiac and according to lucky or unlucky days or omens.

We must also mention that there are many combinations of animals, flowers, reptiles, etc., which frequently occur—for example, the crane, tortoise, pine, and bamboo, all symbolic of longevity. It should be pointed out that these combinations of animals or plants and the like must be harmonious in symbolic significance and that the components are not merely joined together in order to create a beautiful picture. Thus we often see the sparrow and the bamboo, the tiger in a bamboo grove, and the plum blossom and the nightingale. One of the more abstruse associations is the snake, the snail, and the toad. Called *sansukumi,* this group is explained by the equality of power which nature has granted them, for the snake will eat the toad, and the toad will eat the snail, but it is reputed that the slime of the snail will kill the snake. Thus we have a stalemate, a perpetual cycle controlled by the inherent forces of nature (Fig. 200).

As stated, practically every object of nature has many symbolic meanings due primarily to religious concepts of the spirit in all things and secondarily to various superstitions and folklore built up around natural phenomena. A typical example of these complicated interrelations of nature with religion, custom, symbolism, and art can be found in the pine tree (Figs. 135–139). Like practically every other natural object, the pine *(matsu)* plays an integral part in the life of the Japanese people. It is an evergreen which grows abundantly in Japan and is also artificially cultivated into all shapes and sizes. It even has an official title: *goko no taifu.* There are specific pine trees which are venerated as a result of old folklore and certain spiritual and symbolic attributes associated with these trees. Symbolically the pine represents long life and conjugal felicity. When it becomes 1,000 years old, it is said, its thin sap turns to amber. The word *chitose,* the other name for the pine, means 1,000 years. Its needle-shaped leaves drive away demons. It is naturally portrayed in keeping with other symbols of longevity, such as the crane and tortoise. Old folk tales of famous pine trees have been incorporated into Noh plays, such as *Takasago.* This legend relates that one of the sons of Izanagi landed at Takasago, where he met and married a young girl with whom he happily lived to a ripe old age. They died at the same hour on the same day. (Several species of pine have needles growing in pairs and when one needle drops the other quickly follows.) They live on in the spirit of the two old pine trees in Takasago and in Sumiyoshi, and on moonlit nights they retake human shape, go to the beach at Takasago, where they were so happy, and gather pine needles. They are portrayed with a rake, a broom, and a basket, the rake symbolically meaning "to rake in all good things" and the broom "to sweep out all evil." The Takasago song from the Noh play is sung at weddings. *Fukusa* embroidered with the pine and crane, symbols of longevity, are often presented to the newly born.

The pine, because of its happy symbolic representation, is used around temples of gods, before the palace of the emperor, and before the entrance gates at festivals. During the New Year celebrations a pair of pines, the red-stemmed *(akamatsu)* and the black-stemmed *(kuromatsu)*, are placed to the left and to the right of the gateway—the red (on the left) represents the male principle *yo* and the black (on the right) the female principle *in*. The pine was also depicted and used extensively as a result of the influence of Zen Buddhism. The keynote of Zen Buddhism and Zen art was simplicity and meditation in the quiet solitude of nature. Thus the quiet, peaceful tones of the evergreens, especially the pine, became popular in landscaping the tea gardens. Pine trees were also often planted in the gardens of samurai to express wishes for a long and hardy life.

Artistic representation of the pine was correspondingly popular and consisted of allusions to the old folk tales associated with the pines as well as specific designs and patterns depicting the pine. This consisted of everything from heraldic conventionalized patterns of the pine to aesthetic natural portrayal. Young pine trees are represented by the *wakamatsu* design. The three-tiered pine-leaf design is also quite popular. Drawing the pine brings to mind other similarities with nature, such as the appearance of the pine branch with a stork's leg, the concentric arrangement of its leaves like fish scales, or the pine bark appearing like dragon's scales. Certain Chinese aesthetic rules at times governed the drawing of the pine, such as the whorl-spoke dot *(sharinshin)* and the saw-tooth dot *(kyoshinshin)*, the latter being used for distant pine effects. Symbolically the pine was depicted with other emblems of long life and was also shown laden with snow, in which case it represents the blessing of long life even when the snows of winter have fallen (old age).

These illustrations of but a single example of an object of nature, such as the pine, reflect the typical pattern of the integration of Japanese life with nature. Thus again we see the accepted mixing of the natural with the supernatural, the animate with the inanimate through "spirit" and religious beliefs, thereby weaving its intricate symbolic pattern of thinking as reflected in the mythology, folklore, calligraphy, drama, superstitions, customs, art, and everyday way of life of the Japanese people. It is from this thinking that there arises the basically close interrelationship of Japanese customs, mores, and art.

Specifically lacquer artistic representation of nature may be divided into six categories. The first and most prominent is plant and insect life. This encompasses everything from entire landscapes down to the minutest forms of plant and insect life, such as a few blades of grass gently bent by the breeze, an autumnal leaf gracefully floating downward in space, or a colorful praying mantis quietly sitting on a branch of a tree. These smaller aspects of nature are much more ideal for artistic presentation on miniature lacquer surface areas, and avoids overcrowded designs of larger landscapes. It also gives the lacquer artist free rein in depicting in technical detail the minutiae of nature that cannot be physically shown on larger overall designs. The second most frequent nature subject in lacquer art is birds, which are symbolically presented in all forms of motion, from impressionistic designs to extremely detailed ornithological realism. Next in frequency are various animals from large quadrupeds down to various species of amphibians. Sea life, including fish, shellfish, and shells, also forms a group fairly frequently seen in lacquer art. Next come the purely mythological animals, birds, and creatures, such as the dragon, phoenix, *kappa,* and *tengu.* Last, and perhaps the most important group from a subtle aesthetic point of view, are the ethereal aspects of nature or natural elements of nature associated with plant and animal life, namely the moon, wind, rain, water, and clouds. Here is the Japanese lacquer artist's forte, presenting in the most artistic way, combining delicacy, grace and ornamental design, the beautiful vagaries of nature.

Flowers, Grasses, and Trees

In most civilizations, flowers play an important part in the celebration of various festive occasions and are indeed an integral part of the ceremony, and in all societies flowers have a definite language and each species a special significance. In Japan, however, the language and the symbolic significance of plant and flower life are of far greater importance in the daily lives of all of the people than anywhere else in the world. Here flowers are not relegated only to special occasions, but rather perform a daily function. The traditional Japanese house, no matter how poor or wealthy its inhabitants, has a *tokonoma* in which is displayed some family treasure, however humble, complemented by a suitable floral arrangement. Flowers are associated with every act of daily living in Japan. However, their symbolic attributes are so complex that formal rules have been devised restricting and regulating their use, and the art of floral arrangement is one of the most complex skills, and its masters are looked upon with great respect. So rigid are the rules that various restrictions are placed on the number of flowers in an arrangement, the season in which they may be used, the combination of different flowers and leaves in any one arrangement, and the colors and species which may be intermixed. All of these factors plus many others are governed by the specific symbolic significance relegated to each flower. So highly prized is the beauty and appreciation of nature and its foliage and floral treats that the Japanese often make long journeys simply to view their favorite flowers and trees when they bloom.

It is only natural, therefore, that this great appreciation and complex symbolic significance, along with its restraining regulations, be carried over into art. The beautiful colorful art of laquer decoration lends itself exceptionally well to the artistic handling of the natural beauty of the abundant plant life which grows in Japan. However, there is strict adherence to the rules governing the portrayal of flowers and plant life. In order to comprehend some of these restrictions we must first analyze and become acquainted with the symbolic significance of some of the many different varieties of flowers and foliage common to Japan.

FLORAL CALENDAR

Flowers, plants, and grasses are of such great importance in daily Japanese life that a floral calendar is recognized, and these flowers and grasses, when portrayed by themselves in lacquer art, having no other primary symbolic significance, can be regarded as being representative of their own individual months or seasons.

Authorities differ somewhat on a few of the flowers and plants below and their specifically associated months, but in general this is the accepted association and major symbolic explanation.

MONTH	FLOWER OR PLANT	MAJOR SYMBOLIC SIGNIFICANCE
January	pine *(matsu)*	longevity
February	plum *(ume)*	spring
March	peach *(momo)*	longevity
April	cherry *(sakura)*	loyalty (national flower)
May	iris *(shobu)*	victory
June	peony *(botan)* and wisteria *(fuji)*	youth and spring
July	morning-glory *(asagao)*	affection
August	lotus *(hasu)*	purity
September	Seven Grasses of Autumn, which are bush clover or lespedeza *(hagi)*, arrowroot *(kuzu)*, pampas grass *(susuki)*, wild carnation *(nadeshiko)*, maiden flower *(ominaeshi)*, Chinese agrimony *(fujibakama)*, and Chinese bell flower *(kikyo)*	
October	chrysanthemum *(kiku)*	longevity (imperial crest)
November	maple *(momiji)*	autumn; changing affection
December	narcissus or daffodil *(suisen)*	devotion

BAMBOO (TAKE)

There is perhaps no more commonly portrayed single plant than the bamboo, whose image abounds in all art forms and particularly in painting and lacquer ware.

The bamboo is classified as a tree grass, and one expert notes that there are over 400 species of bamboo, of which over 100 are indigenous to Japan. At one time it was estimated that over 1,400 different articles were constructed from bamboo in Japan, and its intrinsic value therefore is readily apparent. Its uses range from food (bamboo shoots, *takenoko*) to almost every conceivable object manufactured by man.

Naturally a plant as important as this one and as common in daily living is surrounded by the Japanese with almost infinite symbolic and emblematic significance.

As a plant, its root always remains below the ground and it is only the stalks which appear and grow upright in groves to varying and sometimes great heights. It is a rapidly growing plant, an evergreen, and practically indestructible. It is symbolic of fidelity, constancy, and long life, and in this respect it is often seen in combination with the crane. When portrayed with sparrows among its branches in the winter, it is indicative of friendship. Bamboo stalks growing close together in clusters represent family loyalty.

In lacquer art, the graceful bamboo stalks are portrayed in all seasons, with infinite artistic variety, bending under the weight of heavy snows, tossing and swaying in the wind, bending beneath the pelting rains, or growing straight and tall as if reaching out to touch the sky. Symbolically the ability of bamboo to bend and sway without breaking even under heavy burdens or in severe storms indicates strength from yielding, while its tall, straight stalks are emblematic of upright conduct and strength of character. There are many legends regarding the bamboo, and one of the most commonly portrayed in lacquer is the "Seven Sages in the Bamboo Grove" (Figs. 119, 120).

CAMELLIA (TSUBAKI)

This is one of the few flowers which bear unpleasant connotations. Since the fading camellia does not drop its petals one by one but suddenly falls from the stem as an entire flower, it was thought in feudal times to suggest the act of decapitation. It was thus a disconcerting reminder—to the samurai in particular—of the possibility of this fate. Consequently, camellias were never to be found in samurai gardens, and they are relatively infrequently depicted in lacquer art.

CARNATION (NADESHIKO)

One of the Seven Grasses of Autumn, it grows wild. It was in the famous *Tale of Genji* that the prince gave his sweetheart a bouquet of wild pink carnations as a symbol of his lasting devotion. Thus carnations are still symbolic of fidelity.

CHERRY BLOSSOM (SAKURA)

This lovely blossom, indigenous to Japan, is accepted as the national flower of Japan and is regarded as the "king of flowers." It is commonly depicted in lacquer art, and indeed variations of the cherry blossom were often adopted as crests by the nobility.

The cherry blossom has a short life, and it is likened to the faithful samurai who was always ready and eager to risk his life for his master. Thus the symbolic inference of loyalty which the cherry blossom bears.

The beauty of the *sakura,* which often grows wild and which is worshiped for its beauty alone rather than for its fruit, inspires the lacquer artist in his frequent efforts to portray this perfect and magnificent tree.

Many thousands of poems have been inspired by the cherry blossom and in April when the cherry trees are in full bloom, thousands of people make excursions to see them in their full splendor.

CHRYSANTHEMUM (KIKU)

Probably the most frequently represented flower in all of Japanese art, the chrysanthemum affords the lacquer artist an opportunity to display his skill through his portrayal of its graceful form. The chrysanthemum, furthermore, is regarded with great affection and admiration in Japan, and the artist has long utilized this flower either in a realistic manner or in a stylized form to adorn his works. Although it is at its height of perfection of bloom during October and November, it is one of the few flowers which blossom all year round, and it is proper therefore to portray it during any season.

The 16-petaled chrysanthemum is the official crest of the imperial house. In this form it resembles the rays of the sun and thus gains even greater significance in the eyes of the Japanese people, whose ancient culture stressed sun worship. The chrysanthemum symbolizes peace and nobility, and its characteristic year-round growth, plus the long life of its beautiful blossoms, which never lose their petals, gives it a further significance of long life and consistency. Occasional representation of chrysanthemums growing close to or floating in a stream is symbolic of an ancient Chinese legend which relates of a member of the court who was banished to the mountains, where he drank chrysanthemum *sake* and lived to be 1,000 years old.

There are several hundred varieties of the chrysanthemum flower cultivated in Japan. The inro in Figure 167 portrays a realistic version of the chrysanthemum while the one in Figure 143 shows how the artist has adopted it into more or less conventionalized forms. A stylized form of chrysanthemum is also often used in lacquer as a diaper pattern or to ornament the sides of an inro or lacquer box. Such ornamentation is seen with great frequency utilizing tiny pieces of colorful *awabi* shell in the fashion of the Somada school with the tiny shell inlays forming a repeat pattern of chrysanthemum flowers.

FERN (SHIDA)

The fern is one of the symbols to be found associated with New Year's ceremonies. As the individual branches grow from one sturdy central stem, the symbolic significance is health, expansion, and numerous off-spring. Shibata Zeshin was fond of portraying the fern in a conventional-ized manner on a matte rough ground (Fig. 202).

FUNGUS (KINOKO OR REISHI)

This is an interesting variety of vegetation appearing with great fre-quency in lacquer art. It is commonly portrayed in the form of the head of the *jui,* or scepter, and is emblematic of longevity, primarily because of its intrinsic durability. It is often combined with other items representative of similar symbology. Occasionally the entire body of an inro will be carved from this material and then decorated with lacquer or inlaid with shell (Fig. 126).

GOURD (HYOTAN)

There are several varieties of gourds which are grown and cultivated in Japan. The one with which we are most concerned and which appears with great frequency in art is the *hyotan,* whose graceful shape is often im-mitated by painters, netsuke carvers, and lacquer artists (Fig. 192).

There are many legends associated with the gourd, and it is a constant companion to many sages, who often use it to evoke their magical powers, as in the legend of Chokaro, who stables his wonderful horse in a gourd which he carries on his back, or in the legend of Kosagi, one of the para-gons of filial piety, as he kneels by the waterfall with his gourd at his side.

Besides being an excellent container for *sake,* a dried gourd is very durable, and this quality has made it symbolic of longevity and health. The gourd was used in ancient times as an amulet to guard against falling and may occasionally be seen to represent the crest of Hideyoshi, who adopted it for his battle emblem.

IRIS (SHOBU)

The iris, a sturdy, easily cultivated flower, is not only emblematic of May, which month it represents in the floral calendar, but is also the main emblem of the Boys' Festival. The long, flat, blade-shaped leaves are remi-niscent of a sword, and thus this flower is emblematic of manly strength and has come to be symbolic of victory. Furthermore, its stiff upright petals are likened to the outstanding character and virtues associated with the ancient samurai warriors, and it can also be used to represent a wish for good health and renewed vitality. Its overall shape and symbolic association of masculinity furnish it with a phallic connotation as well (Fig. 130).

LOTUS (HASU)

The lotus is actually a variety of water lily which grows and thrives in shallow muddy ponds.

An extremely common and important flower in Japanese art, it is predominantly represented as a Buddhist religious symbol (Fig. 204). Buddha is always portrayed seated upon an eight-petaled lotus flower, as are many other Buddhist deities and saints. The circular form of the lotus and its petals, which resemble the spokes of a wheel, symbolizes the Buddhist philosophy of perpetual existence as represented by the wheel, which turns over and over with no beginning and no end.

The major symbolic significance of the lotus, however, is purity. The Japanese never fail to admire the flower, which grows in muddy ponds and yet is unsullied by its murky environment. They respect its strength and liken it to a virtuous man who rises above his sordid surroundings and remains pure.

MAPLE (MOMIJI)

The magnificent variety of changing colors of the maple leaves stimulates the lacquer artist, who loves to capture their beauty for ornamentation (Fig. 215). Symbolically, however, it is just this characteristic changing of color which denotes a change in feeling, and to send a person a branch of maple leaves would indicate one's loss of affection for him and a growing feeling of indifference.

The stag is often portrayed with the maple tree—a combination emblematic of autumn, when both are prominent in the countryside. A white deer in the place of a spotted deer implies a wish for longevity.

MORNING-GLORY (ASAGAO)

A popular flower, it is only occasionally portrayed in lacquer art. As it is a clinging vine, it is symbolic of affection. However, because of its characteristic short life and rapid wilting and fading, it is not a flower to be given as a gift for a happy occasion. Often it is combined in arrangement with the bamboo, whose presence, indicative of long life and endurance, counterbalances the other's weakness. Frequently the morning-glory is portrayed entwined about an old well bucket—a reflection of the famous poem by Chiyo in which she tells how she begged water from her neighbors rather than injure the lovely vine which had overnight grown about her own well bucket. Indeed, the morning-glory was a great favorite with the poets, and many verses were written about it.

ORANGE (TACHIBANA OR DAIDAI)

The orange is rather infrequently represented in art and always in conjunction with some other object or article. For instance a bitter orange, not meant for eating, is depicted among the articles for the New Year's celebration. This variety of the fruit, called *daidai,* is interpreted as a good omen since its name also means "generation after generation." The mandarin orange is included in the *takaramono,* the list of precious things. As this fruit grows from a tree which exudes a lovely, lasting sweet fragrance, it symbolically represents sweetness. When the orange is portrayed with the cuckoo, the symbolic reference is to pleasant memories.

PAULOWNIA (KIRI)

The wood of this tree, which also bears beautiful flowers, is used extensively to make the wooden bases for inro, *kobako,* and other boxes upon which the lacquer artists display their skills.

The flowers of the *kiri* tree are symbolic of rectitude, and conventionalized forms depicting its leaves and flowers were employed as the crest *(mon)* for the empress. The highly esteemed phoenix is reputed to favor the branches of the *kiri* tree, and he is often portrayed thus by the lacquer artist.

PEACH (MOMO)

In accordance with the ancient Chinese legend which tells of the peach tree of the gods whose fruit bears the gift of eternal life, the symbolic significance of peach blossoms and the fruit itself is longevity.

Peach blossoms are also emblematic of the Girls' (Doll) Festival and are prominently displayed at that time. In lacquer art however, the peach is infrequently portrayed.

PEONY (BOTAN)

The peony is usually represented in lacquer art in combination with the *shishi,* and the two are thus symbolically portrayed as the "king of flowers and the king of animals." Furthermore, it is emblematic of regal power and wealth, for its large crimson-colored petals create an impression of great prosperity, dignity, and power (Fig. 203).

PINE (MATSU)

Many species of pine grow in great abundance throughout Japan, and the tree is frequently portrayed in Japanese art. The pine is symbolic of stability and longevity, for this evergreen tree is reputed to live for a thousand years, and legend relates that when it reaches this age it turns into amber. Several varieties of pine have needles which grow in pairs, and when one of the two needles dies or falls from its branch, the other follows soon after. Thus the attributes of connubial fidelity and loyalty are represented by the pine tree. There is a legend of Jo and Uba, an old man and his wife who are reputed to be the spirits of two such ancient pine trees. This couple lived together in such complete marital bliss that after their deaths, which occurred almost simultaneously, they were permitted by the gods to return on moonlight nights to the beach where they had lived and gather pine needles as they had always done together while alive. They are shown together with a rake and a broom, the rake to gather in all good things and the broom to sweep away all evil. Usually they are surrounded by other symbols of longevity, such as the crane and the tortoise. This legend is often portrayed in art, most particularly in netsuke art (Fig. 126).

The pine tree is regarded as a good omen and was often planted in the gardens of the samurai as an example of stability and character and as a good omen for longevity. It is said that the sharp-pointed needles of the pine chase away evil spirits. The gnarled, bent pine indicates old age, and a pine tree covered wth snow is another emblematic portrayal of old age (Figs. 23, 135–139, 201).

The pine is often portrayed with other symbols of longevity, such as the crane, tortoise, and bamboo or with plum blossoms. The combination of pine, bamboo, and plum is given the name *sho-chiku-bai,* and this very popular combination symbolizes the wish for enduring happiness.

PLUM (UME)

Perhaps no tree is more popular for the beauty of its blossoms than the plum. The beautiful plum tree was imported to Japan from China, where it was the national flower. In Japan it is one of the favorite trees, and its blossoms are often portrayed and admired by poets and artists (Fig. 205). In art presentations it closely resembles the cherry blossom, the most easily distinguishable difference being that the cherry blossom (Fig. 21) is slightly indented in the middle of each petal, whereas the plum blossom is completely rounded (Fig. 30). It is the first tree of the year to bloom, and it is often portrayed with the nightingale as being symbolic of the coming of spring and of happiness.

The white blossoms of the plum tree, with their delicate fragrance, have been likened to a beautiful woman and her feminine charms, whereas an ancient, twisted blossoming tree branch is emblematic of strength, endurance, and the vitality of old age. Plum blossoms are often seen in combination with pine and bamboo, and this combination, as we have noted above, signifies lasting happiness and longevity.

SAKAKI

The *sakaki* is a sacred tree closely associated with Shintoism and with legends of the sun goddess Amaterasu. In the *Kojiki* is related the tale of how the sun goddess hid in a cave to express her anger over the misdeeds of her brother. In order to coax her out of hiding and restore light to the world, a large *sakaki* tree was placed near the cave, and on it were hung the offerings of the assembled gods, including *gohei,* the sacred jewel, and the mirror. The subject is frequently portrayed in lacquer art.

The *sakaki* is a species of plant similar to the camellia. It is an evergreen tree and often grows to a height of 10 to 40 feet. Its leaves are small, narrow, and pointed, and in spring it bears small fragrant whitish yellow blossoms.

THE SEVEN GRASSES OF AUTUMN

These various grasses are frequently depicted in lacquer art, usually representing vegetation in fields being tossed and blown by the winds, with a flock of birds flying above or some animal passing through. In combinations the Seven Grasses represent an assortment of graceful shapes of flowering plants and leaves (Figs. 52, 159).

Authorities occasionally differ when naming the individual grasses. However, the following is the most widely acknowledged list of grasses and flowers in this group: *hagi, susuki, kuzu, nadeshiko, ominaeshi, fujibakama,* and *kikyo.* Pictorially they appear as follows: *hagi,* or lespedeza, having small purple blossoms; *susuki,* a beautiful tall slender grass often depicted as if swaying gracefully in the wind; *kuzu,* a lovely purple flower with numerous small blossoms; *nadeshiko,* wild pink or wild carnation; *ominaeshi,* a tiny yellow flower suggestive of gold coins; *fujibakama,* or Chinese agrimony, usually having tiny pink-and-white flowers; and *kikyo,* or Chinese bellflower, having five petals and generally in white or shades of blue.

Many of these grasses were chosen because their names are associated with or can be translated to indicate omens of good fortune, happiness, success, health, and longevity.

WILLOW (YANAGI)

The graceful, supple swaying branches of the willow tree are a common subject for lacquer artists. Considered as a lucky tree because it bends easily and grows quickly, the willow is usually depicted in its natural habitat, growing in a marsh or beside a stream. Symbolically it represents consideration, flexibility, and patience, for it yields willingly to every whim of the wind. Because of its slenderness and gracefulness as it gently sways and bends in the wind, it is considered feminine in nature. A willow depicted with a swallow resting in its branches is symbolic of docility, serenity, friendship, and gentleness.

WISTERIA (FUJI)

This strong yet supple clinging vine, which blooms in the spring, is symbolic of woman, youth, and spring. Its lovely and fragrant lavender or white blossoms are often depicted by lacquer artists and have often been adopted into conventionalized forms as a crest. When presented in conjunction with the cuckoo, the wisteria emblematically heralds the approach of summer. Often lovers attach poems to the flowering buds and return later to see how perfectly the clusters have opened and grown—a fortune-telling device designed to foretell the degree of their future happiness together in life.

Insects

Many, many varieties of insects are to be found in Japan, and, as with all other forms of nature, these insects have been adapted into Japanese art forms. It is commonplace, therefore, to find ants or beetles perched upon a flower or leaf as part of the lacquer ornamentation.

Rather than disliking insects, the Japanese are charmed by them, often keeping them as pets. A popular pastime is catching and collecting such insects as fireflies and crickets. They are placed in tiny cages where they are admired for their beauty or for their song. Furthermore, the characteristics of many insects, such as the moth and the cicada, which emerge full-grown from one state into another—thus symbolically being "reborn" —is in keeping with the beliefs of eternal life and perpetual rebirth in other forms as taught by the Taoist and Buddhist religions.

There are many insects which are portrayed in intricate detail on lacquered objects simply for their shape and to which there is attached no specific symbolic meaning. There is another large group of insects known collectively as the "singing insects" or "insect musicians," which include the cricket *(korogi)*, cicada *(semi)*, "grass lark" *(kusahibari)*, grasshopper *(kirigirisu)*, "pine insect" *(matsumushi)*, "bell insect" *(suzumushi)*, and many varieties of beetles *(kabutomushi)*, which are often seen in lacquer art. Rather than being associated with any significant symbolic meanings, they are represented in tribute to the pleasure which their various sounds bring to the ears of the people in their association with nature and its seasons. The cicada, for example, is heard to sing the loudest on a still, hot summer day while the grasshopper raises his voice during the autumn season, and above all the songs of the night singers, the beetles and crickets, are regarded with particular pleasure. Several of the more popular varieties of insects are endowed with symbolic significance as noted in the alphabetical listing below.

In general, insects, being small, were of ideal size for portrayal in their entirety on miniature lacquer forms. They were usually depicted in minute realistic detail with as much affection as an entire landscape. They also allowed the lacquer artist full play of the use of color: from the beetle, which was usually done in black on black, to the green-colored praying mantis or the iridescent mother-of-pearl tail used for the firefly (Figs. 15, 46, 47, 58, 82, 128, 132, 133).

ANT (ARI)

Represented often in all art forms, these tiny insects are symbolic of the industry and thrift which are easily recognizable as their inherent characteristics. In lacquer art ants are usually done as tiny metallic encrustations (Fig. 206).

BEE (MITSU-BACHI)

Like the ant, the bee is looked upon as a symbol of industry and has been given a place in Japanese lacquer art. A netsuke, for example, may portray a bee resting on a piece of fruit. A swarm of bees hovering about a house is regarded as an omen of prosperity.

BUTTERFLY (CHO)

The natural beauty and magnificent coloring of this graceful, delicate insect have made it a great favorite with Japanese artists, and its image is frequently portrayed in their lacquer work. Symbolically the butterfly is emblematic of summer and is also significant in three other major associations. Two large paper butterflies, one male (o-cho) and the other female (me-cho), play important ritual roles during the wedding ceremony, and the symbolic union of the two is emblematic of the wish of the bridal pair to have a long, happy, unconcerned wedded life.

According to legend and popular superstition, the butterfly—particularly the white butterfly—embodies the soul, either of the living or the dead, and the presence of a butterfly in the house may indicate that a friend will arrive, that a death may soon take place, or that someone has already died and his soul has been entrusted to the butterfly.

The third major symbolic reference is the similarity of the butterfly's characteristics to those of a young girl. Both are frail, fair, lighthearted, given to frivolity, and somewhat fickle in nature. There is an ancient saying that as a butterfly goes from flower to flower seeking honey, the young girl also flits from lover to lover. The colorful clothing and the butterfly-shaped hair ornaments in which young girls dressed themselves added to this comparison.

The kobako and inro in Figures 58, 82, and 128 display the beauty and color which lacquer artists loved to portray in their craft and which is so well suited to portray the rich, and varied colors and designs of the butterfly.

DRAGONFLY (TOMBO)

There are many varieties of tombo, bearing many fanciful names, to be found in abundance in the islands of Japan, particularly during the summer months, of which this insect is symbolic. Legend relates that the first emperor of Japan, Jimmu Tenno, climbed to the top of a mountain and, looking down on the islands before him, likened them to the shape of the dragonfly licking its tail and named them Akitsu-shima, or Dragonfly Islands (*akitsu* being the ancient name for the dragonfly). Thus the dragonfly has long been emblematic of Japan itself.

Although this insect appears to be delicate, it is in reality a powerful fighting insect whose frequent success in battle has given it the symbolic significance of victory and courage. Ornaments such as inro and other objects bearing its image were often used by warriors and boys as amulets. It is therefore often portrayed in all the art forms (Fig. 82).

FIREFLY (HOTARU)

This small popular insect, emblematic of summer, is surrounded by many legends and myths. It is greatly admired by the Japanese, and frequently picnics are scheduled for evening hours in order to be able to view the fireflies. Fireflies are often caught and placed in small cages, and many tales are told of students, too poor to afford light, who studied by the illumination of a swarm of caged fireflies.

To the lacquer artist the firefly offers a challenge, and the inro in Figures 132 and 133 illustrate how subtly and beautifully this subject is handled in lacquer art.

PRAYING MANTIS (KAMAKIRI OR TORO)

A strong, powerful insect whose hunting habits and fighting tactics have made it symbolic of courage, the praying mantis takes its name from the similarity of its stance, in which it raises its forelegs over its head, to that of the attitude of prayer. Its graceful body and waving antenna are frequently portrayed in painting and lacquer art (Figs. 15, 46).

SPIDER (KUMO)

The spider has always been associated with both good and evil—that is, industriousness and magic craft. The Japanese artist, however, is greatly enamored of the spider's characteristic industriousness, and the web which it weaves, with its intricate and delicate beautiful lacy pattern, is one of his favorite subjects. The web itself was occasionally delicately displayed in art, especially for its interesting ornamental value.

Birds

The beauty of the plumage with which nature has endowed most birds makes them excellent subjects for the highly skilled lacquer artist, who captures their delicate softness and luxurious coloring in decorative motifs. Furthermore, their relatively small size and their graceful flight are well adapted to artistic portrayal. The Japanese are very fond of birds and often raise them as pets. The symbology associated with bird life is full and fanciful, as we shall now observe.

COCK (TORI OR NIWATORI)

Because of its close association with the sun, the cock as a symbol is of great importance in Japanese art. It is mentioned in the *Kojiki* as being brought to crow before the cave where the sun goddess was hiding, in order to make her think that the sun had risen without her and thus to coax her from her hiding place. Its crowing at dawn to announce the coming of the sun is interpreted as worshiping the sun goddess. Its dependability and regularity in this respect have made it symbolic of faithfulness, and its constant watchfulness inspires a feeling of protection. Its crow at dawn is said to drive away evil spirits which roam at night, and therefore the crowing cock is further regarded as a protection against evil.

The cock is considered as a symbol of *yang (yo),* the male principle so important in Japanese and Chinese culture. It fights fearlessly and well with its enemies and displays great courage. It has a proud carriage, strong feet, and beautiful plumage and is symbolic of manly beauty and martial spirit. Indeed, few things can compare with the great beauty and courage displayed by the specially bred and reared fighting cock. These are a great favorite with the Japanese artist, and their beauty, with their graceful long tails, lends itself well to portrayal by the lacquer artist, as can be seen in the inro in Figure 110. When depicted in a group with a hen and chicks, the cock represents domestic bliss and wedded happiness.

Another often-seen representation is the cock on a drum. This is symbolic of peace and contentment. There is an old legend which relates that in the 7th century Emperor Kotoku placed a drum outside of the palace gates so that the people could beat upon it when they had a grievance. The emperor was such a wise and just ruler that no one had cause to beat upon the drum, and in the course of time it became overgrown with leaves and served as a roost for the barnyard cock, thus indicating peace and happiness in the land. Another version of the legend states that this drum was used to call warriors to action, but because of the wise emperor peace reigned for so long that the drum was used only by the cock as a resting place.

CORMORANT (U)

Rather infrequently depicted by lacquer artists, but certainly worthy of mention, is the cormorant. Known for his agility and amazing ability as a fisherman, he is symbolic of faithful and constant untiring work for the benefit of his master. An ancient and exceedingly skilled technique, cormorant fishing may still be seen today in Japan. This bird, when grown, is about the size of a small duck, is usually gray to black in color, and can catch approximately 150 fish an hour.

CRANE (TSURU)

This is one of the most popular and frequently depicted symbols of longevity (it is often incorrectly referred to as the stork), for it is reputed to live for 1,000 years. It is particularly well suited for portrayal in Japanese art because of its grace and natural beauty. It is frequently portrayed in motion and usually in combination with either a tortoise, a pine tree, or a *sennin,* all having symbolic meaning. The crane alone symbolizes good fortune, and with the tortoise it stands for good fortune and long life. A flock of flying cranes represents many good wishes. The crane flying across the sun is symbolic of longevity, the sun representing everlasting life—a reference to the sun goddess, from whom, according to legend, the imperial family descended. The crane is often shown with the pine tree to symbolize flourishing and prosperous life and with the bamboo to represent faithfulness and constancy. No wedding decorations would be complete without at least one crane among them to augur fidelity and longevity. In this association the crane represents domestic happiness. Furthermore, the crane is a monogamous bird and will stay with its mate when the mate is unable to fly with the rest of the flock because of illness or other causes. The crane will stay and protect its young until they are able to fend for themselves and is therefore an example for young girls of the quality of motherhood. The crane is also the attribute of the god of longevity, Fuku-rokuju, and serves as the mount for several *sennin* and sages, particularly those of Taoist origin.

So highly regarded were the powers of the crane that even in olden times there were laws protecting it and forbidding anyone to harm it. Although now there are but a few cranes actually to be seen in Japan, they are still a great favorite in Japanese art.

In legend, cranes roam in abundance on the famous Mount Horai, the sacred island mountain of the immortals, wherein live the genii surrounded by all forms of precious jewels and animals symbolic of longevity and immortality. Cranes are often depicted with Jo and Uba, whose story is frequently found illustrated in Japanese art.

CROW (KARASU)

Both the raven and the crow are referred to as *karasu* in Japanese. In Japan, as in most other countries, the mischievous crow is generally regarded as an evil omen. He is supposedly gifted with supernatural powers and is believed to be a messenger of the gods. The *karasu* is often associated with fire. Legend relates that this is the only bird which flies near the sun and that its feathers are black because of having been scorched by the rays of the sun. It is therefore often illustrated in conjunction with the sun.

The black crow is often depicted in combination with the snow-white heron, symbolically representing *in* and *yo,* good and evil, day and night, etc. Furthermore, its very coloring makes it an excellent subject for portrayal, particularly in imitation of *sumie* painting in lacquer. The inro shown in Figure 20 is a good example of this technique. The artist has used a gold-lacquer background upon which, in black lacquer, he has portrayed crows sitting on the branches of the plum tree, another frequent combination which emblematically alludes to the season of fall.

Karasu are also representations of filial piety, for it is said that after young crows have learned to fly they will care for and feed their parents in reciprocity for their attentions when they were young and helpless.

CUCKOO (HOTOTOGISU)

This small bird is usually depicted either flying through rain, in which association it represents the coming of spring and further serves as a reminder to the farmers to sow their rice, or portrayed flying across a crescent moon, as the cuckoo is said to sing only as the moon fades and dawn begins. When depicted with the crescent moon it also brings to mind a legend of the hero Yorimasa, who, so it is related, in the hour just before the dawn of the year 1153, after a constant vigil throughout the night, slew the monster who had been slowly destroying the health of Emperor Konoe—for which deed Yorimasa was richly rewarded. The cuckoo is rarely seen, for it flies so swiftly that usually it can only be heard.

DOVE (HATO)

The dove is symbolic of filial piety, one of the greatest of virtues in the Orient. It is commonly believed that out of respect for its parents the dove perches at least three branches below them whenever resting in the same tree. A wooden dove in the form of a toy with wheels, pulled along by a string behind a child, was a popular folk toy and was often simulated in netsuke art. The dove is the messenger of Hachiman, god of war, and the Minamoto clan of medieval warriors adopted the dove as an emblem for their battle standards.

EAGLE (WASHI)

The eagle has a minor place in Japanese lacquer art and is found most frequently on older lacquer ware. Apparently it was not well enough known to become a popular decorative motif, and there is no agreement as to its symbolic meaning.

FALCON (TAKA)

The word *taka* in Japanese sounds the same as the word meaning heroic, and indeed the falcon is symbolic of power, heroism, boldness, and courage, which characteristics it possesses. It is frequently portrayed in art (Fig. 150).

Falconry was introduced into Japan from Korea about A.D. 350, from which time it became a popular sport, particularly among the upper classes. Falcons are admired for their sharpness of talon and beak, keen eyesight, beauty, power, swiftness of flight, and superior intelligence, which enables them to be highly and skillfully trained.

The falcon is said to symbolize victory as well as generosity. An example of this is the tale that tells of a falcon whose claws were frozen with cold. He caught a small bird and held it in his talons until the body of the bird warmed them, whereupon in gratitude he let the bird fly away unharmed and promised not to fly in the direction in which it escaped for at least 24 hours.

HERON (SAGI)

The heron is a common species of bird in Japan, the best-loved varieties being the white heron and the snowy egret. Like all other white birds and animals, the white heron is symbolic of longevity and is a sacred bird. It is often depicted standing in a pond among lotus leaves, and in this association it denotes purity. It is also often seen acting as the mount for a sage or a god. There is a popular Noh play, *Sagi,* which portrays the story of the emperor Daigo's encounter with a heron.

MANDARIN DUCK (OSHIDORI)

This duck is a great favorite with lacquer artists because its beautifully colored plumage lends itself so very well to their art and also because symbolically the mandarin duck represents connubial affection, mutual consideration, and love, as well as faithfulness (Fig. 216). Because of this symbolic meaning, artistic representation on lacquer wares or in painting always portrays mandarin ducks in pairs, and such a representation is frequently given as a wedding present to assure the married couple of wedded bliss and virtues comparable to those of the ducks. Once mated, these birds remain together for the rest of their lives. If one should die, the other will not remate but will pine and mourn and also die soon after. They are gentle and kindly, thoughtful and peaceful. Indeed, so greatly are they admired for these characteristics that legend reports that the Buddha was at one time reincarnated in the form of a mandarin duck in order to teach their enviable traits to mankind. Wild ducks are known as *kamo* and are also reportedly endowed with the same outstanding wholesome characteristics as the mandarin duck.

NIGHTINGALE (UGUISU)

This is a small bird which is much loved in Japan for its song and its romantic symbolic associations rather than for its beauty. The nightingale, as in Western culture, is the bird associated with romance and poetry. It is often portrayed in association with the plum tree, which is also the favorite tree of Japanese poets. It is regarded as the bird that first sings to announce the arrival of spring.

A further interesting note is that the nightingale is considered to be a very religious bird, for its song suggests the intoning of a Buddhist sutra. For this reason also it is sometimes referred to as "the reading bird."

OWL (FUKURO)

Because of its nocturnal habits, the owl is associated with mystery and evil. As it can see in the dark, it is reputed to have great wisdom and the power of foretelling the future. However, its major symbolic association is that of filial ingratitude, for it has the reputation of eating its own parents on occasion.

The owl is not a common subject in Japanese art, primarily because of its ill-omened associations. However, the great lacquer artist Ogawa Ritsuo was fond of portraying it, and Figure 217 shows an example of his excellent use of the subject for inro decoration. Here we see Ritsuo's typical technique of encrusting part of his design in porcelain into a natural wood ground as well as applying lacquer onto the same plain wood ground.

PEACOCK (KUJAKU)

One of the very few animate creatures that are not related specifically to any symbolic meaning, the peacock, although known to the Japanese, is not indigenous to Japan and was not, in fact, brought to Japan until the late 17th century. It is occasionally seen as the mount of the goddess Benten and more frequently serving in the same capacity for Kujaku Myo-o, the mother of Buddha. There is an old superstition that peacocks kill snakes, and the two creatures are often depicted together for that reason in Japanese art.

Although of no significance symbolically, the peacock is a favorite subject for painters and lacquerers primarily because of its magnificent plumage and majestic tail feathers, which lend themselves so well to portrayal in art. The circular iridescent designs on the feathers are ideal for representation in lacquer art, largely through the use of select pieces of thin multicolored *awabi* shell. The fine feathery edges of the individual plumes are also beautifully and delicately portrayed by the lacquer artists. Occasionally just one or two feathers are artistically depicted rather than the entire peacock itself (Fig. 219). Most commonly such feathers are done in *togidashi* technique, but in Figure 219 they are uniquely done in colorful mother-of-pearl by the great artist Shirayama Shosai.

PHEASANT (KIJI OR KIGISU)

One of the most beautiful of birds, the pheasant is a great favorite with lacquer artists, for whom its splendid plumage is an inducement to a display of their skill. It is often depicted in conjunction with the blossoming cherry tree, having no other symbolic significance except that the regal beauty of the one excellently complements that of the other. The pheasant is associated with Shintoism and on occasion is portrayed as the messenger of the sun goddess. It is a bird of good omen and represents parental devotion and sacrifice, as it is reputed to risk danger and death in order to save its young from harm.

PIGEON (HATO)

This bird, rather rarely depicted in lacquer art, is reputed to be one of the few birds which care for their parents when they are old and is therefore highly regarded as symbolic of filial devotion and protection. Throughout Japan there are many shrines that harbor flocks of pigeons as a constant reminder to those who visit of their responsibilities toward the aged and the rewards that fulfilling these responsibilities will bring.

PLOVER (CHIDORI)

These little birds, always found in large flocks, have long been a favorite subject for writers, poets, and lacquerers, first literary mention of them appearing in the *Kojiki*. They are usually portrayed soaring just above and intermingled with the spray of angry waves and in this situation are symbolic of the struggle to keep above the storms and strifes of life. They were considered as being a fine example for the samurai of the strength to be derived from unity and the need to be constantly active and always on guard (Fig. 207). *Chidori* were a favorite subject of the famous artist Korin, who depicted them in a highly stylized manner which was often copied and repeated by his followers.

QUAIL (UZURA)

At one time this popular bird was kept as a fighting bird, and from this association it is representative of martial spirit. Furthermore, because of its rather patchy and ragged appearance it is also indicative of poverty. One of the most familiar representations of the quail in lacquer shows it with autumn grasses or with millet seed. In these combinations it is simply symbolic of the autumn season.

SPARROW (SUZUME)

This little bird, a different species from that found in Western countries, is frequently portrayed in Japanese lacquer art. A flight of sparrows is representative of grace, friendship, kindness, and industry. Furthermore the song of the sparrow is interpreted as sounding like the Japanese words for "be loyal," and therefore the sparrow is also symbolic of loyalty. In this respect also, it is said to be a faithful and attentive mate. The sparrow is one of the few birds portrayed in all seasons; combined with the chrysanthemum, he represents autumn; with the bamboo and snow, winter; with the bamboo and plum blossoms, spring, and with the peony, summer.

There is a well-known folk legend, "Shitakiri Suzume," or "The Tongue-Cut Sparrow," in which a sparrow is the pet of a farmer and his ill-tempered wife. One day while the farmer is away working the sparrow pecks at the starch while the wife is attending to the wash. She punishes him by splitting his tongue, and the sparrow flies away. When the farmer returns home and learns what his wife has done, he sets out to find his beloved pet. When he finds him he is offered the hospitality of the sparrow's home, and as he is about to leave, the sparrow shows him two chests, one large and one small, and tells him to choose one as a gift. The farmer takes the smaller chest. When he returns home and looks inside he finds it full of gold and jewels. The greedy wife, upon seeing this, in turn sets out to visit the sparrow. She too is offered the hospitality of his home and, upon leaving, her choice of two similar chests. She immediately chooses the larger one and, struggling under its weight, returns home. However, upon raising the lid of the large chest, she is besieged by hideous goblins and spirits who seek to revenge the injured sparrow.

SWALLOW (TSUBAME)

The symbolism associated with this bird is interesting because of its extremes. When depicted with a willow, the swallow is representative of gentleness and meekness. It is also symbolic of spring. However, when portrayed without the willow the swallow is emblematic of an unfaithful mate who is always searching about for new conquests and furthermore is quick to take flight. Yet it redeems itself by being an excellent mother and is symbolic of maternal care. A white swallow is an extremely good and happy omen.

SWAN (HAKUCHO)

Although rarely seen in Japanese lacquer art, this lovely bird is nevertheless endowed with the gifts of prophecy, enchantment, and transformation, such symbolic associations being very ancient in origin.

WILD GOOSE (GAN)

Its lovely plumage combined with its supple grace makes the wild goose a favorite subject for portrayal by lacquer artists. Moreover, the pleasant symbolic associations represented by this bird are added stimulus.

Wild geese are reported to fly in pairs and therefore are representative of happy marriage and fidelity. Their portrayal in a wedge-shaped formation flying across the full moon is symbolic of autumn, and since they can always be depended upon to reappear each season, the wild goose is compared to a faithful spouse. Again, as the rice is ripe in autumn when these birds appear, it is a happy omen to see them. Their rapid motion represents the vigor and vitality associated with the *yang*, or male principle.

Geese fly in a straight line in formal formation and are reputed to break this strict flight pattern only when disturbed by something on the ground beneath them. Mythology relates two tales wherein warriors (Yoshiie and Kiyowara Takenori) were forewarned of the presence of their adversaries by a flock of wild geese flying over the area and suddenly breaking their formation, thus revealing the hiding place of the enemy.

Animals

The Japanese arts abound with all forms of animal life and around each creature is an intricate web of symbolic significance and folklore. The twelve animals of the zodiac are most frequently portrayed although their symbolic significance is not limited to representation of the zodiac cycle alone. Other animals, many of which had never been seen in ancient and medieval Japan, as well as those which are indigenous to Japan, are also often portrayed and are highly symbolic.

BADGER (TANUKI)

Most commonly known in Japan as *tanuki*—"racoon-faced dog"—this animal is credited with great supernatural powers, the ability to change his shape at will, taking both human as well as inanimate forms, and a great propensity for playing practical jokes and tricks on unsuspecting victims.

Folk legends describe the mischievous and playful badger as assuming two main forms. The first has a doglike face, a large bushy tail, and a greatly inflated abdomen resembling a drum: *tanuki no hara tsuzumi,* or the badger's belly drum. Upon this remarkable belly it beats with its front paws, producing an enticing sound that lures unsuspecting mortals to stray from their appointed paths in search of this delightful noise. In a similar manner he often assumes the shape of a teakettle. In his other form he more closely resembles a fox with the exception of a grossly enlarged scrotum simulating a veined leaf, under which he hides or which he wraps around himself as a kimono. In this guise he also pursues his course of playful mischief. There are many legends attached to this fun-loving prankster, among the favorites being "Bumbuku Chagama" (The Lucky Teakettle) and "Kachi-kachi-yama" (The Crackling Mountain).

There is no particular symbolic meaning attached to the badger; however, his fanciful forms lend themselves well to graphic and sculptural portrayal and are a favorite subject for lacquer as well as netsuke artists (Fig. 208).

BAT (KOMORI)

The bat is regarded as a lucky emblem, and its symbolic significance can be traced directly to China, where it is a well-known charm of good fortune, happiness, and prosperity. This association arises from the fact that the characters for "bat" and "happiness" are pronounced alike. Motifs of five bats represent the five blessings of Confucius: longevity, wealth, offspring, virtue, and an easy death.

Gift boxes were commonly decorated with this symbol, which was thought to increase the value of the gift by adding to it the wishes for longevity and happiness. When the bat was portrayed holding coins in his claws, the wish was for increased happiness from greater riches, and when the bat motif was combined with clouds it carried the thought of longevity and of "happiness as extended as the sky is high."

The Buddhist priests, however, placed another connotation on the bat more closely allied with the Occidental feeling regarding this creature. Because it is seen only at night and appears to be flitting about without purpose or direction, they likened it to the restless human conscious in an unsettled, unhappy, chaotic state. This interpretation, however, is not widely accepted.

Beyond its pleasant symbolic connotation, the bat presents a graceful wing shape that easily lends itself to artistic lacquer decoration.

BEAR (KUMA)

This beast was considered to be strong, wise, and rarely vicious, and in general its appearance was regarded as a good omen. Furthermore, it was believed to be able to recognize a kindly person, and legend therefore finds it rescuing, raising, and caring for a lost hunter whom it judges to be a kind and good man. The most famous stories concerning the bear are those of Hachisuke and Kintaro. Although a highly venerated and sacred animal among primitive people (particularly the Ainu tribe, which partook of its flesh in order to acquire some of its great strength and power), it found little favor with later civilizations and is rarely depicted in Japanese art or legend.

BOAR (INOSHISHI OR I)

One of the zodiac animals and a great favorite with Japanese artists, especially netsuke artists, is the wild boar. It is frequently depicted not only in art forms but also in the history, legend, folklore, and literature of the country, the earliest literary mention of it appearing in the *Kojiki*. The boar was held in such esteem that at one time its likeness appeared on the 10-yen note. Boar tusks were frequently used by the netsuke artists for carving.

There are many superstitions surrounding the boar, which has played a popular role with many primitive peoples throughout the world. In ancient Japan, his flesh was reputed to be a charm against baldness and epilepsy. Furthermore popular belief credited him with being a great enemy of the snake, seeking to destroy it at any opportunity. He is said to be fond of its meat and immune to its bite.

In general the boar is highly admired for his great and reckless courage, and it is in this light that he is best known. He is a creature of reckless fighting courage and relentless spirit. When he attacks, he charges straight at his target, never veering, never flinching, never retreating, and never fleeing. For these qualities he is highly regarded as a symbol of conquest and steadfast courage, such as was associated with the samurai and was similarly considered a formidable challenge to the hunter.

CAT (NEKO)

The domestic cat was imported to Japan from China. At one time most of the cats in Japan were of a short-tailed variety, and long-tailed cats were looked upon as evil, deceptive, and crafty animals. Cats with more than one long tail appear in legends; the greater the number of tails, the greater their evil, bewitching powers. It was common belief that cats were able to take the form of humans and thus bewitch them, the most famous story in this connection being that of "Nabeshima no Neko."

Although relatively infrequently depicted in art, the cat is shown in many forms (Fig. 148). *Neko* literally means "rat killer," and it was thought that a painting of a cat was enough to protect the building in which it was hung from rats. Only the cat will be found to be missing from scenes showing the animals mourning the passing of Buddha. Legend has it that the cat was too busy chasing after a rat to come to the bedside of Buddha.

A very familiar characterization of the cat is the *maneki neko,* or beckoning cat, which many merchants and shopkeepers place before the entrance to their stores. This figure, which welcomes and attracts customers to the stores, is therefore held in high esteem by the merchant, for not only does it protect his goods from destruction by rats, but it also aids his business to grow and prosper by enticing the customer into his shop. The beckoning cat was also thought to be a talisman for protecting children from illness, pain, and evil, and its image was often worn about a child's waist. Tortoise-shell tomcats are highly esteemed by sailors, for they are reputed to be able to predict fire and disaster as well as protect from rats and restless ghosts who wander about the sea in search of sailors' souls. In general, the symbolic representation of the cat in art is manifold but primarily one of a magical, supernatural, and not quite comfortable bewitching nature.

DEER (SHIKA)

Most of the symbolic associations concerning this animal coincide with those of the Chinese, in whose language the name given the deer is *lu,* which means "good fortune." In Japan, the deer or stag is emblematic of longevity and good fortune. A Buddhist legend holds that Gautama Buddha was reborn eleven times in the form of a deer and that his first teachings were delivered during his appearance in this guise.

This small, graceful, gentle animal is alleged to live an exceedingly long life. In art the deer is depicted in a manner closely resembling its natural state. During the summer its coat is covered with white spots, while in winter it becomes a solid shade of light brown. According to superstition, after the deer reaches 1,000 years of age its coat becomes gray; in the next 500 years of its life, during which it is said to eat nothing but the sacred fungus, its horns turn black. At this stage it has reached immortality, and it retires to live with other immortal gods and animals on Mount Horai.

Deer are noted for their loyalty and fidelity to their mates and when depicted in pairs are symbolic of marital happiness. A common combination is the deer and the maple, signifying the season of autumn. Occasionally the lespedeza *(hagi)* takes the place of the maple with the same significance.

The deer is the companion of many gods, *sennin,* and other familiar figures in Japanese legend and folklore. However, it is most frequently seen as the constant companion and the messenger of Fukurokuju and Jurojin, two of the household gods of good fortune (Figs. 65, 80, 83).

DOG (INU)

In Japanese folklore there are two types of dog deities *(inugami)* representing both good and evil. Although there are references to dog demons used for the purposes of witchcraft, these are far fewer in number than the tales representing the dog in a far more helpful and protective role. It is a protection against the cunning of the cat, the badger, and the fox, which cannot maintain their supernatural possession qualities in the presence of a dog because of its honest, forthright character. The dog is credited with the power of being able to dispel demons with its bark. Furthermore, it is faithful to its master and shows its gratitude by protecting him not only from demons but also from the hazards of fire, robbery, and illness. An amulet in the form of a dog will serve the same purpose, so great is its power.

The dog has special qualities concerning the very young, and a common toy is a papier-mâché dog or a "dog box" *(inu-bako)* in the form of a sleeping dog which renders fierce and loyal protection. At one time it was the custom when taking an infant out at night to paint the ideogram for "dog" on his forehead in red ink and thus assure him protection from disease and demons. Because the dog is noted for the ease with which it gives birth to its puppies, an amulet in the shape of a dog is placed beside a woman in labor to ease and assist her in childbirth.

Although not imbued with any single specific symbolic significance, the dog is generally considered as a good omen. It is one of the zodiac animals and is held in high esteem. The most popular legend regarding the dog is the "Hakkenden," or "Tale of Eight Dogs."

ELEPHANT (ZO)

One of the most important Buddhist symbols, the elephant and the legends surrounding him were brought to Japan by way of China, where they were originally introduced from India. The elephant's role in Buddhism is intricate, and the mythology relating to him is vast and complex. In Japanese art he is sometimes portrayed as having six tusks. This alludes to a religious belief wherein Buddha appeared six times on earth in the form of a white elephant. Other interpretations have it that each of the tusks represents one of the six great temptations of man according to the teachings of Buddha, which include the human will and the five mortal senses.

Elephants, symbolizing love and mercy, are frequently portrayed with lions, emblematic of strength and wisdom, for although fearful of the lion, the elephant surmounts his fear to join his natural enemy in order to serve Buddha. Furthermore, the combination of these animals cannot but call to mind India, the birthplace of Buddha. The white elephant is particularly revered and often serves as the mount of the Buddhist god of compassion, Fugen Bosatsu, who personifies devoutness, goodness, and prayer. The elephant's ivory tusks are highly admired by Japanese craftsmen, and this material is used with great frequency and variety in their art.

The famous story of the blind men feeling the elephant is often portrayed, in lacquer and netsuke art. This story, in which each man felt a single, different part of the animal and then described what he thought he had felt, is intended to teach that one must know all the facts in order to see the whole truth, and that we should not judge by only part of the whole (Fig. 209).

Generally in Japanese art the elephant is symbolic of knowledge, wisdom, and dignity. He is alleged to be humble, for he always carries his nose turned toward the ground, while the haughty turn their noses toward the sky. Popular superstition has it that he is a quiet, kind, and peaceful animal. He was a great court favorite in India and was frequently used in parades and processions. There are many, many tales of the elephant particularly pertaining to Buddhism. In Japanese folklore three of the most entertaining stories are "Taishun," "Kimi," and "Fugen Bosatsu."

FOX (KITSUNE)

This animal is one of the most generously endowed with supernatural qualities and powers. It is felt by many to be symbolic of the spirit of evil, according to folklore and existing popular superstitions. The fox is indigenous to Japan, although most of the legends surrounding him were first introduced from China during the 10th century.

There are three primary classifications of foxes: the field fox, who steals from the farmer and damages his crops; the good fox, commonly known as the Inari fox; and the evil, demoniacal, man-possessing fox. This last is credited with the greatest supernatural powers. He is possessed of infinite wisdom, is equipped with complete knowledge of the past, and can forsee the future. He is able to look into the souls of humans and read their innermost secrets and thoughts, which knowledge he often uses in his evil exploits and malicious mischief. He often causes many undesirable complications in the course of people's lives. Furthermore, he is capable of the most extensive powers of self-transformation, even into other living creatures, as well as of human possession.

The fox is also purported to attain longevity. The evil and wicked qualities of the fox increase with its age. At the age of 50 years he is able to transform himself into the guise of an ordinary woman; at 100 years he can take the form of a beautiful young woman, in which disguise he seeks to waylay and deceive young men, leading them astray and guiding them to their doom. At this age he can also assume other forms including the possession of human beings. At the age of 1,000 years he achieves immortality, becomes a white or golden color, and possesses nine tails. This nine-tailed fox is known as a celestial fox, and his wondrous growth of tails adds to his crafty, cunning, deceitful ways and also increases his supernatural powers.

Because of the wealth of superstitious folklore regarding the fox, the field fox enjoys some immunity from the hunter, for many truly believe in and fear fox possession. He is hunted for his fur, however, and hunters who shoot a fox are advised to eat some of his flesh, since this is a strong talisman against being haunted by his spirit and will make one immune to fox magic. Other common beliefs are many and varied: foxes are afraid of dogs, for dogs can always recognize a fox no matter what his disguise; groups of three foxes are particularly bad omens; a black fox is a forerunner of good luck, while a white fox hints of an impending crisis or calamity. No matter what shape the fox may have assumed, his true image is always reflected in a mirror or on the surface of a clear, still pond or stream. For this reason a mirror is also good protection against the tricks of this crafty animal.

The white Inari fox, on the other hand, is a kindly beneficent animal closely associated as the mount and messenger of the popular deity Inari, goddess of the harvest, agriculture, and particularly rice. The Chinese ideogram for Inari, literally translated, means "rice plant bearer." The first Inari shrine was established in February 711 in the district of Fushimi, and since that time innumerable similar shrines have been erected throughout the country. In front of all Inari shrines will be found two foxes, one on either side of the entrance—one male, with his mouth open, and the other female, with her mouth closed—representing the principles of in and yo (yin and yang). Frequently one of the pair of foxes holds in its mouth the kagi (the key to the storehouse) while the other has the tama (the sacred jewel).

The great popularity of the deity Inari and her representatives is easily understandable, since the Japanese were an agricultural people whose wealth was often estimated in terms of measures of rice in each family's possession. The Inari fox is often represented in art. It is also considered to be emblematic of February, and it is sometimes worshiped as the god of rice or as possessing the power of giving wealth.

In general, the representations of the fox in art are as many and varied as are its symbolic meanings (Fig. 64). It is frequently depicted as dressed in the clothes of a woman or a priest. Of the many folk tales regarding this animal, perhaps "Kitsune no Yomeiri" (The Fox Wedding) and "Tamano no Mae" (named for a lady-in-waiting of Empress Konoe) are the most outstanding.

HARE (USAGI OR U)

The Japanese artist does not distinguish between the rabbit and the hare, both animals being depicted and referred to under the name of hare. The hare or rabbit is commonly associated with the moon in art and legend, and as in Occidental countries we speak of the "man in the moon," so in Japan do people refer to the "hare in the moon." The origin of this association dates back to ancient mythology. According to Buddhist legend, Buddha appeared on earth as a hare in one of his transmigrations. He was approached by a ragged, hungry traveler who asked for food, whereupon the hare instructed the hungry man to gather fuel and build a fire. When the fire was burning, the hare threw himself upon it and thus sacrificed himself to assuage the other's hunger. The beggar proved to be the god Indra in disguise. As a reward he recorded the image of the hare upon the moon as a shining example and a lasting memorial.

Another source relates that the Sanskrit word for hare is *sason,* which means "the leaping one," and this is associated also with the moon, for as the hare leaps and bounds, so also does the moon periodically change its face. The Sanskrit name for moon is *cacadharas,* which translates as "one who carries the hare." The hare is the emblem of Candra, the original Brahmanic deity, the goddess of the moon, and he is often represented with her in art. Furthermore, he is pictured in the moon as pounding with mortar and pestle to prepare the elixir of life from herbs which must be gathered only in the light of the full moon. In Japan this legend has been altered slightly to conform with Japan's own elixir of life, rice. This popular belief states that the hare in the moon is pounding rice for the rice cakes known as *mochi.* The words *mochi* and *mochizuki* mean literally "rice cakes" and "full moon."

Superstitions regarding the hare relate that the female conceives by running across the surface of water under a full moon on the eighteenth night of the eighth month. If, however, the moon is obstructed from view by clouds or mist, then she will not conceive. In another version the hare conceives simply by gazing steadfastly at the full moon, while still a third tale relates that she becomes impregnated by licking the fur of the male of the species while the moon is full. This motif of the hare beneath a full moon is very common in lacquer art.

The hare is the fourth sign of the Chinese and Japanese zodiacs. He is generally believed to be supernaturally possessed of longevity. He lives for 1,000 years, and at 500 years his coat becomes pure white. He is not, however, emblematic of longevity, nor is he credited with magical or supernatural powers. The combination of hare, water, and moon are symbolic of life and is often referred to in legends (Figs. 141, 146). The best known folk tales regarding the hare are "The White Hare of Inaba," which is recorded in the *Kojiki* and "Kachi-kachi-yama," or "The Crackling Mountain."

HORSE (UMA)

Frequently depicted in art, the horse presents an interesting and varied multitude of symbolic meanings. He is a favorite subject for painters, who often display their skill by executing drawings of the horse utilizing a minimum of strong brush strokes and displaying a free form with the emphasis on movement rather than on realistic detail. In lacquer art, however, he is portrayed more realistically (Figs. 52, 112, 210), since the lacquer medium does not allow for such artistic sweep.

Because it was chiefly used as the mount of military heroes, the horse became symbolically associated with martial power, endurance, strength, and vitality and is regarded in general as being emblematic of manhood. Since each of its hoofs is one single part, thus being an odd number, it is classified as expressing the masculine principle *yang,* further identifying the animal with manhood. Gamboling, frolicking horses are symbolic of a thrifty but free and spirited early manhood awaiting the call of duty. The motion of the horse's gait, with its up-and-down movement, is likened to the up-and-down aspects of life.

The horse is a symbol of fecundity as well as a phallic symbol. In this respect *uma,* the word for horse, was used as a slang expression for a prostitute, for menstruation, and also for penis. The castrating of a white horse was performed in ancient Japan on certain festival days as a symbolic punishment and repentance of women who had confessed to committing adultery during the preceding year. Offerings of horses to the gods were common and soon led to the development of *ema,* pictures and paintings of horses offered to the Shinto shrines as emblems of desire and attainment in place of live horses. Horses have long been esteemed in Japan and many *haniwa* figures of them have been found in ancient tombs. The horse is also mentioned in the *Kojiki,* for it was a "flayed, piebald horse" that Susano-o flung into the room of Amaterasu, which caused her to hide in a cave and thus thrust the world into darkness.

There are many gods and heroes associated with horses in history and folk tales. White horses are sacred to the gods and are usually used by them as mounts. The emperor of Japan, allegedly a direct descendant of the sun goddess Amaterasu, has always ridden only a pure white horse. Bishamon, the militant god among the seven household gods of good fortune is occasionally portrayed riding upon a horse. Although the horse often serves supernatural beings, he does not have supernatural or magical qualities himself. Rather he possesses the virtues of nobility, wisdom, and purity and is a steadfast companion and devoted friend. Many folk tales tell of his refusal to eat when retired or left behind by his master and friend.

To dream of a horse is considered a lucky omen; however, it also symbolizes that the dreamer will soon be taking a journey. The symbolic associations of the horse have led to its widespread use as a crest or badge *(mon)*. The most popular tales regarding the horse are those of Chokaro, Kagesue, and Hakuraku.

LION (KARASHISHI OR SHISHI)

The lion that is so very often depicted in Japanese art is in reality more of a combination of animals than a poor attempt at portraying the realistic animal itself. Lions are not indigenous to Japan, but, as the name itself (*kara*=Chinese, *shishi*=lion) implies, were introduced from China. There are several animals closely resembling one another that are generally classified as *karashishi,* or *shishi,* the Japanese lion. The *koma-inu,* or Korean dog, the *ama-inu,* or heavenly dog, and the Fu dog, emblematic of Buddha himself, are the outstanding examples. In general the *shishi* are shown in pairs, frequently as statues standing at the entrance of both Buddhist and Shinto shrines as well as at secular buildings, such as palaces, statues, tombs, and the imperial palace gates. Wherever it stands, it performs its duty as guardian against all forms of evil, protecting everything in front of which it stands.

In conventionalized appearance, as it is usually shown, the *shishi* has large, protruding, alert eyes, a fierce facial expression, a curled mane, and a bushy, flowing tail. The body is sturdy and compact, with square broad shoulders, conveying a sense of spiritual strength, stability, vigor, and endurance. The overall appearance is similar to that of the small Japanese dog, the Chin spaniel. The Fu dog is similarly depicted but looks more like the Chinese Pekinese dog. *Karashishi* are usually depicted in pairs, the male with his mouth open, standing on the left side, the more demure female with her mouth closed, on the right side. The *koma-inu* closely follows the above description, with the addition of a single horn on the forehead of the male, while the *ama-inu* is a female and has no horn. In general, these various animals, while fairly clearly differentiated in conventionalized forms, are frequently found represented in combination and in variations of design according to the fancy of the artist. Quite commonly a pair of lions will consist of one *karashishi* and one *koma-inu*. Legend has it that the Korean king, following the Japanese conquest of southern Korea in A.D. 201, promised his complete faithful and untiring support of the Japanese people, and as emblems of this proclamation *koma-inu* were erected in front of the imperial palace and Shinto shrines. With the later introduction and adoption of Buddhism, the symbolic significance of the lion was increased, and the *karashishi* was paired with the *koma-inu*. All buildings of any importance were entrusted to the care of the female *karashishi* and the male *koma-inu,* whose combined task it was to guard against evil. These animals were purely mythological in nature and in appearance. They represented religious doctrines, not realistic animals, and they themselves were not gods but rather acted as guardians and symbols of sacred places.

As mentioned, *karashishi* are found in pairs representing *yo* and *in,* the male and female principles so very important in Oriental art: the male with his mouth open, according to Buddhist legend, in order to utter the Sanskrit vowel sound "ah," the female with her mouth closed, sounding the Sanskrit syllable "um." As a pair they are intended to portray the beginning and the end of all religious beliefs and worship. In other words, as they guard each side of the entrance, they indicate the beginning and end on either side, while all that is good lies in between them. At one time the size, posture, and shape of the pair of *karashishi* guardians were prompted by the importance of the building which they guarded. The male of the pair is generally depicted guarding or playing with a smooth round ball (Fig. 74). This is representative of the *tama,* or jewel of omnipotence. However at times the surface of this ball is intricately carved with peony and *shippo* (seven treasures) motifs, in which case the representation is called *mari-to-karashishi,* or "ball and lion." The hollow center of the ball symbolizes emptiness and reflects the Buddhist doctrine which teaches that the mind must first be clear and empty in order to receive wisdom. This hollow ball is occasionally seen as a lantern with the intent of portraying symbolically the illumination which results from wisdom and light.

The female *karashishi* is usually accompanied by one or more cubs— a representation generally agreed to symbolize a happy and congenial family. Legend relates that the female lion, wishing the family line to remain strong and pure, throws her cubs over the side of a mountain, or into a swiftly moving stream in order to test their endurance and strength. Only the strong and worthy ones are able to surmount these rigorous tests, and those that are destroyed are considered to have been too weak to be of true, pure stock.

The *karashishi* is symbolic of great courage and is able to overpower all other animals. Popular superstitions relate that it can travel 500 miles in a night, while others say it can move at 1,000 miles a minute. Its supernatural powers are so great that its roar can tear other animals apart and its sound is likened to the raging noise of the sea during a fierce storm, while its strength and fierceness are compared to the full fury of a gale. Even the wind, reputed to be the most powerful of all the elements, cannot conquer the lion. The male is often depicted with waves, mountains, rocks, or a waterfall to symbolize his conquering of the powers of nature and the elements. He is also symbolic of bravery and strength. However, to dream of a lion is a bad omen indicating that there will be a death in the family in the near future.

Another common combination often found in art is that of the lion with the peony, representing the "king of the beasts" and "the queen of the flowers."

The lion motif is extremely popular and recurrent in the art and folklore of all countries where Buddhism is prominent, and the *karashishi* is often depicted as supporting the lotus throne upon which Buddha sits. It is associated with many legends in Buddhism as well as purely Japanese folklore and mores. It is the mount of Shoki and the attendant of many deities and heroes as well as of Buddha himself or Monju Bosatsu. At New Year's the *shishi-mai,* or lion dance, is always part of the festivities. This dance symbolically exorcises the devils and evil, an important part of the Japanese New Year's festivities. Another famous story featuring the lion is the subject of the Noh play *Shakkyo* (The Stone Bridge).

MONKEY (SARU)

As a species, the monkey is said to have originated in the Orient. However, only the red-faced, short-tailed ape with fine, tawny-colored fur is indigenous to Japan, although all varieties appear with great frequency and fluency in her art (Fig. 236). The Japanese name for monkey, *saru,* is pronounced the same as the verb "to leave." The cry of the monkey is said to resemble the sound "ki" which is the character for the word "joy."

These animals are imbued with magical, superhuman qualities; are capable of transformation; are said to acquire great longevity; and indeed are often shown holding the peach of longevity. Because of their mischievous, playful, and humorous qualities they are frequently depicted in art as imitating human characteristics and postures. They are most commonly portrayed in netsuke art. The *saru-mawashi,* or monkey trainer, used to travel about the country with his troupe of performing animals, and this subject is also frequently portrayed. The monkey is one of the signs of the zodiac. Monkeys are regarded as sensual animals and are often portrayed with phallic interpretations.

Perhaps the most common presentation of monkeys in a group is that of *sambiki no saru,* generally known in the West as the Three Wise Monkeys. They are of Buddhist origin, and their Japanese names involve puns on the word *saru* (which often becomes *zaru* in combined forms). They are called Mizaru, literally meaning "see no (evil)"; Iwazaru—"speak no (evil)"; and Kikazaru—"hear no (evil)." Symbolically the group serves as an example of the right mode of life and warns against the evils of indulging in these temptations. According to Buddhist teachings, the *sambiki no saru* are the attendants and messengers of Koshin, god of roads. The Shinto religion teaches that they are also the messengers of the deity Okuninushi no Mikoto as well as the attendants of several mountain deities. Another interpretation of the three monkeys is that of *sangoku no saru,* which means "monkeys of the three countries"—that is, India, China, and Japan.

"Saru Kurage ni Noru" (The Ride of the Monkey on the Jellyfish) is a tale involving a once popular belief in the medicinal powers of the liver of the monkey. There are many other tales regarding the pranks and adventures of monkeys, some of the most amusing being "Momotaro," "Saru Kani Kassen" (The Battle of the Crab and the Monkey), "Koshin," and "Sanzo Hoshi."

OX (USHI)

In Japanese, the ox, the buffalo, the bull, the bullock, and the cow are all referred to under the name *ushi*. This animal is employed in art in many different settings and associations, and its symbolic meanings mostly result from the placid temperament of the animal as well as its everlasting usefulness and willingness to serve man. The ox is the second sign of the zodiac.

A reclining ox is emblematic of Sugawara Michizane, a great scholar, minister, and statesman of the 9th century who rode away upon a bull when he was driven into exile. Following his death he was found to have been unfairly punished, and posthumous honors were bestowed upon him. He is popularly known today as Tenjin, god of calligraphy and learning.

Oxen are depicted as steeds for many priests and *sennin*. Lao-tzu, the founder of Taoism, rides upon an ox as does Daikoku, who when seen in this relationship is recognized as the god of agriculture. In general, oxen were used as beasts of burden for drawing carts, plowing fields, and carrying bundles or people upon their backs. The ox is shown in very much the same manner as the horse, although it is never used for warlike purposes and is never ridden into battle. By temperament it has a mild disposition and it is a slow but sturdy and faithful worker. As a reward for its tireless service for the good of man, beef eating was forbidden by the Taoist religion. As its principal use in the fields is in preparation for the planting of the rice, it is emblematic of spring, and in this association it is also often seen with peach blossoms.

In art it is often depicted as being ridden by a boy who is usually playing upon a flute. This was one of the favorite subjects of the lacquer artist Shiomi Masanari. The portrayal is partly a tribute to the mild nature of the animal but is more strongly associated with basic Zen Buddhist beliefs, symbolically representing the rewarding peacefulness of spirit which has been acquired through following the codes of the Zen sect. The *ushi* was quite commonly depicted in all of the miniature arts, including sword furniture, lacquer art, and netsuke (Figs. 173, 178).

One of the loveliest folk tales connected with the *ushi* is that which concerns the Tanabata festival. It is said that a dedicated cowherd fell in love with and was wed to a maiden who was a weaver of heavenly garments. After they were wed the couple became so engrossed in each other that she neglected her weaving and he his herd. As a punishment the gods decided that they must live apart. Thus they were sent to live at opposite sides of the Milky Way, and the herdsman, Kengyu, became a star in the constellation Aquila while the weaving lady, Shokujo, became a star in the constellation Lyra. There is only one night each year, the seventh night of the seventh month, when the lovers are permitted to be together. On this night the magpies form a bridge across the celestial stream of the Milky Way so that Kengyu may cross it to be with his wife. All is well if the skies are clear, but if it rains on that night, the birds may be prevented from forming their bridge and the herdsman cannot cross and thus his visit is delayed until the following year. However long the separation may be, the lovers are always in their accustomed places at the appointed hour and always remain faithful to each other.

RAT (NEZUMI OR NE)

The rat, looked upon with great disgust in Western culture, is curiously a great favorite in China and Japan and is considered as a symbol of good luck, particularly the *fuku-nezumi,* or lucky white rat. Indicative of this feeling, the rat is the first sign of the Oriental zodiac and thus is awarded the special significance that always accompanies the beginning of things.

The rat is frequently depicted in art and is most commonly associated with Daikoku, the god of wealth and prosperity, for whom it serves as attendant and messenger. The festival of Daikoku is held on the Day of the Rat. A frequent artistic theme is Daikoku surrounded by bales of tea and rice upon which rats are nibbling. The moral of this scene is that all wealth needs constant care and must be watched and guarded to prevent its being eaten away or stolen (Figs. 160, 212). An old legend relates that the Buddhist gods wished to be rid of Daikoku as the people were still worshiping him instead of themselves, so they sent a demon from Hades to find and destroy Daikoku. As the demon approached, he was seen by one of Daikoku's rat attendants, who grabbed a branch of holly and chased the demon back to Hades. It is said that from this tale originated the ritual of putting a holly branch at the door as part of the New Year's festivities.

One of the most charming legends relates that when the famous artist Sesshu was a boy he was sent to study with some priests. One day, being angry at the boy for wasting his time painting and dreaming instead of studying his lessons, the priests tied his hands to a tree and bade him sit and repent his ways. The boy sat and wept for a long time, and his tears wet the ground around him. In this soft, moist earth he drew with his toes some rats which were so realistic and vital that they came to life and, in thanks, gnawed away at the ropes which bound his hands and freed him. The priests, returning just then, were so awed by what they saw that they forgave the lad his laziness and encouraged him to pursue his real talent. Another tale similar to this is that of the Kabuki heroine Yukihime, who frees herself by drawing a rat in the fallen cherry petals at her feet. The stories of Nikki Danjo and Raigo also prominently feature the rat.

SHEEP (HITSUJI)

One of the animals of the zodiac, the sheep (sometimes depicted as the goat) is rather infrequently represented in lacquer art. This animal was not indigenous to Japan but made its first appearance there when it was introduced by the Dutch and the Portuguese. Under Buddhist doctrine, the Japanese were not permitted to eat the flesh of animals, and woolen goods were not manufactured in the country. Therefore sheep had never been raised in Japan before comparatively modern times.

The serious countenance of the sheep provoked the Japanese artist to poke fun at it, and it is often depicted wearing a whimsical, comical expression. There is no specific symbolic meaning attached to the sheep. It is frequently shown in company with a *sennin* in reference to the story "Koshohei" or "Hakusekisho."

SNAKE (HEBI OR MI)

Since ancient times the serpent has been an object of awe, inspiring worship in many religious sects and imbued with great supernatural powers. For example white snakes were said to be reincarnations of Shinto gods. In the *Kojiki* it is related that Susano-o, brother of the sun goddess, slew an eight-headed serpent from whose tail he withdrew the sword which came to be one of the Three Sacred Treasures composing the imperial regalia.

In Japanese mythology, the snake, rather than being regarded as a repulsive reptile, acquired the characteristics of a fabulous creature and was often attributed the qualities and features of the dragon. Several gods are credited with having the serpent as their messenger, but the truest form of the snake was the attendant and messenger of the goddess Benten. According to ancient legend, on the island of Enoshima there lived a serpent who was rapidly depopulating the countryside, until one day, following an earthquake, there arose an island in the middle of a lake. Upon this island was hidden the serpent's lair. The goddess Benten descended upon the island and married the serpent, thus causing it to cease its wanton activities. In art she is frequently portrayed accompanied by a snake.

In general, the snake has become emblematic of deceit, cunning, and most particularly jealousy. The story of "Kurakaya Doshin" is a good example of this characteristic.

Superstitions hold that human saliva is poisonous to snakes, as described in the tale of "Tawara Toda," and also that iron offers particularly good protection against snake bite. There are still stores in Japan today that sell snakes and snake extracts and medicines made from snakes, which are said to possess remarkable curative powers.

The snake is the sixth sign of the zodiac and is quite frequently and realistically depicted both in netsuke and in lacquer art (Figs. 187, 200, 211).

TIGER (TORA)

Although the tiger is not native to Japan, it is one of the most popularly portrayed and highly symbolic animals in Japanese art, having been introduced into Japan by way of China through Buddhism. According to Chinese beliefs, the tiger sprang from one of the stars of the group known as the Great Bear. For this reason, it is explained, the tiger has the power to control the wind, and, because of the strength and power of its mighty roar, it is regarded by some as being an incarnation of thunder. The tiger is considered to be the king of all four-legged animals. It is classified as one of the four greatest supernatural animals along with the dragon, the tortoise, and the phoenix. Originally under Taoist teaching the tiger was a fearful, evil supernatural creature presiding over the west and autumn, both of which fall under the negative, or *yin,* principle. However, under Buddhist influence the tiger assumed a positive *yang* force, its evil giving way to strength, nobility, and courage. In association with the dragon, however, it reverts back to its old Taoist *yin* principle.

In art the tiger is represented in numerous ways and with a great variety of combinations, each having symbolic significance. There have been complete volumes written describing in detail the tiger and its associations. The most frequent combination is that of the tiger and the dragon. This combination symbolically represents the power of faith, a Buddhist doctrine. It may also symbolize the meeting of the greatest animal power on earth, the tiger, with the greatest animal force in the heavens, the dragon, which controls the clouds. Legend states that when these two forces meet they fight.

A very common symbolic combination in art is the tiger in a bamboo grove (Fig. 213). There are many explanations of this combination. Some say the bamboo never resists the wind, and the wind is a constant companion of the tiger, and therefore this grass is a natural harbor for the tiger. Another explanation is that the wind-tossed bamboo symbolically represents a wild and tangled tossing pit of sin and that in order to penetrate this sinful jungle one needs the strength of a tiger. To have "tiger courage" was the goal of all youths, particularly the samurai. Many possessed tiger charms and amulets to give them strength, to ward off bad luck, and to discourage demons.

In general the tiger's symbolic meaning is "fluid rather than fixed." It is credited with supernatural powers and is reputed to live to the age of 1,000 years. After it reaches 500 years of age it is said to turn white. It becomes immortal at 1,000 years and can take any shape or form it desires.

There is a folk tale which lauds the wisdom of the tiger. It tells of a mother tiger with three cubs who wishes to cross a river. However, one of her cubs is fierce and vicious, and she is fearful of leaving it alone with any of its brothers since it might do them harm. Coming to the edge of the river, she takes the troublesome cub in her mouth and swims to the other side, where she deposits him. She then returns for the second cub. Carrying him to the other side, she then picks up the fierce cub and goes back across the river carrying him with her. She places him on the beach and takes the third cub across to the other side and puts him with his gentle brother. Finally she returns for the troublesome cub and once again carries him across to where his two brothers wait.

The tiger is often seen by the side of a waterfall, since the characteristics of both are their ceaseless strength and their forcefulness. As one of the animals of the zodiac, the tiger is highly esteemed.

Sea Life and Amphibians

Fish, shellfish, shells and even the ocean itself form an important subgroup of nature which is frequently depicted in Japanese lacquer art. These animate and inanimate aspects of the sea played a predominant role in everyday Japanese life, culture, and mythology and hence have often been reflected in Japanese art. The Japanese people, being islanders, are accomplished fishermen, and one of their main food staples is fish. It is even served for breakfast and quite often fish are given as presents. Some fish were believed to be medicinal and were also used as Buddhist symbolic emblems. In general, fish are symbolic of good health, good luck, and plentiful food. Artistic representations of fish swimming in water reflect our own Occidental idea of this happy symbolic relationship of nature or as "feeling fine." Furthermore, this art motif provided the Japanese artist with a wonderful means of portraying the undulating sweep and motion of fish swimming in water (Fig. 218). In lacquer art, in painting, and in metal art this joyous feeling of motion is not only simply and beautifully represented but also incorporates a subtle third-dimensional sweep. Thus part of the fish (usually the head and occasionally the tip of the tail) is seen to emerge from the water while the remainder of the body can be visualized as a shadowy image deeper within the rippling water. In lacquer art this technique is shown most effectively by using various subtle shades of *togidashi*. Of all the fish, the leaping carp has undoubtedly been portrayed the most frequently in Japanese art (Figs. 26, 27). The Korin-Ritsuo school also often delighted in presenting fish and shells in strongly carved, highly raised encrustations. Toyo was fond of representing the lobster, using a coarse red-lacquer ground in imitating the texture of the shell (Fig. 144). The sea in its various aspects was a favorite subject in Japanese painting and in lacquer art. A most popular scene pictures tiny fishing vessels engulfed by the enormity of the seascape, revealing once again the relative insignificance of man among nature (Figs. 118, 134). This parallels the Chinese idea of the tiny hut seen hidden within enormous rugged mountains. Quite often, as a result of Chinese influence, the ocean waves were portrayed in a somewhat conventionalized fashion, perhaps the most famous example of which is Zeshin's wave design. Fishermen pulling their boats up a river was also a favorite subject with lacquer artists, along with the adjacent landscape seen in the distance.

Finally various mythological tales involving marine life and its associated gods were depicted, such as Kinko riding on a fish, or the very popular household god Ebisu, the patron of fishermen. In general, however, such mythological subjects were much more often portrayed in netsuke rather than in lacquer.

ABALONE (AWABI)

One of the most important and most common species of shellfish in Japan, the abalone, or *awabi,* is valued not only for its meat but also for the shell itself. It is a one-shelled mollusk which is found attached to rocks far below the surface of the water. It is gathered mostly by women divers, called *ama,* who are highly specialized in this skill. There are many folk legends surrounding the *awabi,* such as "Muge Hoju no Tama."

The flesh of the *awabi* is very elastic, and when, as in the ancient custom, a thin piece of this meat is attached to special folded paper *(noshi)* which accompanies any gift being given in Japan, its meaning is symbolic of wishing long life to the recipient, as is revealed by an old proverb "May your life be lengthened and stretched like the flesh of the *awabi.*"

In lacquer art, the beautiful, lustrous, many-colored shell is extremely important, as it is frequently used for inlaid designs. A great number of lacquer artists employed this shell in their works, and some, like Aogai Chobei and the more recent Somada school of artists, became famous for their work with this fragile and very beautiful material. It may be that the artist uses the *awabi* for his entire decorative design, or equally as often it is cut up into tiny pieces and inserted in lovely geometric patterns which complement and enhance the major decorative design.

BONITO (KATSUO)

A highly palatable and abundant fish, the *katsuo* is equally prized because its name can be translated to mean "victory fish." Furthermore, in its dried form, in which it is most frequently found in art, its name *katsuo-bushi* means "victorious samurai." For these reasons the bonito symbolically represents success and is often presented as a gift to commemorate any festive occasion. It is portrayed more commonly in painting and in netsuke form than in lacquer.

CARP (KOI)

This fish has great symbolic significance and appears often in lacquer art. The word *koi* also means purpose, and the carp is emblematic of strength, perseverance, courage, endurance, and manly virtue. An ancient Chinese tale relates that fish will swim against the strongest currents and attempt to overcome the greatest obstacles. Only the carp, however, has the fighting strength, perseverance, and endurance to conquer the greatest obstacle of all. This is called the Dragon Gate, and as its reward for conquering this obstacle the carp is transformed into a dragon and then lives forever after in happiness. Thus the carp serves as an example for boys and young men of the rewards that are granted as a result of virtuous efforts. It is only natural, then, that the carp is the emblem of the Boys' Festival, which takes place on the fifth day of the fifth month of each year. Another translation of the word *koi* is love, and two carp are considered emblematic of happy married life, longevity, and numerous offspring.

In general, the carp is represented in lacquer art in the act of leaping and ascending a waterfall, the artist giving special attention to depicting the vigor, energy, and perseverance which this symbolically represents (Figs. 26, 27, 214).

CLAM (HAMAGURI)

This mollusk is surrounded by superstition and symbology revolving mainly about its alleged powers to emit a purplish mist in which one can see depicted the mythological island of Horai (Mount Horai), which is the island of eternal life, and also the fabled dragon palace of Ryujin, which is at the bottom of the sea.

The shell of the clam is used for the shell-matching game *kai-awase* and is frequently portrayed on the lacquer box in which the shells used in the game are stored. The shape of the clam itself lends to its portrayal in the erotic form seen occasionally in netsuke carvings, the most frequent subject being that of a *kappa* with its foot caught in a clamshell.

CONCH (HORA OR HORAGAI)

This sea shell, which was used long ago by warriors as a signal horn, has come to symbolically represent victory in battle. Furthermore, it is one of the eight Buddhist symbols, since it is related that Buddha's descent to earth was heralded by the sound of the *hora* and that when Buddhist priests blow upon it to call their followers for worship, it drives off all demons and evil spirits. It is also one of the attributes of the traveling mountain priests called *yamabushi*. The *hora* is frequently portrayed in lacquer art and also in netsuke form.

COWRIE (KOYASUGAI)

This shell is one of the "precious things" found in the bag of Hotei, and as such it symbolizes wealth and good fortune. It is also called *takara-gai,* or "treasure shell," and in this relationship is frequently represented in art. The ideogram for *ko* may be translated as "child," *yasu* as "easy," and *kai (gai)* as "shell," and it may therefore be interpreted to mean "easy birth" and is occasionally given to expectant mothers as a talisman.

CRAB (KANI)

In 1185 a great naval battle between the Heike and Genji forces climaxed the war between these two clans, and many of the defeated Heike clansmen committed suicide by drowning themselves in the sea. Ever since that time, a legend says, the crabs called Heike-gani bear on their shells the features of a scowling human face, and they are believed to be reincarnations of the dead Heike warriors. Because of its association with warriors, the Heike crab is occasionally used as an amulet for protection against misfortune.

FROG (KAERU)

An exceedingly popular motif in Oriental art, this amphibian is distinguished from the warty toad in that his skin is smoother, his hind legs are more muscular, and he has webbed feet. He is often seen in association with aquatic plants or as a representation of the legend of Ono no Tofu, in which association he symbolically represents perseverance. (See also "Toad" below.)

LOBSTER (EBI)

One of the most common art motifs of the marine-life group is the lobster or crayfish. Because of its bent body it is likened to a very elderly person, and indeed a lobster is one of the most important symbols of longevity. It is one of the gifts given at New Year's along with the orange, fern, and charcoal and in this association represents the wish that "you may become so old that your body becomes as bent as the lobster." Furthermore, a boiled lobster is always depicted, for when a lobster is boiled it turns a bright red color, and red is the accepted color symbol of vitality (Fig. 144).

OCTOPUS (TAKO)

Found in abundance in the sea, the octopus and the squid *(ika)* appear frequently as food and also in art, although to a somewhat lesser degree in lacquer ware. Both the octopus and the squid, because of their numerous tentacles, are symbolic of numerous offspring and therefore, by inference, of happiness. Furthermore, the word *tako* may also be translated to read "grcat happiness." There are many legends centering about the octopus. It is often represented in a comical vein as well as in an erotic manner, particularly in netsuke art.

SEA BREAM (TAI)

One of the most popular fish of Japan, the *tai* is often depicted in art either as part of the symbology of the New Year celebration or as the attendant of the household god of the sea, Ebisu. This fish is emblematic of longevity, since it has on its back a hump which brings to mind the bent, hunchbacked appearance of many elderly people. Furthermore, it is related that the *tai* gets this hump by constantly swimming upstream against the flow of the water, and this also signifies, as in the instance of the carp, victory over difficult obstacles.

TOAD (GAMA)

The rough, warty-skinned toad is more of a land amphibian than the common frog. He is reputed to be able to escape from captivity even under almost impossible conditions and is said to possess magical powers and an inexhaustible knowledge of roots and herbs. He is the constant companion of Kosensei, better known as Gama Sennin, who, legend relates, found a sick toad and nursed it back to health. From that time on, the toad became his attribute and shared his extensive knowledge of herbs and roots with the *sennin* (hermit). Figure 56 shows a typical portrayal of the toad and the Gama Sennin.

TORTOISE (KAME)

The tortoise is extremely popular in all Japanese art forms and is of great symbolic significance (Fig. 104). There are two distinct species of tortoises which are commonly portrayed. The first is the realistic tortoise with which we are all familiar, and the second is the long-tailed or so-called *mino-game* (Fig. 138). In actuality the *mino-game* derives its name from the resemblance of its "tail" to the straw raincoat commonly worn by the farmer, *mino* meaning straw raincoat, and *kame (game)* tortoise. It was applied to tortoises upon whose shell grew a long, stringy, plantlike fungus which would float behind them in the water and thus gave them the appearance of having grown a tail. Tortoises are said to live to great ages, and legend has it that after a tortoise reaches 1,000 years of age it grows a tail and may then live to be 10,000 years old. It obviously, then, is a symbol of longevity. In this respect also, the tortoise is often portrayed with the crane, another symbol of longevity, and almost without exception portrayals of the treasure ship which carries the Seven Lucky Gods show it being escorted into port by cranes flying overhead and a long-tailed tortoise swimming alongside. Furthermore, the tortoise, often with the crane, is the attribute of the household god Fukurokuju and the old couple Jo and Uba and often is seen with the mythological Mount Horai. In some instances the *kame* is portrayed holding Mount Horai upon its back, and in this and other legends it is emblematic of strength, endurance, and support.

There are many folk legends related to the tortoise, and one of the most enchanting is the tale of Urashima Taro. As the tortoise is a water animal surrounded by pleasant symbolic overtones, it is only natural that it should be a favorite object of attention of fishermen and sailors, who have their own special god, Kompira. When a fisherman catches a tortoise he is supposed to give it some *sake* to drink (for tortoises are said to be extremely fond of *sake*) and then set it loose, instructing it to report his good deed to Kompira, who will reward him with a bountiful catch on his fishing expedition. In this respect it is common to find a tortoise depicted in lacquer as a decorative motif on a *sake* cup.

Mythological Creatures

In all the civilizations in the world where mythological creatures exist in folklore, none are as beloved or as intricately developed and as deeply established as those of Japan. Here the mischievous antics of such creatures of the imagination as the *tengu* and the *kappa* occur with great frequency in all of the culture and the art forms. So highly detailed are the descriptions of these creatures that they are easily recognizable by their standard appearance no matter in which medium they are portrayed.

DRAGON (RYU, TATSU)

The Japanese word *ryu* (sometimes *ryo*) is derived from the Chinese word meaning "powerful." (*Tatsu* is the native Japanese reading.) The dragon represents the fifth year of the twelve-year cycle of the Oriental zodiac, the month of March, the hours between 7 and 9 a.m., and the direction east-southeast. It is by far the most popular mythological creature represented in Japanese graphic and glyptic art. The reason is undoubtedly twofold: the first being its great mythological and symbolic significance and the second being its almost ideal artistic adaptability, both in expression and in form. Thus its fierce face and undulating scaly body provided the Japanese lacquer artist an ideal subject in which to give full imaginative vent to power of expression and swirls of motion. Furthermore, in the graphic arts, such as painting and lacquer, dragons were often portrayed along with eddies of water and swirls of dense, ominous clouds—a perfect combination for decorative effects (Figs. 109, 230).

The dragon of Japanese mythology was adapted and modified from Chinese concepts which in turn reflected Indian and Taoist influences. It originally embodied the principles of the male and the female, the *yang* and the *yin,* and was associated with the powers of water, both of rain and of the sea, each of which was of equal importance respectively to the Japanese farmer and fisherman. With the advent of Taoism the dragon became endowed with magical powers, being able to transform itself into innumerable things. Under the influence of Buddhism it finally became endowed with spiritual and philosophical qualities and became the protector of divinities and a symbol of the transience of life and the perpetual state of change and evolution. Under the influence of Shintoism it related to the omnipotence of the imperial household.

Specifically the dragon may assume any dimension. It can fill the universe with its body or become so small as to be invisible. Thus the drag-on's many-sidedness embodies the idea of the male and the female principle and the utmost attainment of the embodiment of wisdom. The continuous changes and variations of life are symbolized by its unlimited powers of adaptation, accommodating itself to all surroundings and therefore having no end, like the everlasting cycles of life. The dragon's breath is changed into clouds from which rain pours down and lightning flashes forth. It is also believed to carry water from the earth to the skies, and therefore in periods of drought it is worshiped in various ways.

There are many kinds of dragons. In general they are powerful, fierce, omnipotent, and representative of celestial power. While physically par-tially embodying the serpent, they basically differ from this creature, since the dragon in general is representative of benevolence and in art, al-though depicted as powerful and fierce, is not loathsome or repulsive. The dragon is one of the four fabulous animals. It is chief of all scaly animals and presides over authority. (The phoenix is chief of feathery animals and presides over virtue. The unicorn is chief of all hairy animals and presides over literature, while the tortoise is chief of all shelled creatures and pre-sides over divination.) The dragon ascends into the heavens in the spring and descends into rivers in autumn, being known respectively in Japanese art as the ascending and the descending dragon.

Pictorially the Japanese dragon resembles the Chinese dragon. It is a composite of various powerful qualities of the animal kingdom. Its head is similar to that of a camel and has elongated jaws, deerlike horns, a promi nent broad-nostriled nose, heavy scaly eyebrows and beard, two long, thin, curved bristles emanating from the corners of its mouth, sharp tusks, oxlike ears, and round intense eyes. Its body is serpentine, with scales like those of a fish and sharp dorsal spines. It is often seen with flames emanat-ing from its armpits and groin. The end of its tail has numerous sharp spines. There are four short legs and feet combining the paw of the tiger and the talons of the hawk. There are usually three claws, except for the imperial dragon, which has five claws. The Chinese dragon has four claws but is otherwise similar to the Japanese dragon. From the description of the dragon it can be seen that its fierce face and scales and spines are also ideally suited for the powerful chisel strokes of the sculptural metal artist, and it was the favorite subject of the famous early Goto school of metal artists.

Among the various dragons are the celestial dragon, who guards the gods; the spiritual dragon, who produces wind and rain; the earth dragon, who marks the courses of streams and rivers, and the dragon of hidden treasures, who watches over the wealth hidden from mankind. The water dragon is considered symbolic of the scholar, the earth dragon of the statesman, and the sky dragon of the emperor. Dragons are also identified by their colors, which range from red, violet, and blue to green, yellow, white, and black. The yellow dragon is identified with the imperial household. The white dragon's breath is believed to become gold. The saliva of the violet dragon turns to crystal balls.

There are numerous popular legends associated with the Dragon King (Ryujin), who is reputed to live in a palace at the bottom of the sea. His chief messenger is depicted as a white serpent carrying the sacred jewel *(tama)*, which controls the ebb and flow of the tides and represents omnipotence. This jewel, which was once stolen from the Dragon King, is often illustrated in Japanese art as having just been caught in the claws of a dragon. The Dragon King is represented as a bearded old man with a dragon on his back, the dragon's head forming his head covering. When aroused, the Dragon King is responsible for the storms of the sea.

The rain dragon is known as Amaryu and is said to be black. Fukuryu is the dragon of good luck and is represented climbing to the top of Mount Fuji—a symbol of success in life.

The dragon fears iron and is also capable of being slain, as noted in legendary tales. It is also a lustful creature, and the fabulous animal known as *kirin* is said to be the offspring of the dragon and the cow. Dragons are associated mythologically with various gods and sages. A dragon emerges from the sea at the command of Kannon and is the steed of the goddess Benten.

In Japanese art the dragon is traditionally never displayed in its entirety, for to see the entire dragon is to invite instant death, the punishment for looking upon too much divinity. Thus in art its undulating form is represented weaving in and out of clouds or water. The dragon is also commonly depicted in art, more commonly in metal art, entwined about a sword. This alludes to the story of the god Susano-o, who, after destroying the eight-headed serpent, found a beautiful sword within its tail.

Finally the dragon is associated symbolically in art most frequently with the tiger and the phoenix. The tiger, while usually a *yang* force, in this association represents the material or *yin* forces and is bested by the dragon, which represents the spiritual or celestial or *yang*. The breath of the tiger creates the wind, and together with the clouds of the dragon, rain is created. The dragon-phoenix combination again represents the *yin-yang* principle, the dragon representing the positive *yang* and the phoenix the negative *yin*.

PHOENIX (HO-O)

The phoenix (in Chinese, *feng-huang*) is one of the four divine animals, head of all feathery creatures, and presides over the southern quadrant of heaven. It is a composite of the attributes of other animals. Traditionally it is six feet tall and has a six-foot plumage, the head of a pheasant, a cock's comb, the features of the dragon and the fish, and the beak of a swallow, below which are feathery tufts. It has the neck of a tortoise, from which issue flamelike appendages. It has relatively long legs and strong claws, and its extremely extended feathers are represented as long, narrow individual streamers. The plumage varies with the artist's imagination, in general becoming more extended and ornate by the 19th century. The feathers are of five different colors with an iridescent sheen of green-blue, yellow, red, white, and black signifying the five cardinal virtues of uprightness, honesty, justice, fidelity, and benevolence. The phoenix, which resembles both the peacock and the pheasant, exists as the male *ho* and the female *o*. It subsists only on the seeds of the bamboo and drinks only at sacred springs. It perches only on the *wu* tree, which is the Japanese *kiri (Paulownia imperialis)*, which incidentally is the crest of the empress and was once that of Toyotomi Hideyoshi.

The phoenix sings beautiful melodies and is followed by all other birds. It appears only upon auspicious occasions, such as during the reign of a benevolent ruler. Many varieties of this fabulous bird are described, depending on its color or of one of the five directions. In the Taoist religion the bird is said to transport the worthy to paradise. The phoenix represents the female, or *yin*, qualities and often appears in association with the dragon. It is the bird of good luck and longevity and symbolizes imperial power. It is a very gentle bird and is known as the sacred golden pheasant and the heavenly phoenix.

The phoenix is a very popular design in textiles and is also seen fairly frequently in lacquer work. It is often drawn in association with bamboo and *kiri* leaves. Its tail feathers are sometimes depicted similar to those of the peacock, sometimes extremely long and wavy, even scroll-like, and occasionally short or curved in circular fashion about the bird as simple conventionalized "powderings" (Fig. 220).

KAPPA (WATER IMP)

The *kappa* (also *kawako, kawataro, suiko*) was originally an amphibious goblin deity of the mouths and pools of rivers. He is of pure Japanese origin, being a mythological creature. He is said to be found in abundance on the island of Kyushu. He has the trunk of a turtle, with a turtle shell on his back, but the rest of his body resembles that of a three- or four-year-old boy. His legs are half human and half froglike in appearance, being hairy, scaly, or bumpy. His head is like that of a monkey, with short, strong jaws. On the top of his head is a circular depression filled with water: the source of his strength. Radiating about this depression is a fringe of rough straight hair. Bobbed hair in Japan is called *o-kappa* (honorable *kappa*), and Japanese children of old had haircuts similar to that of the *kappa*, with the crown shaved and the rest bobbed. The *kappa* has large eyes and long claws and webbed hands and feet.

This river imp is believed to lie in wait on the sandy bottoms of rivers and to bite children who enter the water. It is fond of fresh blood. It is quite strong and draws people and domestic animals under the water and devours them. Because of its amorous nature young women fear it, and it likes to fight young men. However, it can be defeated. While basically a malevolent creature, it is always a gentleman, quite polite and ceremonious, and keeps its word. Therefore, when you bow to it upon an encounter it bows back and loses the elixir in its head dish, and thus its strength, and can then be readily subdued.

The *kappa* is frequently depicted in netsuke art with one foot caught in the shell of a clam: an erotically suggestive warning to young men that once a woman has a man in her clutches it is hard for him to get loose, even if he is as strong as a *kappa*. The *kappa* is a gourmet and is particularly fond of cucumbers. Parents who fear that their children may be drowned are said to appease it by throwing a cucumber into the river. The *kappa* is portrayed relatively rarely in lacquer art as compared to netsuke art.

TENGU

The *tengu* (literally, "heavenly dog"), or bird-man, may be classified as a forest goblin or mythological animal. He is basically a Japanese version of the Indian *garuda* or *suparna* and evolved from the Chinese dog who warred against Buddhism. He ultimately assumed Japanese characteristics and is associated with considerable Japanese folklore. The *tengu* lives on high inaccessible mountains and in forests in the topmost boughs of trees and uses a leaf of the *yatsude* shrub for a fan. He is a Shinto god venerated by woodsmen and hunters, who bring offerings to him. Numerous temples have been erected to him, and he is said to punish those who disturb the woods. The *tengu* flies about freely and can perform wonders. He has the power of transformation, but basically he is not malevolent. He has great strength and is capable of breaking trees with a single blow. He is skilled in the use of weapons and in the art of fencing and is familiar with the secrets of birds and beasts. He is also said to pull out the tongues of lying children and to kidnap both children and adults in the forest.

There are two different kinds of *tengu*. The first type is the ordinary, or *konoha tengu,* which has a human face and form, with wings and a long nose. In art the nose is often treated erotically, especially in association with Uzume, or it is humorously portrayed as a carrying pole. *Konoha tengu* occasionally wear capes. One opinion is that the *konoha tengu* may be a prototype in caricature form of European men with long noses. A *konoha tengu* mask which represents Prince Sarudahiko, who led the imperial party of Prince Ninigi no Mikoto from heaven to rule the earth, is worn in certain Shinto festival processions. The *konoha tengu* are higher in rank than the *shotengu* (little *tengu*) or *karasu* (crow) *tengu*.

The second type is the *karasu tengu*. They are birdlike in form and face, with a strong curved beak and tigerlike claws, and are often armed with clubs.

The great military leader Minamoto Yoshitsune reputedly learned fencing from the *tengu* king, who is depicted as an aged bird-man with a long mustache and a long gray beard and, as a mark of rank, carries a fan of seven feathers and wears the tiny hat of the *yamabushi,* or itinerant priests. He is called Kuramayama no Sojobo or Dai Tengu.

In netsuke art the most common portrayal is called *tengu no tamago* (*tengu*'s egg) and reveals the *tengu* hatching from a relatively large egg. *Tengu* are by far more commonly portrayed in netsuke art than they are in lacquer art.

Natural Elements

No discussion of the symbolic significance of nature as represented in Japanese art could be complete without mentioning the importance of the background elements supplied by nature herself, such as rocks, rain, wind, water, and clouds. Many times we overlook these elements as they quietly blend into the landscape or add the finishing touches to the picture. However, most of them are also portrayed in a symbolic manner and in harmony with the mood of the lacquer painting. Thus the quiet waters of the running brook along whose shores flowers and grasses are growing in abundance symbolizes a calm, contented life which, like the twisting contours of the brook, avoids most obstacles by diverting from the straight path and going gracefully around them.

Clouds are a common pictorial element in lacquer work and are portrayed in different styles, depending on what they are to signify. For instance, when they are placed low and in horizontal masses across the outline of a mountain they are usually rain clouds, or if they are somewhat thinner and closer to the ground in diverse patches they indicate mist or fog. High-flying fleecy clouds show good weather while whorls of clouds are the attribute of the dragon and usually represent his presence (Fig. 54).

Wind is expressed in varying degrees by the angles of the grasses or flowers which it is bending or by the bent-over figure of a man fighting to make his way through the force of a gale.

Rain is symbolic of fertility. This can easily be understood in a country such as Japan where agriculture is so significant. Again in art, the angle of the "rain" lines varies from vertical, widely separated, almost perpendicular lines indicative of a soft summer rain to slightly heavier, somewhat opaque lines indicating a spring shower and to heavy lines at extreme oblique angles, placed close together to indicate a heavy downpour with strong winds.

Snow is symbolic of winter and of the hardships which accompany the winter months. And, as snow comes at the end of the year, it is also symbolic of old age.

Rocks and stones constitute an important part of every Japanese garden, and the lacquer artist uses them frequently in his drawings. Their symbolic significance is varied and in accordance with the overall shape of the rock as well as its place in the picture. Rocks are emblematic of obstacles, ruggedness, and reliability. Deeply imbedded rocks suggest strength of character. A rounded stone signifies peace, a tall one which is wider at the base suggests constancy and stability, while a rectangular rock is emblematic of labor and usefulness. Rocks are usually portrayed in *takamakie* technique to suggest their bulk and texture (Figs. 221, 222).

Mount Fuji, the queen of all mountains, is surrounded with as dense a layer of mythology and legend as it is with clouds. Its outstanding symbolic significance is everlasting power and strength and triumph over all obstacles. It is thus a symbol of success in life. The beauty of its cone shape, with the white cap of snow and the layer of clouds around its summit, is often portrayed in all art forms (Fig. 45).

Curiously the sun, which is so important in Japanese mythology and whose image is the emblem on Japan's national flag, is rarely seen in her art. Rather, through representative symbols only is its importance recognized. The moon, however, is a favorite subject and is portrayed in all its phases by the lacquer artist (Figs. 117, 141, 223, 224, 227, 241). The ways in which the moon is portrayed are endless: silhouetted against the moon a lone leaf or feather floats to the ground; among the grasses a rabbit sits staring at the moon; on the still water of a calm brook the moon casts its reflection. All these and endless others have inspired lacquerers in countless portrayals of the moon, a subject which lends itself most beautifully to lacquer art, particularly in the use of delicate shadings in *togidashi* technique. The full moon is symbolic of autumn and also of feminine purity. Furthermore, it resembles the halo which surrounds the head of Buddha and is thus revered. The new crescent-shaped moon is emblematic of the beginning of things and is a good omen, while the final crescent symbolizes the end and is viewed with regret.

Thus we can see by the few examples outlined above that inanimate things and the forces of nature itself are often imbued with symbolic significance, and the lacquer artist uses these nuances to enrich the beauty and meaning of his works. The variety of subject material is inexhaustible, and, as we have seen, almost in their entirety the subjects embody some poetical reference or symbolic significance.

The Fine Arts

Depictions of aspects of the fine arts are occasionally encountered in lacquer art. By the fine arts in this case we refer to calligraphy, music, poetry, and the drama.

Ink, inkstone, and writing brush are all emblems of scholarship and advancement. The ink cake in particular is treasured for generations, its quality and age being said to influence the depth and gloss of the ink. It is upon black inkstones that the black ink is prepared by adding water and grinding the ink cakes. The Chinese ink cakes are often ornamented with beautiful designs and pictures. The fine designs are usually made by compression within molds. They are occasionally gilded. Ink cakes used by famous calligraphers are highly prized. Imitations of these ink cakes were a favorite subject of well-known Japanese lacquer artists, such as Ritsuo and Zeshin. Here the subtle black-on-black design could be ideally used, and even the chips and cracks of the ink cakes were simulated to perfection (Figs. 59, 60).

Second in popularity in lacquer art is the portrayal of various musical instruments. These include drums *(taiko)* of various types such as those used for Shinto festivals as well as war drums. Flutes *(fue)* also exist in various forms, including those used in the Noh drama and the more complicated-looking, eerie, dissonant-sounding *sho* used for sacred music. The *sho* consists of seventeen bamboo stems of varying lengths encased in a lacquered bowl with a protruding mouthpiece.

Among the stringed instruments is the *koto,* an ancient instrument imported from China which is a sort of horizontal harp, usually with thirteen strings. It has a resonating case about two meters long that rests on the floor. The use of this instrument was reserved for the upper levels of society, and it was part of the formal education of noblewomen to learn to play it.

The most popular Japanese stringed instrument is the *samisen,* which has three strings and resembles the American banjo. Its rectangular resonating case is covered on either side with cat or dog skin. The strings are plucked with a large plectrum *(bachi)*. This cheerful-sounding instrument is the favorite of the geisha.

The *biwa,* also an ancient instrument imported from China, is a sort of mandolin with four strings and is plucked with a plectrum. It is used for vocal accompaniment.

There are also various types of gongs and bells used in Japanese music. The Japanese lacquer artist took delight in simulating musical instruments in accurate detail, including the grain of the wood and the fine lines of the strings (Fig. 13).

The drama was occasionally depicted in Japanese lacquer, including the masks of the Noh and the gorgeously colored and ornamental robes of the Kabuki. Occasionally portrayed also are actors and scenes from favorite Noh dramas (Figs. 2, 225).

Finally, poetry was represented in Japanese lacquer by means of ideograms referring to famous poems. Fairly frequently an inro or *kobako* imitated the shape of a book of poems, the sides appearing like the edges of the pages of a closed book (Fig. 229).

Games and Festivals

Various games and innumerable festivals played an important role in Japanese society. Among the games is that of *go,* which somewhat resembles the game of checkers but in its intricacy is more akin to chess. The game of *shogi* is frequently depicted in Japanese lacquer with two men seated opposite each other carefully studying the game board which lies between them (Fig. 232).

The game of *ken,* which is similar to the Western game of "paper, scissors, and stone," symbolically indicates that nothing is absolute. It is usually depicted by three figures, each representing a different power, seated in a circle. A similar game called *tohachiken* involves a man, a fox, and a gun. Occasionally three gods of different philosophies are similarly presented. Such games or allusions to them are often seen in netsuke art rather than in lacquer art. The same applies to *sumo* wrestling and neckrope wrestling *(kubihiki),* which are better portrayed in sculptural netsuke form. Reference has already been made to the various more serious aristocratic games of verse-matching and perfume- and incense-guessing, as well as to the tea ceremony.

There are many Japanese festivals throughout the year, the most noted being the five festivals known as *go-sekku,* which fall on the odd days of the odd months (the *yo* of *in-yo*)—that is, the first day of the first month, the third day of the third month, the fifth day of the fifth month, etc. The most important festival, as previously noted, is the New Year's festival. The traditional New Year's decoration is the *kadomatsu,* an arrangement of pine branches and bamboo placed before residences and public buildings. Across the top of the gate or house entrance and also before the household shrine is stretched the sacred rope of straw, the *shimenawa,* along which are strung *gohei* (zigzag-folded paper decorations), fern leaves, a bitter orange *(daidai),* and a small bent lobster—all symbolizing good luck, longevity, and prosperity. The pine tree denotes long life; the bamboo, constancy; and the fern, expanding good fortune. The bitter orange has a special significance as a New Year's decoration because its Japanese name, *daidai,* also means "generation after generation" and thus suggests family continuity. The traditional flower arrangement for the new year is made up of pine, bamboo, and plum *(sho-chiku-bai).* Among the games and sports particularly related to this festival are battledore and shuttlecock, kite flying, and a card game of matching lines from the famous poetry anthology *Hyakunin Isshu.* Another traditional New Year's symbol is the treasure ship *(takarabune),* which carries the Seven Lucky Gods as passengers along with a cargo of precious things. The emblems of New Year's are fairly frequently portrayed on lacquer ware.

The third day of March is the Doll Festival (sometimes called Girls' Festival), known as Hinamatsuri. For this occasion the symbolic flower is the peach blossom. A display of dolls in the home—particularly if there are girls in the family—is a feature of this festival.

Tango-no-Sekku, the traditional Boys' Festival, which occurs on the fifth of May and is now celebrated as Children's Day, is the second most popular festival depicted by lacquer artists. Its symbolic flower is the iris, whose leaf suggests the blade of a sword. In celebration of this occasion large paper or cloth carp—emblematic of ambition and perseverance—are flown from poles above the homes of families with young sons, and dolls representing military heroes and other models of masculine virtues are displayed inside the house along with miniature swords, helmets, and spears.

The seventh day of July is Tanabata, the festival of the Weaving Girl (symbolized by the star Vega), who, according to legend, meets her herd-boy lover (the star Altair) but once a year when heavenly magpies build a bridge for them across the Milky Way. On this day, love poems are written in honor of the lovers and suspended on boughs of bamboo. A herdsman with his ox waiting patiently under the stars, a scene quite often portrayed in lacquer ware, is an allusion to this lovely legend of Tanabata.

The ninth day of September is the Chrysanthemum Festival (Choyo), when outdoor parties are held for the purpose of viewing and enjoying the chrysanthemum blossoms.

Abstractions and Symbols

The Japanese have long been acclimated to abstractions and symbols both in their daily routine and in their art. Abstractions and ideational thinking are reflected in centuries-old Oriental religion and philosophy. The complexity of symbolism present in the daily lives and customs of the Japanese also reflects a variety of abstractions. The same applies to their art and allied fields such as the theater and poetry. Their very language and calligraphy represent the height of ideational thinking along with abstract visual form, balance, and motion, which can be considered almost as preparatory groundwork for the arts. Thus in calligraphy each ideogram is carefully written within a hypothetical square so as to produce a well-balanced, asymmetrically pleasing, aesthetically abstract beauty, combining color (washes), strength, form, and movement. Even a simple dot is artistically written so as "to give the strength of a rock falling from a high cliff." Such strokes have been transcribed, incorporated, and interwoven into the brush strokes of painting. For example, in painting the bamboo, the strokes for the stem resemble the character "one." Other strokes of calligraphic origin used in ink painting include those known as "rats' tails" and "fish tails." Calligraphy was not only adopted in painting indirectly by means of brush strokes in the pictorial element but also often directly as a poem or its equivalent alongside the painting. The carefully written artist's signature and seal were also considered to be an integral part of the painting. Painting therefore incorporates symbolism, nature, and calligraphy, all in abstract ideational forms. A thorough understanding of such abstract thinking therefore enables us to better appreciate the aesthetics and goals of Japanese art. It should be noted that considerable stress is placed in Japanese museums upon calligraphy and sword blades, entire rooms being devoted solely to such displays. Both of these art forms, so highly respected, represent the quintessence of abstract beauty which incorporates form, balance, and motion. Such love of form and motion is reflected in Japanese sculptural art as well, as can be seen in the emphasis placed upon the draperies and forms of the subjects rather than on purely facial and anatomical facets. While the powerfully expressive sweep of rapid brush strokes is not suitable for the slow, painstaking work required by the sticky lacquer medium, these secondary influences of form, balance, and motion found their way into lacquer art. It must be remembered that technically in lacquer art the design was primarily dusted onto the tacky lacquer base rather than being applied with a brush. Therefore the broad sweep of the brush strokes or the density of the stroke is not evident in lacquer art. Good lacquer art actually consists of fine lines with sharp marginated borders. If softness of outline was desired this could be accomplished by using the *togidashi* technique or by careful blending of colors. Strength was obtained similarly by careful use of colors, materials, and various degrees of raising of the lacquer. Occasionally calligraphic and brush strokes were simulated in lacquer (Figs. 233, 234), and we have seen how even the black washes of *sumie* painting were beautifully imitated (Fig. 231). While pure calligraphy was not suitable for lacquer work, it was occasionally adopted to a limited degree —for example, by using a few scattered ideograms, usually alluding to a poem, intertwined into the pictorial element. Occasionally the design itself consisted of pure calligraphic symbols, such as the characters for longevity (Figs. 24, 235).

The use of stylized family crests, the adoption of Chinese geometric designs along with varying degrees of conventionalizations of animal and plant life, and the use of decorative symbolic figures, such as the eight Buddhist symbols or the seven precious things, added a further abstract, symbolic, and strong decorative quality to Japanese lacquer art. Similarly, what may appear to be a purely decorative diaper background is also often of significant symbolic meaning tied in with the pictorial element. Thus the common swastika-fret design is generally associated with the bat, and both symbolically refer to longevity. Again, the seven precious things are often seen as ornamental border designs for one of the Seven Lucky Gods, since the seven precious things also represent good luck. Therefore in Japanese lacquer there is not only a symbolic relation of one figure to another but also of the pictorial element to the ornamental background. In such a symbolic way the design of the netsuke is in keeping with that of the inro, and the outside design of a *kobako* with the inside design of its tray or the individual incense boxes which it contains. Similar compatible symbolic meanings are seen within a single pictorial element, such as one figure in relation to another, the male to the female, the negative to the positive, even numbers to odd, lucky to unlucky, and colors to their subjects—yellow, for example, relating to the emperor. Each and every part of a lacquer work therefore is not only thoroughly integrated as to ornamental design but also in reference to symbolic meaning. An entire lacquer work is like a symphony which to the public gives an overall pleasing effect but which to the serious musician represents a preconceived sonata form of organized pieces or movements binding the entire work into a logical whole. Similarly the basic effectiveness of the lacquer piece consists of its individual notes of intricate workmanship and its harmony and rhythm upon the overall design, color, and texture. Finally, what better counterpoint could there be than the delicate balance—aesthetically, symbolically, and structurally—between the pictorial and decorative elements as well as between the various components of the design itself?

CALLIGRAPHY

Since calligraphy is one of the oldest and most highly respected forms of Japanese art, it is only natural to expect to find it in lacquer work. In general it appears as ideograms for good luck, longevity, happiness, and the like. Occasionally these are intricately intertwined in the lacquer design itself and frequently allude to a poem.

THE CIRCLE

Very frequently seen on lacquer in the form of a prayer wheel, the circle, an integral part of Zen symbolism, represents the achievement of perfection and enlightenment, as well as transmigration.

COLOR

As in most cultures, various colors have special meanings for the Japanese, and this is evidenced by the use of these colors in their art. Gold is a great favorite and is often found in lacquer work. In ancient medicine and philosophy, gold was considered to be the metal with the greatest active force and was thought to contribute to the longevity and vitality of man. It was also claimed to be a rejuvenator. White and purple are traditionally colors of mourning and are rarely employed. Red, however, is frequently used because it is the color of vitality and well-being. By long tradition, yellow is the color reserved for the emperor.

CRESTS (MON)

Lacquered articles are frequently adorned with stylized insignia known as crests, or *mon*. In medieval times many families, particularly the court nobles and feudal lords, as well as the samurai and military leaders, adopted individual crests which served as identifying family emblems and have been passed on from generation to generation. These crests were derived with symbolic significance relating to omens of good fortune, such as the crane or tortoise; as emblems of longevity; as associations or pictorial representations of the family name, such as formalized ideograms of the name, or as religious, commemorative, or military associations, such as the dragonfly, which is symbolic of victory. Whatever their symbolic derivation, the crests themselves are beautiful, simple, and decorative. The large majority of them are derived from nature, and even in their formalized presentation the Japanese love of the beauty of nature emerges in realistic adaptations which are easily recognizable.

The crest emerged into prominence during the Kamakura period (1185–1392), and by the Edo period (1615–1868) it had become the fashion, even among commoners, to mark clothing and other belongings with this family emblem. Feudal lords and court nobles were easily identified by their individual *mon,* and thus it was only natural that inro, *kobako,* and *suzuribako,* as well as all other lacquered utensils, often bore such crests. Most of the lacquered articles bearing the crest of a daimyo did not bear the signature of any artist, and thus we can surmise that such articles were either commissioned by the daimyo or made as a gift for him.

The imperial household adopted a crest representing a sixteen-petaled chrysanthemum, which has a twofold symbolic explanation. First, the circular blossom with its sixteen pointed petals is drawn to simulate the disk of the sun, the petals appearing as its rays. This of course is an allusion to the sun goddess, who reputedly founded Japan and of whom the emperor is said to be a direct descendant. Second, the chrysanthemum is noted as the national flower of Japan and is symbolic of longevity.

In general, crests are drawn as small simplified conventionalized designs enclosed in a circle. The crests often form an overall design or are merely used as a diaper or key pattern to set off the major design (Fig. 38).

EARLOBES

All gods and divine beings in Japanese art are represented with enlarged earlobes. Even though the identity of a god may be somewhat obscure in its lacquer portrayal, when the figure bears the symbolically elongated and enlarged earlobe, it is undoubtedly a divine being.

THE EIGHT BUDDHIST SYMBOLS

Occurring with great frequency in lacquer art, either singly, in varying combinations, or as a group, are the fish, the lotus, the knot, the umbrella, the canopy, the jar, the conch, and the wheel. Each of these primarily Buddhist emblems is symbolically significant.

The fish *(gyo)* indicates the lack of restraint that characterizes the enlightened Buddhist, implying that he can move about in his life and thought as easily as a fish does in water.

The lotus *(hasu)* is the "flower of life," symbolizing purity and the divine origin of Buddha. (See section on flowers, page 309; also Fig. 204.)

The knot *(nade-takara-musubi)*, often depicted as an eightfold interlaced design, symbolizes infinity as well as longevity. In the eightfold knot, the folds represent the eight commandments of Buddha.

The umbrella *(karakasa)* has a twofold symbolism, standing both for wealth and for world enlightenment through the teachings of Buddha.

The canopy *(tengai)* represents the covering that was placed over the head of Buddha when he attained immortality.

The jar *(tsubo)* is an emblem of the container in which the material remains of Buddha were placed after his death.

The conch *(hora)* is a visual representation of the voice of Buddha.

The wheel *(rimbo* or *horin)* has a multiple significance. In its turning, it represents transmigration or the unceasing movement from one life to another. In its round shape, it also stands for the sun. A very common motif in lacquer art is a circular disk surrounded by a halo of flame, and in this instance the symbol is that of the Buddhist Law, which, like the sun, casts its rays in all directions and, like the wheel, is a study in perpetual motion.

FANS (UCHIWA, OGI, SENSU, SUEHIRO)

The variety of fans encountered in Japanese art is infinite. Fans may, however, be divided into two major categories: the round flat fan with a protruding handle which does not close and the folding or many-ribbed fan in which the central rivet from which the ribs open and close also serves as the handle. In general when the round fan is portrayed in lacquer art as being held in the hand, it is symbolic of power, whereas the folding fan may refer to the tea ceremony or be a symbol of expanding wealth and good fortune.

FLY WHISK

Very often portrayed in lacquer art, the fly whisk, called *futsujin* or *hossu,* is a whisk with a short handle and long white hairs. It is of Buddhist origin and was carried by the priests to symbolically clear away the dust of the world. In lacquer ware the *futsujin,* particularly the long white hair, is occasionally executed in *takamakie* but more often is inlaid in another material. Its graceful sweep lends itself well to the lacquerer's art (Fig. 142).

GOHEI

It is only natural that this very important Shinto symbol should appear in lacquer work. The *gohei,* which means "august presence" in Shinto ceremonies, represents the presence of the *kami,* or deity. It is symbolic of purity, and its ceremonial purpose is to banish evil influences. Originally the *gohei* was intended to represent offerings to the gods. In lacquer art it is generally portrayed as either a branch of the sacred *sakaki* tree upon which are hung small rectangles of white paper, or as a straw rope, again adorned with rectangles of white paper, white being the color of purity.

HIBACHI

The *hibachi* is the brazier in which charcoal is burned to warm the traditional-style Japanese house. It is portrayed in lacquer art as a symbol of domestic happiness.

JUI

The *jui* is a short scepter fashioned in the shape of a wand. The handle is often decorated with a lotus flower, while the other end has the irregular cracked surface and shape of the sacred fungus. It is frequently depicted in lacquer ware in various materials—for example, wood or intricately carved cinnabar as seen in the inro in Figures 39 and 40. Symbolically it represents blessings and the power of faith.

MANJI

One of the most commonly depicted decorative motifs, often found as part of a diaper design, is the *manji,* or swastika. Of ancient origin, this design appears in art motifs as far back as the 13th century B.C. and is associated with a variety of symbolic explanations. In the Orient it is generally regarded as a Buddhist symbol, being described as an emblem of Buddha's heart and his great love for all, which is so powerful as to counteract all evil deeds of mankind. Other authorities consider the *manji* to be of cosmic origin relating to the sun. A more generally accepted explanation is that the ancient form of the *manji* was similar to the Chinese ideogram meaning "ten." As it became more elaborate, the meaning changed to "ten thousand," and as such it is an emblem of longevity, which is its widely accepted symbolic significance. It is often employed in diaper patterns and as part of the overall design in combination with other symbols of longevity, such as the bat. Many Buddhist deities have the *manji* as their crest and bear the design on their gowns or other apparel.

MIRROR

The mirror *(kagami)* plays an important role in Japanese mythology and religion. In the *Nihongi* it is related that the sun goddess Amaterasu was born from a mirror, and when she hid in anger in a cave, it was a mirror hung upon a tree which helped to lure her out of hiding. Furthermore, the Three Imperial Treasures, without which no emperor could rule, were the mirror, which was emblematic of wisdom; the sword, which symbolized strength; and the jewel, which represented technique. The mirror is therefore sacred to the Shinto religion, and its presence in a Shinto shrine represents the person of Amaterasu herself. In art the mirror may be employed to represent the sun.

The mirror is said to reveal the soul, and a clear mirror reflects purity and cleanliness of soul, whereas a clouded mirror reflects evil. In lacquer art the mirror is a frequent motif and, according to traditional belief, plays an important part in protecting the good from evil. It is a particularly good source of protection against the mischievous fox and is frequently portrayed in tales relating to his deeds.

MOKUGYO

The *mokugyo* is a small wooden bell in the shape of two conjoined stylized fish, the handle of the bell being formed by their heads. The bodies of the fish are frequently covered with carved scales simulating those of real fish. The bell is rather flat, is hollowed out, and contains a small free-rolling wooden ball which acts as the clapper. It is associated with Buddhist temples and is carried by a priest. Legend relates that this type of bell was supposed to be struck by the worshipers before beginning their prayers so as to call the attention of the gods to their prayers. It is in the shape of a fish because it was believed that fish never slept, and so too should religion always remain awake in the soul of man. Figures 121 and 122 depict an *oni* carrying over his shoulder a stick with a temple bell on one end balanced by a *mokugyo* on the other end.

NUMBERS

In all societies there are various superstitions surrounding such abstractions as numbers, and Japanese culture is no different in this respect. The Japanese custom is to always use a specific number of articles for every individual ceremony, such as the tea ceremony or the incense ceremony. These numbers are often chosen because the ideograms for them may be interpreted as lucky omens, and conversely numbers may be rejected because of unpleasant connotations. For instance, the number 4 is considered as being unlucky because one reading of the ideogram for this number is *shi,* and *shi* also means "death." In general, odd numbers are considered good omens and are lucky, while an even number is a negative or *in* principle and frequently is considered as unlucky. Still, odd numbers may be unlucky. For example, the age of nineteen *(juku)* is considered unlucky because *juku* can also mean "repeated sorrows." Thirty-three *(sanjusan)* is also an unlucky age because *sanjusan* has the alternate meaning of "hopeless miseries." Forty-two is another unlucky age, for it can also be interpreted to mean "death."

On the other hand the number 3 is one of the most lucky numbers, for it is an odd number and therefore represents the *yo,* or male principle, and is also interpreted as representing the basic elements of air, earth, and water. The number 9, which is a multiplication of the lucky number 3 by 3, is considered as being possibly the most perfect number. The numbers 5 and 7 are also auspicious numbers, as 5 represents the five basic elements and 7 is the number of days in a week.

Such numbers as 1,000 or 10,000 are symbolic of longevity. Frequently we find these superstitions illustrated in the art forms by means of objects with ideograms which can also be interpreted as good omens, as well as such less subtle groups as the Seven Lucky Household Gods or the Seven Luminaries (Fig. 24). The 1,000 monkeys and 1,000 birds are relatively common subjects executed frequently on miniature lacquer objects (Fig. 236).

ROSARY

The *juzu,* or Buddhist rosary, is a common religious symbol used by both priests and laymen. Originally it had 108 beads. However, for common use the people adopted shorter strands of beads. These beads were originally made of wood, but soon all types of materials were employed. When the rosary is portrayed in lacquer art it is usually inlaid in a contrasting material, such as ivory or coral.

SHICHIYO

This unique and interesting Oriental art motif has cosmic significance. The design of seven circles in an irregular line connected by short straight lines represents the sun, the moon, and the planets Jupiter, Mars, Mercury, Saturn, and Venus. The sun is the male principle, and in Oriental mythology is the source of all life. The moon is the female principle, while the planets represent wood, fire, water, earth, and metal, the basic elements of human life.

TAKARAMONO

The *takaramono* are a group of objects, symbolic in nature, collectively and singly expressing the desire for wealth, comfort, happiness, and prosperity. These objects are closely associated with the Seven Lucky Household Gods and indeed are said to be carried by Hotei in the large sack with which he is always depicted. The objects in this group are native to Japan, and it is felt that the idea of the *takaramono* was created during the secluded and prosperous Tokugawa period.

Various authorities differ as to the number and combination of the items included in the *takaramono.* The complete list is said to include 21 objects, but there are about 10 of these which appear with greater frequency. They are listed here in two groups, in alphabetical order by their Japanese names and accompanied by brief explanations of their symbolic meanings, the first group of 10 being the most commonly portrayed objects. A number of the *takaramono* appear in Figure 237.

1) *choji* (cloves): emblem of sweetness and health and a safeguard against illness and impurities in the air.

2) *fundo* (weight): a measure or weight used by merchants and symbolic of successful commerce.

3) *kagi* (key): key to the treasure chest or storehouse of treasures; emblematic of wealth and security.

4) *kakuregasa* (hat of invisibility): a magic hat which protects its wearer from danger by making him invisible and therefore immune to harm.

5) *kakuremino* (straw coat of invisibility): a straw coat (actually a raincoat) which protects its wearer from all dangers by rendering him invisible and therefore free from attack and harm.

6) *kanebukuro* (purse): a purse containing an inexhaustible supply of money; therefore a symbol of endless wealth.

7) *makimono* (scrolls): the most ancient form of Japanese scrolls, emblematic of great wisdom; also one of the attributes of Jurojin and Fukurokuju.

8) *shippo* (precious things): one of the little understood items in the group; most often described as a combination of the "seven precious things" (gold, silver, emerald, coral, agate, crystal, and pearl) into one object which was probably in the form of a flat, oval coin or a jewel. The term *shippo* is occasionally used in place of the word *takaramono* and in this usage represents all the precious things. *Shippo* is also the Japanese term for enamel work.

9) *tsuchi* (Daikoku's mallet): mallet of riches or creative hammer of wealth, the attribute of Daikoku by which he can produce wealth. It is often said to contain the objects included in the *takaramono*. Its sides are decorated either with the *tomoe*, the symbols of the male and female principles which are responsible for all creation, or with the *tama*, the sacred jewel. The *tsuchi* is symbolic of wealth and good fortune.

10) *tama* (sacred jewel): one of the most important and most often portrayed of the *takaramono*. The symbolism surrounding the *tama* is highly involved and vast in scope. It is said to be the force which controls the tides; it is a Buddhist emblem of glory; it is known as the sacred jewel; it is said to dispel evil spirits; and its name may be translated to mean "everlasting" or "soul." Among the *takaramono* it is usually portrayed as a pear-shaped object having three rings near the top. It is often depicted as wearing a crown of flames. In this representation it is considered as being a precious jewel and emblematic of riches.

There are many other objects included among the *takaramono*. These are not necessarily of lesser importance, but they appear with somewhat less frequency. It should be understood, however, that the *takaramono* may be portrayed in any combination, the number represented at one time usually being seven. The following is a list of other objects included among the *takaramono*.

1) *hagoromo* (feather robe): emblematic of the *tennin* (angels) who, according to mythological tales, soar through the air in robes of feathers. It indicates a desire for perpetual youth.

2) *ikari* (anchor): emblem of security and safety.

3) *koban-no-hako* or *senryobako* (treasure chest): a chest containing 1,000 gold coins, emblematic of plenty; frequently represented by a single *koban*, a large, flat, oval-shaped coin of Tokugawa Japan.

4) *kotoji* (*koto* bridge): the bridge of the *koto*, a Japanese musical instrument which closely resembles the harp. The *kotoji* is symbolic of harmony.

5) *kotsubo* (jar): a jar or pot containing money, valuables, or other such treasures as the *tama*, the *koban*, and the *sangoju* (see below). It is emblematic of security.

6) *orimono* (brocade): rolls of brocade fabric such as was used for the clothing of court lords and the nobility, thus symbolic of luxury and splendor.

7) *sangoju* (coral): the precious coral, symbolic of beauty, perfection, and rarity.

8) *tachibana* (orange): emblematic of sweetness.

9) *takaragai* (cowrie shell): an ancient form of money, symbolic of wealth.

10) *uchiwa* (round fan): a nonfolding fanlike object often carried by several of the Seven Lucky Household Gods. It is symbolic of authority and was carried by military leaders in ancient times. It is reputed to insure the safety of those who carry it.

11) *zeni* (coin): a round iron or copper coin bearing little monetary value; symbolic of moderate wealth.

The various items of the *takaramono* are portrayed with great frequency on lacquer work, particularly in the form of diaper designs or arabesques employed to augment the basic design. They are rarely portrayed as an entire group, but selected items are employed in smaller groups. One of the most common portrayals of the *takaramono* is as cargo upon the ship of good fortune, the *takarabune*. The *takarabune* is a treasure ship which, according to legend, sails into port on New Year's Eve bearing the Seven Lucky Household Gods as passengers and the objects of the *takaramono* as cargo. A small boat, its single sail billowing in the wind, it is symbolic of all good things, including wisdom, happiness, longevity, and prosperity in the new year which it ushers in (Fig. 25).

TOMOE

The *tomoe* is a comma-shaped form closely resembling the ancient *magatama*, or curved jewels. It is also seen in a double form called *futatsu-domoe* and in a triple form called *mitsu-domoe*. It is often used as a crest or as part of a diaper design and is also seen as a decoration on the mallet of Daikoku and the drums of the god of thunder Raiden. The symbolic explanation of this series of designs is controversial and extensive. Most authorities feel that the single *tomoe* has phallic significance; that the *futatsu-domoe* represents graphically the principles of *yo* and *in* (male and female), and that the *mitsu-domoe* symbolizes the three primary elements of nature—fire, air, and water—enclosed in a circle which represents the sun. The *mitsu-domoe* is the form most frequently portrayed in lacquer art. It is considered to be a protection against the forces of nature and is a good omen, as is witnessed by its close association with the lucky god Daikoku (Fig. 238).

TORII

A familiar symbol of Shintoism, the *torii* is rather infrequently represented in lacquer art. It is basically a gateway which is formed by two upright beams and a horizontal beam connecting them. Originally, according to legend, a perch in the shape of the *torii* was used by the cock who helped to lure the angry sun goddess out of hiding. This perch was called *torii*, which means literally "bird perch." In recognition of its place in this legend, the same shape and name was later adopted by the Shinto priests to serve as the gateway to their temples. Passing under the Shinto *torii* was symbolic of cleansing oneself of evil and darkness, as the cock who daily sits upon this perch to crow announces the passing of darkness (night) and the coming of light. This significance, however, has been lost, and the *torii* now serves merely as a gateway and landmark. Although Japan abounds in *torii* of all sizes and descriptions, it is an infrequent art motif.

YO AND IN

According to Oriental philosophy all things are covered by the interplay of the basic principles of *yo* and *in,* which are the male or positive, active power and the female or negative, passive power. In lacquer art this belief is illustrated although in a subtle fashion. Thus when two animate creatures are depicted, one always represents the positive *yo* principle and the other the negative *in* principle. The difference between the two is visually slight, but one (the *yo,* or masculine power) is slightly larger and has an open mouth, while the *in* (or female power) is slightly smaller and has a closed mouth (Fig. 20). Even inanimate objects, such as flowers, trees, or fruits, are classified and portrayed with *in* or *yo* characteristics. This underlying principle is a basic Oriental belief and enters into all art forms.

215. INRO. Maple leaves. Signed: Koma Yasutada. The design is executed in red and gold hiramakie along with inlaid mother-of-pearl and gold kirigane. The background is a silver geometric wave pattern on a black ground. $3\frac{1}{4}'' \times 2\frac{3}{8}'' \times \frac{3}{4}''$. 5 cases and lid.

216. INRO. Mandarin duck. Signed: Toyo. The design is done in red, gold, and silver togidashi against a background of oki-hirame on a roiro ground. $3\frac{1}{8}'' \times 2\frac{7}{8}'' \times \frac{7}{8}''$. 3 cases and lid.

217. INRO. Owl. Signed with seal of Ritsuo. The owl and the leaves are in encrusted pottery, and the tree trunk is in brown lacquer. Plain wood ground. $3\frac{1}{16}'' \times 1\frac{3}{4}'' \times \frac{3}{4}''$. 3 cases and lid. (See Fig. 237 for side views.)

218. INRO. Fish swimming in a stream. Signed: Shiomi Masa-nari. The fish are minutely detailed in gold and reddish-gold togidashi. The gently swirling stream is in gold togidashi on a roiro ground. $3\frac{1}{4}'' \times 2'' \times \frac{7}{8}''$. 4 cases and lid.

219. INRO. Peacock feathers. Signed: Shosai. The feathers are done in minutely carved pieces of iridescent red and green mother-of-pearl inlaid on a rich roiro ground. $3\frac{5}{8}'' \times 2\frac{3}{8}'' \times \frac{3}{4}''$. 4 cases and lid.

220. Inro. Phoenix. Signed: Koami Nagataka. Finely detailed phoenix, clouds, and paulownia leaves done in low takamakie (gold, silver, and red), gold and silver kirigane, gold hyomon, and mother-of-pearl on a striking gold and silver oki-hirame ground. Probably a daimyo inro. $3\frac{1}{8}'' \times 2\frac{11}{16}'' \times 1\frac{3}{16}''$. 3 cases and lid.

221. Inro. Bamboo and rock. Signed: Hokkyo Komin. The bamboo is in soft gold togidashi, the rock in gold-brown medium takamakie, and the earth in gold and mother-of-pearl powderings—all on a rich roiro ground. $3\frac{3}{8}'' \times 2\frac{3}{16}'' \times 1\frac{3}{16}''$. 4 cases and lid.

222. Inro. Bamboo, rock, and stream. Signed: Koma Kyuhaku Yasuaki, with the notation "certified by his grandson Koma Kyuhaku Yasuaki." Extremely subtle design in varying tones of togidashi in gold and reddish-gold hues on a rich, dark roiro ground. $3\frac{5}{16}'' \times 1\frac{11}{16}'' \times \frac{3}{4}''$. 5 cases and lid. (See Fig. 243 for detail showing signature.)

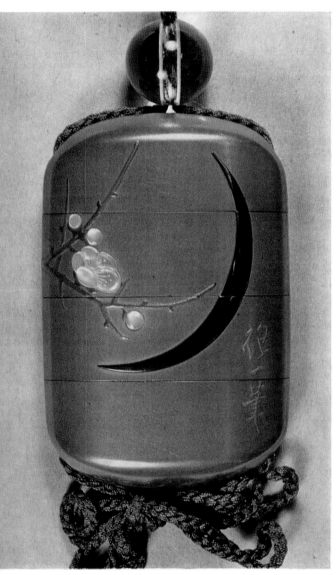

223. INRO. Plum blossoms and moon. Signed: Yoyusai and (on reverse side) Hoitsu. The plum blossoms are done in mother-of-pearl, the branches in low takamakie, and the large crescent moon in inlaid silver. Gold fundame ground. $2\frac{3}{4}'' \times 1\frac{15}{16}'' \times \frac{3}{4}''$. 3 cases and lid.

224. OPPOSITE SIDE of inro in Fig. 136. The full moon is done in a semitransparent dull silver, the pine needles in gold, and the lespedeza leaves in reddish gold, all in togidashi on a roiro ground.

225. INRO. Noh dancer portraying a shojo. Signed: Jugyoku (netsuke artist). The shojo is done in moderately raised encrustation of malachite, silver, and gold, along with high black and red takamakie. $3\frac{3}{8}'' \times 2\frac{7}{8}'' \times 1\frac{5}{16}''$. 3 cases and lid.

226. INRO. Coastal scene. Signed: Hasegawa Shigeyoshi. The tiny coast and distant mountains are in polished black hiramakie. In contrast, the vast ocean and sky, which comprise by far most of the design, are reflected by the empty, polished rich brown ground. $2\frac{1}{2}'' \times 1\frac{15}{16}'' \times \frac{13}{16}''$. 4 cases and lid.

227. INRO. Gate of the Yoshiwara. Signed: Yoyusai. The design of the gate, the weeping willow, and the cuckoo is done in polished black hiramakie. The crescent moon is in silver. The ground is polished green lacquer. $3\frac{3}{16}'' \times 1\frac{7}{8}'' \times 1\frac{3}{16}''$. 5 cases and lid.

228. INRO. Night scene. Signed: Koma Koryu. Two men (one evidently a samurai) in black togidashi, silhouetted against the night, are looking up at three tiny bats done in dull black hiramakie. $2\frac{3}{4}'' \times 2\frac{3}{16}'' \times \frac{15}{16}''$. 3 cases and lid.

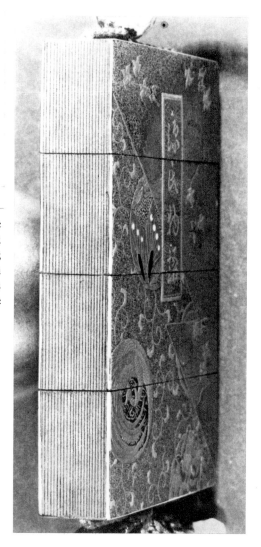

229. INRO (two views). Book: *Genji Monogatari*. Signed: Jokasai. The design employs plovers against a background of waves and clouds; medallions representing phoenixes, a butterfly, and various plants; and arabesques of leaves. The title appears on one side (above) in formal style and on the other (right) in flowing script. The ground is gold, and the edges of the pages are imitated in silver togidashi. The zigzag pattern of the basic design is especially interesting. $4\frac{1}{4}'' \times 2\frac{7}{8}'' \times 1\frac{3}{16}''$. 3 cases and lid.

230. INRO. Dragon and waves. Signed: Sukenaga (netsuke artist). The design is cut in low relief in a natural yew-wood ground. 2⅝″×1⅝″×¾″. 3 cases and lid.

231. INRO. Crow on tree trunk. Signed: Koma Kansai. The design simulates a sumie painting in sumie togidashi on a silver ground. The maple leaves are in red togidashi. 3¹¹⁄₁₆″×1⅞″×1³⁄₁₆″. 5 cases and lid.

232. INRO AND DETAIL. Two men playing game of shogi. Signed: Koma Koryu. The design is in silver, gold, red, and black togidashi on a roiro ground.

Detail shows shogi board. Note the minute calligraphy and the mokume simulating the grain in the wood. $3\frac{1}{2}'' \times 2\frac{1}{4}'' \times \frac{3}{4}''$. 4 cases and lid.

233. INRO. Copy of painting by Kakando Ganku depicting long-legged wading birds. Unsigned. The birds are in gold togidashi on a black ground which is turning tortoiseshell brown from age. $2\frac{7}{8}'' \times 2\frac{3}{4}'' \times \frac{15}{16}''$. 2 cases and lid.

234. INRO. Tekkai sennin. Unsigned. The design is done in gold and black togidashi on a roiro ground. $3\frac{1}{4}'' \times 3\frac{1}{8}'' \times 1''$. 2 cases and lid.

235. INRO. Character for longevity. Signed: Takamasu (Tatsuke). The stylized character is in gold hyomon embossed with different types of diaper, cloud, and wave patterns. Roiro ground. $2\frac{7}{8}'' \times \frac{5}{8}'' \times 1''$. 4 cases and lid.

236. Inro. "Thousand-monkey" design. Unsigned. The monkeys are in silver, red, gold, and black hiramakie on a polished red ground. $3\frac{1}{16}" \times 2\frac{13}{16}" \times \frac{7}{8}"$. 3 cases and lid.

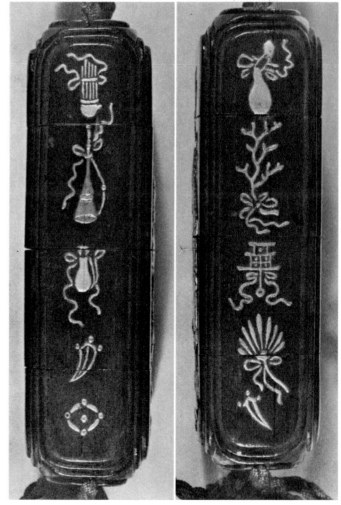

237. Side views of inro in Fig. 217, illustrating Buddhist symbols in gold hiramakie on a natural-wood ground.

238. OPPOSITE SIDE of inro in Fig. 165, illustrating a tomoe and two phoenixes in silver and gold hiramakie and gold kirigane on a gold and red fundame ground.

239. DETAIL of an inro, showing combined signatures of metal artist Ishiguro Masatsune (left) and lacquer artist Koma Kyuhaku (right).

240. KOGO. Hagi (bush clover) leaves. Unsigned. Kamakura period. The design, type of lacquer, pewter edges, and gross fissuring and flaking of the lacquer on the outer and inner surfaces of the kogo indicate its extreme age. Authentication papers lend further validation. $2\frac{3}{4}''$ square by $1\frac{1}{2}''$ high.

241. INRO. Landscape. Signed: Koma Kansai. An excellent replica of the Southern Sung style of painting done in delicate tones of sumie togidashi on a silver ground. $3\frac{3}{16}'' \times 2\frac{1}{2}'' \times 1''$. 4 cases and lid.

242. INRO. Maple leaves. Signed: Yoyusai. The design is in gold and silver hiramakie on a gold ground and incorporates the signature of the painter Hoitsu, from whom it was copied. $2\frac{3}{4}'' \times 2\frac{1}{4}'' \times \frac{7}{8}''$. 3 cases and lid.

243. DETAIL of inro in Fig. 222, showing signature of Koma Kyuhaku Yasuaki (Koma II) at right and certification by his grandson Koma Kyuhaku Yasuaki (Koma IV) at left.

244. INRO. Sparrows in bamboo grove. Unsigned. Gold togidashi on black ground. Note the formal design done in matte gold outlined in black, in the style of the Ashikaga period. Late 17th century. $3\frac{3}{16}'' \times 2\frac{1}{4}'' \times 1\frac{1}{8}''$. 4 cases and lid.

245. AUTHENTICATION on inside of lid of box made to contain a lacquer tray. It reads: "Authenticated by his son Umezawa Ryushin and his pupil Ikeda Sensai as being the work of Shibata Zeshin."

7 ❖ Lacquer Artists

ALTHOUGH LACQUER DECORATION BEGAN CENTURIES BEFORE the advent of the inro, almost none of these early pieces bear the name of the artist. Little is known, therefore, about the early lacquer artists, since we have no record of their signatures. It was not until the Fujiwara period (897–1185) that any artists in any field were known by name, the artist working in anonymity mainly for the Buddhist temples and for the nobility prior to that time. It was during the 16th century, when the country settled down to a more peaceful period after more than a hundred years of civil war, that art in general and lacquer ware in particular began to flourish. Master craftsmen lived and worked under the protection and sponsorship of local daimyo who showed interest in enriching the handicrafts of their people. Great artists were particularly favored under the Tokugawa government, which was established in 1603. They often received specific stipends from the government and were usually exempted from payment of taxes. In short, they were heartily encouraged to continue and perfect their artistic achievements. Subsequent to this period artists became recognized as individuals, opened their own workshops, and established schools for the training of apprentices. Thus early works of art, including early inro, were not signed with any regularity until about the early 17th century. We do not often find signatures on larger pieces of lacquer ware during any period. The early works of art were commissioned by wealthy nobles, military rulers and the imperial family, and it was a breach of etiquette to sign one's name to an item so executed. At a later date, when art became more popular and inro were worn extensively by many classes of people, signatures were considered proper. If it were not for the signatures found on inro, we would not have even the small amount of knowledge that we now possess. In general, inro were made by lacquer artists. Almost all of the great lacquer artists from the 16th century onward made inro at some time or other. Artists would frequently combine their talents when decorating inro, and it is not uncommon to find more than one signature on an article. Metal artists were called upon to execute metal plaques or inlays, and often a metal artist's name will appear on the inro in conjunction with that of the lacquer artist (Fig. 239). Again, lacquer artists frequently turned to the designs of great painters (Fig. 241) or to the writings of master poets and illustrated a poem for their inro design. Many lacquer artists were themselves master painters, such as Korin and Zeshin, and their works often served as designs for other artists as well as for their own lacquer ware. Frequently only the name of the painter or designer will appear on the inro (Fig. 242). Each artist had his specialty, and the finished article was the important objective, not the artist's individual fame or personal achievement. He had no hesitation, therefore, in combining his talents with those of another who was outstanding in his particular field to design or execute a piece of work of the highest quality needed to enrich the final product. Of course these combinations of signatures have often been misleading, and it must be understood that generally the lacquer artist borrowed the design from the painting, rather than the painter making his design for the inro, although occasionally the reverse did exist.

Another very misleading aspect of signatures is the frequent use of the *kakihan,* or written seal. In former days it was the custom for the head of the family alone to have a *kakihan*. This seal was handed down from generation to generation, just as it was customary to hand down the same name to succeeding generations. In fact the seal was considered all the more valuable by virtue of its being an heirloom. Thus the founder of a school of lacquer artists would pass on his *kakihan* and name to his most capable student. As a result we often have difficulty in determining which member of a school or family actually executed a specific object. Then, too, as in all forms of art, forgeries were frequent. Not only did artists sign the name of a master to their works, but pupils also would sign their teacher's name, not necessarily intending to falsify their works by pretending that they were his, but as a means of paying homage and respect to their teacher. Often a pupil was given the privilege by his master of using the master's name after his work had reached a qualifying level of excellence. At times he was permitted to use part of the master's name and, as often happened, ultimately the entire name. To further complicate the situation, artists often abbreviated their names or wrote them in "grass" (cursive) style, and this makes interpreting signatures all the more difficult. As a part of their training, students would frequently be required to duplicate work which had previously been executed by their teacher. Again, masters often had their most skilled students prepare background work to which they added finishing decorative touches and which were signed with the master's name. There were also unquestionably out-and-out forgeries, sometimes a signature being added many years later to a previously unsigned object. In determining the authenticity of a signature one needs an expert who cannot only read Japanese but is also capable of evaluating the handwriting characteristics of the signer in terms of depth of engraving (as on netsuke); strength, ease, and freedom of symbol formation; quality of calligraphy, etc. Furthermore, we must evaluate the artistic validity of the lacquer in terms of quality of craftsmanship, style of workmanship, techniques of use of materials, and age of materials as determined by the method of decoration. Pewter and lead, for instance, were used on older works while metal alloys, such as *shakudo* and *shibuichi,* appear on more modern work. Also to be considered are design, coloring, and pigments used, etc. In general the color on the older work is more subdued, and conversely, brighter, more contrasting colors are found on more recent works. Similarly, very old *makie* was of a coarser grain, and white lacquer was not used until the 19th century. All these factors must be taken into consideration and evaluated in relation to the life and working span of the artist involved (Figs. 240, 244). Some artists engraved their signatures in fine hairline engraving, some signed in gold lacquer, some used inlaid plaques or only *kakihan,* and some were noted for not signing at all—so that an article bearing their name is very likely a forgery. Such knowledge can often determine approximately what member of a school or family made an individual piece even when the family name alone is signed.

Occasionally a lacquer piece was authenticated by another lacquer artist, usually a descendant, such authentication being inscribed on the piece itself (Fig. 243). More frequently such authentication, either by the artist's family or one of his pupils, was done on the wooden box which was usually made to house the finished lacquer piece (Fig. 245).

Often on an old piece of lacquer ware and particularly on netsuke with engraved signatures, we find that over the years part of the signature may have worn down and become illegible. A small amount of powder dusted over the area, the excess carefully being removed, will often make the signature become, temporarily at least, readable.

As mentioned above, multiple signatures are not uncommon, particularly when there has been a combining of talents in order to produce an object. "Metalwork by," "lacquer by," "designed by"—all are frequently found along with the age of the artist, the locality in which he worked, or perhaps the poem or painting from which he took the inspiration for his lacquer picture.

In general, inro, especially late inro, were signed. Individual artists such as Toyo, Zeshin, Shiomi Masanari, Yoyusai, and Hasegawa Shigeyoshi were famous for their inro (Figs. 226, 227). Similarly the Kajikawa and Koma families were noted for their inro (Fig. 228). On the other hand, the Yosei family produced relatively few inro. Lacquered articles of the tea and incense ceremonies, along with *suzuri-bako* were less often signed, and other utilitarian lacquered boxes were even more rarely signed. Some of the best pieces were made for or upon commission of the shogunate, the imperial household, or the local daimyo and were never signed. Thus a lacquer box must be judged purely on its quality, an unsigned piece being in no way an indication of inferiority.

On inro the signature is most often found on the bottom surface, while the second most frequent place is alongside the design. Shiomi Masanari usually signed on the bottom of the outer surface of the cord channels. Rarely, the signature is found inside the lid. Similarly, it may be unexpectedly found hidden under the inkstone of a *suzuri-bako*.

Names

The Japanese have a much more complex system of names than do Occidentals. This is even further complicated by the use of art names as well as written seals by the artists. Furthermore, the artist quite often changed his art name from time to time or at other times assumed part or all of the name of his master. The various names used by the Japanese include the ancient clan name *(kabane)* and the surname *(uji)* as well as two types of first names: the common name *(zokumyo)* and the real name *(nanori* or *na)*. Moreover, there existed the infant name *(yomyo)*, the nickname *(azana)*, the art name *(go)*, and posthumous names *(kaimyo)*.

CLAN NAME (KABANE OR SEI)

Ancient aristocratic names are relatively few and represent the original major clans or branches of these clans. Prior to the Taika era (645–50) these clans formed the social-economic-religious-legal structure of Japanese society. Legal responsibility and land fiefs resided in the hands of these clans, which were perpetuated by means of ancestor worship and clan-god *(ujigami)* worship. Thus the Yamato clan (named after the Yamato district), being originally the most powerful clan, perpetuated itself into the lineal descendants of the imperial household, claiming their birthright from the ancient Shinto gods. The heads of all the major clans, such as the Taira, Minamoto, and Fujiwara, were responsible to the emperor or head of the imperial household.

FAMILY NAME OR SURNAME (UJI OR MYOJI)

The family-name system came into being in the early 8th century and was enforced by the code of Taiho (701) during the Taiho era. By this time, with the dispersion of the clans, the family type of social-economic-legal system based on Chinese codes came into being. The family, rather than the clan, began to play a predominating role in the structure of Japanese society. Under this system a house registry *(koseki)* was established, and the head of a family now could fill an official position and hold property. The promulgation of ancestor worship based on both Buddhist and Shinto concepts was instrumental in perpetuating the family unit. The greatest calamity was to have no male heir to continue the family line in order to perpetuate ancestor worship. Since the spirits of the ancestors could receive only the offerings of persons of the same clan, marriages between persons of the same clan were favored. Similarly, in order to prevent extinction of family lines, as well as forfeiture of the family feudal property, a system of adoption was instituted by the Taiho code. The adopted son had to be within the fourth degree of kinship, and he legally assumed the name of his new household. In feudal times, the use of a family name was permitted only to the aristocracy, court officials, the military class, and a few village heads. Most of these names were of geographical origin, being either place names like Soga, Heijo, and Ashikaga or descriptions of localities like Yamamoto (foot of the mountain) and Tanaka (among the rice fields). With the Meiji Restoration in 1868, all people were ordered to adopt family names. This resulted in the adoption of the same name by entire family relationships or even whole villages or the conversion of nicknames into family names or, again, the use of locations for names, such as Ogawa (little river), Yamada (mountain farm), and Oki (big tree). The family name is usually of two characters chosen for their euphony. The second character is often *ta, da, yama, kawa (gawa), moto, mura, saka,* etc.

COMMON NAME (ZOKUMYO OR TSUSHO)

The general name which resembles the Western first or Christian name was the only name permitted to commoners. Such names often ended in *ichiro* or *taro* (eldest son), *jiro* (second son), *saburo* (third son), etc. If used without a prefix they meant respectively "big male," "second male," "third male," etc., *ro* meaning man.

At other times the common name ended with *emon, suke, nojo, bei,* etc., which formerly designated official posts. Names for boys often ended in *o, ro,* and *kichi,* all meaning "manhood." Other names were composed of numerals indicating the year or month of birth or the father's age when the son was born, etc. Thus Ichizo meant "13" and Goroku "56."

INFANT NAME (YOMYO)

This name, usually short and simple, was bestowed on boys of the nobility and the samurai class on the sixth day after their birth. The name often ended in *maru.* At the age of fifteen, with the performance of the *gembuku* ceremony, the *zokumyo,* or common name, was assumed.

REAL NAME (NANORI OR NA)

This also corresponds to the Western first or Christian name. However, only the upper classes were allowed to use a *nanori* in addition to the common name, or *zokumyo.* Such names were used only on solemn occasions and often appeared in signatures in preference to the *zokumyo.* The *nanori* was usually used in combination with the clan name. Thus in the name

Minamoto no Yoritomo, Minamoto is the clan name, *no* is a word showing possession, and Yoritomo is the *nanori,* or real name. Other examples
of *nanori* are Masashige, Yoshisada, and Yoshitsune. Such names usually
consist of two characters and refer to parts of speech, such as nouns,
adjectives, and verbs. The number of such names is inexhaustible and
includes names using characters for peacefulness, eloquence, truth, bravery, luck, uniformity, very, after, rice, arrow, foot, etc.

NICKNAME (AZANA)

The *azana* are elegant names of the type taken by Chinese scholars and
include such names as Mokei and Shisei. They are similar to the art names
discussed in the following section.

ART NAME, PSEUDONYM, OR GO

These were names used by artists independent of their ordinary names
and signed independently or in conjunction with their regular names.
Some artists used several such names at different times in their careers.
This applied equally to painters, ceramists, and lacquer and netsuke artists.
Part or all of the pseudonym was often given to an apt pupil or an adopted
pupil of an artist. Usually the second half and quite often the first half of
the master's name was adopted. For example, Shomin was the pupil of
Komin, the *min* being the same character. Similarly Koami VI was called
Chosei; Koami VII, Choan; and Koami VIII, Chozen. Here the *cho* is the
common element. The art names usually end with references to the master's
studio—for example, *do* (hall), *sai* (studio), *ken* (house), *sha* (house), *tei*
(pavilion), *an* (lodge), *ro* (upper story), *bo* (chamber), *zen* (garden), etc.
These suffixes are usually preceded by two characters. Often the names end
in *shujin, koji,* or *okina,* meaning respectively "master of the house,"
"scholar," and "aged man."

WOMEN'S NAMES (NA OR NAMAE)

These are usually short euphonious names written in *hiragana* (except
for the aristocracy, who used Chinese characters) and are taken from the
name of some flower, bird, plant, or female virtue—for example, *cho* (butterfly), *matsu* (pine), *nui* (embroidery), *yume* (dream), and *natsu* (summer).
These names are often prefixed with *o,* meaning "honorable." Thus Otake
means "honorable bamboo." The *o* is omitted if the name has more than
two syllables. Since the early Meiji era the *o* has been replaced by the suffix
ko, meaning "child," as in the name Takeko. Craftswomen's names were
often followed by *jo,* meaning "lady." Otherwise their names paralleled
those of their male counterparts.

MISCELLANEOUS NAMES

Various other types of names with specific uses include the following:

1) *haimyo* and *gago:* variations of the *go* (art name) used by comic poets and entertainers.

2) *geimei:* art names used by professional public entertainers.

3) *okurina,* or posthumous names: honorific titles of revered people, heroes, and emperors—for example, Jimmu Tenno.

4) *homyo* or *kaimyo:* posthumous names chosen by Buddhist priests for their followers and inscribed on their funeral tablets.

The Seal

The seal, in a strict sense, was a small block of practically any material on which was engraved a distinguishing mark or design in order to legally identify a family. Colored ink was used for stamping. Similar types of markings were seen as identifying marks on lacquer and netsuke work. In these cases the mark or seal usually consisted of an inlaid ceramic, metal, or ivory plaque with the artist's special design on it. Ritsuo used inlaid ceramic plaques in his lacquer work, and the netsuke artist Tokoku used a similar type of gold-silver rectangular inlaid plaque. This should not be confused with similar inlaid plaques such as those used by the Shibayama artists, which merely consisted of the artist's regular signature. The Kaji-kawa school used a bottle-shaped design in red lacquer in slight relief to identify their lacquer works. All of these seal-like designs were used either with the artist's signature or separately.

The Kakihan

This is the artist's written individual mark as opposed to the impressed or engraved seal. The word literally means "written seal." The *kakihan* consists of a relatively simple engraved calligraphic type of mark comparable to the Occidental initials or monogram. It was usually associated with the artist's first name and, like the seal, either followed the signature or appeared alone. It was commonly used in the handicrafts, especially by makers of sword furniture, and less often by lacquer and netsuke artists.

Titles

Great artists were occasionally given honorary titles, but such titles were less commonly conferred on lacquer or netsuke artists. There were times, however, when outstanding lacquer artists were not only given honorary titles but were also raised to the status of samurai, as in the cases of Toyo I and Zokoku. The calligraphic symbol of the title follows the signature and *kakihan.* The most common titles are

1) *hoin:* the highest title, meaning literally "seal of the law." Never bestowed on any netsuke artist.

2) *hogen:* the next highest title, meaning "eye of the law."

3) *hokkyo:* the lowest title, meaning "bridge of the law."

4) *tenka-ichi:* a title meaning "peerless in the realm" or "first under heaven." It was given to maskmakers and mirror makers as well as to members of the Deme family, outstanding carvers of mask netsuke.

Hoin, hogen, and *hokkyo* were honorary Buddhist titles. Among lacquer artists the title *hokkyo* was given to Komin, Korin, Koami Dosei, and Ryukei.

Miscellaneous Inscriptions

Occasionally the lacquer or netsuke artist added various phrases or expressions to his signature, such as "made by," "carved by," "engraved by," and "made by request." Other information might also be inscribed on the article—for example, the artist's age, when the article was made, or where it was made. All such information followed the signature.

Order of Items in Signatures

The order of items in the artist's signature is normally as follows: 1) art name, 2) family name, 3) clan name, 4) first name, 5) seal or *kakihan,* 6) honorary title, 7) miscellaneous information. Part or all of the above order was used, but often the order was not followed at all, practically any order being permissible. Sometimes one syllable of the art name was used along with the first syllable of the first name. Finally, two signatures are occasionally found, usually representing the artist from whom the design was taken and artist who executed the lacquer ware.

Signatures may be in Chinese characters or Japanese phonetic symbols or in abbreviated forms. Also each symbol may have numerous pronunciations depending on the word order, on whether the word originates from literature, history, art, mythology, etc., and on other factors. Furthermore, words written the same way may have different meanings, especially in Japanese. Besides the basic scripts of *kanji, hiragana,* and *katakana* there are many other kinds of writing and script. In general, a sign may mean many different words. Making things even more confusing we find many different names which, when translated into English, mean the same thing —for example, *zokumyo=tsusho=*ordinary name, *myoji=uji=*family name, *nanori=jitsumei* or *jitsumyo=* fifteen-year name (name taken at *gembuku* ceremony and used only by nobles and privileged craftsmen), *go=geimei=* artist name or professional name, *yomyo=osanana=*boys' names, *sei=kabane=*clan names, *azana=torina=*artists' pseudonyms, etc.

The entire structure of the Japanese written language is highly complex. Evolved originally from Chinese, there have been innumerable modifications and combinations, and one author states that there are 23 different kinds of writing and that there may be as many as 244 different signs representing one syllable. The meaning of a character may be changed in accordance with its position in combination with other characters, the meaning of the other characters, the particular subject to which they relate, and many other factors. Standard Japanese is read from top to bottom in vertical columns running from right to left.

Style and Placement of Signatures

As previously stated, the earliest inro were usually unsigned, mainly because they were made by artists who were in the employ of the imperial family, shogun, local daimyo, and the like. Furthermore, many early inro were made by the Chinese method of carved red *(tsuishu)* and carved black *(tsuikoku)* lacquer, and, in general, lacquer ware made in this fashion is rarely found with a signature. As inro became more widely used and were adopted by ever increasing numbers of people of all classes, artists began to sign their names in order to identify their works. At first these signatures were merely scratched into the lacquer with a pointed tool, usually inside the lid. About the year 1640, signatures were for the first time executed in raised gold lacquer. It also became fashionable to place the signature on the bottom outer surface, usually off to one side and running lengthwise with the surface. There is no rule about placement, however, and, as previously noted, the artist sometimes signed on the inside of the cover, on one of the cord risers, or within one of the cases. Again, the signature may be in the form of a seal or *kakihan* or an inset plaque of pottery, as in the case of Ritsuo, or a plaque of metal or mother-of-pearl. It was not until the early 18th century, however, that it became generally popular for artists to sign their works.

Schools and Families of Lacquer Artists

For the most part, lacquer work may be classified in regard to the places and manner in which it was produced as well as by the influences of the different schools and families which developed and carried on the art. Lacquer arts were so strongly appreciated and encouraged that Emperor Daigo (early Heian period) enforced strict regulations that lacquer artists should not be permitted to change their profession and that they were responsible for training students in the art to carry on the tradition.

In all the arts, including painting, metalwork, and lacquer, the head of the school generally required his students to adhere strictly to his style and technique. This tended to cause stilted conventionalism rather than being conducive to the stimulation of new trends and the development and invention of new ideas and styles. On the other hand, it was this feudal system that gave rise to the great lacquer families who carried on their trade and passed their secrets on from generation to generation.

Religious influences are also seen in the existence of great families in the field of the lacquer arts. According to Confucian doctrines, there could be no intermarriage between classes, and therefore few artisans strayed from the profession of their fathers. Of perhaps even greater importance, as we have seen, was the Shinto tenet regarding ancestor worship. In Japan the perpetuation of the family name is considered to be of much more importance than the perpetuation of a blood relationship. When a family had no heir, it was the custom to adopt a near relative or even a stranger into the family so that the name would be carried on. When a family had no male heir, a boy was adopted into the family to marry the daughter of the house. According to Shinto teachings, every effort must be made to carry on the family name and to provide someone to attend to the worship of the family ancestors. This same principle of course applied to the perpetuation of lacquer schools and families.

Perhaps the most famous of the lacquer families were the Koma and the Kajikawa. These families are especially interesting to us because of the fact that they developed almost exclusively as inro makers. Members of the Kajikawa school usually signed their works only with the family name. This was also true of the Shunsho family, which existed for eleven generations. While the Koma also used the family name, they were more often given to adding a personal name as well. However, many generations of the Koma family had the same personal name, so that this is not a positive means of identification. Artists of the Shibayama school, which gained popularity in the late 18th century, signed their works with the family name only, which was usually engraved on a rectangle of mother-of-pearl and inset into the bottom surface of their inro. The Somada artists usually did not sign their lacquer ware, while the somewhat lesser known Tatsuke family usually signed both personal and family names.

From the foregoing facts we can conclude that definitive, extensive information regarding lacquer artists is nonexistent, the records scanty, and the signatures inadequate. We know that lacquer artists worked many generations before the introduction of inro, and their influences in perfecting this art cannot be disregarded. In the following alphabetical listing of artists will be found the names of some who worked prior to the inro era but who were nevertheless important in its growth and development by virtue of their contribution to the art of lacquering. For example, during the late 13th and early 14th centuries, the Hyoshi Temple was built in Omi. There is a record dated 1316 listing the following lacquer artists who worked on building this temple: Hirabunshi, Kunimitsu, Myoren, Rengetsu, Ryoen, Shokaku, Suketoki, and Teikei. Furthermore, some artists who were famous in other fields, such as painting, netsuke carving, and metalwork, are given brief mention, since their names have also appeared with some frequency on inro and other miniature lacquer works.

A List of Miniature Lacquer Artists

This list is compiled in the order of the art name in capitals, followed by the family name—when it is known—in ordinary type, except when the artist is best known by both family and art name, in which case the family name comes first—for example, SOMADA MITSUMASA. When two artists have exactly the same name, they are distinguished by a number in parentheses following the name—i.e., (1), (2), etc. Cross references are also given in capitals.

The names of the more renowned metal artists, netsuke carvers, and painters (whose designs were commonly used for lacquer decoration) are included when these names have been found on inro and other miniature lacquer works. In general, knowledge of a majority of the artists is fragmentary, in many instances only the approximate period in which they worked being known. Many other lacquer artists' signatures are to be found on inro and miscellaneous lacquer pieces, but their names are not included in this list, since absolutely no information is available about these artists.

For the purposes of this listing we have used the modern spelling of the Japanese names. However, some spellings and pronunciations, even though outdated, are so consistently used by collectors that for their convenience we have chosen to cross-index these names under both their old and their new spellings.

ANTO.   See KOMA ANTO.

ARIYOSHI.   18th-century inro artist.

ASAHI.   Metalworker of the 18th century who also occasionally made metal inro.

AWA Kurimoto.   Lacquerer of the mid-19th century.

AYABE.   Lacquer artist of the 18th century.

BAIGETSU.   Inro artist of the 17th century.

BAIGYOKUSAI.   Inro artist of the 18th century.

BAKUSAI.   See SOTETSU VII.

BANKO.   Inro artist of the 19th century.

BANZAN.   Inro artist of the early 18th century.

BOKKO.   Inro artist of the 19th century.

BOKOKU Ando.   Late-19th-century artist. Studied under Kano Tessai in Kyoto. Did excellent work in carved lacquer and originated a style similar to *tsuishu* but was primarily a wood carver.

BUNCHO. 1861–1909. Son of Kawanobe ITCHO and brother of Kawanobe IKKO. All three did excellent lacquer work.

BUNGORO Nagata. Lacquerer of the second half of the 18th century.

BUNKO (also known as Jukakusai). Mid-19th-century artist, best known for his paintings.

BUNRYUSAI Kajikawa. See KAJIKAWA III and KAJIKAWA BUNRYU-SAI.

BUNSAI. Celebrated lacquer artist of the late 18th and beginning of the 19th centuries. Younger brother of KOMA KANSAI II.

BUNZO Izumi. Inro artist of the early 19th century.

CHIKANAO. Inro artist of the late 18th century.

CHIKATSUNE. Inro artist of the late 18th century.

CHIKUSEN Imanaka. A carver of Tsu City who worked in the mid-18th century. Was sometimes called Shinkyo. Carved mainly flowers, rivers, and mountain landscapes as decorations for inro, *yatate,* and furniture. Occasionally carved netsuke. Was employed as a purveyor by the feudal clan of Tsu.

CHINEI. Mid-18th-century artist who worked in Nagasaki. Decorated inro, using primarily the *chinkin-bori* technique.

CHINGI. Artist of the late 17th century. Decorated inro, using mainly *chinkin-bori* technique.

CHINGISAI. Late-18th-century lacquer artist.

CHINKEI (also known as Kaikeisai). Artist of the early 18th century who used *chinkin-bori* technique for his inro decoration.

CHOAN. Another name of the lacquerers Koami Nagafusa and Koami Naga-yasu. See KOAMI VII and KOAMI XI.

CHOBEI. See TATSUKE CHOBEI.

CHOGEN Koami. 1572–1607. Lacquerer of the late 16th and early 17th centuries.

CHOHEI Nomura. An outstanding lacquer artist who worked during the late 18th and early 19th centuries. Also known by the name Jirobei. Younger brother of Nomura KYUKEI. Worked in Edo. His style is strong and bold, somewhat in the manner of Ritsuo. He frequently inlaid shell, mother-of-pearl, and other materials on lacquer ware. He was also adept at *tsuishu* work and often used thick colored lacquer for his ground. His works were frequently forged.

CHOHO. See KOAMI IX.

CHOIN. See KOAMI XVI.

CHOJU. See KOAMI X.

CHOKA. Lacquerer of the early 18th century who worked mostly in *tsuishu.* Also made netsuke.

CHOKAN. Early-18th-century lacquerer who was a naturalized Korean. Lived in Nagasaki and was especially well known for his work in *chinkin-bori.*

CHOKAN Onko. Early-18th-century artist who lived in Edo. Also known as Kakukakusai.

CHOKAN Sano. 1791–1863. Also known as Nagahamaya Jisuke. Master lacquerer who was said to be a descendant of the naturalized Korean lacquerer

Chokan. Settled in Kyoto in 1825 after traveling throughout Japan. Was especially well known for his black and purple lacquers.

CHOKEI. Lacquerer of the early 19th century. Was a student of Ritsuo and did encrustation in the style of Ritsuo. Also carved netsuke.

CHOKICHI (also known as Ryuetsusai). Excellent inro artist of the late 18th century. His works are rare.

CHOKO. See KOAMI XV.

CHOKOKEN. See KORIN.

CHOKYU. See KOAMI XII.

CHONOSUKE Kurimoto. Lacquerer of the 19th century.

CHOSEI. See KOAMI VI.

CHOSHU. Inro artist of the early 19th century.

CHOSHUN. Inro artist of the 19th century who was reputed to be an excellent craftsman.

CHOZEN. See KOAMI VIII.

CHUBEI Nomura. Lacquerer of the 19th century.

CHUBEI Tanda. Lacquer artist of the 18th century. Also known as Iwamoto Chubei. Native of Edo. During the second half of the 18th century he was in the employ of Lord Hachisuka, daimyo of the province of Awa. Using colored lacquer as well as oil paints, he created somewhat conventionalized designs of flowers. To replace *nashiji* lining on lacquer articles, he created a technique whereby he rubbed pulverized gold foil on the interior surfaces. The technique, however, proved to be impractical and was never adopted by other artists. He founded the celebrated Iwamoto family of lacquerers.

CHUHO. Inro artist of the late 18th century.

CHUMU Namikawa. Lacquer artist of the mid-19th century. Also known as Jimei.

CHUYU. See INAGAWA CHUYU.

DENJIRO Kobayashi. Lacquerer of the second half of the 19th century.

DOCHO. See KOAMI I.

DOEN Kondo. Lacquerer of the early 18th century.

DOGAI. See KOAMI XIV.

DOHO. See IGARASHI DOHO I and IGARASHI KISABURO.

DOI. See SHOGEN Doi.

DOJIN. See RITSUO.

DOSEI. See KOAMI II.

DOSHI Kondo. Excellent lacquerer of the 17th century. Frequently worked for the *chajin* Kobori Enshu during the middle of the 17th century. Invented a lacquer technique called *iji-iji-nuri*.

DOSHO. See SHIBAYAMA and SHIBAYAMA DOSHO.

DOSHU. See KORIN.

DOSO. See KORIN.

DOYO Shimizu. Lacquer artist of the early 18th century. Also known as Michitomo.

EIHACHI. Lacquer artist of the mid-18th century.

EIKI Nishimura. Lacquer artist of the late 18th and early 19th centuries. Executed fine works in Wakasa-nuri.

EISEN. Lacquer artist of the 19th century.

EISHO. One of the names of the painter Toki Saibi, another of his names being Hakka (or Hakkwa). 1780–1844. Student of the painter Maruyama Okyo, whose realistic school of nature painting greatly influenced early-19th-century lacquer works.

EISHO. Lacquerer of the 18th century.

EISUKE. See TATSUKE EISUKE.

EIZAN Kikugawa. Painter of the *ukiyo-e* school who executed designs for lacquer ware. Born in Edo in the mid-18th century. Was particularly skillful in creating designs of flowers and birds.

EKISO. Inro artist of the 19th century who did encrustations in the Shibayama style

ENSHU. See KOMA ENSHU.

ETSUJO Kakujo (or Kwakujo). Metal artist of the early 19th century. Real name: Kakujo Mitsuyasu. Son of Tomisaburo. His works were after the fashion of the Goto school, and he occasionally made metal inro.

FUJIN. Noted lacquer artist of the 17th century who lived in Kaga Province from 1615 to 1680.

FUJISHICHI Ikushima. Well-known artist of the early 17th century. Lived in Nagasaki. Was particularly skillful in *raden* work.

FUKUMATSU Shirayama. Excellent inro artist of the 19th century.

FUKUZO. Early-15th-century lacquerer who is credited with revitalizing the lacquer technique called Negoro-nuri, also called Wajima-nuri (after the district where he worked).

FUMIO Katsurano. Inro artist of the early 19th century.

FUN'UNSAI Hayakawa. Inro artist of the 19th century.

FUROSAI. Lacquer artist of the mid-19th century.

FURYO. Inro artist of the early 19th century.

FUSAI. Inro artist of the 19th century.

FUSATAKA. See KAJIKAWA IV.

FUSEN (or UKIFUNE, which is another reading of the characters). Inro artist of the late 18th century.

FUSHUSAI. See GYOKUHO.

FUYU Kuwano. 18th-century artist who lived in Edo. Also known as Kimura Shigeharu.

GAMBUN (also known as Hakugei). 19th-century netsuke artist who occasionally did *kanshitsu*.

GARAKU. Primarily a netsuke artist who lived in Osaka during the latter part of the 18th century. Also called Taguchi Risuke. Carved mostly in ivory. Favorite subjects were deer and tortoises.

GEKKEI. 1742–1811. Artist. Primarily known as a painter under the name of Matsumura Goshun.

GEMBEI (also known as Seikai). 17th-century artist from the district of Tsugaru, where his father was a samurai. Lived in Edo during the latter part of the 17th century and studied under the celebrated lacquer artist Seikai Tarozaemon. Returned to Tsugaru and invented a technique of lacquer decoration called Tsugaru-nuri.

GENRYOSAI. Artist of the late 18th and early 19th centuries. Best known as a netsuke carver.

GENSHIRO Shimizu. Inro maker of the early 18th century who was employed by the shogun. Lived in Edo and made inro for imperial use.

GENSHOSAI (also known as Masaharu). Inro maker of the mid-19th century.

GENSUKE Tanabe. Expert lacquer artist who worked in Tokyo during the late 19th century.

GENZO. See KOMA X.

GETSUGEN Mochizuki. 1691–1754. Skilled lacquer craftsman. Also known as Genju and Gyokutan.

GICHIN Kobayashi. Inro artist of the mid-19th century.

GOBEI Kanda. Master lacquerer of the second half of the 19th century. Well known for his picnic boxes (jubako) made in Shunkei-nuri lacquer. He allegedly used a red-hot iron to sign his works with three characters.

GONROKU Matsuda (1). Lacquer artist of the late 19th century whose works are of a classical nature.

GONROKU Matsuda (2). Lacquer artist of the 20th century, born in 1896 and still working. Attended Tokyo Fine Arts School and was later a professor there. Was nominated as a member of the Imperial Academy of Art. A former teacher at the Tokyo University of Arts, he is among the outstanding lacquer artists still working at this time.

GORO Haneda. Outstanding lacquer artist of the mid-15th century. Lived in Nara and specialized in making tea-ceremony articles. Said to be the inventor of the type of lacquer tea caddy known as *natsume*.

GOZAN. Lacquerer of the early 18th century.

GYOBU Taro. Lacquer artist of the early 18th century who lived in Edo. He is credited with having created the lacquer technique known as *gyobu nashiji*.

GYOKKEI (also known as Yutokusai). Inro artist of the early 19th century.

GYOKKOKU (also known as Baishu). Best known as a painter who worked in the mid-19th century.

GYOKUHO (also known as Fushusai and Hidekatsu). Inro artist of the late 18th century.

GYOKUKU (also known as Yutokusai). Inro artist of the early 19th century.

GYOKUMEI. Inro artist of the mid-19th century.

GYOKURIN. Lacquer artist of the KOMA school. Worked in the early 19th century.

GYOKUSAI (1). Late 18th and early 19th centuries. Celebrated mainly as a netsuke artist. Worked chiefly in wood and displayed remarkable skill in carving figures that balanced on one foot. Carved equally well in ivory.

GYOKUSAI (2). Known as Tachibana Masamitsu. Lacquer artist of the 19th century.

GYOKUSEN. Lacquer artist of the mid-18th century.

GYOKUSHINSAI. Inro artist of the early 19th century.

GYOKUZAN. It should be noted that there is a great variety of opinion regarding the identity of several artists who used this name. Many authorities believe that the three artists Asahi, Jitokusai, and Tachibana were in reality the same person. There is, however, no conclusive evidence to support this theory. See the following five entries.

GYOKUZAN (1). See JITOKUSAI.

GYOKUZAN (2). See SHOSENSAI.

GYOKUZAN Asahi. 1843–1923. Best known for his carving of netsuke and *okimono,* particularly in the form of skulls. Worked in Tokyo and carved chiefly in ivory. Originally a priest, he took up ivory carving as a hobby when he was twenty-four, and it soon became his chief occupation. In his early career he carved toads, crabs, and snakes, but in his later work skulls were the main subject. He became a professor at the Tokyo Art College and received many honors and much attention for his realistic carvings. He was possibly the most outstanding carver of his time. A few inro have been attributed to him.

GYOKUZAN Omura. Lacquer artist who worked in the second half of the 18th century in the employ of the shogun. Was a pupil of Koma Koryu. Died *c.* 1789.

GYOKUZAN Tachibana. Outstanding lacquer artist of the late 18th and early 19th centuries who frequently worked in cherry bark. Lived in Edo.

GYOKUZANSAI Matsukawa. Lacquer artist of the 18th century.

GYOSEI Koami. See KOAMI GYOSEI.

GYUKI. Lacquer artist of the 17th century.

HADAGORO. Lacquer artist of the second half of the 15th century who worked in Kyoto. Invented a type of decoration called Hokkaimon-nuri after the name of the locality where he worked.

HAKKAKUSAI. Lacquer artist of the early 19th century many of whose designs were styled after the woodblock prints of Hiroshige.

HAKUGYOKU Kano. This name has been found on inro made in the 19th century. It is another name of the painter Nankai, who probably made the design rather than the lacquer ware itself. He received the honorary title of *hoin.*

HAKUHO. Inro maker of the 18th century who specialized in the decoration of his works in *togidashi* technique, using black lacquer for his decoration in *sumie* style.

HAKUSAI Inoue. Well-known lacquer artist who worked in Edo during the late 18th and early 19th centuries.

HAKUSEN. Lacquer artist of the 18th century.

HAKUUNSAI. Artist of the late 18th and early 19th centuries, born in Edo. Best known for his skillful netsuke carving, particularly in the *manju* and *kagamibuta* styles. His son, who worked in Kyoto, succeeded to his profession and adopted the same name. Both artists are frequently referred to by the name of Ichijo.

HANROKU Tsuchida.   Lacquer artist of the early 18th century who is reputed to have been a descendant of Tsuchida Soetsu. Lived and worked in Edo.

HANYUSAI.   Inro artist of first half of the 19th century.

HANZABURO.   Excellent lacquer artist of the late 17th century. Worked in Kyoto. Was equally skilled in lacquering and in encrusting mother-of-pearl. His outstanding style was readily adopted by many later artists.

HANZABURO Ofuji.   Lacquerer of the mid-19th century.

HANZAN Mochizuki.   Skillful lacquer and inro artist of the second half of the 18th century. Believed to have been born in Edo in 1743. Said to have been a pupil of Ritsuo, although this would seem unlikely if his birth date is correct, since Ritsuo died in 1747. More likely, as a great admirer of Ritsuo, he copied his style, although his works are not as powerful, since they are somewhat lacking in daring and originality and are rather more delicate and finely detailed in nature. Hanzan adopted the art name of Haritsu II and frequently signed his works on a small inlaid porcelain plaque, using the same seal as Ritsuo. He occasionally used the art name Gosha. Studied pottery making under Yosei and encrusted his inro with ceramics, mother-of-pearl, and other materials, his favorite subjects being shells and fish. His inro frequently have black linings, with the risers decorated in *chinkin-bori*. Also made netsuke, decorating them with lacquer and encrustations in the same manner as his inro. Died in 1790 and was succeeded by his pupil Kyozan, who called himself Haritsu III.

HARITSU II.   See HANZAN.

HARITSU III.   See KYOZAN.

HARITSU Ogawa.   See RITSUO.

HARUFUSA.   Inro artist of the 18th century.

HARUI KIYOSHI.   Skillful lacquerer of the mid-19th century who worked in Kyoto.

HARUMASA (1).   Also known as Jirobei. Lacquerer of the 18th century, born in Kyoto in 1736. Later worked in Nagoya.

HARUMASA (2).   Also known as Matashiro. Lacquer artist best known for his work in *togidashi* technique, usually on a red background. Worked during last part of 18th and beginning of 19th centuries. Died in 1832.

HARUMASA Shiomi.   Excellent inro artist of the late 17th century who lived in Kyoto. Reputed to have been the father of the famous artist Shiomi Masanari.

HARUMASA Yamamoto.   Very skillful lacquer artist who worked in Kyoto during the second half of the 17th century. Died in 1682.

HARUNAGA.   Inro artist of the 19th century.

HARUNARI.   See HIRATA HARUNARI.

HARUTSUGU.   See SHUNSHO IV.

HARUYUKI.   See HIRATA HARUYUKI.

HASEGAWA KORINSAI (1).   Lacquer artist of the 18th century.

HASEGAWA KORINSAI (2).   19th-century artist, probably the same as HASEGAWA SHIGEYOSHI.

HASEGAWA SHIGEYOSHI.   Well-known inro artist of the late 18th and early 19th centuries. Particularly skilled in making gold-lacquered inro and lacquered netsuke. Famous for his *togidashi* work and *takamakie* in color. Belonged to the Kajikawa school and often used a seal similar to theirs—in the form of a small vase with handles. Sometimes used the art names of Korinsai and Sei. Was a native of Tsuyama (in the present Okayama Prefecture).

HASHIICHI I. 1817–82. Expert lacquer artist who concentrated on lacquering sword sheaths until a law forbidding the wearing of swords was passed in 1870. After this date he turned his attention to decorating inro, trays, and other miniature lacquer objects, initiating a style known as *takemozo-nuri* in which he made perfect imitations of bamboo in lacquer. His real name was Hashimoto Ichizo, and he was the son of Hashimoto Matajiro, from whom he learned the art of decorating sword sheaths. One of his pupils succeeded him and took the name of HASHIICHI II.

HASHIICHI II (Hashimoto Hashiichi II). 1856–1924. Adopted son and successor of HASHIICHI I. Skillful lacquer artist who worked in the style of his foster father.

HEIJURO (also known as Tsuishu). Lacquerer of the early 17th century who did excellent sculptured *(tsuishu)* lacquer work. Was in the employ of Tokugawa Ieyasu and lived in Edo.

HEIZAEMON Akatsuka. Expert lacquer artist of the late 19th century who worked in Edo. Was succeeded by his son Akatsuka JITOKU, who was also a skilled craftsman.

HIDA Sakamoto. Lacquer artist of the 19th century.

HIDARI ISSAN. Skillful wood carver of the late 18th century from the province of Aizu. Particularly noted for carving realistic tortoises in wood as netsuke or inro. Also fond of carving wooden snails. His signature is often accompanied by a written seal reading "Toku."

HIDEKATSU. See GYOKUHO.

HIDESADA (also known as Shinshinsai Toshi). Lacquer artist of the 18th century.

HIDETERU. Lacquer artist of the 18th century.

HIDETSUGU. There were many lacquer artists of this name who distinguished themselves during the 15th, 16th, and 17th centuries. All of them worked for the outstanding tea masters of their time and made *natsume*. See the following six entries.

HIDETSUGU I. Worked during the late 15th century in Nara for the *chajin* (tea master) Jo-o, whose designs he often utilized in his works.

HIDETSUGU II (also known as Yoji). Worked during the late 16th century for the famous *chajin* Sen no Rikyu. Was also employed by Hideyoshi and received the honorary title of *tenka-ichi* for his outstanding lacquer work. He was sometimes called Noro.

HIDETSUGU III (also known as Zensho). Worked for the *chajin* Furuta Oribe during the latter half of the 17th century.

HIDETSUGU IV (also known as Rinzai). Master lacquerer who made *natsume* in an individualistic style for the *chajin* Kobori Enshu during the second half of the 17th century. His boxes were characterized by a top section as deep as the bottom half. Another feature of his work was that the covers of his boxes fit deeply and snugly into the bottoms, thus forming an airtight compartment for keeping the tea fresh. This style of box was called *nakatsugi*.

HIDETSUGU V (also known as Yosai). Lacquerer of the mid-17th century.

HIDETSUGU VI (also known as Choan). Lacquer artist of the early 18th century.

HIKOBEI Nishimura. Lacquer artist who worked in Kyoto between 1720 and 1773. He is sometimes called Zohiko (*zo* being the word for elephant) because of a design of an elephant for which he became famous.

HIRATA HARUNARI. A member of the famous Hirata family of enamelers, this artist worked during the late 18th century. He held a special appointment to the court of the shogun Tokugawa Ienari and was a very skillful artist.

HIRATA HARUYUKI. Member of the famous Hirata family of enamelers who occasionally executed work on inro and other miniature lacquer ware.

HIROMICHI. A very skillful inro artist of the 18th century.

HIROTADA. See TATSUKE HIROTADA.

HIROTADA Yanagawa. Lacquer artist of the 19th century.

HIROTOSHI (also known as Ichiyosai). Founder of a school of metal artists about 1800. He was a student of Tamagawa Yoshinaga II and in turn had many students. The school he founded is known by the name of Uchikoshi, and its style somewhat resembles that of the Nara artists but is characteristic in its abundance of detailed encrustations, particular attention being given to the clothing of the figures portrayed. Legendary subjects are usually represented in the works of the school. Hirotoshi frequently worked in conjunction with lacquer artists in executing inro decorations.

HISAHIDE. See TATSUKE HISAHIDE.

HISAHIDE Tamura. Lacquer artist who worked in the early 19th century.

HISAIE (or Hisaiye). Lacquer artist of the mid-18th century.

HISAIYE. See HISAIE.

HISAMOTO Umehara. Lacquerer of the first half of the 17th century.

HISATAKA (also known as Jurakusai). Lacquer artist of the early 19th century.

HISATOYO. Lacquer artist of the early 19th century.

HITSUJI. Lacquer artist of the late 18th century.

HOBI Yamada. 1872–1933. A leading lacquer artist of Tokyo, son of the famous lacquerer Homin. Was strongly influenced by the Yamato-e school of painting, and this was reflected in his lacquer work. Had many students.

HOCHU Yasui. Well-known Tokyo lacquer artist of the late 19th century.

HOETSU. 1757–1828. Student of KOETSU, whose style he followed. Was an excellent lacquerer and encruster.

HOGEN (also known as Isen). Skillful early-19th-century lacquerer who died in 1828. Used the word *fuji* as his seal.

HOITSU Sakai. 1761–1828. Famous painter and lacquerer born in the province of Harima (the present Hyogo Prefecture). A priest, he was also a well-trained and talented artist who studied the Kano and Tosa styles of painting as well as the style of Ogata Korin, which he strongly favored. His own style is quite free, his favorite subjects being flowers and birds. Many lacquer pieces of the 19th century adopted his designs, and such pieces were often marked "design after Hoitsu" whether the artist signed them or not. Among Hoitsu's students were Kiitsu, Kishin, Koitsu, Ikeda Koson, Shuitsu, and Oho. He also used the names Oson, Nison'an, Toryo, Dojin, and Ukaan.

HOKEI Matsuki. Artist of the 19th century who specialized in *tsuishu* lacquer work. Worked in Edo (Tokyo). Frequently made netsuke of carved *tsuishu* lacquer.

HOKUSAI Nakajima. 1760–1849. The celebrated woodblock-print artist. Although he was primarily a painter, his name is occasionally found on inro. Many of his designs were used for inro decoration.

HOKUUN (also known as Sanshosai). Early-19th-century lacquerer who executed his works mostly in *togidashi* technique.

HOMIN Uematsu (or Uyematsu). Outstanding lacquer artist of the late 19th century, he worked in Tokyo from about 1845 to 1899. He was born in Yotsuya in Tokyo and when young was called Yakichi. First studied lacquering under Ueda Kisaburo and later under Kajikawa Seibei. Produced lacquer ware in a quiet, refined style. He died in 1902. Among his many outstanding pupils was Yasui Hochu.

HON'AMI Koetsu. See KOETSU Hon'ami.

HORIO Ikawa. Inro artist of the late 19th century.

HOSENSAI. Lacquer artist of the late 18th and early 19th centuries.

HOSHIN (also known as Genryosai). Late-18th-century lacquer artist who worked in the style of Ritsuo.

HOSHUKU. See KORIN.

HOYU. Lacquer artist of the mid-19th century.

HYAKKAKU Iwase (also known as Kyosui). 1816–67. Lacquer artist of the 19th century.

HYAKUSEN. Lacquerer of the late 18th and early 19th centuries.

HYAKUSHI. Lacquer artist of the early 19th century.

HYOMON. Lacquerer of the second half of the 12th century who invented a lacquer technique which was named after him.

HYOSAI Kimura. 1817–85. Skillful lacquer artist born in Omi. Well known for his work in Negoro-nuri and black lacquer. Was a student of Shibata Tobei of Kyoto.

HYOSAI II (also known as Yasaburo). The younger son of Kimura Hyosai, he was called Hyosai II. Worked during the middle and late 19th century in Kyoto. Was an excellent lacquer artist.

ICHIBEI. Lacquer artist of the early 18th century who lived in Osaka. Was particularly skillful in both lacquering and shell-inlay decoration.

ICHIDAIYU Shibara. Highly skilled lacquer artist and inro maker of the mid-17th century. He was employed by Maeda, lord of Kaga Province, and his inro are frequently referred to as Kaga inro. He was succeeded by his three sons, TOZO, TOMONOSHIN, and ICHINOJO, who were also expert lacquer artists.

ICHIHOSAI. See IPPOSAI.

ICHIJO. See HAKUUNSAI.

ICHINOJO Shibara. Youngest son of Shibara Ichidaiyu. Excellent lacquer artist who worked during the 18th century. Was also a noted musician.

ICHIRAKU. Well-known netsuke artist of the mid-19th century. Worked chiefly in wood, which he decorated with colored lacquer. His signature is usually inscribed in lacquer.

ICHIRAKU Tsuchiya (also known as Hotoken). Artist of the early 18th century who made *sagemono*, frequently in woven basketwork. Also made netsuke, usually in the form of gourds.

ICHIYOSAI. See HIROTOSHI.

ICHIZAN. Inro and netsuke artist of the early 19th century. Frequently carved netsuke out of walnuts.

IESADA. Inro artist of the 19th century.

IGARASHI. This family is one of the oldest and most outstanding families of lacquer artists. They were in the service of the Ashikaga shogunate in the mid-15th century, and their descendants retained a similar position for many succeeding generations. They were well known in Kyoto along with their contemporaries, the famous Koami family. Their style of lacquer decoration was adopted in later years by the Kajikawa school.

IGARASHI DOHO I. Most outstanding and best known member of the family; fifth in direct descent from IGARASHI SHINSAI; son of IGARASHI HOSAI. During the early part of the 17th century he moved from Kyoto to Kanazawa, where he entered the service of Lord Maeda of Kaga Province and contributed greatly to the production of the local lacquer ware known as Kaga *makie*. His works are characterized by neatness and clarity of style. He returned to Kyoto and died there in 1678.

IGARASHI HOSAI. Lacquerer who executed skillful work in the Igarashi tradition. Father of IGARASHI DOHO I.

IGARASHI KISABURO. This artist was actually a member of the KOAMI family but was adopted by IGARASHI DOHO I and took the art name of Doho II. He served Lord Maeda of Kaga Province. His works show a combination of the Igarashi and Koami styles. He was succeeded by Doho III, who worked at the beginning of the 18th century.

IGARASHI SHINSAI. This artist founded the Igarashi school about 1470 and served as official lacquerer to the shogun Ashikaga Yoshimasa.

IHEI. Little-known artist who worked in Kyoto during the early 18th century.

IKKAN. Inro artist of the 18th century.

IKKIU (Ikkyu). See KAZUHISA.

IKKO (1). Skillful 19th-century lacquer artist who worked in the style of Ritsuo. Used encrustations of many diverse materials to decorate inro, pipe cases, and other miniature lacquer objects. Also carved netsuke.

IKKO (2). Born 1852. Son of Kawanobe ITCHO and younger brother of BUNCHO, with both of whom he frequently worked. Together they executed many excellent pieces of lacquer ware.

IKKOKUSAI Ikeda (Ikkokusai III). Master lacquer artist of the 19th century who worked in Hiroshima. Particularly skilled in lacquer decoration in color carved in relief.

IKKYU (or Ikkiu). See KAZUHISA.

INABA. See KOAMI NAGAYASU II.

INAGAWA. This is the family name of several lacquerers who worked during the 18th and 19th centuries. One of the most skillful Inagawa artists of the 18th century was a pupil of the Kajikawa school who adopted a seal in the form of a small vase similar to the Kajikawa seal and added this to his signature. The Inagawa family was particularly noted for its excellent *togidashi* work.

INAGAWA CHUYU. 18th-century lacquerer of the INAGAWA family.

IPPOSAI. Reference is made to a number of artists bearing the name Ipposai, but no details regarding their lives exist. Among these artists are KANZAN, KOGYOKU, KOYO, Ichihosai (another reading of the characters for Ipposai), Shiomi, and TENKO.

ISEN. Art name of the painter Kano Eishin, who occasionally executed designs for inro.

ISHIKAWA HOYUSAI. 1852–1913. This artist was primarily a sculptor, having descended from a line of decorative shrine sculptors. He adopted the art name of Juzan, was appointed a court artist, and was a professor at the Tokyo Academy of Fine Arts. Studied painting with Kano Sosen and carving with Kikugawa Masamitsu. Executed netsuke, *okimono,* and pipe sheaths with equal skill.

ISOI JOSHIN. Lacquer artist of the late 19th century who excelled in lacquer in the *kimma* technique.

ISSAI. 19th-century artist of the ZESHIN school who was outstanding for his lacquer work, particularly *manju* netsuke.

ISSAN. See HIDARI ISSAN.

ISSETSU. Lacquer artist of the 19th century.

ISSHI. Lacquer artist of the 19th century who decorated his works with inlaid materials in the style of the Shibayama school.

ISSHU. 19th-century artist who excelled in carved red lacquer in the manner of *tsuishu* work.

ISSHUNSAI. Inro artist of the mid-19th century.

ISUKE. See KORIN.

ITCHO Kawanobe. 1830–1910. Distinguished lacquer artist of Tokyo who studied the Koami style of lacquering under Takei Toshichi. He was appointed a court artist in 1896 and assisted in the lacquer decoration of the interior of the Imperial Palace. He also became a member of the faculty of the Tokyo University of Arts. He often worked with his two sons IKKO (2) and BUNCHO and created many fine pieces of lacquer ware.

ITCHU Hanabusa. Artist of the 19th century whose designs often appear on inro.

ITTOSAI. 18th-century lacquer artist who executed many unusual works.

JAKUMEI. See KORIN.

JIEI. See KAJIKAWA BUNRYUSAI.

JIGOEMON (1). Known as Yoshinaga. Lacquer artist of the late 15th and early 16th centuries who lived in Jogahana in Etchu Province. He initiated a technique of lacquering which became known as Jogahana lacquer. This technique was based on *mitsuda-e,* an oil lacquer technique which he had learned during a stay in Nagasaki while he was studying Ming-dynasty painting. He studied the art of lacquering under MATABEI Sasaki, who founded his school during the Tensho era (1573–92). This school later began using the family name of OHARA.

JIGOEMON Hata (2). He was a member of the Jogahana school of lacquer artists. He went to Nagasaki, where he studied Chinese lacquer techniques and perfected the use of *mitsuda* lacquer. One of his students was TOKUZAEMON, who was the grandson of the founder of the school, MATABEI Sasaki.

JIGOEMON Ohara (3). The sixth OHARA family lacquer artist.

JIGOEMON (4). Known as Shigeyoshi. 1729–1805. This artist represented the seventh generation of the Jigoemon line of lacquerers. He invented a type of white lacquer which was named the "white lacquer of Jogahana" after the district where he worked. He was succeeded by his sons Muneyoshi and Yuzo, and all of them used the family name Ohara. Yuzo represented the ninth generation of the Ohara family. After the sixth generation they all used the name Jigoemon Ohara.

JIKKYOKU Kimura. A celebrated 18th-century lacquer artist who worked in the style of Ritsuo.

JIROBEI Nagano. Lacquer artist of the mid-19th century.

JIROEMON. Lacquerer of the 18th century who specialized in carved *tsuishu* work.

JIROZAEMON (also known as Tsuishu). Expert lacquer worker of the 18th century who specialized in carved *tsuishu* lacquer. Worked in Kyoto from about 1716 to 1735. He was considered by some to be even more outstanding in *tsuishu* work than Monnyu, the originator of this style of carving.

JISAKU Sawada. See SAWADA Sotakusai.

JITOKU Akatsuka. 1871–1936. Leading lacquer artist. He was the son of HEIZAEMON and succeeded to his father's trade. In 1930 he was made a member of the Imperial Academy. He trained many students in his dignified and artistic style.

JITOKUSAI Gyokuzan (1). 18th-century lacquer artist who worked from about 1789 to 1804. He was a pupil of Koma V (Kyuzo IV). He frequently signed his work as Jitokusai Gyokuzan.

JIYOSAI. 19th-century lacquer artist of the school of Yoyusai.

JOFU. Lacquer artist of the TATSUKE family.

JOHO. Member of the TATSUKE family of lacquerers.

JOI (also known as Nagaharu). 1700–61. One of the most outstanding metal artists. He worked in Edo and studied under masters of the Nara school. Although he usually made small sword furniture, we occasionally find his works encrusted on lacquer ware and inro as well as on some *kagamibuta* netsuke. He used *shibuichi* primarily and also occasionally encrusted his work with different metals. He is best known, however, for his work in middle relief. He also used the names of Toshichi and Issando. His signature is very often forged, and authentic pieces by him are relatively rare. The characters of his genuine signature are small in size, and each is clearly engraved. In addition, he often used a gold seal. His favorite subjects were legendary characters and animals and, above all, Shoki and *oni*. Of his many students, one of the best was his niece Jowa, who made many excellent copies of his works.

JOKA. Lacquer artist of the late 17th century. Believed to be the same person as Yamada JOKASAI.

JOKASAI Yamada. One of the most masterly lacquer artists of the late 17th century. An outstanding member of the KAJIKAWA school. He lived in

Edo and, along with Koami Nagafusa, served as inro maker to the Tokugawa shoguns. He also made *kobako* and, upon occasion, lacquered sword ornaments. Early in his career he was known as Terada Joka, and his works, which are very hard to distinguish from those of other Kajikawa artists, are frequently signed "Joka." Later works were sometimes signed "Jo-o." His pieces are consistently well executed, and we frequently find encrustations of metal in relief in a base of *nashiji*. He was, however, an expert in many various styles of lacquering. As the founder of the Yamada family of lacquerers, he had many followers and was succeeded by his son and his grandson, who also worked for the shoguns. The last Jokasai was Tsuneo (1811–79). A very skillful craftsman, he worked for the shogunate. He frequently lacquered sword furniture. The school of Jokasai includes such expert lacquerers as Kakosai, Shokasai, and Torosai.

JOKOSAI. A skillful inro maker of the late 18th and early 19th centuries who excelled in *togidashi* and *sumie* techniques for decoration of his lacquer ware.

JOSEN Tsunekawa. Lacquer artist of the early 19th century.

JOSHO (also known as Kokosai). A member of the TATSUKE family of lacquerers.

JOZAN (also known as Jukakusai). Lacquerer of the early 19th century.

JUBEI Fujita. Lacquer artist of the mid-18th century.

JUEI (also known as Toshinaga, another reading of the characters of his name). An artist who worked at the end of the 18th and the beginning of the 19th centuries. He was also a netsuke carver.

JUGYOKU (also known as Chounsai). Lacquer artist of the mid-19th century. Was a student of Ryukei and worked in Edo. Also carved netsuke.

JUICHI Kanai (also known as Seikichi). 1838–98. Lacquer artist.

JUKKYOKU Kano. Early-18th-century lacquer artist who worked in Edo. When he was young he used the name Kimura. His later works are signed Kano.

JUSENSAI. Lacquerer of the early 19th century.

JUSHU. Lacquer artist of the early 19th century.

JUTOKUSAI. Inro artist of the 18th century.

JUZAN. See ISHIKAWA HOYUSAI.

JUZO Mochizuki. Noted lacquer artist of the early 18th century who lived and worked in Edo.

KADOMICHI. Inro artist of the late 19th century.

KAGAWA SOSEKI. Lacquer artist of the late 19th century who did excellent work in Zonsei technique.

KAGEHARU Yamamoto. See SHUNSHO II.

KAGEMASA. See SHUNSHO II.

KAGETOSHI. Lacquerer of the 18th century.

KAGETSUSAI. Inro artist of the 19th century.

KAHEI. Lacquer artist of the early 18th century.

KAIGYOKUSAI (also known as Masatsugu). 1813–92. Born in Osaka, this artist was one of the most skillful netsuke carvers of his time. He also occasionally carved wooden inro and pipe cases. (See chapter on netsuke for further details.)

KAJIKAWA.   One of the most skillful families of lacquer workers, specializing in inro. Starting in the 17th century, the Kajikawa worked for the shogunate and continued to do so for many subsequent generations until well into the 19th century. Along with their contemporaries, the KOMA family, the Kajikawa were the best-known inro makers of their time. Unfortunately it seems to have been the common practice to sign only the family name along with a seal in the form of a small vase or perfume bottle having two handles and feet—usually executed in red lacquer. Because of this custom it is practically impossible to assign a particular piece to any specific member of the family. There are from about ten to twelve slight variations of this seal, but we have no way of assigning these variations to any one person. A few of the seals, however, have been identified as those of specific members of the family. For the most part, the works carrying the name of Kajikawa are expertly executed. But the signatures were often forged and were equally often used by pupils of the real masters.

The early Kajikawa were particularly outstanding for the linings of their inro, which are usually to be found in a rich *nashiji* in which can be seen rather large and irregularly shaped pieces of gold leaf. This is referred to as *gyobu nashiji*. The Kajikawa are also credited with inventing a lining in which an irregular surface is prepared and covered with gold leaf and then covered again with reddish lacquer which produces a variety of tones from red to a rich brown, depending upon the depth of the lacquer that covers the gold leaf.

The skills of the Kajikawa embraced all varieties of lacquering from *togidashi* to elaborate *kirigane* work, and the artists were equally skilled in executing magnificent black-and-gold lacquer work. The later members of the family often worked in conjunction with the Shibayama artists, and we frequently find two signatures appearing on one inro. They often used encrustations of metal or mother-of-pearl for decoration on a gold-lacquer background. These encrustations were often executed by skillful artists in their special field, and their signatures often appear on the inro along with the Kajikawa signature, especially on later works.

The Kajikawa artists also often made netsuke, particularly of gold lacquer, to match their inro. In general, most of the Kajikawa work was extremely detailed, finely executed, and of high artistic standard. Later works, however, tended to be somewhat overornate, using primarily gold-lacquer backgrounds.

In addition to the individual Kajikawa artists listed below, the following are members of the family who worked during the 18th century: Hisataka, Ryusho, Takafusa, Toshihide, Yoshichika, Yoshimitsu, and several who took the art name of Kyujiro. There are many other artists of this school whose names appear on inro but about whom we have no specific information and whom we are unable to date accurately.

KAJIKAWA I (Hikobei).   Artist of the early 17th century who is known to have been working for the shogunate around 1637. He appears to have been the first of the Kajikawa school, but his skill was surpassed by that of his son and pupil KAJIKAWA II (Kyujiro I).

KAJIKAWA II (Kyujiro I).   Outstanding lacquer artist who worked in Edo approximately from 1661 to 1684. He was the son and pupil of KAJIKAWA I (Hikobei) and is thus known as Kajikawa II, although he is generally credited with being the founder of the Kajikawa family. His real name was Tomohide, but he adopted the art name of Kyujiro. He was particularly well known for his *gyobu nashiji* work and for his excellent black lacquer. He worked for the Tokugawa shogunate and received an honorary title for his outstanding skill. He is probably the most famous artist of the Kajikawa school, and the name Kyujiro was adopted by many subsequent artists of the family. Kyujiro's early works were similar in style to those of Soetsu and his gold lacquer is as superb in quality as that of Korin. Most of his lacquer pieces are unsigned, undoubtedly because they were made for the shogunate and the daimyo. In general, his work is beautifully finished and shows a preference for fine *kirigane* techniques. The decoration of writing boxes, particularly the inside of the covers, was a well-suited area for displaying his talents, which he developed to their greatest advantage.

KAJIKAWA III (Bunryusai).   As the third Kajikawa, he was an outstanding lacquerer who is known to have been working for the shogunate around 1675. He is particularly noted for his excellent inro decorated in *togidashi*. He frequently used the designs of the famous painter Kano Tan'yu as inspiration for his inro decoration. There also appears to have been another artist by this name who worked at the beginning of the 19th century. (See KAJIKAWA BUNRYUSAI below.)

KAJIKAWA IV (Fusataka).   He was probably the fourth Kajikawa. He served the shogunate and worked during the 18th century.

KAJIKAWA V (Hidetaka).   The son of Fusataka, he was the fifth Kajikawa, succeeding to his father's profession. He worked in Edo for the shogunate during the 18th century.

KAJIKAWA BUNRYUSAI (also known as Jiei).   A famous 19th-century artist of the Kajikawa school.

KAJIKAWA HOGETSU.   A skilled lacquerer of the 19th century who followed the style of Korin.

KAJIKAWA TADAZUMI.   Lacquerer of the 19th century.

KAKOSAI (1).   Also known as Shiori. A well-known lacquerer of the Kajikawa school who worked during the early 19th century. He frequently worked in conjunction with one of the Shibayama artists. His pieces were signed with a seal in the form of a vase with handles, closely resembling the Kajikawa seal.

KAKOSAI (2).   Also known as Shozan. Lacquer artist of the 19th century.

KAKUJUSAI.   Metal artist of the late 18th and early 19th centuries of the Goto school. Occasionally executed metal inlays for lacquer ware.

KAKUSENSAI.   Lacquer artist of the late 19th century.

KAMBEI Matano.   Lacquerer of the mid-17th century.

KAMON Shimizu.   An excellent lacquer artist of the late 19th and early 20th centuries who lived in Kanagawa.

KAN.   See RITSUO.

KANETOMO (also known as Yoshi).   A famous lacquer artist of the 18th century who worked for the Tokugawa shogunate.

KANKO Shiba.   Lacquer artist of the late 18th century.

KANO.   A famous school of painters whose designs are frequently found on miniature lacquer ware.

KANSAI.   See KOMA KANSAI I and II.

KANSEI. See KORIN.

KANSEN. A painter who also prepared inro designs.

KANSHI. See RITSUO.

KANSHICHI (1). A lacquer artist of the mid-18th century who was noted for his work in sculptured *tsuishu* lacquer.

KANSHICHI (2). Also known as Seigai. An exceptional lacquer artist of Edo who lived and worked during the Genroku era (1688–1703). He was particularly skillful in producing stylized designs of rippled blue brush-mark waves on a gold ground and hence adopted the name Seigai, which means "blue sea." He was frequently but rather unsuccessfully imitated until Zeshin adopted his wave design and popularized it many years later.

KANSHOSAI (1). See TOYO.

KANSHOSAI (2). Also known as Hakugyoku. Artist of the early 19th century who was given the honorary title of *hoin*.

KANSUKE. See KOMA VII.

KANYOSAI. Outstanding lacquer artist of the early 19th century.

KANZAN (also known as Ipposai). Lacquerer of the 19th century. See also IPPOSAI.

KASHOSAI. Lacquer artist of the 18th century.

KASUKE Suzuki. Lacquerer who worked in Tokyo during the Meiji era. He was particularly skillful in producing "fancy lacquer" in much the same style as that of Hashiichi I and II.

KATATANI. Lacquer artist of the early 19th century.

KATSUFUSA. Metalworker of the 18th century who occasionally made metal inro.

KATSUNOBU (also known as Shoji). Metalworker who occasionally made metal inro.

KAZUHISA. Metalworker of the 19th century. The characters of his name may also be read as Ikkyu (or Ikkiu).

KAZUTOYO. Lacquerer of the 19th century.

KAZUTSUNE. See TATSUKE KAZUTSUNE.

KAZUYUKI Shibayama. 19th-century artist who worked in the Shibayama style.

KEIDO. Skillful wood carver and inro artist of the 19th century.

KEIGAI. Early-19th-century lacquerer who worked in the style of Ritsuo.

KEIZAN. Lacquer artist of the 19th century.

KENJI Senoda. Lacquer artist of the late 19th century.

KENYA. Artist of the first half of the 19th century who was one of the last students of the Ritsuo school. He was born in Kyoto but moved to Edo, where he remained and worked. Like Ritsuo, he was a skillful ceramist and often made works in much the same style as Ritsuo and Kenzan, whom he also admired. He frequently made ceramic inro, netsuke, and ojime. There were three generations of artists who used the name Kenya.

KENZAN Ogata. 1662–1743. Famous potter and noted lacquer artist, the brother of KORIN. His real name was Ogata Shinsho, but he used many different names as signatures on his works, among them Shinsei, Shisui, Shokosai, and Shizui. He adopted the name Kenzan from the name of a kiln which he owned near Kyoto. He was also a painter, and his works are characterized by strength of line and coloring. He was particularly outstanding for his landscapes and his paintings of flowers. Always seeking to enlarge his artistic knowledge, he traveled frequently throughout Japan. His decorative effects are much in the same style as those of Korin: impressionistic, daring, and original. His signature, usually in black or brown, is executed in large characters. His works are frequently imitated and his signature falsified.

KICHIEMON Kobata.   Lacquer artist of the early 19th century.

KICHIGORO Yasukabe.   Lacquer artist of the first half of the 17th century.

KICHOSAI.   Lacquerer of the 18th century.

KIKAKU (also known as Nankosai).   Lacquer artist of the mid-19th century.

KIKU.   Lacquer artist of the 18th century.

KIKUGAWA.   Skillful lacquer artist of the early 19th century.

KIMURA SHIGEHARU.   See FUYU Kuwano.

KINJI (also known as Kinjiro).   Well-known artist of the Kajikawa family who worked during the late 19th century. See also KAJIKAWA.

KINJO Sawamoto.   Lacquer artist of the 19th century.

KINKOSAI.   Lacquerer of the early 19th century.

KINSAI.   Lacquer artist of the 18th century.

KIPPO.   Early-20th-century lacquerer skilled in carved lacquer work.

KISABURO.   See IGARASHI KISABURO.

KISABURO Ueda.   Lacquerer of the mid-19th century.

KIYOHARU.   Skillful lacquerer of the 19th century whose works are rare.

KIYOKAWA.   Outstanding lacquer artist of the late 18th and early 19th centuries who was well known for his fine inro.

KIYONAGA.   See KIYOTOSHI.

KIYONAO.   Inro artist of the 19th century who was skillful in carving and inlaying various and often unusual materials.

KIYOTADA.   See KIYOTOSHI.

KIYOTOSHI Fujiwara.   Metal artist of the 19th century who often made metal inro. Also known as Kiyonaga, Kiyotada, or Tanaka.

KIYOTSUGU.   Metalworker of the 18th century who was a pupil of Otsuki Mitsuoki, the well-known maker of sword furniture. Inro with the signature of Kiyotsugu exist.

KIZAN.   A relatively unknown artist of the late 19th century who was also called Kambayashi Zenshi. Throughout his life he was interested in the art and technique of lacquering and constantly experimented with new techniques, including dry lacquer. He studied the art under Hashimoto Ichizo II. Although he developed several lacquer techniques on his own, they proved too complex and too lengthy to be of commercial value. Kizan signed his works with a seal and a *kakihan*. As a rule his works were relatively small in size, and, rather than offer them for sale, he preferred to give them away to those who would appreciate them. He also carved netsuke.

KIZO.   Lacquerer of the 17th century.

KOAMI.   This is perhaps one of the oldest schools of lacquer artists. First

mention of their works dates back to about 1429, when they were court lacquerers. They retained their highly respected position for about nineteen
successive generations. During all these years they remained in the employ of
the court and the aristocracy and made lacquer articles for imperial ceremonies,
for the residences of the shoguns, for court nobles, and for feudal lords. The
works of this famous family are, on the whole, classical in style. The earlier
Koami lacquer artists did especially fine work in *takamakie* and frequently used
the designs of such master painters as Tosa Mitsunobu, Sesshu, Noami, and
Soami, while later members of the family used designs of the Kano school for
their lacquer decorations. The Koami artists are said to have been among the
first to make use of the designs of painters in this fashion.

KOAMI I (Docho). 1410–78. Founder of the Koami family. His real name was
Toki Shirozaemon, but he later adopted the name Koami. He is also known as
Michinaga. As a boy, he entered the service of the shogun Ashikaga Yoshimasa
and made lacquer articles for the use of the court. He used the designs of such
master painters as Noami, Soami, and Tosa Mitsunobu in his work.

KOAMI II (Dosei). 1429–1500. The eldest son of Docho (Koami I), he succeed-
ed to his father's profession and became Koami II. He was employed by the
Ashikaga shogun and received the honorary title of *hokkyo* for his fine work.
Also known as Michikiyo.

KOAMI III (Sozen). 1457–1527. The third in succession, he was the great-
grandson of Docho and was also known as Munekane. He worked for the
Ashikaga shogunate during the late 15th and early 16th centuries. Also known
as Sokin.

KOAMI IV (Sosho). 1479–1553. The eldest son of Sozen, he was also known as
Munemasa and Sosei.

KOAMI V (Sohaku). 1484–1557. As the younger brother of Sosho, he succeeded to his position, becoming the fifth in line. He was also known as Munenori.

KOAMI VI (Chosei). 1529–1603. The son of Sohaku, he worked for the military
dictator Toyotomi Hideyoshi and was commissioned to make lacquer articles
for the court. For his outstanding work, he received the honorary title of *hokkyo*.
Also known as Nagakiyo and Kurimoto.

KOAMI VII (Choan). 1569–1610. The first son of Chosei, he was also known
as Nagazumi and Nagayasu. He succeeded to his father's profession and in
1603 became Koami VII. When he was only fifteen years old, the military
dictator Toyotomi Hideyoshi saw a sample of his work and commissioned him
to make lacquer furniture and other articles for the court. While traveling in
1610 he fell from his horse and died as a result of this accident.

KOAMI VIII (Chozen). 1589–1613. He was also known as Nagayoshi. The
third son of Chosei, he became the eighth Koami in 1611 but died at an early
age in 1613.

KOAMI IX (Choho). He was also known as Naganori. The fourth son of
Chosei, he became the ninth Koami. At the beginning of the 17th century he
worked for a while in Edo for the shogun Tokugawa Ieyasu, but because he
desired to be a priest rather than a lacquerer, he retired from his profession.
He died in 1622.

KOAMI X (Choju). 1599–1651. The fifth son of Chosei, he was also known
as Kiyokawa and Nagashige. He had been adopted into another family but

returned to the Koami family and in 1623 became the tenth in line, working for the shogun Iemitsu in Edo. He was an expert lacquerer and frequently used designs of the Kano-school masters for his works. He was perhaps one of the best known and most outstanding masters of the Koami family.

KOAMI XI (Choan). 1628–82. As the eleventh Koami, he worked with his father Choju and succeeded him after his death. He was also known as Nagafusa. He worked for the shogun Ietsuna. Like his father, he was a particularly skilled craftsman. He retired from his profession to become a priest, and he then used the name Choan.

KOAMI XII (Chokyu). 1661–1723. Also known as Naganari, Choko, and Chodo. He was the son of Choan (Koami XI) and worked in Edo for the fifth Tokugawa shogun.

KOAMI XIII (Shoho). Also known as Masamine.

KOAMI XIV (Dogai). No other information is available about the fourteenth head of the Koami family.

KOAMI XV (Choko). Son of Dogai (Koami XIV).

KOAMI XVI (Choin). No other information is available about the sixteenth head of the Koami family.

KOAMI XVII (Nagateru). No other information is available about the seventeenth head of the Koami family.

KOAMI XVIII (Nagayuki). No other information is available about the eighteenth head of the Koami family.

KOAMI CHOKEN. Reputed to have been the nineteenth direct descendant of Docho (Koami I).

KOAMI GYOSEI. A member of the Koami family who worked during the 18th century. His works are excellent but very rare.

KOAMI NAGAHARU. Worked during the late 18th and early 19th centuries.

KOAMI NAGATAKA. Worked during the 18th century and made lacquer netsuke as well as other lacquer ware. He produced very delicate, brilliant works.

KOAMI NAGATO (Chogen). 1572–1607. The second son of Chosei (Koami VI), a versatile man and a skillful lacquer artist. At the age of sixteen he was already skillful in the art of the tea ceremony and was acquainted with Furuta Oribe, whom he greatly admired.

KOAMI NAGAYASU II. A member of the Koami family who is thought to have been a relative of Chokyu or Shoho. Also known as Inaba. Worked for the shogunate during the last part of the 18th century.

KOAMI TADAMITSU. Worked during the latter part of the 18th and the beginning of the 19th centuries. Was particularly adept at inro decoration.

KOAMI TADAYOSHI. Lacquer artist of the Koami family.

KOCHOSAI. Lacquer artist of the 19th century.

KOEI. Lacquer artist of the early 19th century.

KOEN. Lacquerer who worked toward the middle of the 13th century and is said to have invented Kamakura-bori. He was a descendant of the celebrated sculptor Unkei.

KOETSU Hon'ami. 1558–1637. One of the earliest and most outstanding lacquer artists of whom we have record. It is generally agreed that the time of Koetsu— that is, the late 16th and the early 17th centuries—is the period when inro first became important as works of art. Born in 1558, Koetsu became the founder of an impressionistic school which flourished in Kyoto. He was a talented painter who studied the painting of the Tosa school, but his originality and his genius for invention would not permit him to be just a follower. Instead he created his own personal and highly individual style. He preferred painting flower and plant subjects and rarely executed figures or birds. His artistic efforts were also felt in many other fields. He was an expert calligrapher and a noted ceramist, often using faience to decorate his lacquer works. A competent *chajin,* he frequently made tea-ceremony utensils of great simplicity and artistic taste, both in pottery and in lacquer. He was a skillful forger and polisher of sword blades. In addition, he was an exceptional master lacquerer.

He invented a style of encrustation on lacquer that used such diverse materials as mother-of-pearl, faience, lead, pewter, and *awabi* (abalone) shell. His inlays of mother-of-pearl are formed by small pieces of shell cut into vertical strips and inlaid side by side in small sections to create the design. His works are characterized by expert planning and boldness of design, and they display an independent style as well as great artistic taste. He was a strongly decorative artist whose somewhat extravagant designs occasionally tend to be grotesque, though they are usually tempered by tasteful simplicity.

Although Koetsu used different art names during his lifetime, such as Jitokusai, Taireian, and Tokuyusai, his lacquer works are generally unsigned, and authenticated pieces are rare. His name and signature are frequently forged. In particular, his larger lacquer works are rarely signed.

He died in 1637, having broken free from the traditional and conventional schools and having created a new style and a new concept of lacquering that were further developed by such expert artists as Tsuchida Soetsu (one of his pupils) and Ogata Korin.

KOFU.   Lacquerer of the late 18th and early 19th centuries.

KOGYOKU (also known as Ipposai).   Skillful lacquer artist who worked at the end of the 18th and the beginning of the 19th centuries. He was also an expert netsuke carver.

KOGYOKUSAI.   Artist of the late 18th century who was a skillful netsuke carver.

KOHEI Shiomi.   Noted lacquer artist of the early 18th century who worked in Kyoto. He introduced a new kind of *hirame nashiji* in which the gold dust was polished to a much greater smoothness than was the custom.

KOHO (also known as Seisei).   Artist of the 19th century who was a skillful lacquerer.

KOHOSAI.   Artist who worked at the beginning of the 19th century.

KOJI (also known as Reishosai).   Lacquerer of the 19th century.

KOJU.   Lacquer artist of the 19th century.

KOKEIREI.   Lacquer artist of the early 19th century.

KOKOSAI Tatsuke.   See TATSUKE KOKOSAI.

KOKUSAI.   18th-century lacquer artist who specialized in carved black lacquer (*tsuikoku*).

KOKYO.   See TATSUKE TAKAMITSU.

KOMA.   Without a doubt the Koma family is one of the most outstanding families of lacquer artists. They were court lacquerers for many successive generations covering a period of almost 200 years. Although there are said to have been members of the family in the employ of the shogun Ashikaga Yoshimasa in the 15th century, it is generally agreed that the actual founder of the Koma school was Kyui, who worked during the 17th century. Eleven generations of the Koma family worked for the Tokugawa shoguns in Edo.

The works of the Koma lacquerers are especially distinguished by their refinement of style, their variety of techniques, and their excellence of craftsmanship. Generally speaking, the Koma artists favored a particular shape of inro for decoration. Such inro are rather flat, fairly wide, rectangular in shape, with slightly convex rounded ends, and gradually flatten at the side edges where the internal cord channels are hidden. This style of inro body is relatively flat and wide in comparison with its overall height and is refined in character and almost classic in style without being extreme in nature.

Another outstanding and distinctively Koma characteristic is the application of colored lacquer in such a manner that a design when studied in direct light appears to be gold but when seen sideways or obliquely appears to be a metallic red. This effect of changing color is attributed to a thin film of fine gold lacquer which is applied over the surface and skillfully polished out so as to appear only under certain lighting conditions. This gold powder is also sometimes added to the lacquer itself so as to produce this startling change when seen sideways. The Koma artists also originated a rich vermilion lacquer of astonishing brilliancy that has a steely metallic sheen when viewed obliquely. This effect is found in their *takamakie* work and particularly on their superb *togidashi* work.

For the most part, the artists of this school favored colored linings and risers, particularly gold, red, and black, in lieu of the more commonly found *nashiji,* and frequently they used combinations of color, such as red linings and gold risers.

Unlike the KAJIKAWA family, the Koma artists had no seal or *kakihan.* They often signed their work with both the family name and the personal name, but there were a great many artists of this school who adopted the same personal name, and therefore we have great difficulty in accurately assigning a date to their individual works or, indeed, in distinguishing between the different artists. There is also, unfortunately, no truly accurate record of their family genealogy. The following list, originally compiled by Shibata Zeshin, appeared in an article in *Kokka* (vol. V).

KOMA I (Kyui). 1600–63. The first Koma, he was noted for his inro and was in the employ of the shogun Tokugawa Iemitsu in Edo from about 1636 until his death in 1663. He was followed by eleven generations of lacquer artists.

KOMA II (Yasuaki or Kyuzo I). Probably the second Koma. Details concerning him are unknown.

KOMA III (Kyuzo II). ?–1715. Also known as Yasumasa, Ankyo, and Kyuhaku I. He was appointed court lacquerer to the shogun Tokugawa Tsunayoshi in 1681, and it is felt that his work excelled that of his father Kyui (Koma I). He is reputed to have studied under Kajikawa Kyujiro. He produced mainly inro and was particularly skillful in *hiramakie* and rich black lacquer backgrounds. He is generally regarded as the founder of the Koma family, and the high standards of his lacquer ware established the family's reputation for fine-quality work of refined taste and elegant style. Along with Koami Chokyu, he was in charge of the lacquer department during the building of the Tosho-gu shrine in 1689.

KOMA IV (Kyuzo III). ?–1732. Also known as Yasuaki and Kyuhaku II. He was appointed court lacquerer to the shogun Tokugawa Ietsugu in 1715. He was the son of Kyuzo II (Koma III).

KOMA V (Kyuzo IV). ?–1758. The son of Kyuzo III, he succeeded to his father's profession and was appointed court lacquerer in 1754.

KOMA VI (Kyuzo V). ?–1794. Also known as Kyuhaku III. He was the son of Kyuzo IV. In 1762 he was appointed court lacquerer and worked for the shogun Tokugawa Ieharu. He was chosen to work on the restoration of the Tosho-gu shrine in Nikko in 1778.

KOMA VII (Kansuke). ?–1795. The adopted son of Kyuzo V, he was appointed court lacquerer to the shogun Ieharu in 1786. He was a particularly skilled craftsman.

KOMA VIII (Rokuemon). ?–1803. The son of Kansuke (Koma VII), he was appointed court lacquerer to the shogun Tokugawa Ienari and worked on the restoration of the Tosho-gu shrine at Nikko.

KOMA IX (Kyuzo VI). ?–1816. Also known as Kyui II and Seiemon, he was the son of Rokuemon (Koma VIII). He was appointed court lacquerer to the shogun Ienari in 1803 and retired in 1815.

KOMA X (Genzo). ?–1842. Also known as Genki, he was the tenth in succession. He is thought to have been the adopted son of Kyuzo VI. Appointed court lacquerer in 1815, he retired in 1840.

KOMA XI (Seibei I). ?–1858. The adopted son of Genzo (Koma X), he was appointed court lacquerer to the shogun Ieyoshi in 1840.

KOMA XII (Seibei II). The son of Seibei I, he succeeded to his father's profession in 1847 and is said to have been the last of the official lacquerers to the court.

Unfortunately the preceding six or seven artists did not maintain the high standards of the Koma name, and little is accurately recorded of their works. Other artists who were pupils of the masters were given permission to adopt the family name, and their works lived up to the quality and standards originally associated with this fine school. Thus we find, in addition to the above names, several others who bear the Koma family name. These are listed below.

KOMA ANTO. Koma inro artist of the 19th century.

KOMA BUNSAI. The second son of Kansai I, he was also a skillful lacquerer and succeeded to his father's profession. He was particularly noted for his black lacquer, both carved and plain, and also made clever imitations of cloisonné enamel on black lacquer. He was also a noted painter, having studied under Tani Buncho. He worked in the late 18th and early 19th centuries.

KOMA ENSHU. A member of the Koma family who worked at the end of the 18th and the beginning of the 19th centuries.

KOMA KANJU. A student of Koma Bunsai who worked during the early 19th century.

KOMA KANSAI I. ?–1792. An exceptionally skilled artist of Edo and the outstanding pupil of Koma Koryu (1), he was not a Koma by birth. His real name was Sakanouchi Jubei, and he also used the names Tanso and Tansei. He was given permission by Koryu to use the family name, and it was he who finally brought the work of the family back to its original high quality. He was an excellent lacquerer and also composed comic poems. He was particularly masterly in *chinkin-bori* and gold-lacquer techniques. He died on April 12, 1792.

KOMA KANSAI II. 1767–1835.   The eldest son of Kansai I, he was also known as Sakanouchi Jubei II. He followed his father's profession and was a lacquerer of great merit—not, however, excelling his father. Although his works are of the highest quality, it was not until one of his pupils, Shibata ZESHIN, attained success that Kansai II received the recognition that he well deserved. He worked for the shogun Ienari. In 1824 he retired from his profession as a lacquer artist and took the name Kosai.

KOMA KANSAI III.   He was the eldest son of Koma Kansai II and followed in his father's profession. He took the name of Kansai III in 1824 after his father retired and continued to work in his father's style.

KOMA KORYU (1).   Also known as Kimura Shichiemon, he was a pupil of Kyuhaku III and was also his brother-in-law. A very skillful craftsman of Edo, he was adopted by his master and permitted to use the family name. He worked from about 1764 to 1789 and had many outstanding pupils, among whom were Omura Gyokuzan and Nomura Kyuho. Many of his works are signed Koryusai. His most famous pupil was KOMA KANSAI I.

KOMA KORYU (2).   Lacquerer at the end of the 18th and the beginning of the 19th centuries.

KOMA KYOSEN.   Lacquer inro artist of the 19th century.

KOMA SADASHIGE.   Lacquerer of the early 19th century. Details of his life are unknown.

KOMA SHIGEMITSU.   Lacquer artist of the Koma school who worked during the 19th century.

KOMA TSUGIHARU.   Lacquerer of the early 18th century.

KOMA YASUAKI.   Artist of the late 18th century.

KOMA YASUMASA.   Lacquer artist of the late 18th and early 19th centuries.

KOMA YASUNORI.   Lacquer artist who worked at the end of the 17th century.

KOMA YASUTADA.   Lacquerer who worked during the late 18th and early 19th centuries. He was an expert artist and produced some excellent lacquer ware. He was particularly good in *togidashi* techniques.

There are many other signatures bearing the family name of Koma, but we have no accurate information concerning the artists. Among the names are Koma Nagachika, Koma Ryusei, Koma Sozan, Koma Yasutomi, Koma Yasuyuki, Koma Yasukuni, Koma Kanya, and Koma Kyusai.

KOMAI.   A 19th-century artist who worked in Kyoto and was known primarily for his metalwork. He was particularly skillful in encrustations of diverse metals, particularly iron, and was outstanding for his execution of geometric designs, which he favored.

KOMIN Nakayama (also known as Sensen). 1808–71.   He became a pupil of Hara Yoyusai and worked in Edo. He was an expert craftsman and was particularly skilled in making imitations of old lacquer ware. He also made elaborate netsuke of fine quality. Because of his outstanding talents he received the honorary title of *hokkyo*. He was one of the renowned lacquer artists of his time. One of his pupils was Ogawa Shomin.

KOMYO.   Lacquer artist of the 19th century who was particularly skilled in executing designs of birds.

KONKAN (also known as Hakuhotei). 1743–1801.   Primarily a metalworker, this artist made some excellent metal inro and many metal encrustations on lacquer inro. He is said to have been one of the most renowned animal carvers, his works being exceedingly realistic. He also carved figures of people and deities.

KORIN Ogata. 1658–1716. Unquestionably one of the most eccentric, brilliant, and original artists as well as the best-known impressionist of the 17th century in Japan, he was born in Kyoto into a family of cultured and artistic background. His great-grandmother was a sister of Koetsu; his grandfather worked for the shogun Ashikaga Yoshiteru; his father Soken was a silk weaver in one of the imperial factories and was also a noted painter of the Koetsu school; and his younger brother Kenzan was a talented artist and an expert potter.

Korin became interested in painting when he was young and studied under Yamamoto Sotei. Later he moved to Edo, where he studied under Kano Tsunenobu and still later under the masters of the Tosa school. He was also greatly influenced by the styles of Sotatsu and Koetsu, whom he admired. In his paintings he displays freedom and originality. His brush strokes are firm and bold; his colors are usually brilliant but in perfect harmony. His works are impressionistic. He loved to paint animals and flowers and was particularly fond of the iris and the chrysanthemum, which we often find depicted in his paintings.

Korin's artistic interests lay in many directions, for not only was he an excellent painter but he was also well versed in the complexities of the tea ceremony and was a miniature-landscape gardener, a gifted potter, a talented designer, and, of course, a master lacquerer. Perhaps one of the most important reasons for the originality of Korin's work was the fact that, unlike most of his contemporaries in art, Korin was not under the patronage of any shogun. Therefore he was free to develop his artistic tastes as he desired instead of being required to manufacture art objects in accordance with the tastes and traditions admired by his sponsors.

Korin's style is one of great freedom, boldness of conception, and originality of design and execution, both in his use of diverse materials and in his impressionistic and at times abstract creations. This is particularly true of his lacquer work. He adopted a style of encrustation in high contrast, using shell, pewter, and lead, among other materials. In contrast to the works of Koetsu, whose style he studied and to some extent followed, his inlays were fashioned in large sections—cut and encrusted as a single mass, the entire body of a bird or a flower sometimes being encrusted in this fashion—rather than in small sections, as was popular at that time. His designs were so impressionistic as to be abstract at times. His lacquer work is best appreciated in his larger pieces, such as writing boxes, which lend themselves better to this decorative effect, inro and *kobako* being too small to show his designs to their fullest advantage.

Another characteristic of Korin's lacquer for which he is well known is his gold-background work, which is outstanding for its rich, soft, reddish color and the warmth of its tone. Being independently wealthy, Korin could well afford to use the best quality of gold for his works. His gold lacquer is usually applied in rather thick layers. Within this gold ground are tiny specks which sparkle like points, giving a rich, lively luster to the ground. This technique of gold points has been imitated and therefore cannot be considered an unfailing method of identifying his true works. Because of his extreme and wholly original style, there were many imitations of his work; in fact, there are probably more forgeries of his name on art objects than of the name of any other Japanese artist. Great care should be taken to determine the authenticity of objects bearing his name, since his true works are rare. In general, his signature is allegedly scratched inside the cover of a piece or written in broad characters. He used many different names during his career, his favorites being Seisei, Chokoken, Doshu, Doso, Hoshuku, Isuke, Jakumei, Seiseido, and Sekimei. He was also known as Kansei and Taisui. Because of his outstanding artistic talents, he received the honorary title of *hokkyo* in 1701.

Korin was at all times a decorative artist. Sometimes his works are not particularly pleasing in their overall effect because of their extreme nature, but they are always expertly conceived and designed. He died in April 1716 at the age of fifty-eight, having exerted much influence of the artists of the 17th and 18th centuries, as well as those to follow later. Among his many pupils was Ritsuo.

KORINSAI. See HASEGAWA KORINSAI (1) and (2).

KORITSUSAI Umehara. See KORYUSAI Umehara.

KORYU (1). Lacquerer of the 18th century. Probably the same as KOMA KORYU (1).

KORYU (2). See KOMA KORYU (2).

KORYUSAI (1). See KOMA KORYU (1).

KORYUSAI (2). A Japanese painter of the second half of the 18th century who occasionally executed lacquer designs. His real name was Oda Shobei. He was a samurai, and because of the quality of his artistic works he received the honorary title of *hokkyo*.

KORYUSAI Umehara. Lacquerer of the 19th century who assisted in the decoration of the Tosho-gu shrine at Nikko. There were several lacquerers with the family name of Umehara.

KOSAI (1). A 19th-century lacquer artist of the school of Zeshin.

KOSAI (2). See TOYO.

KOSAI (3). See TATSUKE KOSAI.

KOSETSU. A 19th-century artist whose real name was Yamashita Oijo. He became a priest and began to study lacquering when he was a young man. He was particularly skilled at carving lacquer, sculpturing leaves and flowers in thick layers of colored lacquer. He became a chief priest in Kyoto and continued his study of lacquering, chiefly in the style of Koetsu. He made many tea-ceremony utensils, netsuke, and other lacquer articles.

KOSHICHI Tomita. A noted lacquer worker of the late 19th early 20th centuries who lived in Kyoto.

KOSHO. Lacquer artist of the 19th century.

KOUNSAI. Lacquer artist of the 19th century.

KOYEI. See KOEI.

KOYETSU. See KOETSU.

KOYO (also known as Ipposai). Lacquerer of the 19th century.

KOZAN (1). Lacquer artist of the 19th century who was also an encruster and a netsuke artist. He was also known as Shohosai and was a pupil of Ritsuo. His lacquer work is excellent.

KOZAN (2). See YOYUSAI.

KUKEI Shimizu. Lacquerer of the 17th century from Kaga.

KUZUI. Lacquer artist of the 19th century.

KUZUI Hamano. One of the well-known metalworkers of the Hamano school. He worked during the 18th century and occasionally did metalwork for inro decoration.

KWAKUJO. See ETSUJO.

KWAN. See RITSUO.

KWANSAI. See KOMA KANSAI I and II.

KWANSHI. See RITSUO.

KWANSHOSAI. See KANSHOSAI (1) and (2).

KYOKUSEN. Lacquerer of the mid-18th century. He was also skilled in wood carving.

KYOKUZAN. This artist was primarily a netsuke carver who worked during the late 18th and early 19th centuries. His name has also appeared on inro.

KYOSUI. A skillful lacquerer of the late 18th and the beginning of the 19th centuries. He also made lacquer netsuke.

KYOZAN Sakai. 1662–? This lacquer artist was a student of Hanzan. He created some excellent work and continued to be active until the middle of the 18th century. He was the third in succession to Ritsuo and styled his work after Ritsuo's. He was also known as Ritsuoso and Haritsu III, although his real name was Sakai Chubei.

KYOZUI Hamano. See NORIYUKI.

KYUBEI Shimizu. A lacquer artist of the 17th century, he worked for Lord Maeda in Kaga Province. He is said to have been a pupil of Igarashi Doho I and took the art name of Ryukei. He created many excellent works exhibiting great delicacy of style.

KYUEMON Nosawa. A skillful lacquerer of the 17th century who was particularly adept at *raden* work. He was a pupil of Ikushima Fujishichi and lived in Nagasaki.

KYUHAKU I. See KOMA III.

KYUHAKU II. See KOMA IV.

KYUHAKU III. See KOMA VI.

KYUHO (also known as Dokoitsu). Lacquer artist of the 19th century who was particularly noted for his gold-lacquer inro.

KYUHO Nomura. Late-18th-century lacquer artist who was a pupil of Koma Kansuke (Koma VII). He worked in Edo and made excellent inro. He was also known as Genzaburo and succeeded Nomura Kyukei.

KYUKEI Nomura. Lacquerer of the 18th century who worked in Edo. Also known as Nomura Jiro. He was the brother of Nomura Chohei and was succeeded in his profession by Nomura Kyuho during the latter half of the 18th century. He studied the art of lacquering under Koma VI.

KYUKOKU (also known as Sanjin). Lacquer artist of the late 18th and the early 19th centuries of the school of Ritsuo. He was particularly adept at the *chinkin-bori* technique.

KYUKOKU Nomura (also known as Sanjin). Inro artist who worked at the beginning of the 19th century.

KYUKOKU Ogawa. Lacquer artist of the 17th century who is reputed to have been the teacher of Ogawa Ritsuo.

KYUSAI. 20th-century Osaka netsuke artist who carved *kanshitsu*.

KYUSHI. Lacquerer of the 18th century.

KYUZO I. See KOMA II.

KYUZO II. See KOMA III.

KYUZO III. See KOMA IV.

KYUZO IV. See KOMA V.

KYUZO V. See KOMA VI.

KYUZO VI. See KOMA IX.

MAE (also known as Taiho). Lacquer artist of the late 19th century. He did expert work in the *chinkin-bori* technique.

MAO LUN. Somada-style inlay artist of the mid-18th century who was most likely Chinese.

MASAAKI Tatsumi (also known as Jirobei). Talented inro artist of the 18th century.

MASAHARU. See GENSHOSAI.

MASAHIDE (also known as Gasan). Metal artist of the early 19th century who belonged to the Ishiguro family. He often made metal inro.

MASAICHI. See MASAKAZU.

MASAKAGE Shiomi. Early-18th-century lacquerer; member of the Shiomi family of lacquerers.

MASAKAZU. Primarily a netsuke artist, he worked during the late 18th and early 19th centuries. He used many different materials for his carvings, including wood, ivory, porcelain, and horn. Occasionally he made *manju* netsuke and disks for *kagamibuta* and also carved inro. He was an excellent artist. He is also known as Masaichi and Shoichi, which are alternate readings of the characters for Masakazu.

MASAKUNI. Artist of the 19th century. Although this name has appeared on inro, it may be that it refers to the designer rather than the actual maker, since there was a painter of the same period named Tosa Masakuni.

MASAMI. Lacquerer of the 19th century.

MASAMINE. See KOAMI XIII.

MASAMITSU Kikugawa. Born in 1822, he was primarily a netsuke carver but often worked in lacquer. His name has appeared on inro. His son Gyokumin succeeded him in his profession.

MASANAGA Sawaki. Metalworker of the 18th century who often made metal inro. He was a member of the famous Nara school of metal artists.

MASANAO. Outstanding netsuke artist who occasionally carved inro. (See chapter on netsuke for further details.)

MASANARI Shiomi. Famous lacquer artist of the 17th and early 18th centuries. Born in Kyoto about 1647, he was a student of the Koma school and specialized in *togidashi* work. He had several art names, among them Kohei, Masazane, and Shoin. His works are characterized by great refinement, delicate workmanship, and extraordinary clarity and transparency of color. The quality of his *nashiji* is unsurpassed.

His works are usually signed on the lower edge of the riser in finely written characters in slightly raised red lacquer, enclosed in an elongated rectangle and looking almost like a seal. His other art names were Masanobu and Shosei.

Quite often his work is confused with that of Shunsho, who also excelled in *togidashi* work. Masanari was particularly skilled in executing designs of animals. He was also a talented painter of the Kano school. From Kyoto he moved to Edo and died there about 1725. He had several followers who used the same name, one of whom worked in the 19th century and was also an excellent lacquerer. His works were frequently forged.

MASANOBU (also known as Shikosai). His real name was Adachi Tomoshichi. Born in 1838, he was a samurai of Owari Province. He later studied carving under Sato Masayoshi and became very skilled in executing fine pierced openwork and tiny detailed scenes in relief on ivory. His name has appeared on ivory inro.

MASASHIGE. Inro artist of the late 18th and early 19th centuries.

MASATOMO Shimizu. Well-known lacquerer of the 17th century.

MASATOSHI. Lacquer artist of the early 19th century.

MASATSUGU. See KAIGYOKUSAI.

MASATSUGU Obata. Lacquerer of the second half of the 17th century.

MASATSUNE (1). Lacquer artist of the first half of the 18th century.

MASATSUNE (2). Also known as Matsugoro, Hirai, and Shokasai. Lacquer artist who worked during the mid-19th century.

MASAYORI. Lacquerer of the 18th century.

MASAYOSHI (Suzuki Shozaemon). Noted inro maker of the mid-18th century who lived in Kyoto.

MASAYOSHI Ishiguro. Metal artist of the late 18th and early 19th centuries who belonged to the Nara school. He originated new designs in metalware, and his work is occasionally found on inro.

MASAYUKI. See SHUNSHO III.

MASAZANE. See MASANARI Shiomi.

MATABEI Iwasa. Artist of the 17th century, he is credited with being one of the founders of the *ukiyo-e* school. Primarily a painter, he is also known to have executed inro decoration.

MATABEI Sasaki. Lacquer artist of the late 16th century who was the founder of the OHARA family of lacquerers. See also JIGOEMON (1).

MATASHIRO. See HARUMASA (2) and SHUNSHO VII.

MATAHEI. See MATABEI.

MATSUDA GONROKU. See GONROKU Matsuda (1) and (2).

MATSUMURA GOSHUN. See GEKKEI.

MEIBUN Hakuge. Netsuke carver who worked during the 19th century. He was most likely a student of Gambun, and his works are marked by details of worm holes and encrusted ants in the manner of Gambun. He occasionally executed inro decoration.

MEICHO. Lacquerer of the 19th century.

MEIO (also known as Joka). Lacquerer of the 17th century.

MEISAI Kajiyama. Lacquer artist of the school of Zeshin who worked in Tokyo during the 19th century. He was particularly skilled in *chinkin-bori* work and also executed designs of birds and plants on a natural wood background.

MEISAN. Skilled lacquer artist of the 19th century.

MICHIKIYO. See KOAMI II.

MICHINAGA. See KOAMI I.

MICHITOMO. See DOYO Shimizu.

MITSUAKI. See SOMADA MITSUAKI.

MITSUHIDE. Lacquer artist of the late 18th century.

MITSUHISA. See SOMADA MITSUHISA.

MITSUMASA (1). See SOMADA MITSUMASA.

MITSUMASA (2). One of the art names of Teijo, a metal carver of the Goto family. His work is occasionally found on inro.

MITSUNOBU (also known as Koshin). Lacquerer of the 19th century.

MITSUNOBU Tosa. 1434–1525. This painter was a celebrated member of the Tosa school, which specialized in the Yamato-e style of painting. He made drawings for the shogun Ashikaga Yoshimasa from which lacquer pieces known as Higashiyama *makie* were created.

MITSUOKI Otsuki. Outstanding sword-furniture and metal artist of the early 19th century. He was particularly skillful in executing animal and fish subjects and had many students. His name is found on inro for which he made metal inlays.

MITSUTADA Fujii. Lacquer artist of the early 19th century.

MITSUTAKA Fujii. Lacquer artist of the second half of the 19th century. Son of Fujii Mitsutada. He was a skillful maker of inro.

MITSUTOSHI Yamamoto. Skillful inro artist of the late 18th and early 19th centuries who worked in Kyoto. Also called Nagahide.

MITSUTSUGU Uno. Artist of the early 18th century who made inro for the daimyo of Hikone, for whom he worked. He was a samurai and created some outstanding works.

MOCHIYOSHI. Lacquer artist of the early 19th century.

MOEI Nakaoji. Skillful inro maker of the early 19th century whose works are relatively rare. He excelled in *togidashi* technique. His art name can be read either Shigenaga or Moei.

MONNIN. Lacquerer of the late 15th century who specialized in sculptured *tsuishu* lacquer.

MONNYU. Lacquer artist of the 15th century who is credited with advancing the art of sculptured lacquer. He lived in Kyoto and is known to have worked there around 1465. He specialized in *tsuishu* and *tsuikoku* lacquer work and also introduced *guri* techniques after the Chinese fashion.

MORIKAZU (1). Lacquer artist of the early 19th century who lived in Kyoto.

MORIKAZU (2). Also known as Shukurinsai. Lacquer artist of the 19th century.

MORIKIYO (also known as Ransai). Lacquerer of early 19th century having title of *hokkyo*.

MORIMASA Gamo. Lacquer artist of the mid-19th century.

MORIMITSU Kiyokawa. Lacquerer of the late 18th and early 19th centuries.

MORISHIGE Shoami. Metal artist who was a member of the outstanding SHOAMI family. He occasionally did metalwork for inro decoration.

MORITOMI Shoami. Metal artist of the early 19th century who often made sword furniture. He was a member of the SHOAMI family, who had been metalworkers from the 15th century on. He occasionally did metalwork for inro decoration.

MOTOBUMI. Lacquerer of the early 17th century.

MOTONOBU Higashiyama. Metal artist of the 19th century who occasionally executed inro decorations.

MOTOSADA. 19th-century lacquer artist who specialized in *chinkin-bori* work.

MOTOTADA Ishiyama. An amateur metalworker who occasionally made metal inro. He was a court noble.

MOTOTOMO Saito. A student of Motozane, this artist was a metalworker of the beginning of the 19th century who occasionally made metal inro. He was a member of the Saito family of metal artists.

MUCHUAN. See RITSUO.

MUNEHIDE (also known as Kosensai). Lacquer artist of the 19th century.

MUNEKANE. See KOAMI III.

MUNEMASA. See KOAMI IV.

MUNENORI. See KOAMI V.

MUNEOKI Kuroji. A metal artist who occasionally executed metalwork for inro decoration. He was a member of the Yakoya family.

MUNETADA Nishimura (also known as Zohiko). Lacquer artist of the second half of the 18th century who worked in Kyoto.

MUNEYOSHI Ohara. 1755–1813. This noted lacquer artist was a son of Jigo-emon (Shigeyoshi). He was the eighth representative of the Ohara family and was succeeded by his brother Yuzo.

NAGAFUSA. See KOAMI XI.

NAGAHARU. See JOI.

NAGAHARU Hirose. A well-known lacquer artist who worked during the latter part of the 18th and the beginning of the 19th centuries. He also used the art names Nagamitsu and Nagatsugu.

NAGAHIDE (1). Lacquerer who specialized in the Wakasa-nuri technique.

NAGAHIDE (2). See MITSUTOSHI Yamamoto.

NAGAKIYO. See KOAMI VI.

NAGAMITSU. Lacquerer of the late 19th and early 20th centuries.

NAGAMITSU Hirose. See NAGAHARU Hirose.

NAGANARI. See KOAMI XII.

NAGASHIGE (Kiyokawa). See KOAMI X.

NAGATAKA. See KOAMI NAGATAKA.

NAGATERU. See KOAMI XVII.

NAGATOMO. Lacquer artist of the 19th century.

NAGATOSHI. There were three well-known and skillful lacquer artists who used this name, all of whom worked at the end of the 18th century.

NAGATOSHI Matsuda. Lacquer artist of the 18th century.

NAGATSUGU. See NAGAHARU Hirose.

NAGAYASU. See KOAMI VII.

NAGAYUKI. See KOAMI XVIII.

NAKAGAWA. Lacquer artist of the 18th century.

NAKATSUGU. See TATSUKE TAKAMITSU.

NAKAYAMA. See SHIBAYAMA.

NANKA (also known as Ichimuken). An artist of the mid-18th century who was primarily a netsuke carver. He specialized in minute details, such as a complete map of Japan etched on a *manju* netsuke. He also executed this type of work on inro. His drawings and characters are so clear that the names of all the stations on the Tokaido are legible in spite of the small surface area. He usually did his fine engraving in black *ke-bori* on ivory grounds.

NAOMASA Yanagawa. A metal artist of the 18th century who made metal inro. He was a member of the Yanagawa family.

NAONORI Hamano. A metal artist who worked in Edo in the mid-18th century. He occasionally executed lacquer decoration in the form of metalware. He was also known as Konakamura and was a student of Yanagawa Naomasa.

NAOTSUGU. Metal artist of the 18th century who made metal inro.

NAOYUKI. See RITSUO.

NARIKADO Hirata. A metalworker and enameler of the Hirata family who executed lacquer decorations. He worked during the first half of the 18th century.

NEMOTO. Lacquerer and encruster of the 19th century.

NIKOSAI. Lacquerer of the early 19th century.

NOBUHIDE (also known as Fusensai). Inro artist of the early 19th century.

NOBUYOSHI Somada. 18th-century artist who lived in Kaga. He was a lacquerer and specialized in encrustation of *aogai* shell in the Somada-school fashion.

NOMURA. The name of a family of lacquer artists who were descendants of Nomura Yoshiyuki Shirobei, a lacquerer of the 17th century.

NORINOBU. Metal artist of the beginning of the 19th century. He made sword furniture, and his metalwork is sometimes found on inro. His real name was Hamano Kuzui II.

NORINOBU Kano. A painter of the Kano school who designed inro decoration.

NORISUE Kiyohara. One of the earliest lacquer artists of whom there is record. He is reputed to have worked in the late 12th century.

NORIYUKI. Metal artist of the Hamano school whose work appeared on inro during the second part of the 18th century. He was also known as Kyozui.

OGATA. Surname of a famous family of lacquer artists of the 17th and 18th centuries. See KENZAN and KORIN.

OGAWA. See RITSUO and SHOMIN.

OHARA. Surname of a family of lacquer artists. See JIGOEMON (3), (4), MUNEYOSHI, and YUZO.

OSAI. Lacquerer of the mid-19th century who worked in Kyoto.

OSHIN. Lacquer artist of the mid-19th century.

OSUMI Seki (also known as Shoko). Lacquer artist of the mid-19th century.

OTEKI Nagano. See YOKOBUE I and II.

REISAI. See ZESHIN.

REISAI Shibata. A noted lacquerer of the 19th century, he was the eldest son of Shibata Zeshin and succeeded to his father's profession.

REIYA. See ZESHIN.

RENJO. Lacquer artist of the early 19th century.

RICHO. Lacquer artist of the mid-19th century.

RICHU. A Chinese lacquer artist of the late 18th century whose name has appeared on inro.

RIHEI Yamamoto. 1735–66. Lacquer artist of the second half of the 18th century.

RINANKEI. Lacquer artist of the 19th century.

RINCHOKEN. Lacquer artist of the early 18th century who was especially noted for his work in *chinkin-bori* technique.

RINZAI. See HIDETSUGU IV.

RISHUSAI. Lacquer artist who worked at the beginning of the 19th century.

RITSUO. 1663–1747. This famous artist of the late 17th and early 18th centuries was a man of many talents and interests. He was a strong-minded, unconventional person of eccentric nature. Born in the province of Ise, he was a student and contemporary of Korin and a lacquerer of the impressionistic Koetsu school who introduced a slight Chinese flavor into his works. He was also a talented painter of the Tosa school, a samurai well versed in the use of arms, a metalworker, a wood carver and sculptor, an expert potter (having studied the craft under Kenzan), and a clever poet who was a friend and student of Basho. He was also an expert lacquerer who studied lacquering under Ogawa Kyokoku.

Having a restless nature, he loved to travel rather than remain for any length of time in one place. He is well known by the name Ogawa Haritsu, *haritsu* meaning "broken hat" and referring to a tattered cane sun hat in which he would wander about. At one time in his life, Ritsuo, in spite of all his talents, was so poor that he was forced to sell clay dolls in the streets in order to support himself. Later in his life he worked for the daimyo of Tsugaru.

He was a creative artist of great boldness and distinction and introduced into his works (which were always of his own design) a combination of his many talents. Above all, he decorated his wares with encrustations in colorful relief of many materials: ivory, jade, mother-of-pearl, tortoise shell, coral, *tsuishu* sculptured lacquer, and others, and particularly faience and pottery. He was very clever at creating pottery and lacquer ware which resembled perfectly the color and texture of wood, stone, bronze, and other metals. He rarely used a lacquer background but preferred to encrust his decorations on plain or lightly lacquered natural wood, fine basket-woven bamboo, or cherry bark. Generally he preferred using a background of rough, aged, wormholed wood in an attempt to overcome any coarseness or gaudiness that might be created by his rather large colorful inlays. Indeed, frequently only the linings and risers of of his inro are lacquered. His works display great originality and artistic arrangement of color and texture and material. His favorite subjects included broken Chinese ink cakes, dried fish, badgers, and old mirrors partly covered with moss and mold. His works became known as Haritsu ware.

Ritsuo also made netsuke, frequently of black wood and often in *manju* style, in which he would encrust decorations of ceramics and other materials. He also made *kagamibuta* disks of pottery.

His works are signed with a characteristic seal which is a small rectangular green porcelain plaque containing the character *kan* (in old-style romanization, *kwan*). Sometimes he added a second, similar seal containing the characters for Haritsu. It should be noted that Mochizuki Hanzan, who was his best pupil and later succeeded him as Haritsu II, also used the *kan* seal.

Ritsuo used many different names during his career. His real given name was Kin'ya, which he later changed to Heisuke. One of his earliest art names was Dojin; later ones were Shoko, Sou, Bokanshi, Ukanshi, and Muchuan. His best known art names, however, are Naoyuki, Ogawa Haritsu, Kan (Kwan), Kanshi (Kwanshi), and Ritsuo. He had many followers, and his works were often imitated and his seal forged.

ROJIN (also known as Kyonei).   Mid-19th-century lacquer artist.

ROKUEMON.   See KOMA VIII.

ROSHU (also known as Seiryuun or Hoshi Ryuun).   Artist of the first half of the 19th century who lived in Edo and was particularly skilled in *tsuishu* sculptured-lacquer carving.

RYOGAKU.   Lacquerer of the 19th century.

RYOSEI. 1599–1667.   Lacquer artist of the early 17th century. He was the eldest son of Koami Nagato.

RYOUNSAI.   Lacquer artist of the 19th century.

RYU (also known as Hogen).   Artist of the late 18th century.

RYUEI.   Netsuke artist of the 19th century who occasionally made inro.

RYUGYOKUSAI.   19th-century artist who was primarily a netsuke carver.

RYUHEISAI Asada.   Lacquer artist of the late 19th century who lived in Kyoto.

RYUKEI (1).   Skillful artist of the early 19th century from Edo. He was primarily a netsuke carver but also often worked in lacquer. His works are executed with detailed realism. Because of his outstanding talents he was awarded the honorary title of *hokkyo*.

RYUKEI (2).   See KYUBEI.

RYUSAI Yoshida.   An excellent lacquer artist of the 19th century of the school of Zeshin. He made reproductions of ancient works in Nara.

RYUSHIN Umezawa.   Lacquer artist of the 19th century. He was the youngest son of Zeshin, and his work is executed in the Zeshin style.

SADACHIKA.   Lacquer artist of the 18th century.

SADAJI.   An artist of the school of Ritsuo.

SADAMASA.   Lacquer artist of the early 18th century.

SADAYASU Kiyohara.   Noted lacquer artist of the 12th century.

SADAYASU.   Skilled lacquer artist of the 18th century.

SADAYUKI (also known as Teizui, which is another reading of the same characters). Primarily a netsuke carver who worked during the 19th century.

SADO Suzuki. Lacquer artist who worked during the second half of the 19th century.

SAICHI Matsui. Lacquerer of the 19th century.

SAJI TADASHI. Young lacquer artist of the 20th century who worked in Tokyo.

SAKENAGA. Lacquer artist of the early 19th century.

SAMPEI. Lacquer artist of the 19th century. He was also a noted potter.

SANEKIYO (also known as Kaan). Lacquer artist of the first half of the 18th century.

SANESHIGE. Lacquer artist of the 18th century.

SANKURO Yamauchi. Talented lacquer artist who worked during the late years of the 17th century. He is credited with having originated Noshiro Shunkei lacquer ware. He lived in the district of Hida and later migrated to Noshiro in Akita Prefecture.

SANZAEMON Narita. Lacquerer of the first half of the 17th century. He lived in Takayama (Hida district) and invented Hida Shunkei lacquer ware.

SATO. Lacquerer of the mid-19th century.

SATSUGA Yamada. Lacquer artist who lived and worked in Edo in the mid-18th century.

SAWADA Sotakusai (also known as Jisaku). 1830–1915. A fine lacquer artist who worked in Kanazawa. He studied the art of lacquering from Umeda Sagoro and later originated his own school. He was particularly skillful in Kaga-style lacquering. His eldest son, Ryotaro, became his successor and took the name of Sotakusai II.

SEIAMI. A famous lacquerer of Kyoto who worked during the early 16th century. A specialist in lacquering tea-ceremony utensils, he was in the employ of the *chajin* Sen no Rikyu and (later) Furuta Oribe, as well as the shogun Hideyoshi, from whom he received an honorary title for his outstanding work. He was also known as Shoho and was succeeded for three generations through the 16th and 17th centuries.

SEIBEI. A very skillful inro maker of Osaka who lived during the early 18th century. He was particularly noted for the accuracy of fit and design of his inro cases, which could be interchanged without any detrimental effect on the design. Indeed, so well did each case fit that any change was not noticeable. On his way to Edo to work for the shogun, he fell from his horse and met an untimely death at an early age.

SEIBEI I. See KOMA XI.

SEIBEI II. See KOMA XII.

SEIEMON. See KOMA IX.

SEIETSU Tsuchida. Lacquer artist of the impressionistic Koetsu school.

SEIHO. Lacquerer of the late 19th century.

SEIJI. Lacquer artist who is known to have been a student of Ritsuo.

SEIJO (also known as Kiyonao). Metal artist of the Goto school who worked during the mid-19th century and occasionally made metal inro.

SEIKAI. See GEMBEI.

SEIKANSAI. Lacquerer of the mid-19th century.

SEIKAWA. Lacquer artist of the late 18th and early 19th centuries.

SEIKEN. See SHUNSHO X.

SEIRO. Lacquer artist of the 19th century.

SEISEI. See KORIN.

SEISEI Shiomi. Lacquer artist who worked at the end of the 17th and the beginning of the 18th centuries. He worked in Kyoto and was noted for his originality and style. He specialized in *togidashi* lacquer work in gold and in color.

SEISHI (also known as Noriyuki). Lacquer artist of the 20th century presently executing miniature articles of excellent quality, particularly in *togidashi* and *hiramakie* techniques.

SEISHIN Hishida (also known as Gennojo). Lacquer artist who worked during the second half of the 17th century.

SEKIGAWA. Inro artist who used designs and plaques of the Hirata family, famous cloisonné workers, for encrustations on his works. He worked at the end of the 18th century.

SEKISAI. A very skillful lacquer artist of the early 19th century who was well known for his *chinkin-bori* work.

SENJUSAI. Well-known inro artist of the 18th century.

SENREISAI. Celebrated inro artist of the 17th century. He was well known for producing excellent lacquer as well as skillful encrustations. Another artist by the same name worked during the 19th century.

SENSEI (also known as Seino). Skillful lacquerer who worked in Tokyo during the late 19th and early 20th centuries. He is said to have been the teacher of Shirayama Shosai.

SENSEN. See KOMIN.

SESSEN. Artist of the late 18th and early 19th centuries who was a painter and also executed inro designs. His real name was Tsukioka Ban'u. He worked in Edo and was also known by the art names of Chogaro and Honjo. He was a student of Torin III and of Settei.

SESSHO Nara. Lacquer artist of the mid-17th century.

SHIBATA. See ZESHIN.

SHIBAYAMA. A famous family of inro artists founded at the end of the 18th century whose works are marked by minute encrustations of diverse materials. This style became increasingly popular during the 19th century, when the trend in lacquer decoration shifted toward gaudy and elaborate detail. This type of encrustation entailed great technical craftsmanship which contrasted with the simple, tasteful, refined, and subtle qualities of older works. However, the care and attention given to the carving of the smallest details—so as to make the tiny faces, hands and other objects completely realistic—is indeed an artistic achievement in itself. It was this school that introduced encrustations of mosaic carvings of different materials which simulated flesh-colored lifelike images. The encrustations of the Shibayama family differed from the inlaid work of previous schools in many ways. In contrast to the Chinese mode of encrustation of shell flush with the lacquered surface, such as practiced by Aogai Chobei, this later work was inlaid in high relief in a manner similar to that of the school of Korin. Korin, however, used large, bold inlays to create an overall impression and made no attempt to carve the inlays other than to satisfy the needs of the decorative effect. The Shibayama artists, on the other hand, carefully sculptured their encrustations, giving the tiny pieces a three-dimensional appearance. The pieces were intricately carved and minutely detailed, and frequently they were tinted so as to appear as realistic as possible. The word Shibayama has come to be a generic term for this type of work rather than being merely a family name.

Although many artists of this school made netsuke in the same style, their work is most frequently found on inro, particularly on a gold background. Generally the gold lacquer was prepared by one artist and the encrusted work added by another, and many of these inro bear two signatures: one of the lacquerer and the other of the encruster. Members of the family often worked with lacquerers of the late Kajikawa school who would prepare and finish the lacquer ground. The eldest Shibayama worked with Shokasai, Kanshosai, the Kajikawa, and other early-19th-century inro makers. These works are usually encrusted with the name Shibayama carved in a small pearly-white rectangular plaque, the name of the lacquerer being signed independently. The early artists carved their figures to give a three-dimensional effect and used many different materials to best suit their needs, such as colored ivory or soapstone for hands and faces and bits of metal, tortoise shell, malachite, jade, or coral for the trimming of clothing, for jewelry like bracelets and earrings, and for the pupils of the eyes. The lacquer background carried out the decorative effect and added the finishing touches to the design. The early works are detailed yet tastefully designed. As this type of work became more and more popular, however, less care was given to artistic and subtle decoration, and more attention was focused on elaborateness of detail. The decorations tended to become too busy, too crowded, and too gaudy. Indeed, many artists now had helpers who did nothing but prepare the lacquered background, which became merely a surface upon which to encrust the design.

Shibayama work continued to flourish well into the present century, with increasing deterioration of quality as artists felt the need to cut costs and increase production and as inro and similar objects came to be produced for commercial markets rather than for utilitarian purposes. Very late works of the school usually appear on ivory backgrounds and bear the Shibayama name only, if indeed any name at all. For the most part these objects lack the exquisite details of depth of dimension and subtlety of coloring and expression and consist, instead, of flat, conventional forms cut out of colored pieces of mother-of-pearl and poorly and shallowly inlaid. The designs on the inlaid shell—for example, flower petals—are not carved but are merely formed by shallow grooving of the shell. They are easily distinguished from the earlier works by their lack of individuality and by the omission of subtle and artistic detail.

SHIBAYAMA DOSHO (also known as Senzo).   This artist is generally credited with being the founder of the family. He worked during the second half of the 18th century. His real name was Onogi Senzo, and he was originally a farmer, living in Shibayama in Shimo-osa Province (in the present Chiba Prefecture). He later moved to Edo, where he worked as an artist and established the Shibayama school. He had many followers and was succeeded by his grandson Ekisei.

SHIBAYAMA EKISEI.   Grandson of the founder of the Shibayama school, this skillful artist worked during the late 18th and early 19th centuries.

SHIBAYAMA NAOYUKI.   Worked as an encruster during the 19th century.

SHIBAYAMA SOICHI.   Worked as an encruster during the 19th century.

SHIBAYAMA YASUMASA (also known as Ekisei).   Worked as an encruster during the 19th century.

SHIBAYAMA YASUMUNE.   See YASUMUNE.

SHIBAYAMA YASUNAO.   See YASUNAO.

SHIBAYAMA YASUNOBU.   Worked as an encruster during the 19th century.

SHIBAYAMA YASUTAKA.   Worked as an encruster during the 19th century.

SHIBAYAMA YASUYUKI.   See YASUYUKI.

SHIBAYAMA YOSHIN.   Skillful artist and encruster of the 19th century.

Although the Shibayama family of artists is not very old, we have practically no information regarding its many members and followers because of the tradition of signing the family name only. Other known members of the Shibayama family who worked during the 19th century include Shibayama Ekisei II, Kazuyuki, Somei, Yasumune, Yasunao, Yasuyuki, Ekiji, Ekishin, and Ekishu. Followers of the Shibayama school who worked during the 19th century include Ekiso, Isshi, Nakayama, Tozan, Michiyama, Nakamura, Shibatama, and Tamashiba.

SHIBUYA.   Lacquer artist of the late 18th century.

SHIGEAKI.   Metalworker of the 18th century who frequently made metal inro.

SHIGEHIDE.   Lacquer artist of the late 18th and early 19th centuries.

SHIGEKATA (also known as Bashoken).   Lacquerer of the 18th century.

SHIGEMASA.   Lacquer artist of the 18th century.

SHIGEMITSU.   See KOMA SHIGEMITSU.

SHIGENAGA Nakaoji (1).   See MOEI.

SHIGENAGA (2).   Inro artist of the 19th century. He excelled in lacquering in *togidashi* technique. His work resembles that of SHIGENAGA (1), but he signs his name with a different character for "NAGA."

SHIGENORI.   Lacquer artist of the 18th century.

SHIGEOKI.   Inro artist of the late 18th and early 19th centuries who worked in the style of Ritsuo.

SHIGETANE.   Artist of the 18th century who did excellent lacquer work.

SHIGETSU (also known as Masanori).   Inro artist of the 19th century who was particularly skilled in *togidashi* work.

SHIGETSUGU.   Lacquer artist of the 19th century.

SHIGETSUNE.   Metalworker of the 18th century who is known to have made metal inro.

SHIGEYOSHI.   See HASEGAWA SHIGEYOSHI and JIGOEMON (4).

SHIKO Ishii. 1872–1927.   Well-known lacquer artist of his time who had many pupils.

SHIMODA.   Skillful artist of the late 17th century. He lived in Kyoto and had many pupils who followed his style.

SHIN.   See ZESHIN.

SHINSABURO Koami.   Lacquerer of the 19th century.

SHINSAI. Son of Shibata Zeshin. Worked during the 19th century, following his father's style.

SHINZAEMON (also known as Sorori). Lacquer artist of the 16th century who was primarily a lacquerer of sword sheaths. He was in the employ of Hideyoshi and worked for the court.

SHIOMI. See IPPOSAI, MASANARI Shiomi, and TOMOHARU Shiomi.

SHIROBEI. Skillful lacquer artist who lived and worked in Kyoto around the end of the 17th century. He was well known for his decorations using encrustations of mother-of-pearl and had many pupils who copied his style.

SHISUI (also known as Rokkaku). 1867–1950. One of the outstanding lacquer artists and teachers of the art of lacquering in modern days. As a student he worked under Ogawa Shomin, and his early works were influenced by Shomin's classical style. From 1904 to 1908 he worked for the Boston Museum. Upon his return to Japan he became a lecturer and later a professor at the Tokyo School of Fine Arts. He became interested in the techniques of ancient lacquer ware and created a complex lacquer technique of his own upon which he worked until his death.

SHOAMI. A noted family of metal artists founded in the 15th century. Different members of the family had separate workshops and adopted different styles. They established various schools throughout Japan and worked for many generations, producing a great variety of styles and techniques of metalware. Members of the family occasionally executed metalwork for inro decoration.

SHOBEI Yamamoto. Well-known lacquer artist of the late 18th century who worked in Nagoya.

SHOGA Enami. Lacquer artist and inro maker of the 18th century.

SHOGEN Doi. Lacquer artist of the 17th century.

SHOGETSU. Lacquerer of the 17th century.

SHOGYOKUSAI. Lacquerer of the 19th century who was in the service of the Matsudaira family.

SHOHEI Hagiwara. Metal artist of the second half of the 19th century whose name is occasionally found on metal inro.

SHOHO (1). See KOAMI XIII.

SHOHO (2). Lacquerer of the 19th century.

SHOHO (3). See SEIAMI.

SHOHOSAI. Noted inro maker of the 19th century.

SHOJIRO Suzuki. Lacquerer of the late 18th century.

SHOJO. See TATSUKE SHOJO.

SHOJU. Lacquer artist of second half of 19th century.

SHOKASAI (also known as Yasutada). Outstanding inro artist of the early 19th century. He belonged to the Kajikawa school of lacquering and worked in Edo. He frequently worked with members of the Shibayama family, who did encrustations for his inro. He was a very skillful artist.

SHOKO. See RITSUO.

SHOMIN Ogawa. 1847–1891. Born in Edo, he was an outstanding lacquer artist of the second half of the 19th century. He came from an artistic background, his father being a metal artist as well as a lacquerer. He studied painting with Ikeda Koson and at the age of sixteen became a pupil of the noted lacquerer Nakayama Komin. He was an expert in imitating the works of the old masters and later worked for the imperial court, where he reproduced and reconstructed many old lacquer works for the court collection. His decorations frequently included cypress and pine trees (the character *sho* in his name means "pine tree"). He was also well known for his lacquer imitations of bamboo and natural wood. In 1889 he helped to organize the Japan Lacquer Art Society, and later he was appointed head of the lacquer department at the Tokyo School of Fine Arts.

SHOMOSAI (also known as Masamitsu). An outstanding inro artist of the late 18th and early 19th centuries. He was well known as a lacquerer and often worked with artists of the Shibayama school, who executed encrustations for his inro decorations.

SHORI (also known as Kakosai). Lacquerer of the early 19th century.

SHORIN. Lacquer artist of the 19th century.

SHORINSAI. Lacquer artist of the late 18th and early 19th centuries.

SHORITSUSAI (also known as Tatsuei). Lacquer artist of the late 18th and early 19th centuries.

SHORYUSAI. Lacquer artist of the 18th century who was a specialist in executing designs in *sumie togidashi*.

SHOSABURO (also known by the title *makie-shi*, meaning "lacquerer"). Lacquer artist of the early 18th century who lived in Fukuromachi, Kanagawa.

SHOSAI Shirayama. 1853–1923. An expert lacquerer who worked in Tokyo during the late 19th and early 20th centuries. He became a professor of the Tokyo School of Fine Arts and, because of his outstanding talent, was made a court artist. He worked for the emperor Meiji on the interior decoration of the Imperial Palace, then under construction. Only the most outstanding lacquer artists were selected to participate in this undertaking. He had studied lacquering under Seino Sensai, and his works display intricate, minutely detailed, and beautiful workmanship in a great variety of lacquer techniques. They are characterized not only by perfection of technical craftsmanship but also by extremely refined, subtle, and tasteful designs. Shosai is well known for the outstanding quality and exceptional brilliance of his gold *nashiji*. He also made perfect imitations of the designs and styles of Yamamoto Shunsho. He is regarded as one of Japan's greatest modern lacquer artists.

SHOSENSAI (also known as Gyokuzan). Inro artist of the 19th century.

SHOSHINSAI Iwami. Lacquerer of the 18th century.

SHOTAI. Skillful lacquer artist of the 20th century who was a pupil of Shirayama Shosai.

SHOTO. Lacquerer of the late 18th and early 19th centuries.

SHOUNSAI. Skillful lacquer artist of the 19th century. He was the father of the outstanding lacquer artist Ogawa Shomin.

SHOYA. Lacquer artist of the late 18th century.

SHOZAN (also known as Kakosai). Outstanding inro maker of the late 18th and early 19th centuries.

SHU. Lacquer artist of the early 20th century. He came from a family of Shinto priests and was himself a priest before he studied lacquering. He was particularly skilled in gold lacquer work and developed a style of his own. He worked mostly in Kyoto and in 1931 was appointed a teacher at the Imperial Art Academy. He made lacquered netsuke as a hobby.

SHUGETSU. Lacquer artist of the 18th century.

SHUGYOKUSAI. Artist of the early Shibayama school.

SHUHO Enami. Lacquer artist of the 18th century.

SHUKO. Lacquer artist of the late 18th century.

SHUKOSAI. Lacquerer of the 18th century who was also a netsuke carver.

SHUMIN Funabashi. Lacquer artist of the 19th century who worked in Edo.

SHUMMEI (also known as Haruaki, which is another reading of the characters for Shummei). 1786–1859. One of the outstanding metalworkers of the early 19th century. His real name was Kono Haruaki. He studied metal art under Naoharu, and his style is somewhat similar to that of the Goto school, although more flexible. His works are executed in low relief and often have encrustations of varying materials. They are free in style, and the subject matter is depicted in a realistic manner. He occasionally executed metalwork for lacquer decoration. For his outstanding talent he was awarded the honorary title of *hogen*.

SHUNKEI. Lacquer artist of the late 14th century. He invented a lacquer technique which bears his name: Shunkei-nuri. He lived at Sakai near Osaka and worked during the reign of the emperor Gokameyama (1383–92).

SHUNKYO. A Chinese artist of the 18th century whose designs are found on inro.

SHUNSEI. Lacquer artist of the 17th century. He was a pupil of the first Shunsho and followed his style.

SHUNSHO (also known as Yamamoto Shunsho). An outstanding school of lacquer artists founded in the mid-17th century. Members of the family continued to work for at least eleven generations. They are particularly well known for their *togidashi* work, which is unsurpassed. Their works are marked by great refinement of taste, delicacy of coloring, variety of tints and tones, and background surfaces of highly polished, mirrorlike brightness. The entire lacquer object was so skillfully polished and finished that it had a radiant, sparkling quality and appeared almost as if to glow. The perfection of the lacquer and the rich, velvety quality of the ground give testimony to the skill and painstaking work done by members of the Shunsho family.

Their *togidashi* work differs from that of most other schools in that it is not marked by sharp, rigid outlines but has a lovely soft quality that could be obtained only through endless polishings guided by expert judgment and experience. The design seems to flow out of the background rather than to appear sharply etched against it. Frequently the entire design is created in tints of gold and brown only. All surfaces of the objects are expertly finished, no detail of riser or lining having been overlooked or slighted. Little attempt is made to use encrusted decorations, and lacquer in high relief is not found on Shunsho works.

Members of the school, particularly the early artists, rarely signed their works, but, when they did, they used the family name or seal only, thus making it virtually impossible to distinguish one artist from another. The later Shunsho artists popularized *ukiyo-e* subject matter in their lacquer work, using *togidashi* technique and many beautiful colors which were striking but somewhat gaudy.

SHUNSHO I (Yamamoto Shunsho). 1610–82. Born in Kyoto, he was the founder of the school. During his youth he was a student of the Chinese classics and also a poet, as well as a painter of the *ukiyo-e* school. However, he became interested in the art of lacquering, and it was this art in which he excelled. His high quality and superb workmanship was a guide for the generations who succeeded him. He was also known as Shuboku.

SHUNSHO II (Yamamoto Kageharu, also known as Kagemasa). Son of Shunsho I, he succeeded to his father's profession and worked in Kyoto, where he died in 1707. He was followed by his son Masayuki (Shunsho III) and his grandson Harutsugu (Shunsho IV), who were also expert lacquerers.

SHUNSHO III (Masayuki). 1654–1740. Son of Shunsho II, he continued to work in Kyoto as a very fine and talented artist. He was also known as Josho.

SHUNSHO IV (Harutsugu). 1703–70. Son of Shunsho III, he continued in his father's profession, working in Kyoto. He was also known by several other names, among them Hachizaemon, Sekizan, and Tozan.

SHUNSHO V (Jirobei). Born in 1734, he was a very talented and famous inro artist. He moved from Kyoto to Nagoya, where his descendants continued to work.

SHUNSHO VI (Masanori). Son of Shunsho V, he succeeded to his father's profession and continued to work in Nagoya, where he died in 1803.

SHUNSHO VII (Matashiro). 1774–1831. An outstanding artist who made many fine inro. He was also known as Bokusai, Masayuki, and Seishi.

SHUNSHO VIII (Masanori). Details unknown.

SHUNSHO IX (Masakane). Younger brother of Shunsho VIII. Died in 1877.

SHUNSHO X (Shosho, also known as Seiken). Because of illness he was unable to continue his work and retired from his profession. Died in 1878.

SHUNSHO XI (Masakane). The second son of Shunsho IX, he was the eleventh direct descendant of Shunsho I.

SHUNSUI (also known as Ganshosai). Lacquerer of the early 19th century, he was known to be a talented inro artist.

SHUNZO Fujikawa (also known as Bunkido). Lacquer artist of the 19th century who lived in Takamatsu. He was the younger brother of the well-known lacquer artist Zokoku.

SHURAN. Early-19th-century carver of *tsuishu* lacquer.

SHUTOHO Mizutani. Inro artist of the late 18th and early 19th centuries.

SHUTSUYOSAI. Lacquer artist of the late 19th century.

SHUZAN Yamamoto (also known as Ribei). 1743–91. Lacquer artist.

SOAMI (Kangaku). 1472–1525. One of the most famous artists of the late 15th and early 16th centuries. He was the grandson of the well-known Buddhist priest Naomi and, like his grandfather, was an expert painter as well as a poet and a *chajin*. He was in the service of the Ashikaga shogun Yoshimasa and executed designs for lacquer which were called Higashiyama *makie*. In painting, he was particularly noted for his flowers, birds, and landscapes. As a master lacquerer, he was skilled in *hiramakie* technique. He was also known as Shinso, Shosetsusai, and Shosessai. His real works are rare, but his signature is often forged. He was succeeded in his profession by several members of his immediate family.

SOCHO Sekino.   Lacquer artist of the first half of the 17th century in Kyoto who is credited as having been the first to sign his inro in lacquer, previous signatures always having been engraved or etched into the lacquer. Some authorities claim that this artist's name was Seki Munenaga Hosunsai.

SOCHOSAI.   Lacquer artist of the 18th century.

SOETSU Tsuchida.   One of the most celebrated lacquer artists of the 17th century. He worked in Kyoto and was also known as Hanroku. He was the outstanding pupil of Koetsu and is best known for his magnificent inro decoration. Soetsu employed acetate of iron for his black lacquer backgrounds, which have gradually changed color through the years and have become a rich, dark brown. Since he used this compound exclusively, this is one means of identifying an authentic article by Soetsu. Another characteristic of his work is that he used small vertical strips of mother-of-pearl, carefully fitted together side by side, to form his encrusted designs. He believed that shell so cut could be more carefully molded to fit the curved background surface than the more commonly used mother-of-pearl cut into the desired shape and encrusted in one piece. He used diverse materials, such as pewter, lead, and other alloys for his encrustations. His works are marked by great refinement of style and perfection of finish. They are usually designed in the impressionistic style of the Koetsu school.

Soetsu frequently signed his inro, not only with his name but also with his age at the time of executing the work. According to the records, there are many inro marked "81 years," "85 years," and even greater ages. Soetsu worked during the last part of the 17th century, but the exact dates of his birth and death are not known.

SOHAKU.   See KOAMI V.

SOIN Ozaki.   Lacquer artist of the late 16th and early 17th centuries.

SOKIN.   See KOAMI III.

SOKYU Negoro.   18th-century artist of Osaka. He was a dentist by profession and made lacquer ware and netsuke as a hobby. He was a very skillful carver and adopted the name Negoro from the lacquer with which he decorated his works.

SOMADA.   The Somada style of lacquering developed in the mid-18th and 19th centuries. The early Somada artists were lacquerers to the head of the Maeda family. The Somada school specialized in skillful, intricate mosaic encrustations of rich, highly colorful iridescent *aogai* shell and often tiny pieces of gold and silver foil. This type of lacquer decoration was similar to that of the Chinese Ming style used by Aogai Chobei, although it developed into a much more lavish and decorative technique than had previously been employed. The Somada artists used tiny flakes of rainbow-colored shell, sliced paper-thin and imbedded flush with the lacquered surface. Their black-background lacquer is deep in color and usually of excellent quality. No pattern, landscape, flower, figure, or animal was too complex to be executed in this technique by these highly skilled craftsmen. For their decorative surfaces, members of the school chose chiefly inro and other small boxes, such as *kobako*. Their works are rarely signed, and if they are signed at all it is with the family name only. The word "Somada" has come to be a generic term used to describe this style of lavish and highly colorful encrustation. The style is also often referred to as "green-shell decoration" because of the sparkling, radiant quality of the shell which was used. The late works of the school have a tendency to be too elaborate and decorative, as though the artist had been determined only to exhibit his superb technical skill instead of producing primarily an artistic lacquer creation. Members of the Somada school often made netsuke in the same style, and occasionally large storage boxes and small cabinets were also produced. We also find matching works of inro, ojime, and netsuke all executed by the same artist in this highly colorful, decorative style.

SOMADA GEMPO.   An outstanding craftsman of the 19th century. He was particularly skillful in creating mosaic pictures using tiny flakes of shell and metal cut in geometric patterns.

SOMADA HISAMITSU.   Artist of the early 19th century who lived in Daishoji in Kaga Province (the present Ishikawa Prefecture). He was the brother of Somada Mitsuaki.

SOMADA KIYOSUKE.   Artist of the beginning of the 18th century who is credited with founding the Somada school. He lived in Etchu Province (the present Toyama Prefecture).

SOMADA MITSUAKI.   Artist of the early 19th century, brother of Somada Hisamitsu and Somada Mitsumasa. He is noted for his inro in the Somada style.

SOMADA MITSUHISA.   A very skillful and talented craftsman of the 19th century. He was a younger brother of Mitsuaki, and after Mitsuaki's death he succeeded to his profession. He executed much work in a highly artistic and facile manner.

SOMADA MITSUMASA. 1775–1856.   One of the most outstanding artists of the Somada school, he lived in Etchu Province (the present Toyama Prefecture). After his death his work was carried on by his brother Mitsuaki.

SOMIN Yokoya (also known as Chojiro, Jihei, Tomotsune, and Tonin). 1669–1733. A very famous metal artist of the 18th century who invented a style of metal carving which imitated the various strokes used in *sumie* painting. He lived in Edo and worked for the shogunate, producing mostly sword furniture. His grandson Tomotsugu (died in 1788) became Somin II, and his works so closely follow the style and quality of those of Somin I that it is impossible to accurately separate the two. There are also known to be metal inro which bear this signature, which was the same for both artists. Somin I and II also frequently made metal plaques for *kagamibuta* netsuke.

SONTOKU.   Lacquer artist of the 18th century who did fine Somada-style work.

SONZEN.   Lacquerer of the mid-18th century.

SOSEI.   See KOAMI IV.

SOSEKI.   See KAGAWA SOSEKI.

SOSHIAN.   Lacquer artist of the late 18th and early 19th centuries.

SOSHO (1).   See KOAMI IV.

SOSHO (2).   See TATSUKE SOSHO.

SOSHU.   Lacquerer of the early 19th century.

SOTETSU I (Tosai). 1617–95.   Famous lacquer artist born in Kyoto. He was a pupil of Koetsu, and his works are executed in an impressionistic style. He was particularly well known for his lacquer works in *yozakura-nuri* technique. One of his art names was Nakamura. He was succeeded by six generations, all of whom adopted the name Sotetsu.

SOTETSU II (Yusai).   Lacquer artist who worked during the late 17th century and died in 1706.

SOTETSU III (Kyusai). 1699–1776.   This artist, representing the third generation of the Sotetsu line, was also known as Shitto, Shoboko, and Yusai.

SOTETSU IV (Shinsai). 1742–91.   Fourth-generation artist in the Sotetsu line.

SOTETSU V (Shippo, also known as Hyosai).   Worked during the early 19th century.

SOTETSU VI (Chosai).   Worked during the early 19th century.

SOTETSU VII (Bakusai, also known as Tokugen).   Worked about the middle of the 19th century.

SOU.   See RITSUO.

SOYAN.   A very skillful lacquer artist of the 19th century.

SOYETSU.   See SOETSU.

SOZABURO Asano.   A skillful lacquer artist of the late 19th and the early 20th centuries who lived in Kanazawa.

SOZEN.   See KOAMI III.

SUETSUNE Nakahara.   Well-known lacquer artist of the 12th century.

SUICHIKUKEN.   Lacquer artist of the mid-19th century.

SUKENAGA Matsuda.   Outstanding artist of the late 18th and early 19th centuries. He was primarily a netsuke carver who lived in Takayama in Hida (the present Gifu Prefecture). He also occasionally carved wooden inro.

SUNRYUSAI.   Lacquer artist of the 18th century.

TACHIBANA MASAMITSU.   See GYOKUSAI (2).

TADAMITSU.   See KOAMI TADAMITSU.

TADAYOSHI.   See KOAMI TADAYOSHI.

TAGUCHI RISUKE.   See GARAKU.

TAIAMI.   Lacquerer of the mid-15th century from Kyoto. He was particularly skillful in *togidashi* and *takamakie* techniques. There were many generations of his family who succeeded to his profession and continued his fine work. Unfortunately we do not know any details concerning the individual artists.

TAIGYO Yamada.   Lacquer artist of the early 19th century.

TAIMIN.   19th-century lacquer artist of the school of Zeshin.

TAIREIAN.   See KOETSU.

TAISAI.   Lacquerer of the 19th century whose works are executed in the style of Zeshin. He was a pupil of Taishin.

TAISHIN Ikeda. 1825–1903.   One of the most outstanding lacquer artists of the late 19th century. Born in Edo, he became a pupil of Zeshin at the age of eleven and displayed remarkable talent. He is well known for the delicacy and refinement of his works. He was also a skillful painter and often made excellent lacquered netsuke. In 1896, in recognition of the quality of his lacquer work, he was made a court artist. His works so closely resemble those of Zeshin that they are frequently mistaken for them, although close examination reveals that they lack the light touch, the freedom, and the refinement of Zeshin's creations.

TAISUI.   See KORIN.

TAKAHASHI SETSURO. Lacquer artist of the 20th century working in Tokyo.

TAKAHIRO. Lacquer artist of the 19th century.

TAKAMASU. See TATSUKE TAKAMASU.

TAKAMITSU. See TATSUKE TAKAMITSU.

TAKANO SHOZAN. Lacquer artist of the late 19th century who lived in Tokyo and whose works are of a classical nature.

TAKANORI. See TATSUKE TAKANORI.

TAKASE. Metal artist of the 19th century who occasionally executed metal inro. His works are generally decorated with diverse encrustations of materials in high relief.

TAKATADA Tamura. Well-known lacquer artist of the 18th century.

TAKEMUNE Enami. Lacquer artist of the mid-17th century. He was an outstanding artist, and along with Koami XII (also known as Naganari) he was commissioned to work on the famous Tosho-gu shrine in Nikko in 1689.

TAMAKAJI. See ZOKOKU.

TAMPO Tsujiya. Lacquer artist of the second half of the 18th century. He moved from Kyoto to the Takaoka district of Etchu Province (the present Toyama Prefecture). He was particularly skillful in lacquer work in the Chinese style of carved red relief lacquer and Zonsei lacquer work.

TANAKA. See KIYOTOSHI.

TANGO Enami. Lacquer artist of Edo who worked during the early 18th century.

TANREI. Lacquerer of the late 18th century.

TANSO. Lacquer artist of the 19th century.

TAN'YU Kano. Outstanding painter of the first half of the 17th century who worked in Edo. In recognition of his great talent he was given the honorary titles of *hogen* and *hoin*. He frequently executed designs which served as inro decoration, and therefore his name has appeared on inro.

TATSUGORO Okubo. Expert lacquer artist of the early 19th century, originally from Omi Province (the present Shiga Prefecture).

TATSUKE. One of the somewhat lesser known families of lacquer artists, said to have been founded by Aogai Chobei during the second half of the 17th century. As a group, the Tatsuke artists produced work of consistently high quality which displayed pure Japanese flavor and refined taste.

TATSUKE CHOBEI. 1605–49. This famous inro artist, better known as Aogai Chobei, worked in Kyoto during the second half of the 17th century. His real name was Takatada, but he adopted the art name of Aogai, which literally means "blue shell." He was a member of the Tatsuke family.

Chobei was renowned for his inro decorated with colorful encrustations of mother-of-pearl inlaid flush with the lacquer. He adopted this Chinese style of encrustation using the iridescent blue-green shell of the *awabi (Haliotis japonica)* in contrast to the milky-white opaque shell of the *omugai* (nautilus) and *sazae (Turbo cornutus)*, which were abundant in Satsuma and which had long been in use for *raden* encrustation. Chobei's shell decoration was imbedded rather than merely encrusted, as were other *raden* decorations of this period. He apparently had no immediate following of students, and it was not until the Somada school developed in the 18th century that a similar type of mother-of-pearl encrusted (that is, imbedded) work using the iridescent *awabi* shell was revived.

TATSUKE EISUKE.   Noted inro maker of the 18th century, brother of Tatsuke Chobei(Aogai Chobei). He lived in Kyoto and worked for the Lord of Satsuma. He was very skillful in making inro decorated with designs of animals.

TATSUKE HIROTADA.   Member of the Tatsuke family. Details unknown.

TATSUKE HISAHIDE (also known as Nagahide, Tokei, and Toshihide I). 1756–1829.   Member of the Tatsuke family who was born in Kyoto and worked there during the latter part of the 18th and the beginning of the 19th centuries.

TATSUKE JOFU.   Member of the Tatsuke family who worked during the mid-19th century.

TATSUKE JOHO.   Member of the Tatsuke family who worked during the 18th century in the style of the Koma and Kajikawa schools.

TATSUKE JOSHO (also known as Kokosai).   Member of the Tatsuke family who worked during the 19th century.

TATSUKE KAZUTSUNE.   Member of the Tatsuke family. Details unknown.

TATSUKE KOKOSAI.   See TATSUKE JOSHO.

TATSUKE KOKYO.   See TATSUKE TAKAMITSU.

TATSUKE KOSAI (also known as Yasutsune).   Member of the Tatsuke family who worked toward the end of the 18th century.

TATSUKE SHOJO.   Member of the Tatsuke family, daughter of Takanori. Lacquer artist of the 18th century, expert in *makie*.

TATSUKE SOSHO.   Follower of the Tatsuke school who worked during the 19th century.

TATSUKE TAKAHIRO.   Member of the Tatsuke family who worked during the first half of the 18th century.

TATSUKE TAKAMASU.   Member of the Tatsuke family who worked during the late 18th and early 19th centuries.

TATSUKE TAKAMITSU (also known as Kokyo and Nakatsugu).   Member of the Tatsuke family and well-known inro artist who worked in Kyoto during the late 18th century. His inro are often large and of unusual shape. He was still working at the age of eighty-three.

TATSUKE TAKANORI. 1757–1833.   Member of the Tatsuke family and inro artist who worked in Edo. He was also a talented painter of the Kano school. His daughter Shojo, like him, was an expert *makie* artist.

TATSUKE TOSHIHIDE I.   See TATSUKE HISAHIDE.

TATSUKE TOSHIHIDE II (also known as Jorei and Hirokuni).   Member of the Tatsuke family and lacquerer of the late 18th and early 19th centuries. He was the brother of Tatsuke Hisahide (Tokei).

TEIJI.   Netsuke carver, potter, and lacquerer of the mid-19th century, student of Ritsuo. He used encrustations of pottery for decoration of his lacquer ware. His signature appears on a ceramic plaque inlaid on his lacquer objects.

TEIKAN (also known as Sadamoto).   Lacquer artist of the 18th century.

TEIRAKU.   Lacquerer of the 19th century.

TEIRIKUSAI.   Lacquer artist of the 18th century.

TEMMIN (also known as Shojo).   Metal artist of the late 18th and early 19th centuries. He was an excellent artist and made *manju* and *kagamibuta* netsuke as well as occasional inro. He had many pupils, one of the most famous being Shuraku.

TENKO (also known as Ipposai). Lacquer artist of the early 19th century.

TESSHO (also known as Shukasai). Lacquer artist of the 19th century.

TOBEI Shibata. Noted lacquerer who worked in Kyoto during the early part of the 19th century. He was the teacher of Kimura Hyosai.

TOGAN Fujishige. Outstanding lacquer artist of the 17th century who specialized in creating lacquered tea-ceremony utensils. He lived and worked in Nara. It is said that he was the first to use lacquer for repairing broken ceramic objects.

TOGI. Lacquerer of the 18th century.

TOJU. A very skillful lacquer artist of the late 18th and early 19th centuries. He was a pupil of Toyo and often used Toyo's art name of Kanshosai.

TOKA. Lacquer artist of the 18th century.

TOKEI (1). Lacquer artist of the mid-19th century. He frequently used the drawings of Kyosai as designs for his lacquer decorations.

TOKEI (2). See TATSUKE HISAHIDE.

TOKOKU Suzuki. Skillful artist who worked in Edo in the mid-19th century. He was an outstanding netsuke artist who occasionally made inro with decorations of various finely detailed inlaid materials. (See chapter on netsuke for further details.)

TOKOKU Takamachi. Outstanding lacquerer who worked toward the close of the 18th and at the beginning of the 19th centuries.

TOKOSAI. Lacquer artist of the 19th century whose inro are executed in the manner of the school of Jokasai.

TOKUBEI Tatsumi. Lacquer artist of the 19th century.

TOKUJO (also known as Shokasai). Lacquer artist of the 19th century.

TOKUOI Sasayama. Metal artist of the mid-19th century. He was a skillful craftsman and a student of Otsuki Mitsuoki. He occasionally executed inro decorations.

TOKUSAI. Metal artist of the 18th century who made metal inro.

TOKUSAI. See KOETSU.

TOKUZAEMON. Lacquer artist of the late 17th century. He was the grandson of Matabei Sasaki and a pupil of Jigoemon Hata. See also JIGOEMON (1) and (2).

TOMOCHIKA. Famous mid-19th-century netsuke artist who occasionally carved inro.

TOMOFUSA (also known as Kambei). Artist of the 18th century who primarily executed lacquered netsuke. He lived in Tsuyama in Sakushu (now part of Okayama and Tottori prefectures).

TOMOHARU Nagata. Lacquer artist of the mid-18th century who worked in Kyoto and later moved to Edo, where he died at the age of eighty. He was a student of the Korin school, and his works are excellent studies in the impressionistic manner.

TOMOHARU Shiomi (also known as Kohei, Kohei Masanari, Shiomi Masakage, and Shiomi II). 1681–1764. Born in Kyoto, this artist was the son of Shiomi Masanari and became Shiomi II. His work is similar to that of his father, and he used the same signature. See also MASANARI Shiomi.

TOMOHISA Yamichi. Metal artist of the end of the 18th century. He was a member of the Yamichi family of metal artists and worked in Hagi. His specialty was metal inro, and he was particularly skillful in producing landscape designs without using any encrustations.

TOMOICHI. Lacquer artist of the 18th century.

TOMONOSHIN. Lacquer artist of the late 17th century. He was the second son of Shibara Ichidaiyu and was a skillful lacquerer. He was a talented musician as well and played the flute.

TOMOTADA (also known as Yanagawa Zenzo). Metalworker of the late 18th and early 19th centuries. He made inro and netsuke as a hobby. His works are elaborate and are executed with great skill.

TORI. Family name of many skillful painters of the *ukiyo-e* school. Members of the family occasionally executed designs for inro decorations.

TORIN (also known as Gyokusensai). Lacquer artist of the 19th century.

TORYUSAI. Skillful inro artist of the 19th century.

TOSA Hara. Lacquerer of the 18th century.

TOSEN Watanabe. Outstanding lacquer artist of the end of the 18th and the beginning of the 19th centuries. He was a pupil of Toyo, and his works are executed in a style similar to that of his master. He was also called Shofusai.

TOSHI. A pupil of Toyo who worked during the late 18th and the early 19th centuries, sometimes using the art name of Kanshosai or the family name of Yamada. He was a very skillful lacquer artist who also executed lacquer netsuke.

TOSHICHI Takei. Lacquer artist of the 19th century. He worked in the style of the Koami school. One of his pupils was Kawanobe Itcho.

TOSHICHI Tsuishu. Skillful artist of the early 18th century noted for his sculptured red lacquer. He worked in Nagasaki and is considered one of the best artists of his time. See also TSUISHU.

TOSHIHIDE I. See TATSUKE HISAHIDE.

TOSHIHIDE II. See TATSUKE TOSHIHIDE II.

TOSHIMAYA IHEI. Primarily a netsuke artist, he worked in Osaka during the early 18th century. He was particularly skillful in executing ashtray netsuke of fine braided copper or gold.

TOSHINAGA. See JUEI.

TOSHIRO. Outstanding lacquer artist of the early 19th century.

TOSHIYOSHI. Lacquer artist of the early 19th century.

TOSHU (also known as Kikugawa Manyoshi and Kanshosai). Lacquer artist of the late 18th and early 19th centuries. He was the grandson of Toyo and produced fine-quality work in the style of Toyo.

TOSHUSAI. Lacquer artist of the 19th century.

TOSUI Kogi. A painter from Osaka who worked at the end of the 19th century. He occasionally made sketches which were used as inro designs. He was a student of Nishiyama Hoen and Yokoyama Seiki.

TOSUKE Takei. Lacquer artist of the 19th century who studied under Inaba Koami.

TOTEI Ninomiya. A doctor of Edo during the late 18th century who made lacquer inro as a hobby. He was a skillful artist and is particularly well known for his work in *chinkin-bori*. He is said to have used rats' teeth for the engraving of his designs, thus producing very fine, delicate incised *chinkin-bori* work. He was partial to designs of flowers and foliage for his inro decorations.

TOTSUHEI. Lacquer artist of the late 18th century who was a pupil of Ritsuo.

TOU. See YASUCHIKA.

TOYO Iizuka. One of the master lacquer artists of the mid-18th century, who worked from about 1764 to 1772. He was primarily an inro artist but occasionally made lacquered furniture and lacquered netsuke. He was particularly skillful in *togidashi* work and often executed *sumie togidashi* on gold-lacquer backgrounds. His inro indicate that he was equally adept in other lacquer techniques, and as a whole his works are highly imaginative and artistic. He was in the employ of Lord Hachisuka, the daimyo of the province of Awa, who made him a samurai in recognition of his outstanding talent and devotion to his art.

Of Toyo's many art names, the best known is Kanshosai. He is also known as Genroku, Kosai, and Toyosai. His inro are generally signed with his name and *kakihan* and frequently with his age as well. He was succeeded by several generations who adopted and used his name. Many of them continued to work for the daimyo of Awa. Their works are identical in style and similar in excellence to those of Toyo I, and we cannot distinguish them accurately from his, since they used the same signature and *kakihan*. Furthermore, Toyo's works are often imitated and his signature forged.

TOYOSUKE Oki. A talented artist who worked during the first half of the 19th century. He was originally a potter, and he invented a process of covering unglazed pottery with lacquer and decorating it with lacquer designs. This work is known as Toyosuke-raku or Horaku-yaki. The quality of his decorative work reveals him to have been a skillful lacquer artist as well as a ceramist. He died in 1858. His son adopted his name and continued working in the same style.

TOYOYOSHI Yamada. A skillful lacquer artist of the 18th century who produced works similar to those of the Koma school of lacquering.

TOYU. Lacquer artist of the 18th century who worked in the Koma style.

TOZAN. Lacquer artist of the 19th century. He was particularly skillful in executing encrustations in the Shibayama style.

TOZO. Lacquer artist of the late 17th century. He was the eldest son of Shibara Ichidaiyu and was a skillful lacquerer as well as a talented musician.

TSUCHIDA. Surname of many outstanding lacquer artists, the most famous being SOETSU.

TSUCHIYA. See YASUCHIKA.

TSUGIHARU. See KOMA TSUGIHARU.

TSUISHU. One of the names of the outstanding family of lacquer artists who specialized in sculptured lacquer carving. See TOSHICHI and YOSEI.

TSUJI MITSUSUKE. Artist of the 20th century working in Tokyo.

TSUNEKAWA. Lacquer artist of the 17th century.

TSUNENOBU Kano. Outstanding painter of the Kano family. His designs were often used as inro decorations.

TSUNETADA Sano. Lacquer artist of the mid-19th century.

TSUNEU. Lacquerer of the 19th century.

TSUNEYOSHI (also known as Shokosai). Lacquer artist of the 19th century.

UCHIKOSHI (also known as Iichiyosai). A school of metal artists founded in Edo about 1800 by Ichiyosai Hirotoshi. Their work is similar to that of the Nara artists, but it is richer in minute details executed in colorful encrustations. The school had many followers, and their works are frequently found on inro.

UKIFUNE. See FUSEN.

WAKAI. Lacquer artist of the 19th century. He specialized in executing designs of plants and birds, particularly crows, in black lacquer on a background of natural wood. His works are skillfully presented and are very beautiful.

YAHEI. Well-known lacquer artist of the late 17th and early 18th centuries who worked in Kyoto. He had many students who produced work in his style.

YAKYU Somada. Lacquer artist who was particularly skilled in encrustations of richly colored *aogai* shell.

YAMADA. Outstanding family of lacquer artists of Edo founded in the late 17th century by JOKASAI. They often applied lacquering techniques to the execution of sword furniture and *tsuba*. There were many artists who used the same name.

YAMAMOTO SHUNSHO. See SHUNSHO.

YAMAZAKI KATSUTARO. Lacquer artist of the late 19th century who worked in Tokyo.

YASABURO. See HYOSAI II.

YASUAKI. See KOMA II, KOMA IV, and KOMA YASUAKI.

YASUAKI Kobayashi. Lacquer artist of the late 18th and early 19th centuries. He was in the employ of the daimyo of Yanagawa and executed many outstanding inro.

YASUBEI Yamamoto. Outstanding lacquer artist of the early 19th century. He was particularly skillful in the technique of mosaic lacquer.

YASUCHIKA Tsuchiya (also known as Tou). 1669–1744. Outstanding metal artist. He was one of the most famous masters of the Nara school of metalworkers and made metal inro as well as occasional netsuke as a hobby. His works are executed in medium relief with an abundance of rich encrustations. His metalwork is frequently found encrusted in lacquer inro. He occasionally carved inro in *ke-bori* style. There were six generations bearing the same name, a name that was frequently forged.

YASUKAWA. Lacquer artist of Osaka who worked during the early 18th century.

YASUKUNI. Lacquer artist of the KOMA family.

YASUMASA. See KOMA YASUMASA.

YASUMUNE Shibayama. 19th-century artist who executed inro designs with decorations of colorful encrustations in the manner of the SHIBAYAMA family.

YASUNAO Shibayama. Member of the SHIBAYAMA family who worked during the 19th century. He was well known for his skillful encrustations.

YASUNOBU Nishikawa. Member of the Utagawa school of painters who executed work in the *ukiyo-e* style. He was born in Edo at the end of the 18th century. His real name was Utagawa Kuniyasu. He made many prints and also illustrated books and produced several designs for use as lacquer-ware decoration.

YASUTADA. See KOMA YASUTADA.

YASUTOSHI (also known as Shinryosai). Lacquer artist of the 19th century.

YASUTSUNE. See TATSUKE KOSAI.

YASUYUKI Shibayama. Lacquer artist of the 19th century. He was a member of the SHIBAYAMA family and executed skillful work for inro encrustations.

YOKEI (1). Lacquer artist of the end of the 18th and the beginning of the 19th centuries. He was known for his encrustations in the fashion of the Somada school.

YOKEI (2). Also known as Saikindo. Lacquer artist of the 18th century.

YOKOBUE I (also known as Nagano Yokobue or Oteki). Lacquer artist of the 18th century who lived in Kyoto.

YOKOBUE II (also known as Nagano Yokobue or Oteki). Son of YOKOBUE I, he succeeded to his father's profession and worked in Kyoto during the early 19th century. He specialized in making lacquer furniture and rarely executed smaller lacquer objects, such as inro and *kobako*.

YOKOBUYE. See YOKOBUE I and II.

YOKOFUE. See YOKOBUE I and II.

YOMO. Lacquer artist of the late 18th century.

YOSAI (1). Skillful lacquer artist of the 18th century who specialized in sculptured *tsuishu* lacquer.

YOSAI (2). Lacquer artist of the 17th century, a contemporary and student of the school of Ritsuo and Hanzan. His inro are decorated with ceramic encrustations and frequently have risers in *chinkin-bori*.

YOSEI. A family of lacquer artists who specialized in and excelled at producing sculptured lacquer of the Chinese Ming style. They were equally skillful in *tsuikoku* and carved *guri* lacquer work. Their *tsuishu* work far surpassed the Chinese work in richness of color, beauty, skill of carving, and variation of design.

About the middle of the 14th century the shogun commissioned some articles in *tsuishu* lacquer and was so pleased with them that he bestowed upon the artist the name of Tsuishu Yosei, which was derived from the names of Yomo and Chosei, the two outstanding Chinese *tsuishu* artists of that time. This name was subsequently used by nineteen successive generations of the family.

Sculptured lacquer inro by the Yosei artists are relatively scarce, particularly those of fine quality. This type of work is rarely signed. Although we have a comparatively accurate chronological record of the names of the members of the Yosei family, we know practically nothing about them as individuals. The following is a list by generations.

YOSEI I (Tsuishu). Worked for the Ashikaga shogun Yoshiakira during the middle of the 14th century, from about 1356 to 1361.

YOSEI II (Tsuishu). Worked for the Ashikaga shoguns, succeeding to his father's profession. He was active during the late 14th century, from about 1381 to 1384.

YOSEI III (Chotei, also known as Nagasada). Was in the employ of Prince Tosan and worked during the middle of the 15th century. He died in 1488.

YOSEI IV (Choshi, also known as Nagatsugu). Worked at the end of the 15th century.

YOSEI V (Chohan, also known as Nagashige).   Active during the early 16th century.

YOSEI VI (Choho, also known as Nagafusa).   Worked for the Ashikaga shogun Yoshiharu during the middle of the 16th century. He was a skillful artist.

YOSEI VII (Choshin, also known as Nagachika).   Active during the late 16th and early 17th centuries. Was in the employ of Hideyoshi and executed many articles to his order. He moved to Kamakura, where he died in the early 17th century.

YOSEI VIII (Choso, also known as Nagamune and Heijuro).   He inaugurated a technique of sculptured *tsuishu* lacquer with green shell inlay which is known as Kamakura *tsuishu*. He died in 1654.

YOSEI IX (Chozen, also known as Nagayoshi).   Worked during the mid-17th century and died in 1680.

YOSEI X (Choze, also known as Nagakore).   At the request of the Tokugawa shogun Tsunayoshi, he moved to Edo and executed much work to his order. He was an excellent artist and was given a piece of land in Edo by the shogun as a reward for his outstanding work. He died in Edo in 1719.

YOSEI XI (Chosei, also known as Nagamori).   One of the most outstanding artists of his time. He worked during the first half of the 18th century and died in Edo in 1735.

YOSEI XII (Choin).   Worked during the middle of the 18th century and died in 1765.

YOSEI XIII (Chori, also known as Nagatoshi).   Worked during the middle of the 18th century and died in 1779.

YOSEI XIV (Chokin).   Worked during the second half of the 18th century and died in 1779.

YOSEI XV (Choryu, also known as Nagakage).   Worked during the end of the 18th and the beginning of the 19th centuries. He died in 1812.

YOSEI XVI (Choei, also known as Nagahide).   Worked during the first half of the 19th century and died in 1848.

YOSEI XVII (Choho, also known as Nagakuni).   He was given the name of Nagato during the middle of the 19th century by the Tokugawa shogun Ieyoshi, for whom he worked, and from that time on his works were signed Tsuishu Yosei Nagato.

YOSEI XVIII (also known as Kokuhei and Nagato).   Worked during the second half of the 19th century and died in 1890. He adopted the name of Nagato.

YOSEI XIX. 1880–1952.   One of the outstanding lacquer artists of the first half of the 20th century. He continued to execute the fine-quality *tsuishu* lacquer for which the family was famous. He also trained many students.

YOSHIAKI Ozawa.   Inro artist of the late 18th and early 19th centuries.

YOSHIDA GENJURO.   Lacquer artist of the late 19th century. He worked primarily in colored lacquer.

YOSHIMITSU.   Outstanding lacquer artist who executed mostly inro. He worked during the second half of the 18th century. His works are similar in style to those of the Kajikawa family, and he was particularly well known for his *hiramakie* decorations.

YOSHINAGA Hara.   Lacquer artist of the early 16th century.

YOSHITOMI. Lacquer artist of the mid-19th century.

YOSHIYUKI Nomura. Lacquerer of the late 17th century.

YOYUSAI Hara (also known as Kozan). 1772–1845. Born in Edo, he was one of the most skillful lacquer artists of his time. He was sponsored by Lord Matsudaira and executed many fine lacquer articles for him. His works are fashioned after those of Korin. He had many students and followers, the most outstanding being Nakayama Komin and his pupil Ogawa Shomin. He was particularly skillful in executing decoration in *hiramakie* and also made lacquer netsuke. He frequently used the paintings of his equally famous painter friend Hoitsu for the designs of many of his inro and other lacquer ware. While his designs were often taken from those of the Korin school, his works were not in the Korin lacquer style, being mainly in flat *makie* and delicately artistic rather than grossly impressionistic. His name was often forged and his work imitated. There was another artist with the same name who worked in Edo during the second half of the 19th century.

YUHO. Lacquer artist of the early 19th century.

YUJI Nagata. Noted lacquer artist of the 18th century, working in Kyoto from about 1711 to 1736. He was of the impressionistic school and executed inro decoration in the style of Korin, whom he greatly admired. He was a talented artist and a skillful craftsman.

YUKASAI. Lacquer artist of the mid-18th century.

YUKEI Ishikawa. Lacquerer of the late 18th century.

YUKICHI Ishii. Lacquer artist of the end of the 19th century. He specialized in making works inlaid with jewels in the Chinese style and known as *yusuki* ware.

YUKIMASA. Lacquer artist of the 18th century.

YUKINOBU. Member of the famous Kano school of painters. His sketches have been used as inro designs.

YUSAI. Lacquer artist of the early 19th century whose works are done in the style of the school of Zeshin. He frequently worked in gold lacquer and also produced lacquered netsuke.

YUTOKUSAI (1). See GYOKKEI.

YUTOKUSAI (2). See GYOKUKU.

YUTOKUSAI (3). Lacquer artist of the end of the 18th and the beginning of the 19th centuries. He frequently produced inro of colorful designs and intricate detail on gold-lacquer background.

YUZO Ohara. 1787–1859. Member of the Ohara family of lacquer artists. He was the son of Jigoemon Shigeyoshi and the younger brother of Muneyoshi. His lacquer works are realistic in style, one of his favorite subjects being the catfish.

ZAIMITSU Ukiki. Lacquer artist who worked during the early 19th century.

ZENKYO Noji. Skillful lacquer artist who specialized in executing lacquered tea-ceremony utensils.

ZESHIN Shibata. 1807–91. 19th-century lacquer artist and painter of Edo (later Tokyo), outstanding for his originality, versatility, and expert craftsmanship. His real name was Shibata Kametaro, which he later changed to Shibata Junzo. Although he is best known as Shibata Zeshin, he is also known by several other art names, among them being Shin, Tairyuko, and Reisai (or Reiya, which is another reading of the characters), the name he used during his early career.

He was born on February 7, 1807, and at the age of eleven began the study of lacquering under the guidance of Koma Kansai II. He was equally talented as a painter, and his paintings are highly esteemed. An avid student of art, he studied under such master painters as Suzuki Nanrei and Okamoto Toyohiko. He was an admirer of the works of the old masters and studied them with great care. His paintings, as well as his lacquer works, display great artistic feeling and refinement.

Zeshin made many contributions to the field of lacquering. He revived a little-known 18th-century technique of painting which employed lacquer for the coloring instead of ink or ordinary pigments. Although this purely pictorial work is considered to be a "trick medium," the dignity and masterly control of materials that he displayed in creating these pictures cannot be overlooked.

Zeshin excelled in all lacquer techniques, and his works compare favorably with those of the most skillful lacquer artists. He produced many inro as well as other lacquer objects and also carved and lacquered netsuke. Particularly outstanding are his works that imitate the styles of the old masters while retaining their own individuality. These lacquer objects are by no means copies of the originals, nor do they intend to be. Zeshin often executed a sculptured surging wave design, usually in brown *hiramakie,* fashioned after the work of Seigai Kanshichi although by no means a direct copy of it. His own distinctive quality and genius are present in his works at all times.

Zeshin was fond of creating lacquer which simulated the texture of other materials, such as metal, leather, pottery, or a cake of *sumi* ink. He was expert in using colored lacquer and frequently employed a rich, dark-brown lacquer for his backgrounds. At the same time, he rarely used a background of gold lacquer. He was also quite fond of matte grounds, especially of a dark-gray, olive-green color known as "tea-dust green." Some of his works are encrusted with diverse materials. In whatever medium he employed, he displayed a complete mastery of the materials he used.

He paid strict attention to the details of small things, and his designs are usually simple and frequently humorous. He portrayed plants and flowers, animals, people, and legendary subjects with equal skill. In general his works are bold, artistic, imaginative, well planned, and meticulously executed, with great emphasis on finish and realistic detail. Many of his inro were made with matching lacquer netsuke.

Zeshin was a very prolific artist and produced great quantities of excellent work. He had many students, one of the most outstanding being Ikeda Taishin. Possibly his students prepared much of the background for his larger pieces while he decorated and finished them. This would also tend to explain the abundance of his lacquer articles. Of all his works, it is the larger articles, trays, and boxes that occasionally do not measure up to the flawless professional quality that is associated with his name. These defects, however, are mainly in the grounds, which were probably not prepared by Zeshin himself. Also, many of his larger pieces have tended to warp.

Another distinguishing characteristic of Zeshin's work is the beautiful balance of his lacquer designs executed by means of diverse lacquer techniques. Thus if the major part of a design was intended to give bulk and strength, it would be done in high *takamakie*. To give better aesthetic balance, however, the *takamakie* would be supplemented by giving part of the design a touch of *hiramakie* or a few delicate strokes of an incised design. These incised designs, incidentally, were fairly characteristic of Zeshin, being done in *chinkin-bori* style but not filled in with gold powder. It should also be noted that the lacquered designs were balanced texturally as well as aesthetically. Thus the grounds were often done in matte and the designs counterbalanced by using various textures ranging from the completely smooth to a rough, pebbly texture, each technique being done in suitably varying degrees of *hiramakie* and *takamakie*.

While his subject matter was quite diverse, Zeshin is perhaps most noted for his whimsical portrayal of small insect and animal aspects of nature. This is seen not only in his lacquer ware but especially in his lacquer sketches, which were done in lacquer on paper and frequently mounted in book form (Fig. 123).

Zeshin generally signed his works, and his signature is scratched into the lacquer surface in fine characters. He often engraved this signature with the needle-like point of a rat's tooth.

In 1890 he was made a court artist, and at the request of the emperor Meiji he worked along with other outstanding lacquer artists on the lacquer decorations of the Imperial Palace, which was then under construction. He had three sons who also became lacquer artists: Reisai, Shinsai, and Ryusai, the youngest, who was also known as Umezawa Ryushin.

Zeshin died in Tokyo on July 13, 1891, at the age of eight-four. He is usually considered to have been one of the finest of the master Japanese lacquer artists.

ZOHIKO Nishimura (also known as Sochu). 1720–73. Well-known lacquer artist who had many followers, all of whom used the same name. There were at least seven generations of artists bearing this name, the last working into the 20th century.

ZOKOKU (also known as Gyokuto, Keizo, Shisei, Tamakaji, and Tamao). 1806–69. The real name of this artist was Fujikawa Tama. He was born in Takamatsu, Sanuki (the present Kagawa Prefecture) and came from an artistic family who had been gold lacquerers and sword-sheath lacquerers for many generations. He worked under the patronage of Lord Matsudaira, and in 1830 he was made a samurai by this lord in recognition of his outstanding work. Zokoku was particularly skillful in sculptured *tsuishu* lacquer decoration and was the inventor of a style of lacquering that bears his name: Zokoku-nuri (see page 125). He was also a clever poet and a good ceramist, occasionally using ceramic encrustations on his lacquer ware. He was succeeded by his son (also known as Zokoku) and his brother Fujikawa Seiji.

ZONSEI. Lacquer artist of the 17th century who excelled in decoration with colored lacquer. He invented a style of lacquering called Zonsei-nuri (see page 125).

ZUIHO. Lacquer artist of the early 19th century.

ZUISHO Hotta. 1837–1917. Artist of the late 19th and early 20th centuries who invented a style of lacquer known as Hotta lacquer. He was also a talented painter and wood carver. His style is strong and powerful.

Signatures of Lacquer Artists

The signatures reproduced here are those of a selected group of representative lacquer artists. It should be noted, however, that it is impossible in some cases to assign a signature to any specific artist—for example, the signatures "Kajikawa" and "Yosei"—because a number of artists used the same name. Each signature is accompanied by a brief caption giving a translation and explaining parenthetically, where pertinent, whether the signature is a seal itself or whether it is followed by a seal or a *kakihan*. The signatures are arranged in the alphabetical order of the names by which the artists are best known; for example, "Jitokusai Gyokuzan" is listed under G and "Yoshi Kanetomo" under K.

1. Chohei (seal).
2. Ekiso.
3. Made by Gyokuzan.

4

5

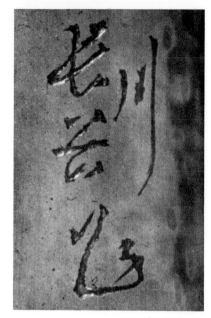

6

7

8

9

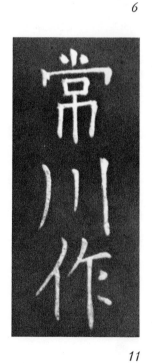

10

11

4. Made by Jitokusai Gyokuzan.
5. Hanzan (seal).
6. Made by Hasegawa.
7. Made by Hasegawa Shigeyoshi (with seal).
8. Hashiichi.
9. Made by Yamada Joka.
10. Jokasai.
11. Made by Josen.

12   13   14   15

16   17   18   19

12. Jugyoku (with *kakihan*).
13. Made by Kajikawa (with seal).
14. Kajikawa Bunryusai (with seal).
15. Kajikawa Fusataka.
16. Made by Kajikawa Toshihide (with *kakihan*).
17. Made by Yoshi Kanetomo.
18. Kanshosai (with *kakihan*).
19. Kanshosai (with seal).

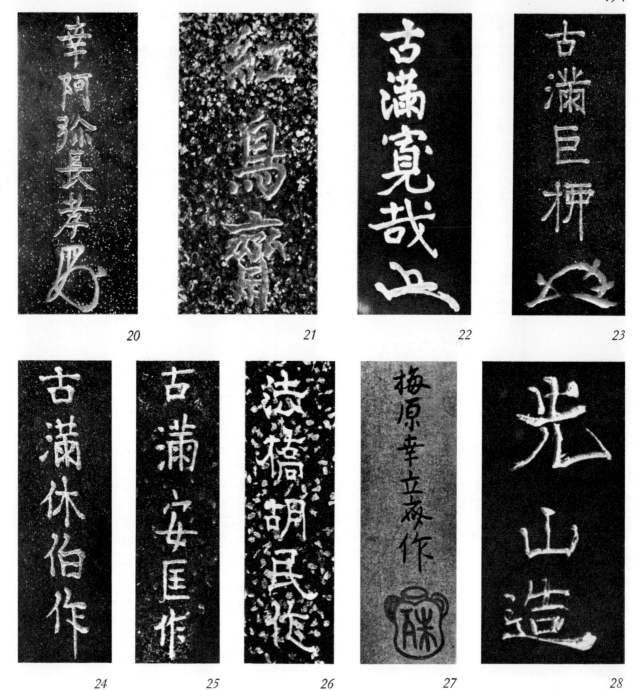

20

21

22

23

24

25

26

27

28

20. Koami Nagataka (with *kakihan*).
21. Kochosai.
22. Koma Kansai (with *kakihan*).
23. Koma Koryu (with *kakihan*).
24. Made by Koma Kyuhaku.
25. Made by Koma Yasutada.
26. Made by Hokkyo Komin.
27. Made by Umehara Koryusai (with seal).
28. Made by Kozan.

29

30

31

32

33

34

35

29. Moei (with seal).

30. Morikazu (seal).

31. Ritsuo (seal).

32. Made by Nakayama.

33. Made by Shibayama (at left); Kakosai (lacquer artist, at right).

34. Made by Shibayama Yasumasa.

35. *Makie* by Shigetsugu (at left); carving by Masayuki (at right).

36 37 38 39

40 41 42 43 44

36. Shiomi Masanari (seal).
37. Shiomi Masanari (seal).
38. Made by Shoho (with seal).
39. Shosai (seal).
40. Shunsho (with seal).
41. Shunsho (with seal reading "Kagemasa").
42. Shunsho (with seal reading "Kagemasa").
43. Shunsui (with *kakihan*).
44. Shunsui (with seal).

45   *46*   *47*   *48*   *49*

50

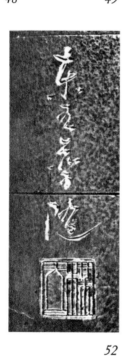

51   *52*

45. Tsuchida Soetsu (with *kakihan*).
46. Made by Somada Hisamitsu.
47. Made by Taisai.
48. Taishin.
49. Made by Tatsuke Takamasu.
50. Takamitsu (seal).
51. Toju (with *kakihan*) at the age of seventy.
52. Tokoku Shinzui (with seal).

53

54

55

56

57

58

59

53. Toshi (with *kakihan*).
54. Toyo (with *kakihan*) at the age of sixty-one.
55. Made by Yokobue (or Oteki, which is another reading of the characters).
56. Yosei (with *kakihan*).
57. Yoyusai.
58. Yutokusai (with *kakihan*).
59. Zeshin.

Genealogical Charts

The following charts outline the genealogy of the major lacquer families and the individual artists as related to their schools.

CHART 1

IGARASHI SCHOOL
(founded c. 1470)

Igarashi Shinsai (15th cen.), founder

Honai (4th generation)

Doho I (d. 1678), son (5th descendant)

Kisaburo (Doho II, 17th cen.), adopted son

Shimizu Kyubei (17th cen.), pupil

Doho III (18th cen.)

C‍HART 2

KAJIKAWA SCHOOL

(offshoot of Igarashi school, founded c. 1637)

D‍IRECT L‍INE

Kajikawa Hikobei (Kajikawa I, 17th cen.)

Kyujiro I (Kajikawa II, 1661–84), son

Bunryusai (Kajikawa III, *c.* 1675)

Fusataka (Kajikawa IV, 18th cen.)

Hidetaka (Kajikawa V, 18th cen.), son

OFFSHOOTS OF KAJIKAWA SCHOOL

SCHOOL OF KAJIKAWA (18th–19th cen.)	Yamada Jokasai (17th cen.)		INAGAWA FAMILY (18th–19th cen.)
18th century:	Tsuneo, son (19th cen.) last direct descendant	SCHOOL OF JOKASAI	Inagawa Chuyu (18th cen.)
Kajikawa Hisataka		Kakosai	
Kyujiro (several artists)		Shokasai (Yasutada)	
Kajikawa Ryusho		Tokosai	
Takafusa		Torosai	
Kajikawa Tomohide			
Kajikawa Yoshichika			
Kajikawa Yoshimitsu			

19th century:

Kajikawa Bunryusai

Hasegawa Shigeyoshi

Kajikawa Hogetsu

Kakosai (Shiori)

Kinjiro (Kinji)

Kajikawa Tadazumi

CHART 3

KOAMI SCHOOL
(15th–19th cen.)

Docho (Michinaga or Koami I, 1410–78), founder

Dosei (Koami II, 1432–1500), eldest son

Sozen (Koami III, 1457–1527), great-grandson of Docho

Sosho (Sokei or Koami IV, 1479–1553), eldest son

Sohaku (Koami V, 1484–1557), youngest son

Chosei (Koami VI, 1529–1603), son of Sohaku

Choan (Koami VII, 1569–1610), first son of Chosei

Chogen (Koami Nagato, 1572–1607), second son of Chosei

Chozen (Koami VIII, 1589–1613), third son of Chosei

Choho (Koami IX, d. 1622), fourth son of Chosei

Choju (Koami X, 1599–1651), fifth son of Chosei

Choan (Koami XI, 1628–82), son of Choju

Chokyu (Koami XII, 1661–1723), son of Choan (Koami XI)

SCHOOL OF KOAMI

Gyosei (18th cen.)

Shoho (Koami XIII), son	Nagayasu II (Inaba, 18th cen.), relative
Dogai (Koami XIV)	Tosuke (Tokei, 19th cen.)
Choko (Koami XV), son	Itcho (Kawanobe, 1830–1910)
Choin (Koami XVI)	
Nagateru (Koami XVII)	Ikko (19th–20th cen.), eldest son
Nagayuki (Koami XVIII)	
Choken (Koami XIX)	Buncho (19th–20th cen.), youngest son

Nagaharu (18th–19th cen.)

Nagataka (18th cen.)

Tadamitsu (18th–19th cen.)

CHART 4

KOETSU-KORIN SCHOOL
(16th–20th cen.)

Hon'ami Koetsu (Taireian of Tokuyusai, 1558–1637), founder

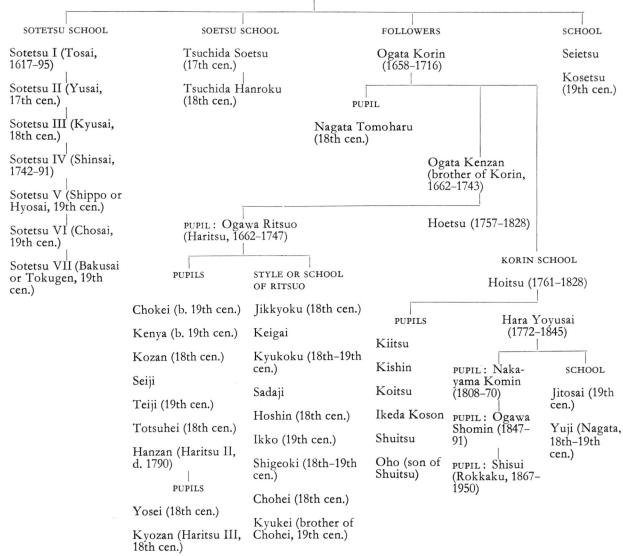

SOTETSU SCHOOL

Sotetsu I (Tosai, 1617–95)

Sotetsu II (Yusai, 17th cen.)

Sotetsu III (Kyusai, 18th cen.)

Sotetsu IV (Shinsai, 1742–91)

Sotetsu V (Shippo or Hyosai, 19th cen.)

Sotetsu VI (Chosai, 19th cen.)

Sotetsu VII (Bakusai or Tokugen, 19th cen.)

SOETSU SCHOOL

Tsuchida Soetsu (17th cen.)

Tsuchida Hanroku (18th cen.)

FOLLOWERS

Ogata Korin (1658–1716)

PUPIL

Nagata Tomoharu (18th cen.)

Ogata Kenzan (brother of Korin, 1662–1743)

Hoetsu (1757–1828)

SCHOOL

Seietsu

Kosetsu (19th cen.)

PUPIL: Ogawa Ritsuo (Haritsu, 1662–1747)

PUPILS

Chokei (b. 19th cen.)

Kenya (b. 19th cen.)

Kozan (18th cen.)

Seiji

Teiji (19th cen.)

Totsuhei (18th cen.)

Hanzan (Haritsu II, d. 1790)

PUPILS

Yosei (18th cen.)

Kyozan (Haritsu III, 18th cen.)

STYLE OR SCHOOL OF RITSUO

Jikkyoku (18th cen.)

Keigai

Kyukoku (18th–19th cen.)

Sadaji

Hoshin (18th cen.)

Ikko (19th cen.)

Shigeoki (18th–19th cen.)

Chohei (18th cen.)

Kyukei (brother of Chohei, 19th cen.)

KORIN SCHOOL

Hoitsu (1761–1828)

PUPILS

Kiitsu

Kishin

Koitsu

Ikeda Koson

Shuitsu

Oho (son of Shuitsu)

Hara Yoyusai (1772–1845)

PUPIL: Nakayama Komin (1808–70)

PUPIL: Ogawa Shomin (1847–91)

PUPIL: Shisui (Rokkaku, 1867–1950)

SCHOOL

Jitosai (19th cen.)

Yuji (Nagata, 18th–19th cen.)

CHART 5

KOMA SCHOOL
(17th–20th cen.)

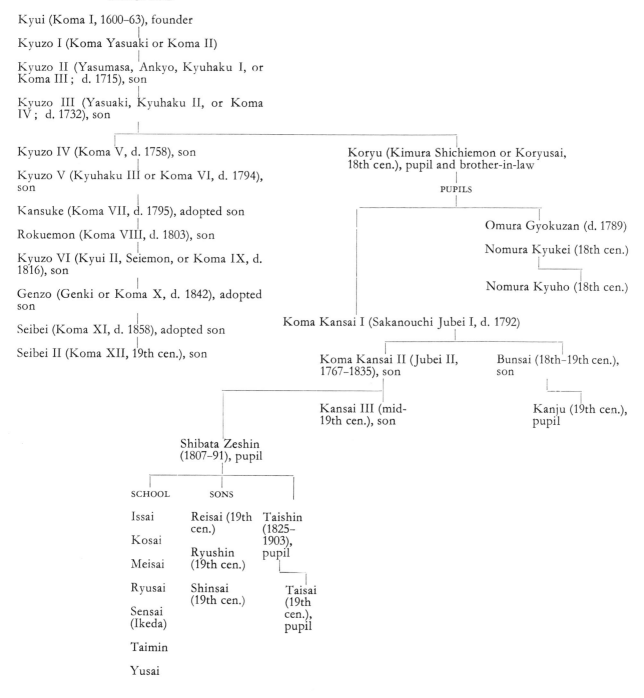

DIRECT LINE

Kyui (Koma I, 1600–63), founder

Kyuzo I (Koma Yasuaki or Koma II)

Kyuzo II (Yasumasa, Ankyo, Kyuhaku I, or Koma III; d. 1715), son

Kyuzo III (Yasuaki, Kyuhaku II, or Koma IV; d. 1732), son

Kyuzo IV (Koma V, d. 1758), son

Kyuzo V (Kyuhaku III or Koma VI, d. 1794), son

Kansuke (Koma VII, d. 1795), adopted son

Rokuemon (Koma VIII, d. 1803), son

Kyuzo VI (Kyui II, Seiemon, or Koma IX, d. 1816), son

Genzo (Genki or Koma X, d. 1842), adopted son

Seibei (Koma XI, d. 1858), adopted son

Seibei II (Koma XII, 19th cen.), son

Koryu (Kimura Shichiemon or Koryusai, 18th cen.), pupil and brother-in-law

PUPILS

Omura Gyokuzan (d. 1789)

Nomura Kyukei (18th cen.)

Nomura Kyuho (18th cen.)

Koma Kansai I (Sakanouchi Jubei I, d. 1792)

Koma Kansai II (Jubei II, 1767–1835), son

Bunsai (18th–19th cen.), son

Kansai III (mid-19th cen.), son

Kanju (19th cen.), pupil

Shibata Zeshin (1807–91), pupil

SCHOOL

SONS

Issai

Kosai

Meisai

Ryusai

Sensai (Ikeda)

Taimin

Yusai

Reisai (19th cen.)

Ryushin (19th cen.)

Shinsai (19th cen.)

Taishin (1825–1903), pupil

Taisai (19th cen.), pupil

KOMA FAMILY AND SCHOOL

Koma Anto (19th cen.)

Koma Enshu (18th–19th cen.)

Gyokurin (early 19th cen.)

Kanya

Koma Koryu (18th–19th cen.)

Koma Kyosen (19th cen.)

Kyusai

Koma Nagachika

Koma Ryusei

Sadahide

Sadashige (19th cen.)

Koma Shigemitsu (19th cen.)

Koma Sozan (Mototoshi)

Toko

Toyu (18th cen.)

Koma Tsugiharu (18th cen.)

Yasukuni

Koma Yasuaki (18th cen.)

Koma Yasumasa (18th–19th cen.)

Yasunari

Koma Yasunori (17th cen.)

Koma Yasutada (18th–19th cen.)

Koma Yasutomi

Koma Yasuyuki

SCHOOL OF KOMA (SHIOMI FAMILY)

Shiomi Harumasa (early 17th cen.)

Masanari (Seisei, Kohei, Masazane, Shoin, or Shiomi I; 1647–1725), son

Masakage (Tomoharu, Kohei, or Shiomi II; 1681–1764), son

CHART 6

SHIBAYAMA SCHOOL
(18th–19th cen.)

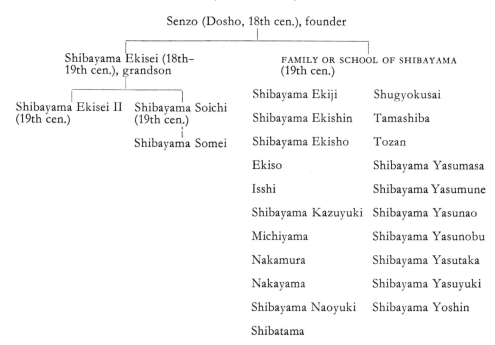

Senzo (Dosho, 18th cen.), founder

Shibayama Ekisei (18th–
19th cen.), grandson

FAMILY OR SCHOOL OF SHIBAYAMA
(19th cen.)

Shibayama Ekisei II
(19th cen.)

Shibayama Soichi
(19th cen.)

Shibayama Somei

Shibayama Ekiji	Shugyokusai
Shibayama Ekishin	Tamashiba
Shibayama Ekisho	Tozan
Ekiso	Shibayama Yasumasa
Isshi	Shibayama Yasumune
Shibayama Kazuyuki	Shibayama Yasunao
Michiyama	Shibayama Yasunobu
Nakamura	Shibayama Yasutaka
Nakayama	Shibayama Yasuyuki
Shibayama Naoyuki	Shibayama Yoshin
Shibatama	

CHART 7

SOMADA SCHOOL
(18th–19th cen.)

Kiyosuke (18th cen.), founder

BROTHERS

SCHOOL OF SOMADA

Mitsumasa (1795–1856)	Gempo (19th cen.)
Mitsuaki (19th cen.)	Somada Nobuyoshi (18th cen.)
Mitsuhisa (Hisamitsu, 19th cen.)	Somada Yakyu
	Yokei (18th–19th cen.)

CHART 8

SHUNSHO SCHOOL
(17th–19th cen.)

Yamamoto Shuboku (Shunsho I, 1610–63), founder

Kagemasa (Yamamoto Kageharu or Shunsho II, d. 1707), son   Shunsei (17th cen.), pupil

Masayuki (Josho or Shunsho III, 1654–1740), son

Harutsugu (Sekizan, Tozan, Hachizaemon, or Shunsho IV ; 1703–70), son

Jirobei (Shunsho V)

Masanori (Shunsho VI, d. 1803), son

Matashiro (Masayuki, Bokusai, Seishi, or Shunsho VII; 1774–1831)

Masanori (Shunsho VIII)

Masakane (Shunsho IX, d. 1877), brother of Masanori

Shosho (Seiken or Shunsho X, d. 1878)   Masakane (Shunsho XI), second son

CHART 9

TATSUKE SCHOOL
(17th–19th cen.)

Aogai Chobei (Takatada, 1605–49), founder

Tatsuke Eisuke, brother

Tatsuke Takanori (18th cen.)

Tatsuke Shojo (18th cen.), son

FAMILY OR SCHOOL OF TATSUKE

Tatsuke Hirotada

Tatsuke Jofu (19th cen.)

Tatsuke Joho (18th cen.)

Tatsuke Josho (Kokosai, 19th cen.)

Tatsuke Kazutsune

Tatsuke Kokosai (19th cen.)

Tatsuke Kosai (Yasutsune, 18th cen.)

Tatsuke Sosho (19th cen.)

Tatsuke Takahiro (18th cen.)

Tatsuke Takamasu (19th cen.)

Tatsuke Takamitsu (Kokyo or Naka-tsugu, 18th cen.)

Tatsuke Hisahide (Nagahide, Tokei, or Toshihide I ; 18th–19th cen.)

Tatsuke Hirokuni (Jorei or Toshihide II, 18th–19th cen.), brother of Tatsuke Hisahide

CHART 10

TOYO SCHOOL
(18th–19th cen.)

Iizuka Toyo (Kanshosai, 18th cen.), founder

Toyo, son

Toshu (18th–19th cen.), son

PUPILS

Toju (18th–19th cen.)

Tosen (18th–19th cen.)

Toshi (18th–19th cen.)

Chart 11

YOSEI SCHOOL
(14th–20th cen.)

Yosei I (Tsuishu, *c.* 1356–61), founder
|
Yosei II (Tsuishu, *c.* 1381–84), son
|
Yosei III (Chotei, d. 1488)
|
Yosei IV (Choshi, 15th cen.)
|
Yosei V (Chohan, 16th cen.)
|
Yosei VI (Choho, 16th cen.)
|
Yosei VII (Choshin, *c.* 1615–23)
|
Yosei VIII (Choso, d. 1654)
|
Yosei IX (Chozen, d. 1680)
|
Yosei X (Choze, d. 1719)
|
Yosei XI (Chosei, d. 1735)
|
Yosei XII (Choin, d. 1765)
|
Yosei XIII (Chori, d. 1779)
|
Yosei XIV (Chokin, d. 1791)
|
Yosei XV (Choryu, d. 1812)
|
Yosei XVI (Choei, d. 1848)
|
Yosei XVII (Choho, 19th cen.)
|
Yosei XVIII (Kokuhei, d. 1890)
|
Yosei XIX (1880–1952)

Glossary

ai-same: lacquer technique in which sharkskin nodules are surrounded with a halo of indigo

Aizu-nuri: lacquer technique used in Fukushima Prefecture

aka-fun: (literally, "red powder") metallic dust

akagane: (literally, "red metal") copper; also called *do*

Aka Shunkei: *see* Shunkei-nuri

aogai: mother-of-pearl

aogai-mijin: greenish iridescent shell powder

aogai-shi: mother-of-pearl inlayer

aogai-zaiku: see *raden*

aokin: gold-silver alloy

aokin-fun: gold-silver powder

ao-urushi: see *sei-shitsu*

ara-tsume: coarsest quality of *yasuriko*

Asakusa *ningyo:* doll netsuke made in Asakusa in the mid-19th century

asa-no-ha: pattern of a series of circles whose points of intersection are connected by lines, forming a star

ashide-e: calligraphy interspersed within a pictorial design

awabi: sea-ear shell *(Haliotis japonica)*; also called *aogai*

Awano Shunkei: transparent lacquer technique used in Ibaraki Prefecture

bagu: decorated horse trappings

bekko-zaiku: tortoise-shell work

benigara: red oxide of iron

bento-bako: picnic or lunch box

bero-ai: Prussian blue

binroji: betel nut

bokuto: wooden dummy sword

bon: serving tray

-bori: see *hori*

bundai: low table used for writing or holding various objects; also called *kadai*

byakuro: pewter

byobu: folding screen

cha-dansu: cabinet used for holding tea utensils

chajin: tea master

chanoki: tea wood

chinkin-bori: (literally, "sunken gold carving") technique in which fine lines are engraved in lacquer or metal and then rendered more visible by powdering (usually with gold) or lacquering with a color different from that of the background

chiriji: technique in which a brown or black lacquer background is powdered with fine gold or silver particles and enriched by scattering a few metallic particles (combination of *nashiji* and *oki-hirame*)

chiri-makie: sprinkling of gold and silver powder onto a tacky lacquer surface

chogai: a pearl-oyster's shell

chomoku: (literally, "carved wood") technique similar to Kamakura-bori

Chosen-matsu: Korean pine

choshi: lacquered *sake* pitcher

choshitsu: Chinese carved lacquer; also known as Pekin or cinnabar lacquer

dai-dai-ichi: largest type of *hirame*

dai-ichi: largest type of *nashiji*

daimyo-nuri: term used for lacquer ware made specially for feudal lords

dairiseki: marble

dakkatsu kanshitsu: technique used for large sculptures in which multiple layers of lacquered cloth were applied over a wood or clay frame

do: see *akagane*

e-nashiji: technique using *nashiji* for the design rather than just for the background

fouchou: Chinese lacquer technique in which silk cloth was placed over a wooden core as a base for the lacquer

fubako: box used for important letters; also called *fumi-bako*

fuchi-kashira: pommel of a sword

fuda-zutsu: box to hold the written guesses in the incense-guessing game

fude: writing brush

fudekake netsuke: netsuke, usually in the form of a reclining human figure, used as a brush rest

fukidome: technique in which lacquer is blown onto the basis to produce large irregular blotches, usually of black on a red ground

fumi-bako: see *fubako*

fundame: flat matte gold-lacquer ground

futa: topmost section, or lid, of an inro

Gigaku: a kind of drama-dance introduced to Japan during the 7th century

gin: silver

gin-kise: overlaying with silver

go: bamboo pots used for receiving lacquer fresh from the tree

Gohana: see Jogahana

gohei: Shinto symbol of folded white pieces of paper, hung from straw ropes or wooden staffs

goki: box for the stones for the board game of *go*

gokin: five basic metals used by metal artists: iron, copper, silver, gold, and tin (or lead)

guri: technique in which alternating layers of colored lacquer or metal are cut into in V-form to reveal the various layers; also called *guri-bori*

guri-bori: see *guri*

gyobu nashiji: technique of placing large, irregular flakes of gold alongside of each other, giving a mosaic effect

haguro: black solution made by boiling iron filings in rice vinegar; needed for preparing *ro-urushi*

hakeme: (literally, "brush marks") lacquer imitating Korean pottery

hako netsuke: boxlike netsuke; also called *kaku* netsuke

hana-bishi: diaper design

hanagai: see *raden*

hari-bako: needle box

hari-bori: needle-carving technique

hashi-ire: case for chopsticks

hashika-bori: the same technique as *koka-ryokuyo,* but having a shallower engraving

heidatsu: technique in which little sheets of gold or silver are affixed to form a design on brown, gray, or red lacquer, which in turn is covered with transparent lacquer

heijin: (literally, "even dust") lacquer background technique using rough sprinklings of gold dust; also called *heijin makie*

heijin makie: see *heijin*

hibachi: charcoal brazier

Hida *ningyo:* doll netsuke carved in Hida; often made of natural yew wood

Hida Noshiro: *see* Noshiro Shunkei

Hida Shunkei: variant of Shunkei-nuri

Hidehira ware: usually found in the form of soup bowls and *sake* cups on which plant designs in red or red and gold appear against a black ground; also called Nambu ware

hidokei netsuke: sundial netsuke

Higashiyama *makie:* lacquer ware made in the late Muromachi period

himekomatsu: species of pine

himotoshi: cord channels of an inro or a netsuke

hina ningyo: dolls for Girls' Festival

hinoki: Japanese cypress

hiragata: inro having a flat shape

hiramakie: (literally, "flat *makie*") name identifying gold lacquer which has a flat surface, the design being almost level with the background

hirame: gold or silver scale dusts made by flattening metallic filings; available in eight different sizes

hirame-fude: pointed stick for applying *hirame* to tacky lacquer surfaces

hirame-fun: flake-gold powder

hirame nashiji: lacquer technique employing various irregular flat pieces of *hirame*

hitori koro: box for hot charcoal, used during incense burning *hiuchi-bukuro:* flint-and-tinder box (bag)

hiuchi netsuke: functional lighter netsuke

ho: Japanese cucumber tree

hogen: honorary title given to some artists

hoin: honorary title given to some artists

hokkyo: honorary title given to some artists

honen: Malayan hornbill; occasionally used for netsuke

honji: applying basic layers of lacquer to the wooden core

honoki: tree of the magnolia family *(Magnolia hypoleuca)*

honzen: tray with legs used at formal dinners

Horaku-yaki: technique in which lacquer is applied to unglazed earthenware; also called Toyosuke-raku

hori (-bori): carving, chiseling, engraving

horiage: see *horu*

horu: chasing; also called *horiage*

hossu: fly whisk

hyomon: technique in which the design is cut out of thin sheets of gold or silver, applied to the lacquer, and then covered with lacquer

ichii: yew tree

Ichimatsu: decoration simulating the pattern of a checkerboard

ichiraku netsuke: basketwork netsuke of metal or rattan shaped like a box, gourd, etc.

iji-iji-nuri: lacquer decoration consisting of a faint network of finely executed designs

ikakeji: similar to *heijin,* but with gold powder put on more densely

Ikkan-bari: technique employing lacquered paper

in (yin): negative, or female, principle

ingyo netsuke: seal netsuke

inro-dansu: box with drawers used for storing inro

inro-shi: artist specializing in making the core of an inro

inu-bako: box made in the form of a sleeping dog and used as a charm

iroe togidashi: togidashi technique using gold, silver, and colored lacquers

iru: casting metal

ishime: lacquer and metal technique in which the ground is coarse-textured like a stone

ishime-nuri: see *nashiji ishime*

isu: tree producing wood in dark-brown and red shades *(Distylium racemosum)*

ito-bako: box to hold strings for musical instruments

itodo: sake cup

itto-bori: faceted style of carving

iyo: smoked bamboo

jidai makie: lacquer products of the Genroku era (1688–1704)

jiki-ban: gold-silver alloy in dust form

jinko: eaglewood

jinoko: lacquer composed of burnt clay and *seshime-urushi*

jisshu kobako: box containing all the paraphernalia used during the incense ceremony

jitsuin: seal

Jogahana: style of decoration done with lacquers of different colors; also called Gohana

joge: top and bottom surfaces of an inro

jo-hana-urushi: shading lacquer

Johoji: technique of drawing the design in yellow or green lacquer on a red or black background and embellishing it with cut metal foil

jokei-in makie: lacquer ware named after an appellation of Shogun Tokugawa Tsunayoshi (ruled 1680–1709)

joken-in makie: ornamentation of different regular seedings in gold and silver of different tonalities

jubako: nest of food boxes

jui: scepter

ju-kashi-bako: nest of sweetmeat boxes

jukogo: three-layered box used during the incense ceremony

juku-bon: scroll tray

kadai: low table used for holding flower arrangements, etc.; also called *bundai*

kaede: a type of maple

Kaga *makie:* lacquer technique developed in the mid-17th century in Kaga Province

kagamibuta: button-like netsuke consisting of a shallow, round bowl of ivory or wood and covered with a metal lid

kai-oke: box for shells used in the shell-matching game

kaishi-ire: container for paper used as napkins during the tea ceremony

kaki: persimmon

kakihan: written seal

kaku netsuke: see *hako* netsuke

Kamakura-bori: lacquer ware made of wood carved in low relief, usually covered with a final red layer of lacquer

kana-gai: technique in which designs are cut from gold or silver foil and imbedded in lacquer

kanamono: metalwork

kanoko nashiji: metallic powder dispersed in spots, resembling the reddish spots of a young deer

Kanshichi-nami: see *seigai-ha*

kanshitsu: dry lacquer

kanzashi: ornamented hairpin

kappa: mythological creature

karabitsu: scroll box; also called *karahitsu*

karahitsu: see *karabitsu*

karakane: bronze

karin: Chinese quince

kashi: oak

kashi-bako: see *kashiki*

kashiki: sweetmeat box; also called *kashi-bako*

kasu: pitch

kasumi nashiji: variation of *mura nashiji*

kata-bori netsuke: figure-carving netsuke

katana-kake: sword rack

katsura: a Japanese Judas tree (*Cercidiphyllum japonicum*)

kawa: hide or leather

kebo: horsehair brush

ke-bori: lacquer and metal technique consisting of hairline chasing by means of knifelike chisels

kendai: slanted stand for holding books or mirrors

keshi-fun: very fine *yasuriko,* made only out of gold or *koban*

keshodai: cosmetic cabinet

ke-uchi-urushi: lacquer used for drawing fine lines

keyaki: zelkova (*Planera japonica*)

kiji: wooden core of an article to be lacquered

kiji makie: lacquer decoration on a background of natural wood

kijiro-nuri: the finest of transparent lacquer techniques

kimedashi: colored lacquer over a wooden base with the wood grain showing

kimetsuke makie: relief *makie* with the design being ornamented with gold or silver flakes

kimma: lacquer technique over bamboo base; also called *kimma-de* and *tenshitsu*

kimma-de: see *kimma*

kin: gold; also called *ogon*

kinchaku: purse

kin-fun: see *kin fundame*

kin fundame: fine gold powder in black lacquer; also called *kin-fun* and *kin-pun*

kingin-de-ga: decoration technique on lacquered or polished wood background, using gold or silver powder mixed with lacquer

kingin-e: ("gold and silver picture") pictorial design technique using powdered gold or silver mixed with glue

kinji: gold-lacquer background

kin-kise: gilding

ki-no-horimono: wood carving

kinoko: fungus

kin-pun: see *kin fundame*

kio: chrome

kiri: paulownia or empress tree (*Paulownia imperialis*)

kirigane: (literally, "cut metal") metallic foil cut into small, various-sized squares or rectangles; used for lacquer inlays

kirin: mythological animal of Chinese origin

kiseru-zutsu: pipe sheath

ki-urushi: raw, filtered lacquer

ki-urushi-ji: chrome-yellow lacquer

kobako: incense box

koban: see *koban-kin*

kobangata: inro with an oval cross section and rounded edges, imitating a *koban,* or oval-shaped gold coin

kaban-kin: gold-silver alloy in dust form; also called *koban*

kobon: incense tray

Kodai-ji *makie:* lacquer work of the Momoyama period in which parts of plants are outlined in gold lacquer, surrounding a *nashiji* filling

kodame chiriji: unpolished, slightly roughened lacquer background of *nashiji ishime*

kodana: small cabinet housing incense ceremony equipment

kodansu: small cabinet

Koetsu *makie:* lacquer ware named after Hon'ami Koetsu, who introduced a specific technique

kogai: metal rod attached to a sword sheath

kogo: incense box

kojubako: box with cover, usually containing two to four smaller boxes *koka-ryokuyo:* variety of *tsuishu* lacquer in red-and-green relief carving

kokutan: ebony

koma-de: lacquer ware decorated with carved circles of different colors

Korin *makie:* lacquer ware named after Ogata Korin, who introduced a specific technique

korozo: a palm nut

koshisage: see *sagemono*

kozuka: handle of a small knife attached to the sheath of a sword

kuchinashi: gardenia, or Cape jasmine

kudan: a fabulous animal

kujaku-seki: malachite, or peacock stone

kuma-urushi: shading lacquer

kunizu netsuke: map-of-Japan netsuke

kuri-iro-fun: (literally, "chestnut-colored powder") metallic dust

Kuroe-nuri: lacquer ware produced in Kuroe, Kii Province

kuro-fun: (literally, "black powder") metallic dust

kurogane: see *tetsu*

kuro-makie: style of lacquer utilizing a highly polished black ground, with the ornamentation also done in polished black in low relief; also called *urushi-makie*

kuruma: carriage used by nobles during the Heian period

kurumi: walnut

kusu: camphor wood *(Cinnamomum camphora)*

kuwa: Japanese mulberry

kyara-bako: box containing scented woods for burning as incense

kyoshinshin: saw-tooth dot design

maki-abise: lacquer technique in which gold dust is heavily heaped onto the raised design

maki-bokashi: lacquer technique of spreading metal powder more thinly in some places than in others

makie: (literally, "sprinkled picture") technique in which the design is built up by repeated alternating applications of coats of lacquer and metallic dustings

makie-shi: lacquer artist specializing in decoration

maki-hanashi: technique in which the gold dustings are left uncovered by lacquer and unpolished

makkinru: decoration technique using mixture of powdered gold and lacquer

manju: button netsuke named after a Japanese cake or bun of similar shape

maru-cha-ire-no-gata: inro in the shape of a round pottery tea caddy

marugata: inro having a round shape

masa-honoki: a variety of *honoki*

matsukawa-nuri: lacquer technique imitating the bark of a pine tree

menso: deer's-hair brush

menuki: ornamental piece on a sword hilt

midare-bako: rectangular or square tray used for clothing when changing one's dress

mikaeshi: reverse side of a cover for an inkstone box

mitsuda-e: decoration technique using a mixture of lead oxide, oil, and colored lacquer, usually with a polished black background

mizu-ire: water container

mokugyo: small wooden bell in the shape of two conjoined, stylized fish

mokume: (literally, "wood eye") lacquer and metal technique imitating wood grain

mokumehada: metal surface technique imitating wood grain or rippling water

mokushin kanshitsu: technique in which lacquer is modeled over a crude solid-wood core

momo: peach

mura nashiji: *nashiji* technique with the metallic powder forming irregular, more or less dense masses in cloudlike effects

murasaki-ko: purple powder lacquer

muro: damp cupboard used for drying lacquer articles

naka-nuri-urushi: lacquer used for middle coats

nakatsugi: type of lacquered tea box

namban: gold-silver alloy in dust form

Nambu ware: *see* Hidera ware

nanako: (literally, "fish-roe ground") metal technique consisting of filling up the background with almost microscopically perfect, evenly placed dots

Nara-bori: carved wood decorated with colors

Nara *ningyo:* netsuke made by Nara doll carvers

nashiji: lacquer technique employing irregular flattened flakes of pure gold or silver or gold-silver dusts buried in transparent lacquer; often translated as aventurine

nashiji-fun: fine gold powder

nashiji ishime: unpolished background in lacquer or metal which imitates the rough skin of the Japanese pear *(nashi);* also called *ishime-nuri*

nashiji-urushi: transparent lacquer used for *nashiji* technique

natsume: tea caddy

Negoro *ningyo:* figure netsuke covered with lacquer in the Negoro-nuri technique

Negoro-nuri: technique used for decoration of table utensils in black or red lacquer

neji-fude: rat's-hair brush

nekogaki: metal technique imitating cat scratches

netsuke-shi: netsuke artist

nezumi-iro-fun: (literally, "gray powder") silver dust combined with charcoal with a trace of vermilion

nigurome: copper-lead-tin alloy

ningyo netsuke: doll netsuke

nioibin netsuke: perfume-bottle netsuke in gourd shape

norimono: enclosed, highly decorated portable chair used to carry the daimyo

Noshiro Shunkei: variant of Hida Shunkei, using a clear yellow and very transparent lacquer; also called Hida Noshiro

nuno: cloth

nunome: lacquer technique imitating cloth

nuri: coating with lacquer

nuribe: ancient clan of lacquer workers; also called *urushibe*

Nuribe no Tsukasa: Guild of Lacquer Workers; established 701

nuri-mono: lacquered objects

nurimono-shi: artist specializing in applying the basic coats of lacquer before decoration begins; also called *nuri-ya*

nuri-ya: see *nurimono-shi*

obijime: narrow cord worn over the obi

ogi: folding fan

ogon: see *kin*

ojime: bead used, together with a cord, to hold the inro cases closed

okiagari-koboshi: self-righting toy

okiagari netsuke: Daruma netsuke

okiguchi: pewter or silver rims on lacquer boxes

oki-hirame: lacquer technique in which relatively large, irregular, flat metallic pieces (usually gold) are encrusted quite regularly next to each other, giving a mosaic pattern

okimono: decorative object of an alcove

okoyaba: lacquer workshop established by the shogunate in the Edo period

omugai: nautilus shell

oni: a devil

otoshi: see *saya* inro

Ouchi ware: lacquer products with a technique similar to Johoji

Owari ware: lacquer products with a technique similar to *heidatsu,* but having a gold background

raden: inlaid mother-of-pearl decoration; also called *aogai-zaiku* and *hanagai*

ramma: openwork panel, transom

rinzu: pattern of a series of straight lines resembling the well-known "key pattern"

ro: wax

roiro: (literally, "wax color") best-quality, highly polished deep-black lacquer

rokuro-zaiku: turning done on a lathe

roseki: soapstone, or "wax stone"

ro-se-urushi: lacquer used as a base for metallic powders and flakes

ro-urushi: black lacquer

ryoshi-bako: see *ryoshi-bunko*

ryoshi-bunko: large writing box; also called *ryoshi-bako*

ryusa: a type of *manju* netsuke

sabi: lacquer used for high-relief designs

sabiji: lacquer technique imitating the surface of old metal

sabi-nuri: dull black lacquer

sagemono: small objects carried suspended from the obi; also called *koshisage*

saishiki-bori: painted figure netsuke

saki: smallest type of *hirame* and *nashiji*

sakura: cherry wood *(Prunus pseudo-cerasus)*

same-nuri: technique of lacquering sharkskin; found mainly on sword hilts

sangoju: coral

sankaku-bori: triangular ivory netsuke

saru-no-koshikake: monkey-stool fungus *(Boletus versicolor)*

sashi-gushi: ornamental comb

sashi netsuke: rod-shaped netsuke of carved wood or ivory *satsu-bako:* box with a tray for holding tea-ceremony utensils

sawari: copper-tin alloy

saya: sword sheath

saya-gata: geometric patterns

saya inro: inro contained in a sheath; also called *otoshi*

saya-maki: scabbard of a Japanese sword, wound with cord and then lacquered

saya-shi: sword-sheath lacquerer

sazae: shellfish *(Turbo cornutus)*

seido: copper with a specially obtained green patina

seigai-ha: lacquer design of stylized waves; also called Kanshichi-nami

sei-shitsu: green lacquer; also called *ao-urushi*

sendan: bead tree *(Melia japonica)*

sennin: hermit

sentoku: alloy, pale yellowish brown in color

seshime-urushi: clear lacquer

setsu: a tree *(Prunus tomentosa)* also called *yusura-ume*

shakudo: copper-gold-silver alloy

shakudo-fun: gold-copper alloy in dust form

sharinshin: whorl-spoke dot design

shibuichi: copper-silver alloy

shido: copper-lead alloy

shigure: metal technique imitating rainstorm

shinchu: brass

shippo: enamel

shirome: white solder

shishiai togidashi: technique combining relief *makie* and *togidashi* to produce flattened, burnished relief and high relief

shita-e: sketch

shita-maki-urushi: undercoat lacquer

shitan: sandalwood

shitan-nuri: lacquer technique imitating sandalwood

shitsuga: (literally, "lacquer painting") technique in which designs are painted on the base with different colors of lacquer

shojo: mythical monkey-type creature with red hair; fond of drink

shokudai netsuke: candlestick netsuke

shu-kin: mixture of gold dust and cinnabar

Shunkei-nuri: transparent-lacquer technique; also called Aka Shunkei

shu-nuri: background of red lacquer

shu-urushi: vermilion lacquer

soken-shi: class of artisans producing sword furniture

Somada: technique in which pieces of mother-of-pearl are imbedded in black lacquer

soroban netsuke: abacus netsuke

suaka: copper with a specially obtained red patina

su-bori: unpainted netsuke

Sugara-nuri: transparent-lacquer technique used on different kinds of wood joined together, showing the variety of grains

sugi: Japanese cedar *(Cryptomeria japonica)*

suigara-ake netsuke: small ashtray netsuke

sukashi-bori: openwork carving

suki-urushi: finest-quality, crude transparent lacquer

sumi: Chinese ink

sumie: painting done with black ink

sumie togidashi: design done with black lacquer powder, imitating *sumie*

sumomo: damson

suri-hagashi: partial abrasion through handling of an upper layer of red lacquer, revealing in spots the underlying black lacquer

suri-urushi: (literally, "rubbed *urushi*") variation of *kijiro-nuri*

suzuri-bako: inkstone box

tabako-bon: tobacco cabinet; also called *tabako-dansu*

tabako-dansu: see *tabako-bon*

tabako-ire: tobacco pouch

tabu: a tree *(Cinnamomum pendunculatum)*

tagayasan: ironwood; a Chinese wood

takamakie: (literally, "high relief *makie*") name identifying raised gold lacquer, including dusting and inlaying of thin metal or mother-of-pearl flakes

taka-maki-urushi: raising lacquer for slight relief

take: bamboo

takemozo-nuri: lacquer technique imitating bamboo

tamago-no-mijin maki: technique in which eggshell pieces are encrusted on the surface of lacquer designs

tama-moku sendan: a variety of the bead tree

tama-tabu: best variety of the *tabu* wood

tana: shelf

tansu: chest with drawers

te-bako: toilet box

tengu: a long-nosed goblin

tenka-ichi: honorary title given to some artists

tenshitsu: see kimma

tetsu: iron; also called *kurogane*

to-beni: magenta roseine

to-bori: foreign carving, usually in the form of ivory seals

tochinoki: Japanese horse chestnut

togidashi: lacquer technique in which the design has been brought out by repeated coating and polishing; also called *togidashi makie*

togidashi makie: see togidashi

togidashi manju: manju netsuke decorated in *togidashi* style

togidashi-zogan: metal technique, similar to lacquer *togidashi,* often used in designs of swimming fish

to-kuwa: a variety of mulberry that grows in China

to-megane netsuke: telescope netsuke

tonkotsu: tobacco box

Toyosuke-raku: *see* Horaku-yaki

tsuba: sword guard

Tsugaru-nuri: type of lacquer ware whose surface gives a mottled effect of red, yellow, green, and black

tsuge: boxwood

tsuikoku: (literally, "heap black") carved lacquer ware with the top layer being black

tsuio: carved lacquer ware with layers made up of many different colors

tsuishu: (literally, "heap red") carved red lacquer

tsuitate: nonfolding, decorative screen

tsuno-ko: calcined deerhorn

tsuribana-ike: hanging vase

tsutsu: wooden tube to hold incense sticks; also a dusting tube used for applying metallic powders

tsuya-keshi: variety of lacquer ware with a dull finish

uchiage: see uchidashi

uchidashi: repoussé or embossing; also called *uchiage*

uchikomi: encrustations of pure gold nuggets

Uji *ningyo:* colored doll netsuke made of old tea wood

uki-bori: fine-relief carving

Ukitsu-nuri: transparent-lacquer technique used around the middle of the 19th century in Nagoya

umi-matsu: petrified underwater sea pine

urushi: a lacquer tree *(Rhus vernicifera)*

urushibe: see nuribe

urushi-e: painting a lacquer picture on paper or silk

urushi-makie: see kuro-makie

usuji: finest quality of *yasuriko*

usu-yasuriko nashiji: metallic filings strewn very sparingly

uta-bako: box for poetry-game cards

utae: (literally, "poem picture") lacquer technique incorporating into the design various Chinese characters of a poem

Wakasa-nuri: multicolor lacquer technique; similar to Tsugaru-nuri

yaki-kin: (literally, "burnt gold") metallic dust in a gold or brassy color

yakugai: pearl shell

yakuro: nonportable receptacle for medicines

yaku-sugi: a variety of cedar

Yamato-e: pictures with Japanese characteristics developed during the Heian period

yama-zakura: wild cherry tree

yang: see yo

yashi-no-mi: coconut

yasuri-fun: see yasuriko

yasuriko: filings or file powders made from pure gold, silver, or gold-silver alloy; also called *yasuri-fun*

yasuriko nashiji: variety of *nashiji* with large metallic filings, densely applied and rolled fairly flat

yasurime: subclassification of *ishime*

yatate: portable writing kit

yin: see in

yo (yang): positive, or male, principle

Yoshino-nobe-urushi: *see* Yoshino-urushi

Yoshino-nuri: black lacquer ware with red ornamentation

Yoshino-urushi: crude, clear lacquer from Yoshino, used for final coatings; also called Yoshino-nobe-urushi

yozakura-nuri: ware characterized by a special type of black lacquer background against which can be seen the contours of a cherry tree, also in black

yushoku: (literally, "oil color") technique in which, after the lacquer is dry, a thin coating of oil is spread over the colored design to prevent fading or flaking

suki ware: lacquer works inlaid with jewels in the Chinese style

yusura-ume: see *setsu*

zen: meal tray

zogan: inlaying, encrusting, damascening

zogan-nuri: lacquer technique imitating cloisonné enamel

zoge-no-horimono: ivory carving

Zokoku-nuri: carved lacquer technique similar to *kimma*

Zonsei: *see* Zonsei-nuri

Zonsei-nuri: technique similar to carved *tsuishu* lacquer; also called Zonsei

zushi: miniature portable shrine

Bibliography

Allen, Maude Rex: *Japanese Art Motives,* A. C. McClury and Company, Chicago, 1917

Anderson, William: *The Pictorial Arts of Japan,* Sampson Low, Marston, Searle and Rivington, London, 1886

Anesaki, Masaharu: *Art, Life, and Nature in Japan,* Marshall Jones Company, Boston, 1932

————: *Buddhist Art in Its Relation to Buddhist Ideals,* Houghton Mifflin Company, Boston, 1915

————: *History of Japanese Religion,* Kegan Paul, Trench, Trubner and Company, London, 1930; reprinted, Charles E. Tuttle Company, Rutland, Vermont, and Tokyo, 1963

Arakawa, H.: *Nihon no Bijutsu* [Art of Japan: Lacquer], Vol. 35, Shibundo, Tokyo, 1969 (in Japanese)

Aston, W. G.: *Shinto: The Way of the Gods,* Longmans, Green and Company, London, 1905

Audsley, George Ashdown: *The Ornamental Arts of Japan,* 2 vols., Charles Scribner's Sons, New York, 1883

————, and Bowes, James L.: *Keramic Art of Japan,* Henry Sotheran and Company, London, 1881

Ball, Katherine M.: *Decorative Motives of Oriental Art,* Dodd, Mead and Company, New York, 1927

Barbanson, Adrienne: *Fables in Ivory: Japanese Netsuke and Their Legends,* Charles E. Tuttle Company, Rutland, Vermont, and Tokyo, 1961

Blacker, J. F.: *The ABC of Japanese Art,* George W. Jacobs and Company, Philadelphia, 1911

Bowes, James L.: *Japanese Enamels,* Bernard Quaritch, London, 1886

————: *Notes on Shippo,* Kegan Paul, Trench, Trubner and Company, London, 1895

Bowies, Henry P.: *On the Laws of Japanese Painting,* Paul Elder and Company, San Francisco, 1911

Brinkley, F.: *Japan: Its History, Arts, and Literature,* J. B. Millet and Company, Boston and Tokyo, 1901, Vol. VII: "Pictorial and Applied Art"

Brockhaus, Albert: *Netsuke: Versuch einer Geschichte der japanischen Schnitzkunst,* F. A. Brockhaus, Leipzig, 1905

————: *Netsuke,* Duffield and Company, New York, 1924 (English translation of the above)

Bruerer, A. A.: "The Influence of China on Lacquer in Japan," *Transactions and Proceedings of the Japan Society of London,* Vol. XII, pp. 158–176, London, 1913–14

Bushell, Raymond: *The Netsuke Handbook of Ueda Reikichi,* Charles E. Tuttle Company, Rutland, Vermont, and Tokyo, 1961

Bushell, Stephen W.: *Chinese Art,* Victoria and Albert Museum, London, 1914, Vol. I, Chapter 6 (Lacquer)

Cammann, Schuyler: *Substance and Symbol in Chinese Toggles,* University of Pennsylvania Press, Philadelphia, 1962

Casal, U. A.: "Inro," *Transactions and Proceedings of the Japan Society of London,* Vol. XXXVII, London, 1941

————: "Japanese Art Lacquers," *Monumenta Nipponica,* Vol. XV, Nos. 1–4, Sophia University, Tokyo, 1959–60

————: "Some Notes on the *Sakazuki* and the Role of *Sake* Drinking in Japan," *Transactions of the Asiatic Society of Japan,* Vol. XIX, Kyobunkan, Tokyo, 1940

Catalogue of Chinese Lacquer, edited by E. F. Strange, Victoria and Albert Museum, London, 1925

Catalogue of Japanese Lacquer, 2 vols., edited by E. F. Strange, Victoria and Albert Museum, London, 1925

Catalogue of Specimens of Japanese Lacquer and Metalwork Exhibited in 1894, Burlington Fine Arts Club, London, 1894

Catalogue of the Seymour Trower Collection, edited by Henri L. Joly, Glendening and Company, London, 1913

Catalogue of the W. L. Behrens Collection, edited by Henry L. Joly, Glendening and Company, London, 1913-14, Part 2

Chamberlain, Basil Hall: "Kojiki: Records of Ancient Matters," *Transactions of the Asiatic Society of Japan,* supplement to Vol. X, R. Meiklejohn and Company, Yokohama, 1882

————: *Things Japanese,* 5th edition (revised), J. L. Thompson and Company, Kobe, 1927

Champoud, M.: *Quelques Notes sur les Inro,* H. Tschudy et Cie., St.-Gall, 1942

Conder, Josiah: *Floral Art of Japan,* 2nd edition, Tokyo, 1899

Descriptive and Historical Catalogue of a Collection of Japanese and Chinese Paintings in the British Museum, edited by William Anderson, Longmans and Company, London, 1886

Dresser, Christopher: *Japan: Its Architecture, Art, and Art Manufactures,* Longmans, Green and Company, London, 1882

Edmunds, Will H.: *Pointers and Clues to the Subjects of Chinese and Japanese Art,* Sampson Low, Marston and Company, London, 1934

Erskine, William Hugh: *Japanese Customs: Their Origin and Value,* Kyobunkan, Tokyo, 1925

————: *Japanese Festivals and Calendar Lore,* Kyobunkan, Tokyo, 1933

Ferry, Ervin S.: *Symbolism in Flower Arrangement,* The Macmillan Company, New York, 1958

Gonse, Louis: *Japanese Art,* translated from the French by M. P. Nickerson (publisher unknown), Chicago, 1891

Griffis, William Elliot: *The Religions of Japan,* 2nd edition, Charles Scribner's Sons, New York, 1895

Grundy, Anne Hull: "Netsuke Carvers of the Iwami School," *Ars Orientalis,* Vol. IV, 1962

————: "Staghorn and Other Quaint Netsuke," *Oriental Art,* Vol. VI, No. 3, London, 1960

Hana no Masegaki (catalogue in Japanese), edited by Morimasa Takei, 8 vols., (publisher unknown), Tokyo, 1917

Hart, Ernest: *Lectures on Japanese Art Work,* Troume, London, 1887

————: "Notes on the History of Lacquer," *Transactions and Proceedings of the Japan Society of London,* Vol. III, London, 1892–93

Hart, Mrs. Ernest: "Impressionism in Japanese Art," *Transactions and Proceedings of the Japan Society of London,* Vol. V, London, 1902

Harukawa, Toshimasa: *Makie Daizen* [Guide to Designs on Lacquer], 5 vols., Osaka, 1751 (in Japanese)

Hearn, Lafcadio: *The Writings of Lafcadio Hearn,* Houghton Mifflin Company, Boston and New York, 1922, Vol. IX: "In Ghostly Japan," pp. 221–241 ("Incense")

Herberts, Kurt: *Das Buch der ostasiatischen Lackkunst,* Econ, Düsseldorf, 1959

Holme, Charles: *A Course of Instruction in Wood-Carving According to the Japanese Method,* Offices of *The Studio,* London (date unknown)

Hozumi, Nobushige: *Ancestor Worship and Japanese Law,* Z. P. Maruya and Company, Tokyo, 1901

Huish, Marcus: *Japan and Its Art,* 2nd edition (The Fine Art Society, Ltd.), Simpkin, Marshall, Hamilton, Kent and Company, London, 1893

Ienaga, Saburo: *History of Japan,* 3rd edition, Japan Travel Bureau, Tokyo, 1958

Inaba, Michitatsu Shin'emon: *Soken Kisho* [Appreciation of Sword Furniture], 7 vols., Shibukawa Seiemon, Osaka, 1781, Vol. VI on *inro* artists, Vol. VII on *netsuke* artists (in Japanese)

Joly, Henry L.: *Legend in Japanese Art,* John Lane, London, 1908; reprinted, Charles E. Tuttle Company, Rutland, Vermont, and Tokyo, 1967

————, and Tomita, Kumasaku: *Japanese Art and Handicrafts,* Yamanaka and Company, London, 1916

Jonas, F. M.: *Netsuke,* Kegan Paul, Trench, Trubner and Company, London, 1928; reprinted, Charles E. Tuttle Company, Rutland, Vermont, and Tokyo, 1960

Joya, Mock: *Quaint Customs and Manners of Japan,* 4 vols., Tokyo News Service, Tokyo, 1951–55

Kaempfer, Engelbert: *The History of Japan,* 3 vols., James MacLehose and Sons, Glasgow, 1906

Kokka: Journal of Japanese Art, Kokka-sha, Tokyo, 1889 (new series beginning with No. 182 in English)

Koop, Albert J., and Inada, Hogitaro: *Japanese Names and How to Read Them,* The Eastern Press, London, 1923

Lee, Sherman E.: *Japanese Decorative Style,* Harry N. Abrams, New York, 1961

Low-Beer, Fritz: "Chinese Lacquer of the Early Fifteenth Century," Bulletin No. 22, The Museum of Far Eastern Antiquities, Stockholm, 1950

————: "Chinese Lacquer of the Middle and Late Ming Period," Bulletin No. 24, The Museum of Far Eastern Antiquities, Stockholm, 1952

Maeda, Taiji: *Japanese Decorative Design,* Japan Travel Bureau, Tokyo, 1957

Masujima, R.: "On the Jitsuin or Japanese Legal Seal," *Transactions and Proceedings of the Japan Society of London,* Vol. XVII, London, 1889

Meinertzhagen, Frederick: *The Art of the Netsuke Carver,* Routledge and Kegan Paul, London, 1956

Morrison, Arthur: *The Painters of Japan,* 2 vols., T. C. and E. C. Jack, London, 1911

Morse, Edward S.: *Japanese Homes and Their Surroundings,* Dover Publications, Inc., New York, 1961

Munsterberg, Hugo: *The Folk Arts of Japan,* Charles E. Tuttle Company, Rutland, Vermont, and Tokyo, 1958

Munsterberg, Oskar: *Japanische Kunstgeschichte,* 3 vols. (publisher unknown), Braunschweig, 1904–7

O'Brien, Mary Louise: *Netsuke: A Guide for Collectors,* Charles E. Tuttle Company, Rutland, Vermont, and Tokyo, 1965

Okada, Yuzuru: *Netsuke: A Miniature Art of Japan,* Japan Travel Bureau, Tokyo, 1951

Orange, James: *Japanese Lacquer: Box of Curios,* Printing and Publishing Company of Yokohama, 1910

Otto, Alexander Francis, and Holbrook, Theodore S.: *Mythological Japan, or The Symbolisms of Mythology in Relation to Japanese Art,* Drexel Biddle, Philadelphia, 1902

Pageant of Japanese Art, Toto Shuppan Company, Tokyo, 1957, Vol. V: "Textiles and Lacquer"

Piggott, Francis: *The Music and Musical Instruments of Japan,* 2nd edition, Kelly and Walsh, Yokohama, 1909

————: *Studies in the Decorative Art of Japan,* B. T. Batsford, London, 1910

Priest, Alan: "Zeshin," *The Metropolitan Museum of Art Bulletin,* Vol. XII, No. 4, New York, 1953

Quin, John J.: *Report of Her Majesty's Acting Consul at Hakodate on the Lacquer Industry of Japan,* Harrison and Sons, London, 1882

————: "The Lacquer Industry of Japan," *Transactions of the Asiatic Society of Japan,* Vol. IX, Part 1, 1906

Rein, J. J.: *Japan: Travels and Researches,* 2nd edition, A. C. Armstrong and Son, New York, 1888

————: *The Industries of Japan,* A. C. Armstrong and Son, New York, 1889

Reinaecker, Victor: "Japanese Lacquer," *Transactions and Proceedings of the Japan Society of London,* Vol. XXXVI, London, 1939

————: "Masterpieces of Japanese Craftsmanship," *Country Life Annual,* 1955

Salwey, Charlotte M.: *Fans of Japan,* Kegan Paul, Trench, Trubner and Company, London, 1894

Sansom, G. B.: *Japan: A Short Cultural History,* revised edition, D. Appleton-Century Company, New York, 1943

Sasaki, Chujiro: *Nippon no Netsuke* [Netsuke of Japan], Koyukan Shobo, Tokyo, 1936 (in Japanese)

Sawaguchi, Goichi: *Nihon Shikko no Kenkyu* [Studies on Japanese Lacquer Works], Maruzen Company, Tokyo, 1933 (in Japanese)

Schurhammer, George: *Shinto: The Way of the Gods in Japan,* Kurt Schroeder, Bonn and Leipzig, 1923

Shibata, Zeshin: "The Koma Family of Lacquer Artists," *Kokka,* Vol. V, Kokka-sha, Tokyo, 1890

Shisui, Rokkaku: *Toyo Shikko-shi* [History of the Lacquer Industry in the Orient], Yuzankaku, Tokyo, 1932 (in Japanese)

Silvester, Norman L.: "Japanese Lacquer," *Bulletin of the Russell-Cotes Art Gallery and Museum,* Vol. XVII, No. 1, Bournmouth, March 1938

Smith, Harding W.: "A Description and History of Japanese Lacquer Down to the End of the Genroku Period (1681–1708)," *Transactions and Proceedings of the Japan Society of London,* Vol. VII, London, 1905–7

Strange, Edward F.: *Chinese Lacquer,* Ernest Bonn Limited, London, 1926

Swann, Peter C.: *An Introduction to the Arts of Japan,* Frederick A. Praeger, New York, 1958

Tei-San: *Notes sur l'Art Japonais: La Sculpture et la Chiselure,* Société du Mercure de France, Paris, 1906

Tomkinson, Michael: *A Japanese Collection,* 2 vols., George Allen, London, 1898

Tsuchiya, Takao: "An Economic History of Japan," *Transactions of the Asiatic Society of Japan,* Vol. XV, Kyobunkan, Tokyo, 1937

Ueda, Reikichi: *Netsuke no Kenkyu* [The Study of Netsuke], 2nd edition, Osaka, 1952 (in Japanese)

Ushikubo, D. J. R.: *Life of Koetsu* (publisher unknown), Kyoto, 1926

Volker, T.: *The Animal in Far Eastern Art,* E. J. Brill, Leiden, 1950

Weber, Franz: *Netsuke,* Vol. 1, Nos. 1–12, Verlag B. M. Leitner, Vienna, 1960–61

Weber, V. F.: *Ko-ji Ho-ten,* 2 vols. (privately published), Paris, 1923

Willetts, William: *Chinese Art,* 2 vols., Penguin Books, Harmondsworth, 1958

Yee, Chiang: *Chinese Calligraphy,* Methuen and Company, London, 1938

Yoshida, Tetsuro: *The Japanese House and Garden,* Frederick A. Praeger, New York, 1955

Yoshino, Tomio: *Japanese Lacquer Ware,* Japan Travel Bureau, Tokyo, 1959

Index